For Honor, Flag, and Family shows the depth of compassion and the complexity of character that led to the prominence of Franklin County's highest-ranking officer, Samuel Crawford. While serving at Fort Sumter, he eloquently delivered his lifelong motto: "I must sustain with honor my flag and the reputation of the name I bear."

— The Author —

RICHARD WAGNER attended Gettysburg College and obtained a bachelor's and master's degree from Shippensburg University. A resident of Franklin County, Pennsylvania, Wagner taught social sciences for 35 years. After retiring, he spent years researching the life of Samuel Crawford, the only Civil War infantry general from Franklin County, Pennsylvania—a crossroads of the Civil War.

For Honor, Flag, and Family

*Civil War Major General
Samuel W. Crawford, 1827–1892*

By Richard Wagner

WHITE MANE BOOKS
SHIPPENSBURG, PENNSYLVANIA

Copyright © 2005 by Richard Wagner

A Note on Samuel W. Crawford's Date of Birth

Throughout Samuel Wylie Crawford's life, confusion existed regarding his birth year, particularly in the Civil War years. Many listed his birth date as 1829, but it was finally correctly listed as 1827 when Crawford, in a letter to the Retirement Board (Adjutant General), dated October 12, 1871, acknowledged being born November 8, 1827, at "Allendale farm," Franklin County, Pa. M1395 NA. Crawford's sevens and nines often looked similar.

ALL RIGHTS RESERVED—No part of this book may be reproduced in any form without permission in writing from the publisher, except by a reviewer who wishes to quote brief passages in connection with a review.

The acid-free paper used in this book meets the guidelines for permanence and durability of the Committee on Production Guidelines for Book Longevity of the Council on Library Resources.

For a complete list of available publications
please write
White Mane Books
Division of White Mane Publishing Company, Inc.
P.O. Box 708
Shippensburg, PA 17257-0708 USA

Library of Congress Cataloging-in-Publication Data

Wagner, Richard, 1935-
  For honor, flag, and family : Civil War general Samuel W. Crawford, 1827-1892 / by Richard Wagner.
     p. cm.
  Includes bibliographical references and index.
  ISBN-13: 978-1-57249-372-8 ISBN-10: 1-57249-372-0 (alk. paper)
  1. Crawford, Samuel Wylie, 1827-1892. 2. Generals--United States--Biography. 3. Physicians--United States--Biography. 4. United States. Army--Biography. 5. Franklin County (Pa.)--Biography. 6. United States--History--Civil War, 1861-1865--Campaigns. I. Title.

E467.1.C84W34 2005
973.7'41'092--dc22 [B]

2005042295

PRINTED IN THE UNITED STATES OF AMERICA

To My "Soul Mate" Karen
Who never complained of another research trip, another chunk of reading and editing, or answering my endlessly ridiculous computer questions. She is the force that stops my world and makes it go. Thanks, Suz.

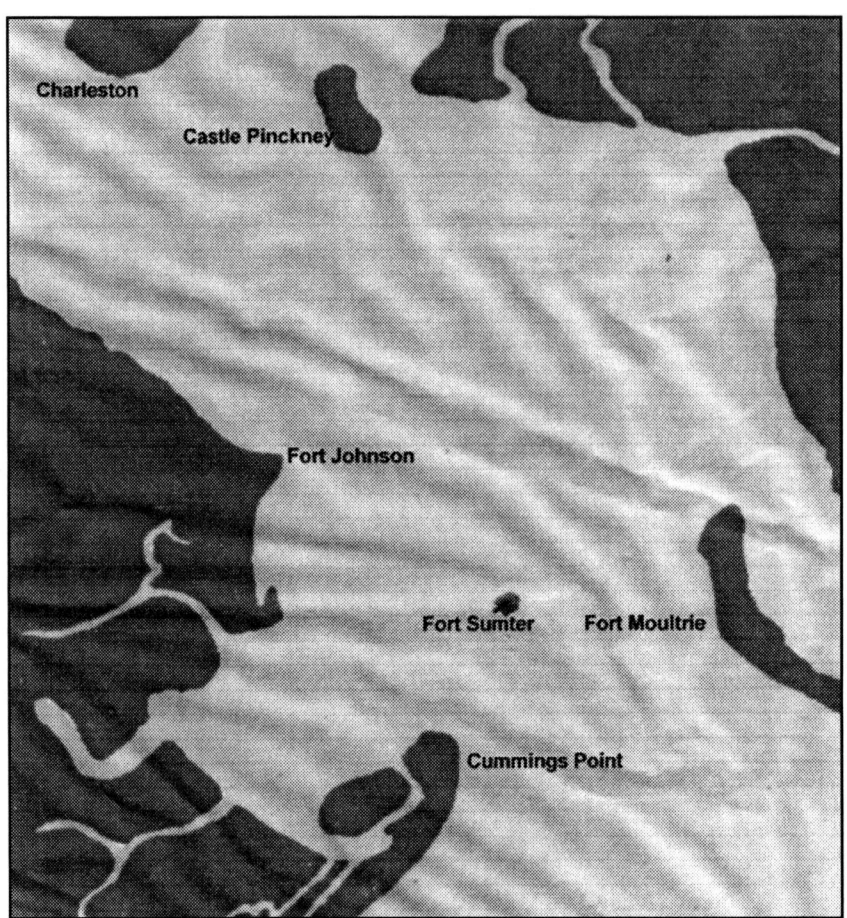

Charleston Harbor.

Map by John Leonard

Honor

"That we come honorably out of these difficulties is my earnest prayer."

S. W. Crawford
Fort Sumter
February 3, 1861

Flag

"We are determined to stand by our flag."

S. W. Crawford
Fort Sumter
January 17, 1861

Family

"My singular hope is that I sustain with honor the reputation of the name I bear."

S. W. Crawford
Fort Sumter
March 14, 1861

They caught our beautiful hens — ever and cooked it — for Gen'l Hill's dinner — it was more than my G. father could stand, he went over to Fort Hill and told Gen'l H. what — he thought of him and all the rebel army. Told him he had no son fighting against them and if he was not so old he would be fighting them himself — Gen'l H. let him talk, then told him to go home and keep quiet and not talk that way before his men or they might do worse than they had

An excerpt of Jennie Washington Wiestling's Diary. This tells the story of her grandfather's conflict with General A. P. Hill.

❧ Contents ☙

Prologue	xi
Acknowledgments	xiii
Introduction	xv

Part One: The Molding Years of Victorian Values

Chapter One. A Summer's Retreat to Alandale	3
Chapter Two. The Mentor, the Plan, and Philo	14

Part Two: The Penn Years

Chapter Three. Back to Philadelphia and Penn	25
Chapter Four. Medical School: University of Pennsylvania	29

Part Three: The Military Frontier

Chapter Five. Military, Medicine, and Adventure on the Frontier	37

Part Four: The Moultrie and Sumter Experience

Chapter Six. The Call to Moultrie	47
Chapter Seven. The Crossing, December 26, 1860	65
Chapter Eight. Fort Sumter: Symbol and Prison	76
Chapter Nine. "God Bless the Poor Noble Fellows"	90

Part Five: The Decision and the Inspector General

Chapter Ten. From Assistant Surgeon to Major, U.S. Infantry	105

Part Six: The Early Years of Infantry Command

Chapter Eleven. Cedar Mountain or Slaughter Mountain	117
Chapter Twelve. Antietam: From a Wheatfield to a Cornfield	127
Chapter Thirteen. Gettysburg, on a Rocky Ridge and Beyond	148

Part Seven: The Spring and Summer of 1864

Chapter Fourteen. Spring in the Wilderness and Spotsylvania	185
Chapter Fifteen. The Summer of 1864	206

Part Eight: A Military End, but an Abiding Relationship
    Chapter Sixteen. An End and a Beginning 231
    Chapter Seventeen. The Years of Passing Flags,
        Friends, and Career 245

Part Nine: The Adventures of a Gentleman Bachelor
    Chapter Eighteen. The World Traveler 255

Part Ten: The Final Years
    Chapter Nineteen. A Life's Commitment 265
    Chapter Twenty. The End Is Near 270

Appendix 279
Abbreviations 287
Notes 289
Bibliography 327
Index 345

ঙ **Prologue** ৫

It was slightly more than a week before Christmas in the year 1912 in Franklin County, Pennsylvania, when Margaret Washington passed away at Alandale, the Crawford family homestead. She was the last of the seven siblings born to Reverend Samuel Crawford, Sr., and his wife, the former Jane Agnew.

Margaret, along with her sister, Anne, and three brothers, John Agnew, Samuel, Jr., and Alex, had witnessed a period in our history rife with change, conflict, and growth. The Civil War touched the family deeply. They provided the Union cause with three sons and a son-in-law. One would not come home and two others would live out their lives in pain. Just how they and, in particular, Samuel, Jr., reacted to and participated in this turmoil is the subject of this book.

Though often perceived as aloof and arrogant, Samuel Wylie Crawford was a multifaceted man with strong human qualities instilled in him by his family. He did not seek material wealth, but rather channeled his energies and treasury into efforts to preserve his nation and the memory of those with whom he served.

Brigadier General Samuel W. Crawford

Crawford personally believed this was his best image. He had it taken by Mathew Brady while visiting his sister, Anne, in New York.

Mollus/USAMHI

Acknowledgments

The gratitude I owe for making this work a reality covers many years and numerous individuals who gave their time, interest, advice, encouragement, and expertise. I leaned on so many experts in so many different fields that the list would be as long as the book.

To all of you, please accept my eternal gratitude. How does one express proper appreciation for the interest of archivists, librarians, associates, family, and friends? I am particularly grateful to my children, "the three amigos"—Pamela, Shawn, and Kirk—for their speculative questioning and ongoing support through the years.

To Charles and Judy Culbertson whose incredible knowledge and writing skills made me realize how much effort goes into a work of this sort. Without their assistance the book would have never seen the "ink of the press."

To Ted Alexander for guiding me through the matrix of historical editing and to Harold Collier and his staff for their patience with this novice, particularly Marianne Zinn and Angela Guyer.

ঌ Introduction ଔ

Samuel Wylie Crawford was born in Franklin County, Pennsylvania, near the village of Fayetteville in 1827. Little could anyone know that thirty-six years later, elements of General Robert E. Lee's Army of Northern Virginia would camp near his home, Allandale, and the commander of the newly formed Third Corps, General A. P. Hill, would make his headquarters just across the field.

His early education gave no hint that he would later become a combat commander in some of the bloodiest and most decisive battles of the Civil War. Crawford was educated at the University of Pennsylvania, entering at the age of 14 and graduating in 1846. From there he attended the Medical School of that institution, graduating with his M.D. in 1850. Next he served on the frontier of Texas and New Mexico as an assistant surgeon in the U.S. Army. During this period he distinguished himself both in scientific research on the flora and fauna of the region, and in a diplomatic mission to Mexico.

By 1860 he was a surgeon with the Federal garrison manning Forts Moultrie and Sumter in Charleston Harbor. During the siege of Fort Sumter he requested and was granted command of one of the fort's batteries, winning a brevet rank of major. Although forced to surrender the fort, all of Sumter's defenders were hailed in the North as the first heroes of the Civil War. Thus, all of the officers at Sumter, Crawford included, were ensured favorable consideration when it came to attaining rank in the Union army.

Crawford experienced a fairly swift rise to command. By the spring of 1862, after brief tours on garrison and staff duty, he was promoted to the rank of brigadier general of volunteers and commanded troops in the Shenandoah Valley Campaign of 1862. There he won praise from General Nathaniel Banks for his administrative abilities.

Also, during that fateful summer of 1862, Crawford won his spurs as a combat commander. At Cedar Mountain his brigade suffered heavy casualties going against Stonewall Jackson's Confederates. He led a brigade at South Mountain and a division at Antietam. At the latter battle he suffered a debilitating and controversial wound that forced him into a lengthy period of convalescence.

Crawford's recovery period lasted until May 1863, when he was assigned command of the Pennsylvania Reserves in the defenses of Washington. In one of his most noteworthy deeds of the war, he led the Reserves in a famous charge across Plum Run on the second day at Gettysburg. Later, in the postwar years, Crawford played an important role in preserving that part of the battlefield.

Crawford won a number of brevets for gallantry during the final campaigns of the war in Virginia, attaining the rank of major general in both the regular and volunteer army. At war's end he continued his service on occupation duty at several posts in the South. Crawford retired from the service in 1873. Two years later he was promoted to the rank of brigadier general on the retired list.

During the war Crawford was not without his detractors. Although he led his men in an exemplary fashion at Cedar Mountain, his performance a few weeks later at Antietam came under a cloud. His superior there, General Alpheus S. Williams, claimed that Crawford "skulked" during the battle and that the wound he received was "self-inflicted." Likewise, contemporaries and modern historians alike have criticized the counterattack of the Pennsylvania Reserves that Crawford led at Gettysburg, claiming that he exaggerated the importance of this affair. Toward war's end at Five Forks, Crawford received blame for sluggishness, despite Union victory at that battle.

His final days were spent in Philadelphia. There he worked on a book about the Civil War and directed efforts to preserve the Gettysburg Battlefield. Crawford died on November 3, 1892. He was buried in Laurel Hill Cemetery, Philadelphia's final resting place for many Civil War heroes.

These are the bare bones of the Crawford story. An army surgeon who found himself an unlikely hero because of Fort Sumter. A battlefield commander who had his good days and bad. A controversial individual who sometimes clashed with superiors and was accused of self-serving glory hunting by some of his contemporaries. Samuel Wylie Crawford has gone down in history as a not so famous general with mixed abilities. A minor hero of Gettysburg, Crawford's statue was one of the last erected on that field to commemorate Pennsylvania's commanders.

Through the years, little has been written about the general. Richard Wagner has brought us the first full-blown biography of Crawford. Besides that, the real good news here is that Wagner writes history the old-fashioned way—with twelve years of research and writing. Indeed, the author's research odyssey into the life of Crawford took him several thousand miles to repositories up and down the East Coast.

Wagner left no stone unturned as he accessed data on this subject that had not seen the light of day for decades, if not longer. One of the most illuminating discoveries in his research was material that shed more light on Crawford's early years and relationship with his family. This information was found in newspapers, letters in the Library of Congress and in a rare find, his niece's diary.

Crawford's student days at the University of Pennsylvania were well chronicled at that institution's archive. These vast holdings also provided important data on his father's tenure as Director of the Academic Department.

General Crawford's war experiences are well documented here. Richard Wagner spent much time at the National Archives and other repositories, sifting through military records, personal letters, and other holdings. He also tapped a source that is all too often ignored by biographers. That is the libraries at the various National Battlefields. These frequently hold extensive files on the soldiers and commanders of the respective battle. Wagner made good use of the collections at Forts Moultrie and Sumter, at Gettysburg, Appomattox and my workplace—Antietam National Battlefield. From these places he gleaned additional information on Crawford, including rare soldiers' accounts of the battles in which the general participated.

In today's Civil War book market, a number of biographies of commanders, north and south, have been published with little substance. Certain authors have embarked on such endeavors even though their subject may not have left any significant body of papers behind to warrant a biography. Accordingly, these books rely on a rehash of battles and events that are already known to most students of the war. I am glad to say that this is not the case with this biography. Wagner has spent the last twelve years in a diligent search for substantive information on Crawford. To be sure there are battle accounts. However, the author has sought to write a full account of Crawford's life, including his prewar scientific endeavors and his postwar travels, including a number of exotic jaunts to the Holy Land.

As a result the reader is treated to a portrayal of a real flesh and blood individual, warts and all. A "Renaissance Man" who did his duty for his country yet made mistakes and did not always endear himself to others.

Wagner's dedicated scholarship provides readers with one of the more detailed Civil War biographies to be rendered in several years.

I believe that readers of this book will conclude, as I have, that this is a valuable study of a too long overlooked Civil War commander.

Ted Alexander
Antietam National Battlefield

Part One
The Molding Years of Victorian Values

The lovely brick dwelling was named Alandale

"If I sell the property, in the case of my death, my family, without a home, would be reduced to begging."
—Reverend Samuel Crawford to
Presbyterian Synod, April 1, 1831

Samuel Wylie Crawford, U.S.A., A.M., M.D., L.L.D.

USAMHI

℘ Chapter One ℛ
A Summer's Retreat to Alandale

I. Looking Forward to the Spirit of the Mountains of Pennsylvania

It must have been a glorious sight that early August morning in Philadelphia as the carrot and ruby sun moved in an orbit that sprayed its rays over the entire front of the Crawford yard. Once again that fireball would sap the strength and destroy the energy of those in Philadelphia. In this city there was very little difference between one summer and the next. They were typically so humid and muggy as to prove nearly unfit for man and animal, but this summer had caused everyone to complain, even "Ma" and "Pa" who rarely voiced displeasure with things beyond their control. With the stifling misery of the last month, Father likely hinted that the unbearable heat was an ally of Satan.

Adding to the discomfort of the stagnating heat and humidity was the size and annoying nature of the blowflies, the reek of the piles of garbage, and the stench of manure in the streets. In addition to the normal irritations of daily living, the ever present prospect of another epidemic of cholera or typhus loomed as a constant and relentless fear.

All of this could not pass quickly enough for the Crawford clan, but they knew relief was on its way. The ghastly qualities of a city's summer life would soon give way to the tranquility of a homestead in the foothills of Pennsylvania. Those mountains symbolized invigorating health and mental harmony. Those valleys and peaks gave a special soothing comfort to all the family members; but to young Samuel Crawford, they would become a lifelong passion. They had a certain "spirit" that revitalized his being.[1]

Much work had to be done before their vacation could get under way. As the family packed, they tried to ignore the distress of Mother Nature.

The climbing, moving, replacing of bags, and especially the lugging of the two seaman's trunks into the rig made shirts fuse to the torsos and pants seem like wet, tangled webs on the legs. In spite of it all, calmness prevailed and time seemed to pass quickly.

Samuel, Jr., was fascinated by the strength and agility of his father as he watched him toss the luggage into the wagon. His father looked more like a stone mason's tender than a minister and academician. The family patriarch and his sister had been orphaned in South Carolina when their parents died of yellow fever. An aunt and uncle from Philadelphia, hearing of their plight, brought them back to that city where the family introduced Samuel, Sr., to the importance of education.[2] Understanding that value, he graduated from the University of Pennsylvania and used the opportunity to enter the ministry. He was subsequently ordained in the Presbyterian Church in 1823, and a year later was "called" to serve as a pastor in the Franklin County Reformed Presbyterian Churches in Fayetteville, Scotland, Greencastle, and Waynesboro, Pennsylvania.[3]

In 1820, about three years prior to arriving in Chambersburg, Reverend Samuel met and married Jane Agnew in New York City. She accompanied him to Franklin County that summer of 1824 with their firstborn, two-year-old John Agnew, and daughter, Margaret, who had not celebrated her first birthday.[4] After living a short time on Federal Hill, west of Chambersburg, the reverend realized the need for a more centrally located home to serve his four churches.[5] Just after his 30th birthday, Samuel purchased a farm on a parcel of land located near Fayetteville, only four miles from the thriving Franklin County seat of Chambersburg.[6] He named his new home Crawford-John. Samuel, Sr., was now closer to his churches; however, the most distant was still 15 miles away.

In late 1824 catastrophe struck the homestead. In later correspondence to the Presbyterian North Synod, Pastor Crawford referred to the tragedy: "Once moved in and comfortable, a fire destroyed much of the house and the family escaped with only the clothes on their backs."[7]

Jane and the two children went to her home in New York City while Samuel remained to superintend and aid in the repair of the home.[8] With drawings and the assistance of parishioners, he remoded the home in the image of his ancestral home in Scotland. With a growing family and the additional cost of rebuilding, his cleric salary proved inadequate; therefore, he turned to academia. He taught the classics and directed the Chambersburg Academy of Learning while maintaining his ministerial duties. When "the mansion" was finally completed, the lovely brick dwelling was named Alandale after his family home place in the Old World of Scotland, Great Britain.[9]

Mother and the two children arrived back from New York in time for Ma to fill one of the empty bedrooms with child number three. Anne Stavely Crawford, named after her maternal gandmother,[10] arrived in 1825. In two more years she would be presented a baby brother named Samuel Wylie and two years later another brother, Alex McLeod Crawford.

In 1830, having preached the circuit and "taught and directed the Chambersburg Academy"[11] as teacher of classics and headmaster, Reverend Samuel's health began to decline from overwork and financial stress. He was unable to meet his growing expenses on his meager $300 a year salary. At one point he wrote, "If I sell the property, in the case of my death, my family, without a home, would be reduced to begging."[12]

Like a message from heaven, he received an invitation from the Trustees of the University of Pennsylvania to become the principal of the Academic Department. It was with pride that at the end of his tenure at the Chambersburg academy, "not one of his pupils offered for examination to any college was ever rejected."[13]

The family moved back to their adopted home, Philadelphia, in the autumn of 1831, and four years later Samuel, Sr., accepted a pastoral call to Fairmont Presbyterian Church in the Philadelphia suburbs. This was one of Reverend Samuel's most satisfying periods of his 83 years as he merged his two loves, academia and theology.

Though they loved the character that was Philadelphia, Ma and Pa, as the children lovingly dubbed their parents, looked for any excuse to go back to the hills that "God had created with his hands."[14] In the summer of '46, with Samuel's graduation from Penn and with the family beginning to splinter, the time seemed right for family bonding in the serenity of the forested valley.

Father probably allowed his second son to drive the team to the station, not only adding an extra graduation present, but also increasing Sam's confidence in handling horses. In 1865 General George Meade would offer Crawford the leadership of the cavalry, but he would refuse.[15]

Margaret, the older sister, whom Sam called Maggie, just recently married Edward Crawford Washington, a distant relative of George Washington. Margaret would come back to Alandale to live some of her happiest moments, the birth of her children, and the saddest, the death of her husband and two children.

The other human cargo in the wagon consisted of Sister Anne, whom Sam referred to as his bossy sister. She was 21, two years younger than Margaret, and also interested in marriage and wifely duties. Anne had attracted the attention of a Mr. Andrew Wilson, and in a few years Anne and

Andrew became "one" and moved to Orange County, New York. Little did they know how changing national circumstances would link the lives of the Crawford family tightly together, in spite of their geographical separation.

This summer the daughters, working with their mother, were most likely anticipating an opportunity to enhance their domestic skills of cooking, sewing, and baking. Ma was "a woman with a sympathetic heart, a strong good sense and actively benevolent."[16] She was patient and was the role model her daughters hoped to be to their children.

The other male passenger, Alex, was the youngest of the living offspring. He had enjoyed his sibling position as his sisters and mother certainly provided him with more than his share of attention, but now going on 17 he most likely thought them slightly silly and certainly overprotective. He wanted most of all to be just like brother Samuel. Alex imprinted much behavior from his elder male sibling, and Samuel would forever be his idol. His older brother frequently referred to him as "Mac" or "Alex."

The two youngest members of the family were with the family in mind and spirit only. The death of the two children had been best remembered by the older John and Margaret, but Samuel was an impressionable 13 when his nine-year-old brother, Cornelius Nathan, passed on. Infant Jane Elizabeth had died shortly after returning to Philadelphia from Alandale in 1833. Samuel was only six years old.[17]

The family's sense of loss was felt when they visited their children's graves in the back of Father's church. Later they would be reinterred in the family plot at Laurel Hill, Philadelphia.[18]

The parents believed it was God's will that the children were taken. Sam had a difficult time with that explanation for the death of a nine-year-old boy and a girl not yet one year old. Perhaps, believing this to be cathartic for his parents, Samuel, Jr., was learning that life was not always fair, but right now it was good.

As they approached the Philadelphia station, Ma would have organized the brood. She was gently firm with them, and they all lent a hand. She knew it would be a long tedious journey to Chambersburg. Traveling had almost become second nature to her since marrying the children's father. Seven children in eleven years had given her experience in both child-rearing and touring.[19] The anticipated visit made the time seem to pass quickly.

As the cars pulled into the station, the Crawford family could not have missed the large sign, "C H A M B E R S B U R G," and probably busied themselves looking for the hired man or Mr. Clark, the tenant, who would take them to Alandale.[20]

II. The Willow by the Stream
Sparked Imaginations and Memories.

The gentleman to take them to the homestead probably helped load the spring wagon and then drove them east. It would be a bumpy four-mile ride.

The last leg of their trip gave Mother an opportunity to tell the driver how the children had grown during the years of absence from Alandale. Samuel was described as almost six feet tall; his whiskers sprouting, and his pitch black hair wavier than ever. Samuel accepted his mother's assessment graciously. Outwardly, he gave the appearance of being somewhat embarrassed, but secretly Samuel enjoyed compliments about his physique and appearance. One writer called him "tall, well formed, strongly knit, and erect."[21] He certainly had that "Crawford nose." Throughout life Samuel struggled with his vanity, but not enough. The almost conceited attitude affected his relations with others mostly in a negative manner.

During the ride to the homestead, the family without a doubt bombarded the driver with so many questions that before they realized it, the closing mile was nearing its end. They passed the George Chambers tenant house in its tranquil setting with the brick house situated deep in the wood lot amid a variety of pines and evergreens that adorned both sides. The woods were neatly trimmed. The large, full, low limbs of the evergreens and maples created an enjoyable relaxing area for an evening picnic, and later, in turbulent times, a fine place to hide horses.[22]

As the carriage rounded the bend, the occupants likely noticed the drive leading into their summer home. They would have been ecstatic as the top of the home became visible and struck them as resembling the mast of a large ship. Almost as quickly, they undoubtedly spied the circular drive and the three-story brick building. Off to their left, they surely noticed the milk shed straddling the stream, as the creek water was used to cool the milk. The mountain stream had always been the first spot to spark both their imaginations and memories. Here they had sailed chestnut barks the world over, they had splashed in the cool creek on those hot August days, and beneath the weeping willow crafted new dreams and shared old ones. It had been many years since the sights of their childhood. The nostalgia created enthusiasm and inner warmth.

Alandale was about to be given rebirth and new life. Then a house, it quickly became a home. The partially ivy-covered brick mansion was about to be revolutionized. The bustle and commotion would bring laughter, thought, and tears, all with a hospitality fitting its heritage.

No doubt father's voice would have broken through the excitement like a foghorn in the night. As was his style, with a few chosen words, they were all assigned their duties. It was unloading of the wagon for the men while the ladies prepared a light dinner.

It is easy to imagine Mother and the girls slicing smoked ham and placing it on an iron grill extending from the hearth. They would complement the ham with fresh tomatoes, cucumbers, and onions mixed with garden herbs that Anne had gathered while singing and taking large breaths of fresh mountain air.

This was a delectable time of the year in rural Pennsylvania. The gardens and orchards flourished with a variety of fresh vegetables and fruits that their mother had learned to serve in an assortment of ways with each meal. With the season barely half over, the promise of more beckoned. Though normally obedient, the children, in their common desire to absorb everything in view, assuredly pushed the limits of "Pa's" patience with their distractions from the assigned chores. However, he would have understood it was not his authority that was being challenged, but merely the circumstances of the moment.

One can envision Samuel looking at his home of yesteryear as his memories flowed. Behind the dormers on the top floor was that special bedroom he and John shared.[23] Traditionally, it was theirs to occupy since they were the eldest sons. Samuel recalled when Alex was born—as youngest, he stayed in the small room next to his parents on the second floor which also housed the girls in an adjacent, large bedroom.

Outside, the four windows, crafted in six panes of large glass, provided light and warmth. The wooden shutters, decorated with shapes and figures and anchored by large iron brackets, were designed for sun, storm, or wind protection.

On the ground level, the stone front porch was centered between two windows. The portico, a half-arched gazebo-like structure, added to the symmetry. Oak posts surrounded by a railing enhanced the overall sense of security. The porch's focal point, a grand, heavy, foot-thick wooden door, welcomed friends and neighbors and discouraged all others. Samuel likely recalled the door key as being the size of a "horse" when he last saw it many years ago.

The second son did a few light, frivolous chores just to appear busy and then slowly rambled toward the southwestern side of the house. The refreshing breeze and the aroma of Mother Earth was a stark contrast to the odors of the city. As he stood under some locust trees, looking east he could see the large barn with its stone base and ground ramp. Suddenly, startled by a giant image in the sky, Samuel dropped to his knees cautiously looking up to see a dreadfully large owl whose habitat he had disrupted.[24]

After regaining his composure, Samuel went to greet the horses in their stalls, with a promise he would visit them often. Out the barn door, turning slowly, he could have surveyed the other buildings that dotted the landscape: the wagon shed, the smoke house, the corncrib, the chicken house, the small blacksmith shop, and the "place of necessity," a luxurious two-seater no less.

In the fields in front of the barn, the vegetable garden bathed in the sunlight. An orchard was located on the rise of the hill where the farm lane opened out into the vast fields. Apples were growing large though still green, peaches were beginning to bleed colors, and the cherries had nearly finished their run. The remaining ones appeared red, juicy, succulent, and far too tempting for Samuel to allow them to remain on the limbs.

He often came the "mountain way" to the backyard. The wild flowers sprinkled the areas between the trees with a variety of colors created in every shade. In the moist spots grew ferns and masses of maidenhair. His parents and God had certainly glorified the land. Sam had been taught to include God into the mixture of all things.[25]

The herb garden in the back of the house was planted in a solitary plot selected because the trees allowed sunshine to filter into the fertile area. Its multitude of fragrances contributed to the farm's ambience. The different herbs were used for culinary as well as medicinal purposes. For Samuel, no matter where he was for the rest of his life, the smell of basil, oregano, rosemary, and sage always brought him back to this place, these moments.

Since composing his senior essay, he could never be exposed to nature again without noticing and studying the birds. Their diversity and sizes, their luminous colors that blended so admirably, their buoyancy in flight, and their songs of joy and praise all fascinated him. Whom were they eulogizing today? What virtuosos in such small packages![26]

Snapping out of his reverie Samuel realized his help was needed with the heavier chores, so he moved toward the wagon, stopping only to get a refreshing drink from the pump near the maple tree adjacent to the front porch. Glancing toward the dormer he could see Alex waving. Alex had arrived; he would stay with John and Samuel in the connecting third-story bedrooms where his world would expand.

Focusing on his task, Samuel aided his father in hoisting the trunk. In this mountain environment, even the seaman's chest with its large rough leather straps seemed lighter than when they had loaded it in the city. The city already seemed so far away in space and time. Life was like that, what was relatively close geographically could be eons apart mentally and emotionally and vice versa.

As they entered the dwelling, Samuel and his father would have been greeted by the natural warmth of the grained woods in the hallway, the gaily flowered wall covering, and intricately designed reflector style wall lanterns. His father and a number of talented parishioners had done it all with the simplest of tools. Proudly, Father often repeated that the finely crafted railing staircase made of deep grained, dark cherry wood mirrored the one in the old country. It curved as it rushed up the stairs to the landing, then swirled again, like an accomplished dancer, and continued its climb to the top, stopping only after encircling the inside of the entire domicile.[27]

From the dormer level a back set of stairs led down to the basement area. This lowest level was designed, almost exclusively, for the large kitchen with its grand fireplace outfitted with iron hardware on which to hang the stew pots, kettles, and assorted cookware.

Let it be known that the kitchen was Jane Crawford's domain. Had we been witnesses, we would have seen her use the facilities to school Margaret and Anne in the culinary arts of the day: the right amount of coals, the proper heat, the best place to swing the stew pot and kettles, and the timing to make a complete meal all come together. Meals were prepared in the back of the huge kitchen area directly opposite the fireplace, placed in the dumbwaiter, and hoisted to the upstairs dining room. The kitchen's multitude of fragrances proved evocative to the family. Different aromas prevailed in different seasons. Each had a special place in their memory bank. The smoked hams, the freshly salted pork, and slabs of bacon were hanging in one of the rooms across from the kitchen. In an adjacent room the earthy smell of potatoes, apples, and turnips in their designated bins proved enticing. On the shelves above the bins were the multihued jars of Mother's home-canned peaches, Seckel pears, crabapples, and cherries.

The aroma of the baking bread conjured the memory of a real home. The baking took place outdoors in the brick-lined ovens built into small mounds of land. In the bottom of the oven was an area large enough to build a wood fire. Later the coals were removed and the bread baked to a golden brown. It is easy to believe that many times the children would have been caught with a slice of freshly baked bread smothered with homemade apple butter or preserves.[28]

While the coals were being readied, Mother would certainly have demonstrated the blending, kneading, and rising processes of the dough for her watchful brood. Once the readied loaves were placed in the oven, she likely scurried away to perform other chores and returned to the oven precisely when the bread was perfectly done. At times the girls were likely overwhelmed by all there was to learn about being a 19th-century housewife.

After the meal, which had been served in the first floor kitchen area with the aid of a dumbwaiter, we can picture Samuel politely excusing himself to pick cherries for tomorrow's breakfast. On his way to the black cherry trees, he passed by the swing where the family would spend many summer evenings discussing a current political event, critiquing a book in the Bible, or conversing about a family problem. The importance of education in this household was a common family value for everyone, male or female.[29]

Samuel almost certainly picked some cherries, but that would have not been his intrinsic motive for these moments. Once he was alone on the top of the hill on the property's southwest corner, he had only his thoughts to accompany him as he went through the motions of gathering fruit. Looking over the fields, he would have noticed the oats with long fibers and a number of grains promising a good crop. Weather had to be an ally with a proper mixture of sun and moisture blended into the fertile valley soil to create the splendor he saw in the fields. The valley was a beautiful deep green, but the value of this place for him was neither the oats, wheat, corn, rye, nor even the cherries; it was the mood this view created. This, unquestionably, was one of his favorite places. Fixing his eyes on a tree line in the distance, he knew from experience that on the other side the Conococheague Creek maneuvered its way through the white birch and elm trees and a smattering of evergreens. Raising his eyes, he could see the Allegheny Mountains and follow their semicircular pattern toward the blunted lavender peaks. From this vantage point the mountains and sky seemed to meet. Here was another place to make memories, create laughter, shed tears, and plan a future.

While Samuel yearned for the mountains of Pennsylvania for his physical well being, it would be the dynamic culture and excitement of Philadelphia that would feed his inquisitive mind.

III. The Entrance Exam

It was in those Pennsylvania mountains on the morning of November 8, 1827, Samuel W. Crawford, Jr., was born at "Allandale Farm." These were the times in Pennsylvania when morning frosts nipped the nose and sunny days warmed the heart. Those early carefree years of play and frolic with his brother John were no doubt particularly memorable. John likely saw Samuel as an inquisitive brother trying to take everything apart to see how it worked. He was sure Samuel would be an engineer due to his prying, snooping, building, and constructing. Perhaps in some families he would have been encouraged to pursue engineering, but it was unlikely in this family of ministers and educators.[30]

Now the two brothers would meet again after what seemed a lifetime of memories. Samuel understood that his brother would want to know what he was going to do with his "Penn education." Samuel could be sure that John would listen intently and permit no intellectual sloppiness; and if impressed by his brother's rationale, John Agnew—or "A.J.", as he was called by the family, because of childhood confusion in his initials by Samuel—would give his younger brother any aid or advice needed.

Samuel's mind assuredly drifted back to those torturous hours of being grilled by his father and brother as they tutored him in preparation for admittance to Penn. Sometimes, he thought it was inhumane punishment. Often, in his father's library they quizzed him on his knowledge of Caesar, Virgil, and Cicero. Then they tested him on his ability to scan both Latin and Greek.[31] They seemed to enjoy making him squirm.

John, a Penn grad of '41 and later a seminary student in Philadelphia, could challenge him on subjects as diverse as the rudiments of ancient and modern geography, as well as the calculation of math problems. Correct grammar and syntax must be a part of the responsive brain. Nothing could be implied in his answers; all must be specific. Even though, at the time, the young Crawford thought their questioning to be harsh, he eventually understood the wisdom of their methods.[32]

This brought to mind the pressure that was applied by the faculty at Grey and Wylie's Academy. Father had selected the school carefully when they first moved back to Philadelphia. Its reputation and emphasis upon the college entrance exam, and the fact Samuel, Sr., had taught in the Academy made it the first choice. Books had always been Samuel's love and only under dire circumstances did he miss a day of school. From the Academy professors he obtained his academic and moral recommendations to accompany his admission to "the University."[33]

A "Penn man" was a product of such machinations. Since both his father and brother had preceded him in earning their distinctions, Samuel probably felt he had no other choice. It was a given he would attend college— "the college." Now, four years later, as he sat perched on the fence gazing at a narrow part of the Cumberland Valley, one can imagine that he reflected on his lack of options for the first time in his life. Not horrific choices, just limited ones. West Point had never been mentioned nor had the ministry—it was just expected. But now he would have greater input into his future options. Whatever the choice, he had to remember as he was constantly reminded: do nothing to tarnish the family name and reputation. They were theologians, men of the cloth, and a family who strived for the good in life by caring genuinely for others.

Imagine the morning he stood before the entrance board, professors and administrators likely robed in their distinctive academic regalia designating prestige and achievement; he would have now realized that his mentors had tried to accomplish that which was in his best interest. He was embarking on an educational experience that would be, as they had promised, "the longest hour of his life." If John Agnew accompanied him to the exam, Samuel likely would have rarely spoken on the way. One moment he felt self-assured; the next scared to his wit's end. His mind undoubtedly reverberated with the phrase "Honor the family name."[34]

It was over! He would be Penn man number three from the family. He had upheld the family name. On the eighth day of September 1842 S. Wylie Crawford, Jr., two months shy of his 15th birthday, would begin classes at the University of Pennsylvania.[35]

On the way home, one can believe the younger brother was likely as talkative as he had been silent on the way to the examination. His brother probably enjoyed the former, but understood perfectly his little brother's ebullience. Of course, John would bring him back to earth by reminding him that he would have to be concerned about one course his freshman year. The classics were taught by Reverend S. W. Crawford, Sr. The family name would be challenged yet once more but by whom? Samuel was confident he could handle the Greek, but what about the complex classics that Father taught?[36]

Samuel entered the University of Pennsylvania when the curriculum was undergoing change, just as pursuits other than the ministry were becoming available. Emphasis was increasingly being placed on practical studies, and the school was no longer just an avenue to the priesthood. This opportunity and his desire to be judged in his own field, by his own merits, led him to serious consideration of the study of medicine. Not only would he avoid comparison with his father and brother and their chosen profession, but in medicine he could aid others. Perhaps he could save someone's brother or sister from the ravages of typhoid or cholera. It was an alternative that must have appealed to his humanitarian nature.

How would Father accept a nonministerial son? Samuel would need and appreciate the emotional support of his guru, John Agnew.

ᛋᛟ Chapter Two ଓ
The Mentor, the Plan, and Philo

I. The Mentor

By the summer of 1846, 24-year-old John Agnew Crawford was preparing to serve as pastor in his first church. He had graduated from the University of Pennsylvania in 1841 with a degree in theology. Three years later, John received his license to preach in the Presbyterian Church. Like his father, the ministry and teaching would prove to be his lifelong career and abiding passions.[1]

In physical appearance John Agnew favored his father. At five feet eleven inches tall he had inherited the typically rigid and trim body structure of the Crawfords. His face was shrouded by a thick beard that gave him the appearance of a mature middle-aged man. From a distance he could easily be mistaken for his father.

Although he was born in Philadelphia, as was his sister, Margaret, they were the first to reside in Crawford-John. In their early years, they vaguely shared the memories of having escaped the flames that destroyed a large part of the farm. Moreover, they could recall the births of Anne, Samuel, and Alex over the six years following the catastrophe. Sadly, they were better able to recall the untimely deaths of their younger siblings, Cornelius and Jane Elizabeth.[2]

II. "I know you hold a higher doctrine."[3]

Being the firstborn, John Agnew was expected to "set the example" for the younger siblings—a responsibility he readily accepted. The burden was offset somewhat by what John perceived as a common sense of respect for his position as scion.

From the earliest years John felt a particular intensity of kinship to his younger brother, Samuel. They probably shared numerous adventures at Alandale, many of which they held in secret between themselves. That same sharing later became one of communion as they discussed intellectual subjects as well. The two surely explored ideas and topics covering a host of the day's current issues. Their intellectual give and take proved enjoyable as they pursued the issue, no matter how intense the sparring. This can be clearly seen in their later letters where the dialogue continued.

John was surely anticipating the two-week respite with the entire family. Deep down he suspected that this event was made possible by their sensitive and crafty mother who sensed this might be the final time the entire flock could be assembled.

Immediately upon his arrival John was likely pelted with innumerable questions about life in Milton, Pennsylvania. He charmed everyone with his responses and smiled assuredly that "he was fighting the good fight and keeping the faith."[4]

John and Samuel took the opportunity to renew and strengthen their brotherly bond. John felt his brother was like a "pot boiling over" in that he was constantly questioning and probing new ideas for discussion. And discuss they did. Whether in their old bedroom or down by the stream or while sitting beneath the cooling shade of the old giant willow tree, one can imagine how they reminisced, John in his congenial manner and Samuel with his inexhaustible nervous energy. At times they were like carefree kids of old once again. Alex likely listened, observed, and intermittently proposed an idea or shared in a thought; he too felt the bonding.

Naturally, A.J. and his younger brother did not share the same fondness for any particular youthful incident, but they were in agreement on one topic. Both recalled fondly the winter Sabbaths when they packed into the family carriage to make the rounds with Father to his charges in Fayetteville, Scotland, Greencastle, and the distant town of Waynesboro. One can just imagine all five siblings climbing into seats, kept warm by their closeness and the coarsely woven horsehair blanket that covered them. They felt snug and secure, far from harm's way.

The camaraderie was fun, but the best part of the daylong trek was not Father's long sermons, nor prayers, but the luscious feasts provided at each church. After the fun, the games, and prodigious amounts of delicious food, the affairs ended with the carriage full of sleeping, well-fed children of all shapes and sizes bouncing obliviously toward home.

Undoubtedly John was Samuel's friend as well as his mentor. They seemed to agree, within broad limits, on most topics they discussed. However, when the topic of John Calvin slipped into the discussions, Samuel withheld comment as he knew this was the one theologian that John believed had the answers to life's meaning. If Samuel disagreed, he likely remained silent.[5]

During a particularly intimate moment, John most assuredly turned from recalling the past to confiding in Samuel that he had a lady interest. John touted her many virtues and the possibilities of marriage. Samuel had no trouble identifying a smitten brother, but he would tell no one as John imposed a vow of secrecy between them.

The silence was eventually lifted when Susan Monroe Gilbert and John Agnew Crawford were wed. The union would result in the births of four more children to add to the Crawford clan.[6]

During the time the two siblings spent together at Alandale, they came to the mutual recognition that an understanding of each other's point of view was a valuable lesson for each to learn. Understanding and tolerance for another and their point of view were so much more important than agreement. Their dialogue and analyses revealed one to be a religious philosopher and the other a probing skeptic.

Their discussion on the institution of slavery was representative of that conclusion. They had been reared in an environment of equality. "Father was a strong abolitionist and one who threw his whole soul into the struggle." Their father was not timid about his stands on social, political, or religious issues.[7]

Both sons believed slavery to be inhumane, degrading, and un-Christian. They further agreed that the general government was the only authority strong enough to deal with the problems that would follow its demise. But when it came to the question of true equality of blacks and whites, the two Crawford siblings parted intellectual company.

Pastor John Agnew firmly believed, as Father did, that all men were created equal in the eyes of God. Race does not matter to God nor should it to his other created. The brothers had grown up in a household whose father preached that every slave should be freed immediately. They certainly had been lectured intensely and often that, in the process of socialization, if each human were given the opportunity to achieve to their fullest potential, inferiority would not be construed along racial or ethnic lines. If society dictates an inferior status and one is forcibly taught to obey and submit, the resultant inferiority is in appearance only. They are human barriers, not God's.[8]

Samuel acknowledged they differed widely in their views, but he held that John was very sincere. However, he believed that John's higher doctrine would not work in the real world. The Negro could not be elevated to the white man's level. Inequality has been, is now, and will always be a part of America's social fabric. Additionally, the person and the culture must be prepared for the slave's freedom and such is not the case at the present. How would either survive? "Our opportunities for observation have been so different," he wrote John, trying to explain the reasons for their differences.[9]

III. Salvation in Medicine or Religion?

The inevitable question about Samuel's future plans probably surfaced a number of times. The possibility of a third "man of the cloth" was sure to make the family proud. Although he dutifully respected the careers of his father and brother, he was uncertain whether the ministry was for him. His nervous nature would surface as he tried to explain to John how he could best serve God by serving humanity. John would not have passed up the opportunity to point out that his brother had just described an important characteristic of the ministry.

Samuel Wylie looked back so he could look forward. The years at Penn had been invigorating for him as he discovered a challenging blend of social activities and academic success. Courses in the classics had challenged and provoked his thinking, and his rhetorical studies had aided him in speech and written communications.

It seemed in his freshman year he began to change his views about certain disciplines. Prior to that time he had seen little value in the study of ancient civilizations, but after being forced to delve more deeply into the subject, he learned to value and respect the lessons to be learned and the validity of the application to help solve contemporary problems. As he continued to immerse himself in modern historical studies, he found himself fascinated with diverse topics. The schemes that led to the Compromise of 1820, the tariff debates, and all such attempts to bridge sectional differences within the Union, were subjects that captured his interest. These subjects, together with a course in political law in his senior year, gave him a background to aid his evaluation and assessment of the current events.[10]

Samuel recognized the unique period of American history in which he was living. Penn had taught him how to separate the important factual grain from the chaff. Interest in country was added to interest in serving humanity. The knowledge, wisdom, and insight he had gained was well worth the "$25 per course fee."[11]

His peers at Penn represented states from almost every part of the nation, 24 in all. The students in the Collegiate Department also represented foreign countries.[12] Debates and discussions were surely methodical and passionate but seldom mean spirited.

Most of the students argued that government should rest upon local and state authority with an emphasis on local authority. Police, militia, schools, and the courts were institutions based upon individuals you knew and trusted. The concept of popular sovereignty that was now emerging on the political scene was a much discussed idea. Samuel expressed empathy for the states' role in national affairs. In 1861 he would write, "states should be treated with equality and justice."[13] He would later learn that state officials were not always satisfied with their limited constitutional powers.

The opposite sector most likely espoused a view toward a greater role for the general government because of the growing complexity of issues, such as the Compromise of 1820. They saw no evil in the federal role. These controversial debates were further complicated by the increasing technological challenges to the nation as a whole. Rapidly changing economic systems, fueled by two totally different engines, pulled the sections in different directions. Additionally, the altering mood of the political environment further complicated the issues. Finally, a moral undercurrent created by perceptions of race and ethnicity gave rise to a sense that the fabric of what they called America was unraveling.[14]

For Samuel a personal decision was now far more pressing than national issues. Was it possible that medicine was his route to salvation akin to the careers which John and Father had chosen? Alleviation of physical pain and misery, though not directly divine, was to him almost a spiritual pursuit.

First, he needed to pass the literary test to allow him to acquire a higher degree. Next, he would complete studies for his master of arts degree, with emphasis on medical readings. Finally, he would make formal application to the School of Medicine.[15]

The only other remaining hurdle for "The Plan" was to gain Father's approval. Realizing how crucial that approval was, John Agnew likely volunteered to sit in with him when he talked with the senior Crawford—Father was a stern taskmaster in these sorts of things. Samuel's confidence would be boosted by Pastor John's presence.

Incredibly, Father and the entire family accepted with little resistance. Father shocked them with his admission that he had attemped to enter the medical field before turning to theology. For the first time the family learned that their father had been tempted by medicine after witnessing the death of his parents in Charleston, South Carolina, from yellow fever. Because he had known the death of his own brother and sister, Samuel could readily empathize with his father.[16]

IV. "The membership committee has the honor to inform…"[17]

Samuel apparently felt quite comfortable with his connection to the University of Pennsylvania throughout his undergraduate years. He worked hard and took advantage of the opportunity the college provided him. In part he applied himself because of his father's position and of his brother's previous accomplishments, but in a larger sense his dedication was due to his personal drive to succeed. Samuel's pride led him to believe that anything less than a person's best was a mark of laziness and a degradation of one's honor. This trait, though not always manifested positively, would be associated with him throughout life, at times making him seem arrogant, haughty, and conceited.

As he successfully worked his way through the maze of courses, he felt compelled to be more than merely a graduate of the institution. Samuel aspired to be recognized as a scholar. Being selected to the Philomathean Society could provide the capstone to his academic achievements. Membership was based on the ability to demonstrate scholarship, character, and leadership. Members were expected to "impact the wider world of ideas in their post-graduate years."[18]

In November of his junior year, Samuel received what he hoped might be an invitation for membership. He opened the envelope with a degree of anxiety, for he conceivably had heard of pranks being played on hopeful seekers to membership in the past. Thinking that it might only be a request to join a study group, he likely scanned the contents with one eye closed.

> Mr. Samuel W. Crawford, Jr.
>
> The Membership Committee has the honor to inform you, on behalf of the Philomathean Society of the University of Pennsylvania that on the evening of the twelfth of November, eighteen hundred and forty-four, you were selected for membership to the above-mentioned society.
>
> The society requests your acceptance in writing.
>
> > With respect,
> > The committee of the Philomathean Society.[19]

The transforming effect of that eight by ten piece of parchment on 17-year-old Samuel's attitude and outlook was palpable. Until then, he felt others saw him as the son of Reverend Samuel or the brother of John Agnew. Now he had achieved recognition of his own merit. Ever mindful that his father would credit the Almighty, Samuel believed his hard work and persistence in his studies were a large part of achieving the honor. However, those thoughts were best left unsaid to his father.

In the beginning, membership in Philo would have undoubtedly required a meeting one evening a month along with a service duty. The amount of time required varied with the objective of the committee assignment. Over time, he became more and more involved in the society. Guest speakers with expertise in social, political, and philosophical matters were not only found to be engaging, but they also provoked thought and controversy. In his senior year, Samuel was selected moderator of the Philomathean Society, and he found it consuming much of his time and energy.[20] However, the position enabled him to influence the society at a time when radical changes were taking place in America. These exhilarating times imbued within him an obligation to give voice to conditions on the national scene.

The highlight of the academic year centered on the Philomathean Society and its debate with the Zelosophic Society. It was a tradition that allowed scholars to demonstrate their intellectual prowess and reap some of the justifiable prestige therein garnered. Samuel's good time at Penn would always be remembered and further enhanced by his association with the Philomathean Society. He had the opportunity to meet many who would go on to illustrious careers. Future Philadelphia notables such as Robertson Wharton and Caldwell Biddle had served with Samuel in the organization.[21]

Some of his last year as a senior sophister was devoted to the research and writing of his senior thesis. After it was finished, he would have to defend it orally. His topic on ornithology was approved, and he made his successful defense in June 1846. He was one of 29 class members to be graduated. Eighty-five percent of his freshman class had successfully completed the degree requirements.[22]

Graduation did not sever his ties to Penn as he would continue an active association with the university throughout his lifetime. Samuel saw the value of what had been accomplished. He had started four years earlier as an immature, inquisitive, and somewhat intimidated 14-year-old. Through his hard work, the school's firm foundation, and family support he was ready for the next stage in his life.

Samuel Wylie Crawford would need all the skills and knowledge he had acquired in order to move on in the challenging medical profession. Like his country, he was young, exuberant, and full of confidence. He displayed that same vigorous attitude that seemed emblematic of the nation. Problems existed, but they could be and would be overcome. After all, this new land of America was a nation of problem solvers.

Reverend Samuel Crawford, educator, minister, and the family patriarch.
Crawford Papers, Library of Congress

John Agnew Crawford, brother and mentor of General Crawford. Like his father, he was a minister and educator.
Courtesy of Falling Spring Presbyterian Church, Chambersburg, Pa.

This wartime photo appears to be of General Crawford and his brother and aide, Alex McLeod Crawford, on the right.

USAMHI

This is Alandale just before the turn of the 20th century. Barely visible are two ladies, Samuel's sister Margaret's daughter and her child. At this time they were Jane and Janet Wiestling.

Courtesy of Kittochtinny Historical Society

Part Two

The Penn Years

"The two buildings on Ninth Street."
—Amey Hutchison,
Archivist, University of Pennsylvania

"Perhaps this medical institution . . . may collect a number of young persons, of more than ordinary abilities, and so improve their knowledge as to spread its reputation to distant parts . . ."
—John Morgan; George W. Corner,
Two Centuries of Medicine

Alandale, the Crawford homestead near Fayetteville, Pa. Samuel W. Crawford was born here in 1827.

Courtesy of Kittochtinny Historical Society Library, Chambersburg, Pa.

The Crawford homestead today. Owned by the Chris Shorb family at the time this book was written.

Author's photo

❧ Chapter Three ☙
Back to Philadelphia and Penn

I. The End of the Days of Endless Wonder

The trip back to Philly surely lacked the emotional anticipation of the trip to Alandale. One can imagine Samuel looking upon the passing countryside as the train chugged toward the connecting point in Harrisburg; he could not help but believe that whatever they did for the rest of their lives no member of the family would think of this summer, or Alandale, without thinking of each other. This retreat, would not, could not, be duplicated ever again. The unforeseen changes coming to the lives of the Crawfords and to their nation would create a world none of them could have imagined.

In a couple of years, Anne married Andrew Wilson and moved to Orange County, New York, where they carved out a piece of life for themselves. Their new home reminded Anne of a miniature version of Alandale; she enjoyed her role as farmer's wife and within a short period of time the role of mother.[1]

II. The Large and the Diminutive City

Upon the Crawfords' arrival back in Philadelphia, Alex was soon ready to try his hand at college life. The time the brothers spent together would prove valuable as they strengthened the shared blood bond and grew closer in what was to prove a lifelong welding of trust and friendship. Driven by fate and circumstances this relationship would grow throughout their lives.[2]

The differences in the two environments must have been rather jarring to Samuel and Alex. Surely life in Philadelphia would prove to be a sensory shock to them. The City of Brotherly Love was a startling contrast to the small towns of Chambersburg and Fayetteville. It would be difficult not to notice the amount of noise. The sounds of numerous carriage wheels added to those varied wharf and factory wagons clamoring and crunching over the roughly paved streets. These sounds were accompanied by the din of multiple conversations, ultimately making Chambersburg sound like "the proverbial tree falling in the forest." In the country town they were entertained by the occasional rush of a few stage coaches arriving or departing, the infrequently ringing courthouse bell to signal the gathering of the town fathers, or the occasional grinding of the farmers' wagons as they made their way to the market or the gristmill.

Another contrast they no doubt detected was the general pace of life. In Chambersburg, the clerk at Miller's Drug Store or the one at Hoke's Dry Goods or perhaps those at Huber's Hardware all had time to thank you and spare a few moments to converse. Weather was the most popular topic and everyone spoke of it with an assured authority. After that, the small talk became unpredictable as to its concern. The purpose of the chitchat was generally friendly, but on occasion a customer got the sense that gossip mongering was the talk's purpose. To know everything about everyone was a small-town occupation. In Philadelphia, life's tempo was rapid and everyone seemed to be perpetually late. They had to go faster and faster in an effort to catch up. No time to waste on matters that seemed trivial. Theirs was an ever-changing industrial city, more of an impersonal world. In the eyes of the Philadelphians, this was the price paid for the progress gained.[3]

Once the pace became second nature, the family became more aware that unique, interesting, and motivating opportunities awaited them. Philadelphia's matrix of cultures represented the diversity that was fast becoming urban North America with the various languages, forms of dress, food, and customs symbolizing the numerous ethnic groups. Thanks to Benjamin Franklin the city was the center of American thought and ideas. Free public libraries were not much further away than the desire to get there.

Father now substituted in his former church in Fairmont where his wife worked by his side. Later he filled the chair of Church History and Pastoral Theology in the Theological Seminary in Philadelphia.[4] Staying in touch with the Fairmont Church meant not giving up his visits to the Fairmont Park area. For him this was the perfect place for a relaxing Sunday afternoon stroll past the Victorian-era mansions, or out to the boat dock where couples enjoyed romantic outings on the Schuylkill River, and later, a walk or carriage ride through Laurel Hill Cemetery.[5]

III. Back to the Other Building on Ninth Street

In the fall of 1847, Samuel, Jr., was back to literary pursuits. His long-range objective to pursue a medical degree was his constant focus. Though neither the ministry nor a college-level teaching post, it was a humanitarian choice nonetheless.

Samuel arranged an appointment with the Dean of the Medical School. It was in the second of the two buildings that he had come to know as Penn. The edifice had an aura that reflected prestige and earned his reverence immediately. As he approached the building, he noticed a stained glass window above the large entrance. In the two floors above, the windows were adorned with small white pillars on either side. As he entered the ornately decorated door, the Penn seal on the back wall gripped his attention along with the orrery that was highly visible. Both made a deep impact on all who passed through.[6]

The dean of the Medical School, Mr. William Horner, certainly let Samuel know that he was familiar with his undergraduate work as he relied on his academic record as well as other administrative data. All the sources revealed much about Samuel's performance as an undergraduate of Penn.

Upon the successful completion of the literary test, Samuel would be eligible to seek the master of arts degree with emphasis on medicine and then apply for medical school in the 1849–1850 academic year. By that time he would have reached his majority, a requirement to be admitted to medical school. He would celebrate his 21st birthday in November of 1848.[7]

Samuel realized that the road ahead would be long and difficult, but he must have been comforted in the self-assurance that he would persevere. Such resolve was a fundamental trait of his personality. Life, for the most part, was a series of tests and readings.

In May of 1847, Samuel Sr.'s sons accompanied him, at his request, to the Laurel Hill Cemetery for the purpose of selecting a family burial plot. Father and sons agreed on a suitable family plot with five burial sites on a hill near some young shade trees. The Schuylkill River flowed a stone's throw away. The location was peaceful and tranquil and a place Reverend Crawford thought would be easy for God to visit. The decision was made: Plot 69 in Section L. It was enhanced by walkways on two sides, allowing the customary strollers to pass near. The regular $100 purchase fee would be halved since Samuel, Sr., was a minister. The bargain was sealed.[8]

Soon after, Samuel's parents were visiting the area during a Sunday stroll and his mother observed that with eyes closed and ears alert she could hear the gently rolling river and the breeze through the nearby shade trees. This was a story that circulated in the family for many years.

Samuel returned to his studies only to be reminded of the stern discipline needed to matriculate at Penn. No sooner had the semester opened when a student was dismissed after he was found with an egg in his pocket. A student-faculty committee had reasoned that the accused was plotting to use the egg as a missile against a professor who he felt had misjudged him. Samuel had reason to be cautious in his actions as well as to intensify his dedication to his studies. In late 1847 all his labors proved worthwhile as he successfully passed the literary test.[9]

His next goal, the master of arts degree, was to be the upcoming academic year's quest. This study would involve numerous courses and readings in mathematics, science, and anatomy; all were subjects for which he had been well prepared by his undergraduate studies. Upon receiving his degree, Samuel was permitted the opportunity to deliver a public dissertation if so desired. No record indicates that he took advantage of the moment. He was undoubtedly already looking forward with special anticipation to his next great challenge.[10]

❧ Chapter Four ☙
Medical School: University of Pennsylvania

I. The Study of Medicine

All through life Samuel had been taught, in both formal and informal settings, to have respect for the written word. However, that same respect brought with it the responsibility to analyze critically to discern the truth of a document. Now, as he read through the instructions and procedures outlined in the requirements section of the medical brochure, he tried to detect exactly what it intended.

He was to begin his lecture series on the first Monday of October 1849. Not only must he be prepared to produce his matriculation card to the dean of admission as evidence of his eligibility, but he needed to pay "$105 for each lecture ticket, payable at the initial lecture."[1]

Furthermore, each class would meet three times weekly with an additional Saturday recitation. The character of the student's recitation would be communicated to the parents. At term's end there were to be public oral exams. After successful completion of the exams, the five-member board of trustees would then determine if the candidate was competent to attend the clinical part of the course. Three negative votes would reject the candidate. After becoming acquainted with those stipulations, the additional $5 matriculation fee, the $10 practical anatomy fee, the $10 hospital fee, and the $30 graduation fee seemed less consequential.[2]

Samuel arrived for his first class on that October Monday. He took leave of the horse-driven bus at Chestnut and Ninth Street and cut toward the twin marble-trimmed brick buildings with their entrance on Ninth Street. He made his way to the southernmost building, which housed the medical school. The multiple doors stood open to allow any breeze to pass as the end of summer hung on tenaciously. The size and ambience of the building made one feel small, insignificant and slightly overwhelmed.[3]

In keeping with his personality, he was probably quite nervous as he presented the required documentation and paid his fees, having counted the money three times. He was to study anatomy under the renowned dean of the medical school, Dr. William Horner. It was the beginning of an affiliation that would grow closer and more personal, as well as academically enriching. Samuel was stunned to hear of Dr. Horner's death in 1853.

In addition to anatomy, Samuel was to attend classes on the theory and practice of medicine by Mr. George Wood; lectures in chemistry and medicine would be led by Mr. James Rogers, and Henry Smith would address demonstrative surgery.[4]

The readings would prove to be extensive, but a medical library publicized as the largest and best stocked in the United States at the time would provide him with ample resources to meet his needs. The courses were often provocative and the professors were well versed in theory as well as practical experience. Much emphasis was beginning to be placed on homeopathic medicine; Samuel was intrigued by the possibilities. He recognized the period as a captivating time in medicine, as he inched his way forward toward his goal with methodical dedication.[5]

Academically, Samuel proved himself qualified for the next step as he received the votes to begin the clinical portion of his medical schooling. Undoubtedly his inner strength would be challenged. Samuel, himself, contemplated his ability to remain calm under the most trying circumstances: Would a sick or dying person have confidence in him? Could he diagnose problems quickly and clearly?

However, the thing that possibly bothered him and his medical associates most was how they might react to the pressure of treating a dying person. All of these imponderables nagged at Samuel and at times made him less optimistic about his abilities. Still, he must have reasoned that if the board had accepted him into the medical school's clinical branch, then they had faith in him and his potential. He had only to believe in himself and move on to test his resolve.

II. The Clinical Side of Medicine

Samuel probably traveled by train or a horse-pulled bus to Blockley Hospital. Learning was compacted. Training and events spun like a whirlwind. The students were faced with the current challenges in both illness and surgery. Wards at this time were off limits to the students.

During his internship, a patient with a compound fracture was brought to the clinic. Upon examination it was determined there was damage to joints and nerves. Treatment was started immediately and involved amputation. Medical practice at the time considered it wiser to sacrifice a limb in order to save a life. The use of ether was common. However, some physicians were using a relatively new anesthetic called chloroform; it required smaller dosages, but was not as readily available. By the time he was in Fort Sumter, it was a staple.[6]

Amputation would be a procedure Samuel would come to know through personal experience. A cone-shaped sponge soaked with the anesthetic was placed over the mouth and nose of the patient and then a towel placed over all. The patient was then instructed to inhale deeply. After some twitching and slight murmuring, the pulse slowed, and the person was under. A tourniquet was then applied to stop the limb's bleeding. The reality of the demonstration proved riveting in a manner the students were unable to imagine in the earlier classroom lecture. Muscle, fat, and nerves were identified by the color and substance. A larger knife was used to cut the muscle. Some skin was cut in a way that it could be used to cover the bone at the end of the operation. The surgeon worked quickly as he severed the bone transversely. To Samuel the sound was like that of Father cutting through the bone in a piece of smoked ham. An assistant used forceps to close the arteries, and the major blood vessels were ligated with quick slashing pulls of surgical thread. The bone was filed smooth and then the piece of skin was replaced to complete the surgery. The wound was then dressed with warm water and a small amount of camphor.[7]

Samuel was becoming more aware each day that his chosen career represented every aspect of the real world. Mercury proved useful in the treatment of syphilis as well as in the treatment of dysentery. However, too much mercury could induce vomiting, stomach pain, or worse, mercury poisoning.

When time permitted, he sat in on Joseph Carson's course on pharmacy; he learned that his medicine chest would combine the chemicals of the day and many of the herbs in his mother's garden. The professor stressed the practical side of medicine.[8]

Samuel surely had heard the constant coughing, wheezing, gasping, and spitting of that "bastard," pneumonia. It drained the bodies and spirits. Finding cures for the diseases that took the lives of Cornelius and Jane Elizabeth would not happen this semester, maybe not in a year or for a number of years, if ever. Along with that realization, he was probably beginning to understand another truth. A doctor only had so much power, and at times it seemed so miniscule. The medical staff's warning to use the power of medicine to the fullest potential and accept, just as realistically, what it cannot do weighed on the students' minds.

It is easy to imagine that Samuel felt the teaching staff was defying him. His passionate attempts to master medicine at times surely appeared to be equally matched by their convictions that he could not meet their standards. Theories learned only a few months ago now seemed incredibly difficult to apply. He likely struggled with the ability to discriminate between the different fevers and diseases. Symptoms were comparable and clouded diagnoses: typhoid mimicked cholera, malaria resembled yellow fever, and the stomach pains of dysentery were similar to those in cholera. A deferred judgment or a misdiagnosis might mean the loss of someone's brother, daughter, or husband. He understood the reality of death, but, in medicine, he was dealing with the process of death.

He surely hoped a cure for cholera would be found quickly, but fast was not the nature of medicine in most cases. The repulsive physical symptoms slapped your face like the wire bristles of a horse brush. The victim's eyes would fall to the bottom of the orbs, dehydration led to shock, the skin wrinkled, and exhaustion ensued with the limbs becoming icy to the touch. Soon the heart was no longer able to push or pull the mire called blood through the veins and arteries. All the while the eyes of the parent or the grandmother were pleading for help beyond the power of the doctor.[9]

He would soon have to learn that some die by the heart and others by the body. In his mind he would have to understand that medicine could only answer so many questions, only have so many cures. One could but use his God-given and individually developed talents and do his best.

III. National Issues

The outside world was in as much turmoil as was Samuel's psyche. Concentration on his medical pursuits left him limited time and energy to devote to understanding national problems. He feared losing the ability to identify his intellectual and moral positions as he had in the Philo years. His nature demanded that he step back, get things in focus, and understand issues holistically.

At Penn, national issues had always been openly discussed and debated by a diverse student body with varying political persuasions. He certainly followed the course of the war with Mexico, as it had commenced in his senior year of undergraduate school. It was now concluded with a treaty that provided the United States with the second largest land mass ever, adding 500,000 square miles of territory. More land meant additional threats to the already precarious balance of political power.[10] The issue of "free or slave" paralleled the development of nationalism or sectionalism. On the

Mexican issue, David Wilmot, a representative from Samuel's state had attached a proviso to an appropriation bill that paid Mexico for some of the land. He used the language to resemble the Northwest Ordinance of 1787 to rekindle the fires of the slavery issue. The document stated that "neither slavery nor involuntary servitude shall ever exist" in any part of the territories that might be acquired from Mexico. Although the United States Senate rejected Wilmot's idea, the slavery issue and the feelings of sectionalism had been more widely raised "with aggravation once more but without solution."[11]

Popular sovereignty—the voice of the people to decide through voting—and its potential sectional pull now made its rounds in territories like Missouri. James Buchanan opposed the idea because he felt a republic gave the citizens the ability to speak through their representatives. In Kansas he feared popular sovereignty would only invite local war.[12]

Manifest Destiny was riding on steamboats, canals, and railroads. Both internal and external commerce and trade were expanding. Technology was growing. Samuel's father enjoyed reminding others that the cotton gin was patented about the time he was born and the reaper invented during his stint at Penn. One would be pivotal to the economic growth of the South, and the other important to the North and West.[13]

Sectional discord was raising its cobralike head more steadily and more consistently. The question was whether it would prove deadly and strike or be charmed back into its basket.

Historically, compromise had been the substance of America's strength as a nation. Major differences had been solved through give and take, but now the seemingly intractable issue of slavery was back. Can morality be compromised?

Despite his more immediate problems as a 22-year-old medical student, Samuel can be seen drawn into the debate. Schooled in reason, he struggled with the dilemma of whether slavery as a moral and property issue could be compromised within the constitutional role of states' rights.

IV. Hypertrophy and Atrophy

In one of the initial meetings with the medical staff, Samuel and his peers would have been reminded of the obligatory thesis requirement. The student's topic had to be approved by his preceptors, written in the students' own hand, and defended orally before April 1, 1850. Again, three votes in opposition to the oral presentation denied the candidate the right to a medical degree. March 28 was the date of Samuel's presentation for his chosen topics, "hypertrophy and atrophy."[14]

He came prepared as he faced his inquisitors and jury. One can imagine Samuel sitting straight and tall, his slender frame belying a maturity that revealed itself in his eyes. By successfully defending his thesis, he felt an inner strength of a kind not felt in any other of his academic achievements.

The success of Samuel Crawford was not shared by the same percentage as in the undergraduate and graduate programs. Of the accepted applicants, fewer than half earned the degree of Doctor of Medicine.[15]

Graduation took place on Saturday, April 6, 1850, in Musical Fund Hall on Locust Street. Reverend John Ludlow conferred the degrees upon the graduates. After the speaker, Hugh Hodge, Chairman of Obstetrics, finished his address, Samuel said good-bye to a few close friends and hurried to his family to thank them once more for their emotional support. In his inner self, he knew he had the tools, now he needed the wisdom to know how to best use them.[16]

Part Three

The Military Frontier

*"Dr. Crawford was assigned the health of
160 men of the 8th U.S. infantry."*
—James Dickson

*"I remember in the frontier days, from the 800 foot high
rocks the Indians watched our every move."*
—Samuel W. Crawford

A modern view of Fort Sumter.

Author's photo

The casemates today at Fort Sumter.

Author's photo

Chapter Five
Military, Medicine, and Adventure on the Frontier

I. He Was Now S. W. Crawford, M.D.

Samuel had been loyal and dedicated to his goal, his school, and his family. That loyalty aided him in obtaining a medical degree. Now 23 years old with credentials, but no career, he began his search to find a profession and renew his sense of loyalty and dedication in another arena.

Driven to medicine by the desire to serve humanity, he had yet another goal: to serve his country. Perhaps the two could be combined. As a military surgeon, he could unite healing and service. Additionally, he could travel, experience different aspects of the country's culture, and expand his knowledge of the languages and science. These would be profitable perks for a young mind bent on exploring and expanding.

Although most Americans looked upon a military career as a worthy profession, Samuel's family was slightly skeptical. Still, the possibility intrigued him.

II. The Assistant Surgeon

After graduation in April of 1850, he traveled to New York City to take the examination of the United States Army Medical Board. His preparation for medicine had been thorough and genuine. He had indeed received an education from one of the finest medical schools in the country. The results of the grueling oral examination showed that Samuel W. Crawford finished number one in the class of 1850.[1]

On March 10, 1851, Crawford accepted a commission as an assistant surgeon in the United States Army with the rank of captain of cavalry. His pay was $70 a month; the service papers listed his age as "23 4/12 years."[2]

Captain Crawford received his initial orders to report to the headquarters of the 8th United States Infantry on the southwestern border of Texas. He would serve in this territory for approximately three years.[3]

En route to his assignment the steamboat ride would prove a captivating experience for a young man not given to ship travel. Having read about the possibility of boiler explosions, Samuel was surely apprehensive about this mode of transportation; but with the exception of a few listings and strangely fearful noises from the engine area, the trip passed without mechanical incident.

As Samuel prepared for a new phase of his life, he would have had time on the voyage to contemplate the changes taking place in America during this decade. He no doubt thought of the discussions that he, John Agnew, and Alex had at Alandale. They had discussed how change was a constant factor in growing America and that these changes seemed to be taking place more rapidly. Perhaps this was only a perception. Those who immigrated to America's shores saw a lot of change. Certainly, the folks who had participated in the American Revolution felt change that was fast and furious; yet the forces that created change seemed even more powerful now.

The present seemed to have a distinctive tension. The compromises of 1820 and now 1850 seemed to relieve some of the anxiety, but the uneasy feeling was still apparent. Would they be able to continue to compromise their differences as the sections grew increasingly diverse? Could slavery be compromised? The fact that some saw it as a property issue and as a moral issue made it seem insolvable. The issue of slavery was everywhere. One heard and read about the tariff, the Northern control of the banks, but ultimately the subject drifted back to the slave issue. A case in point, the Fugitive Slave act was hated by many who looked on it as morally wrong and had no qualms about disobeying it, even though it was law.[4]

III. Frontier Duty

As a frontier soldier and doctor, Captain Crawford would experience the same problems as any frontier campaigner. He would learn that the weather in the Southwest was extreme. Stifling summer heat was made worse by perfidious dust storms. Winter could be bitterly cold due to unimpeded winds and the poorly insulated and barely heated barracks.

In this environment and under these conditions, Samuel would cross paths with some very interesting soldiers. Two he particularly remembered were James Longstreet and James Ewell Brown "Jeb" Stuart, known as "Pete" Longstreet and "Beau" Stuart.[5]

The military duties fluctuated. At times there was nothing but the routine and boredom of camp life. For the enlisted soldiers the long days were spent in manual labor or brigade drill. Occasionally, the routine was broken with the call to escort a wagon train. Sometimes they were ordered to scout new territories. From time to time, they were involved in clashes with the Indians.

The health of 160 soldiers in the 8th U.S. Infantry was Assistant Surgeon Crawford's primary responsibility. Dealing with camp diseases took up more time and energy than battle wounds. He treated fevers, gastrointestinal complaints, diseases, and a host of almost daily accidents. He had broken legs to set, mashed fingers or toes to bandage, digits to lance, and scorpion stings as well as bee stings to treat. Dysentery was a constant and perplexing problem.[6]

For the first time he would have seen firsthand the ill effects of boredom and loneliness on health. Monotony, combined with the lack of contact with family and friends, often left the men fighting the battle of the bottle. Alcohol, the soldier's age-old solution, was a constant problem. Captain Crawford, himself, tried to keep the mind busy and ever growing to stay away from the slippery slope of alcoholism. In 1853 he wrote, if the enlisted man "loses any interest he may have had in his profession, which finally becomes distasteful to him and he falls, in many instances, the easy victim of the liquor-sellers that crowd around the frontier posts."[7]

The primary mission of the United States Infantry, in his assigned region, was to oversee the Comanche Indians. According to the treaty with Mexico, the United States was "honored" to keep the Indians out of Mexico. Most of the army's strength and energy was devoted to seeing that the tribes remained under control and confined to areas in Texas and the Southwest.[8]

The discovery of gold presented additional security challenges for the 8th Infantry. An onslaught of western-bound settlers prompted angry Indians to strike back as they were driven first from their homeland and then from land promised to them by treaty.

In January of 1854, while Samuel was assigned to Fort Davis, Texas, before leaving on a scouting party to New Mexico, he lived under the watchful eye of the Comanche. Seven years later he could still recall the vivid image of the Indians on the rocks eight hundred feet above. The drawing sent to him by his brother triggered his thoughts concerning the Indian problem of those years. He recalled how far and how accurately the Indians could send smoke signals to communicate to each other.[9]

Experience no doubt boosted Samuel's confidence in his abilities as surgeon. After a year and a half, he would leave his first permanent assignment with mixed emotions. He had done his best, but he experienced some failure. Medical school with its rigors of mental discipline and routine had helped him adapt to frontier life. He heard the child's first cry and witnessed the unmistakable rattle of death. Still, he remained proud to be a physician.

IV. Chihuahua Del Trio and Popocatepeti

In the years from January 1854 until October 1856, Samuel augmented his military experiences with his love of science and his desire to study flowers and birds. He made excursions to San Juan de Los Argos to attend the great December fair. The magnificence of the country showed in the blooming fields and spread throughout the mountains and valleys. At the fair, the weavers blended all those same brilliant colors into their blankets, garments, and native costumes.[10]

He would never forget the beautiful province of Chihuahua Del Trio. There he saw specimens he had cited in his senior essay in their natural habitat. Hundreds of species of birds and butterflies were omnipresent in their rare beauty.[11]

Near the headwaters of the Rio San Saba and the unexplored El Paso Del Norte territory, he conducted more botanical and zoological research which he sent to the Smithsonian Institute. The United States Congress ordered this research published the following year.[12]

In 1856 he received permission from the War Department to travel by train through Mexico, and on October 23, 1856, he entered Mexico City where he reported, as instructed, to the American Foreign Minister. In a couple of weeks he would observe his 29th birthday. After a long discussion, the minister requested Samuel's permission to ask the War Department to have him detailed to the embassy. He would be used to assist in negotiating a pending Indian treaty. Captain Crawford's familiarity with the land and his expertise with the language made him a valuable asset to the staff. The exposure gained from the diplomatic experience was to prove a mixed blessing in his military career. Strategically exercised manners and the ability to relate to others to achieve positive results were desirable practices in the diplomatic corps. In the military, on the other hand, those same maneuvers were often looked upon with suspicion.[13]

In the later months of 1856 while on the staff of the American Embassy, Samuel made the acquaintance of a Prussian gentleman with an interest in science who was a representative of his government assigned to explore Mexican volcanoes.[14] Their mutual respect grew each day as they explored the natural history of the country. They decided to tour and to climb Popocatepeti, a volcano about fifty miles southeast of Mexico City. In January 1857 the 30-year-old adventurer and the Prussian scientist probably paid about $97.50 each to join the expedition. The scientist and Samuel, who was armed with a special barometer and other equipment, made their way toward a small ranch base camp at Slamacos. There they met their tour guide and a number of others going on the climb. They left the base camp and began their ascent, overcoming many obstacles en route. Their pace slowed as they approached the snow line. As the snow deepened and the oxygen became rarefied, the others turned back but Samuel and the guide trekked on. The footing became more torturous, the breathing more difficult, and with less than a half mile to go, Samuel feared he also might become a victim. However, with the guide's encouragement he made it to the summit.[15]

Samuel found the exhilaration worth the laborious journey and its toll on his body. He and the guide rested for the night inside the crater as protection from exposure. In the early morning, the guide eased Samuel into the cavity using a number of ropes. He was lowered about one hundred feet where he procured mineralogical specimens of sulfur, basalt, and lava. He also was the first person to carry a barometer to the summit. Before returning he "climbed the sister mountain, Iztuchihuatl, known as the 'white woman.'"[16] He settled the national debate by proving the mountain was no volcano since it had no crater. Popo was the highlight of volcano exploration for Samuel. He sent several volcanic specimens to West Point, and scientific journals would carry many articles about his exploits.[17]

As a result of his part in the expedition, in 1858 Mexico designated Samuel an honorary member of the Mexican Geographical Society.[18]

V. The Wild West

After the volcano explorations, Samuel was ordered to Washington. Armed with messages and dispatches from Mr. Forsyth of the American Embassy, Samuel Wylie made his way to the State Department in Washington, D.C.[19]

On March 6, 1857, he likely heard the news of the Supreme Court's Dred Scott decision, just two days after the presidential inauguration of fellow Pennsylvanian James Buchanan. Buchanan had heard the results of the case from a justice prior to his inaugural. The principles involved in the decision would have profound consequences on Buchanan's policy, the country, and the military career of Captain Crawford.

In 1858, having served more than five years in the medical division of the United States Army, Samuel was permitted to wear his full medical uniform. He slipped out of his more comfortable sack coat and donned his full dress uniform, wearing it for the first time to have his likeness taken. The large medical epaulets with his captain bars sat proudly on his shoulders. A gold cord circled his thin waist. A small, thin, ornamental dress sword dangled by his left side. His pose for the folks back home reflected a military presence. He stood straight as an arrow, with his arms crossed, displaying a slight frown and penetrating eyes. His muttonchops almost touched his jacket collar and his black wavy hair swept forward and then layered across his ears. He held his chapeau bas under his right arm. The folks back home would recognize his inward pride.[20]

On March 4 another Pennsylvanian, born about 25 miles from Alandale, had celebrated an event he had wished for many years—the U.S. Presidency. What he wished for, however, made him the loneliest man in America with the desire to go back to "Wheatland," his home near Lancaster.

President James Buchanan was now less than a month shy of 65 years. He had witnessed change throughout his political career, but never as rapidly as now nor with such staggering consequences. The new president sensed the beginnings of social and political fragmentation. Answers, for him, had always been found in the U.S. Constitution, the Holy Bible, and through prayer. Of a legalistic mind, Buchanan struggled to find a way to use the Constitution to heal the problems of the country's division. His service to his country had been varied and unquestionable. Born in Cove Gap, Pennsylvania, he would go on to serve his rural constituents in the Pennsylvania legislature and as a member of the United States House of Representatives and the United States Senate. Later he would serve as secretary of state, then minister to Russia and England.[21] Buchanan had a rewarding career based on the art of compromise. Significantly, Buchanan had not been in the United States during these last tumultuous years as he was serving as United States minister to Great Britain during 1854–56. His art of negotiating differences was more intensely challenged as the sectional issues grew in complexity. The idea of Federal noninterference that had garnered him just under half the vote in the last election was also increasingly unpopular. He tried to appease the South by supporting proslavery legislation and placing those favorable to Southern interests in his cabinet.

He saw his beloved country splintering and disintegrating before he was able to finish his term. For a long while Mr. Buchanan coveted the presidency; when it happened, his hour had passed.

Samuel Crawford would serve under the Buchanan doctrine for what would prove to be some of the most tempestuous years of his military life. During the Fort Sumter crisis of 1861, Samuel was personally dismayed and appalled by what he called Buchanan's "don't initiate policy."[22] Nevertheless, he maintained a certain degree of political agreement on other

Buchanan matters. To him it was a choice of lesser evils, by his own admission; he opposed republicanism.[23]

Captain Crawford was assigned to Fort Adams, Rhode Island, to await his next orders. He sensed he would be sent to the Midwest, given the conditions of that area at the time.

After 1855, the territory of Kansas had two governmental adversaries, each claiming to be the legal entity. The area had become a massive battleground for both pro- and antislavery forces who settled into the region. Both sides tried to populate the area, set up recognized governments, and intimidate the other side. Violence reigned supreme in 1856 and 1857.

In May of 1856 Lawrence, Kansas, was sacked by the proslavery elements. Days later "John Brown and his sons retaliated by killing in cold blood five pro-slavery folks on Pottawatomie Creek."[24]

In the spring of 1858, Captain Crawford was assigned to accompany an expedition against Indians on the Red River in Texas led by William T. Sherman and General David Twiggs. After a number of Indian skirmishes, Crawford continued the expedition cross country to Kansas.[25]

The duty on this frontier expedition and post reminded him of his first assignment in the Southwest, except the political atmosphere was much more electrical and explosive. The problems, the diseases, and the lifestyle once again reflected frontier life. While the duties of post surgeon were satisfying, it was the frustration created by the seemingly endless cycle of military routine and boredom that was causing Crawford to begin to question the life of a military surgeon. Naturally, he had to realize this was the same for all soldiers on frontier duty.

Was it the almost 10 years in the regular army, the frustration of medicine, or was it the need for a change in venue? Whatever, change was on the way. After a brief visit to the mountains of Pennsylvania and a "short respite"[26] in Newport, Rhode Island, the batteries would be recharged and the doctor would be ready for a new challenge, one that would change his life.

This photo of Crawford is an early one taken in his full dress medical uniform. Notice the wavy hair and the thin waist.

USAMHI

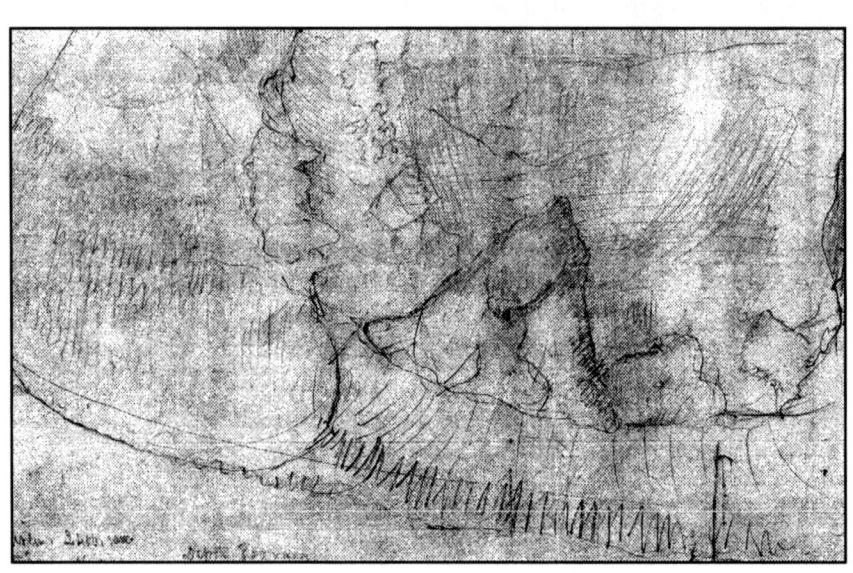

This is a drawing Samuel made of the interior of Popocatepeti Volcano that he climbed in Mexico. Some dimensions are recorded in lower left.

Drawing from Crawford Papers, Library of Congress

ଛ Part Four ଓ
The Moultrie and Sumter Experience

"I am prepared to cry, God's speed to a division in these states if the time has come when all cannot live in the Union with equal rights and in common brotherhood."

"When historians seek a cause for this wanton rebellion, they can look at a government that left a handful of troops to perish while trying to maintain the honor of its flag."
—Samuel W. Crawford

Crawford's drawing of Institute or Secession Hall. "I was in almost daily attendance upon the convention which passed the Ordinance of Secession..."

Crawford, *Genesis of the Civil War* and Crawford Papers, Library of Congress

ᛞ Chapter Six ଔ
The Call to Moultrie

I. A Few Days' Respite

In the summer of 1860 Captain Crawford was reassigned to Fort Adams, Rhode Island. Before reporting to duty at his new post, he had an opportunity to go to Alandale for a brief visit.

Crawford would have noticed a number of changes in Chambersburg since last he visited. He likely would have noticed the relatively new courthouse and recognized a few familiar stores. Chambersburg proved a natural crossroad for trade and travel. Captain Crawford, thinking as a military man, now became aware that the good roads could be used to move large segments of military men and equipment. The town had grown, but it still retained a sense of small-town America. The homes were well kept and displayed a degree of moderate middle class affluence. Chambersburg was special to him in a different way than Philadelphia.

He followed tree-lined Market Street out of town. An hour's leisurely ride would bring him to the homestead. The topography of this green valley was so different as to be shocking when compared to the plains and prairies where he had spent most of the last decade.

Samuel's visit to his home was to be one of rest and relaxation. Margaret and Edward were in Ohio where Edward would eventually join the United States Infantry. Margaret would bring the children back to the old homestead during those years.[1]

Alex had decided to emulate his brother Samuel by trying to become a medical doctor. The army surgeon warned him of the severity of the curriculum and the degree of commitment needed to succeed. But first Alex had to matriculate the college courses, obstacles in themselves.

Back in the mountains of Pennsylvania one can conjure the image of father and son bonding as they probably rode to the Woodstock Mill about a mile east of Alandale. Like others this mill was an essential part of rural America for it was here that his father not only had his grain ground but heard the latest gossip. The Woodstock Mill was the same as Samuel remembered from his youthful visits. The monstrous, slow revolving water wheel still squeaked and groaned as it provided power for the milling process. It was still frightening.[2]

Another morning assuredly Samuel joined his father for a carriage trip eastward to Caledonia and its Iron Works. During the ride, father and son basked in the passing shades of green, sun, and shade. They smelled the earthy fragrances of the forest. The two conversed in a comfortable, relaxed manner probably about national issues.

After the five-mile journey, they came to Thaddeus Stevens Iron Works where Samuel, Sr., sought information from Mr. Sweeny, the manager, concerning the construction of a small furnace like the one near the blacksmith shop.[3] After gathering information, they began the return trip and likely eased into a resumption of their earlier conversation.[4] They would have almost certainly agreed that the Northern and Southern factions of the Democratic Party might help elect the Republican, Abraham Lincoln. Young Samuel had no compunction voicing his belief that Lincoln was a third-rate politician whose election would cause the South to secede. "It is not the time for an uncouth Hoosier to lead these United States."[5] Captain Crawford would afterward proclaim, "Under Seward there is hope."[6]

On a warm morning in late August, Samuel and his father must have been sitting on the front porch discussing nothing earth shattering when Father saw an object in the sky and ran for his glasses. Sam, too, noticed a colorful object in the sky and ran to obtain a better look. The object seemed to be descending toward a nearby field; realizing it was going to land in one of his fields, he ran toward it. As he drew closer, he saw a man waving his cap from a basketlike contraption with an enormous red, white, and blue air bag above his head. The basket car hit the ground and bounced as the gentleman inside held tight to the top of the basket. The man was out of his balloon before Samuel arrived and asked for some aid to secure it. He introduced himself as, "Mr. John Light, aeronaut." He had left the square of Chambersburg and was on his way to Waynesboro. Father came breathlessly up as Mr. Light told of the beautiful view of the valley from the balloon's vantage point. Before Samuel could ask a thousand questions, as he often did, the gentleman spoke of his adventure and that he had inflated the balloon with gas from the Chambersburg Gas Works. The valves allowed him to apply or release gases to adjust his height. The winds today were slight, and when he descended too low, he ran into trouble and grounded. He assured them he would go higher from this point to his destination. Samuel surely showed great interest in accompanying him but had to be discouraged as his carriage was made for one man to move and operate the balloon. Others had gathered and about 3 p.m. the men followed the aeronaut's instructions to assist him in lifting his balloon off terra firma. Samuel envied the courage of the brave and skillful gentleman and hoped one day they made larger cars so that passengers could experience the feel of flight.[7]

Much too soon, Crawford's time to report to Fort Adams, Rhode Island, was at hand. He would turn 33 in a few months and probably considered what the circumstances would be on his next visit to Alandale. Would America be as they had known it, or just another failed experiment in representative democracy? In late August or early September, 1860, Captain Crawford returned to his rather familiar surroundings at Fort Adams.[8]

II. The Aroma of Bacon, Eggs, Ham, and Biscuits

Captain Crawford had missed many things about home while on the frontier but nothing more than the food of the green valleys. When he returned to civilization and real food, he found himself the first person at breakfast, his favorite meal, and the last to leave. Although back on the frontier he was not likely to abandon his habitual eating habits.[9]

The morning probably began with a fresh cool glass of water, preferably in a dark blue tumbler, and a large glass of apple juice made from Macintosh apples, if the season permitted. He sipped slowly and conversed deliberately, allowing the chef to prepare his two flapjacks to a golden brown and a slice of country cured ham tanned slightly around the edges. A cup or two of fresh coffee with a small bowl of seasonal fruits completed the morning banquet.

Given the conditions of the United States in the summer and early fall of 1860 and Crawford's penchant for discussing issues, he most likely queried his friends, army personnel representing many different areas of the country, about events in their hometowns.[10]

Since Samuel had visited Chambersburg, he likely fielded many questions about John Brown. It was, after all, a highly controversial subject and would remain so. Admittedly, Samuel could relay what he had heard and read during his recent visit home. His father, as minister and abolitionist, likely spoke of the incident with frequency. Brown had rented a room in Chambersburg, an active Underground Railroad community, under the identity of a miner. Many of the arms used at Harpers Ferry were shipped to and stored in Chambersburg. Prior to his exit from Pennsylvania, Brown had met with Frederick Douglass in Chambersburg. He was obviously unsuccessful in enlisting the support of Douglass. Later the idea surfaced that Douglass opposed the raid because it was to be conducted on Federal property.[11]

The Harpers Ferry raid lasted only about a day and a half. Ten persons were killed, including a couple of Brown's sons. The raid was quelled by the United States Marines under Colonel Robert E. Lee aided by James Ewell Brown Stuart.[12]

Brown's trial engendered an emotional response by almost all familiar with the attack. Most agreed that the charges of treason and conspiracy filed by Virginia governor Henry Wise were unusual since Harpers Ferry was in Virginia where Brown was not a resident. Furthermore the raid had been committed on Federal property, not Virginia property.[13] The Southern citizens, however, feared slave uprising and wanted to make an example of Brown and his actions. No doubt the debate grew quite intense as the group shared the many faceted possibilities of Brown's actions and execution.

On the fateful day of September 7, Fort Adams activity began early like a typical New England morning. The air hinted at fall, while some of summer's warmth lingered. The trees, with green foliage dominating, had begun to display hints of autumn oranges, reds, and yellows. The morning dew, while evident, was light. It was, they agreed, one of God's most delightful gifts—autumn in New England.

III. "The Secretary of War directs that you proceed . . ."[14]

Samuel sat with friends on the lawn enjoying the beginning of the changing foliage as a telegram delivery man approached the cluster. The message was for Captain Crawford, who excused himself and read the contents in private. The telegram informed him that he was to proceed immediately for duty at Fort Moultrie, South Carolina. "Leaving the table at once, I was soon on my way to Charleston."[15]

Crawford was puzzled by the telegram. The contents were no surprise, but why had the War Department notified him in this manner? The telegraph was not normally used by the U.S. Army for ordinary business. No matter, he bade farewell to his friends and immediately made arrangements for rail travel.

Once under way, Crawford pondered as to "why he was being sent so far south in the sick season?"[16] The heat seemed to increase dramatically once he was south of the Potomac River. The oppressive humidity was only more of a burden. While trying to deal with the discomfort, he overheard someone in the car state, "The papers cannot suppress it, the yellow fever is in Charleston and the Fort's surgeon has just died of it."[17]

The reality of the situation was at once made crystal clear. Assistant Surgeon Crawford was to be the replacement for the fort's surgeon. A sense of grave apprehension hung over him as he moved toward his new assignment.

When his train arrived in Charleston shortly after 3 a.m. on September 8, 1860, a weary Samuel Wylie grabbed his baggage and inquired the direction to the chief hotel. He made his way on deserted streets. Even at this time of the morning the heat and humidity were oppressive. As he registered, the clerk on duty inquired if he was a Union officer to be stationed at Moultrie. Upon Crawford's affirmation, the clerk suggested that he try to make his way to Moultrie, since he would most likely be the only person in the hotel.[18]

"I have never been here but I've been told it's about . . . isn't it five miles?" Crawford inquired. "At least," the clerk yawned in response.[19]

"What means of transportation do you suggest?"

"There is none," the clerk said nonchalantly. "The boats stop running at 2 a.m.; and the horse carriage connecting the steamboat wharf is also closed."[20]

Frustrated, tired, and with his options limited, Crawford took a room. Was it his uniform or the yellow fever paranoia that elicited such a welcome? In either case, he anticipated further incidents.

IV. The New Home of Fort Moultrie

The next morning he made his way leisurely by boat to Sullivan's Island and then by horse car to his new home. A look around his new home gave him an idea of the size and condition of the sea fort. At places he walked the footing was slow and difficult. As he looked up, Captain Crawford noticed a high brick battery with guns directed on the channel. It loomed like a contemporary castle. As he moved inside, he recognized what he thought to be the officer's quarters to the left on the second story. What he took for enlisted men's barracks was on the opposite side. The administrative offices were located toward the back of the fort.[21]

One of the initial introductions was Chaplain Matthias Harris, who would have been concerned about the possibility of yellow fever. He told Samuel of his Maryland roots. His past 11 years spent at Moultrie had been, for the most part, pleasant, if not ideal. Harris was quartered, along with his wife, in a cottage outside the compound in Moultrieville. He chatted freely and rather dominated the conversation, leaving no doubt in Samuel's mind that he was a strong Union supporter. Those beliefs had served him well, but now those opinions were not so popular in Charleston. A storm seemed to be brewing.[22]

The post commander, Colonel John Gardner, sent a messenger to "summon him to the bedside of his servant."[23] The man feared he had yellow fever since he had aided a number of individuals who died from what was thought to be the dreaded disease. One can imagine the assistant surgeon gently touching the servant's head to determine if he had a fever. He would have checked the patient's eyelids and tried to discover if the man had swollen glands and complained of joint pain. He was told that the elderly colored gentleman had been passing urine regularly. Samuel could not be sure immediately if it was the dreaded disease. Eventually he was able to diagnose it as dengue or bone fever, usually marked by vomiting and stomach pain before the fever would break. This disease, though dreadfully painful and longer lasting than yellow fever, was rarely fatal.[24]

Colonel Gardner informed Captain Crawford that his normal medical concerns would consist of seven or eight officers, two understaffed companies of artillery, about seventy men in all, the band, and some soldiers' wives and children.

The commander made it known he wished to talk to him about the previous surgeon. In an extremely low and deliberate tone, Commander Gardner chose his words carefully. Samuel sensed his uneasiness. He told the new doctor of the plight of the previous surgeon, Captain Byrne, and, therefore, the reason Captain Crawford had been sent to Fort Moultrie. Byrne had been sick, and he believed it was yellow fever. He went on sick leave and stayed there for over a month. During that time more soldiers and civilians died. Byrne asked a civilian doctor in town to care for those patients that he had been doctoring. Those in Charleston thought he just did not want to care for them because he was busy caring for his sick wife. They both survived. The soldiers, their wives, and civilians who lost loved ones brought pressure on Gardner to get rid of the surgeon, charging he was interested only in his own needs and interests. Gardner was forced to call for a court-martial. Some witnesses spoke on the surgeon's behalf, and a Charleston doctor informed the court Captain Byrne was not obligated to care for the town folk even though that was traditional. However, he was found guilty of negligence and forced to resign.[25]

Dr. Crawford assured Colonel Gardner that he would try to do his best to care for the soldiers at Moultrie and also assist the doctor in Charleston. Both men agreed that the practice of medicine proved a good means of public relations in these times.

The surgeon spent his initial time familiarizing himself with the hospital, its facilities, and meeting with his steward, Ed Weitfieldt, a 24-year-old soldier from Hanover, Germany, in his second year of service.[26] He would prove to be a worthy and valuable steward in providing aid to the garrison members, often without Crawford's urging. He was reimbursed $22.65 a month, plus rations and clothing allowance. Weitfieldt was required to write legibly and spell accurately. He probably aided the assistant surgeon in minor surgeries and would have been able to bandage and dress wounds.[27] He was Samuel's man "Friday."

V. Captains Doubleday and Seymour

Captain Crawford, usually aware of his surroundings, would have likely observed the brick chapel, the beacon light, a sandy hill, and Colonel Gardner's home. He was soon to meet the second in command, Captain Abner Doubleday, a dark-haired, stocky New Yorker who was the outspoken, and the only, officer, by his own admission, in favor of abolition and Abraham Lincoln.[28] He would later say that Captain Crawford was "genial, studious, and full of varied information."[29] He no doubt informed the surgeon of all the weaknesses of the Buchanan administration and other varied information of his own. Captain Doubleday was suspicious of the Carolinians and, therefore, communicated with his brother in code with information for Lincoln. Later when Mrs. Doubleday lived in Washington she was visited by Lincoln so he could better comprehend the situation in Sumter. Captain Doubleday surely warned Captain Crawford about the mad Carolinians. The two men certainly shared ideas about national problems, and grew to appreciate their differences even if they were diametrical. Crawford probably thought him gruff, but so much of the time he realized the captain had his finger on the pulse of events at Moultrie and the Southern mind. Doubleday thought the captain more of a scholar than warrior, but detected in Samuel's personality the desire to someday make a name for himself as a soldier.[30]

Captain Crawford, in all probability, told Abner Doubleday that his father had been born and orphaned in the Charleston area and the folks had treated him with care. The assistant surgeon, having some family there who were close and prized, indicated the city folk agreeable to him. The pull between the love of family and love of country was real for Crawford as it would be for many in the future.[31] Abner probably chided Samuel for healing those who could turn against him. Captain Crawford and Captain Doubleday would come into close proximity in 1862 at Antietam, again the following year in Gettysburg, and ultimately in a 1865 celebration just across the water at Fort Sumter.

In the process of getting acquainted with his duties and the fort's personnel, he met another rather tough maverick to whom he could relate, Captain Truman Seymour. They were both sons of ministers and both released tension in the following months by drawing. Truman was more adept at his art as he had taught drawing at West Point, but Captain Crawford was a novice who sharpened and polished the new skills learned from this teacher.[32] In the next six months both would have their drawings published in *Harper's Weekly*, both would leave Fort Sumter suffering from illnesses, and both were enthralled with the skills of engineering. Crawford was fascinated by the creations of Seymour who could build almost anything. They, too, would both be in command of divisions in the Appomattox campaign and be the only officers from Fort Sumter to attain the rank of general. They would truly connect Fort Sumter and Appomattox.

As the chill winds of November replaced the warmth of summer, the assistant surgeon became aware that the post commander was an "old and worthy soldier"[33] with a military bearing and sense of courtesy that engendered the respect of all. Yet, in Doubleday's and Crawford's minds, Gardner did not fully comprehend the changing military, which he had been a part of since the War of 1812, and the importance of the Charleston harbor forts in the Southern mind. He seemed "slow to awaken to the reality of his position in these radically changing times." Doubleday wrote that he was "ill-fitted to weather the storm about to burst upon us."[34]

Crawford, upon his arrival at Moultrie, had observed a lack of military discipline. No guards were posted over storehouses or near the highly flammable wooden buildings. The hospital had no sentinel, and entrants to the fort faced little challenge. The situation thus allowed a growing number of spies, professional or amateur, access to valuable military information. Even local newspaper reporters discerned every move within the compound.[35]

Commander Gardner was often absent from inspections and drills. It was believed that he longed for the good old days when duty at the fort transpired in a country club atmosphere, when relations with its neighbors were cordial, and "the military band furnished the attractive feature and the parapet was the daily promenade of the fashionable throng."[36] It had been a time of shiny brass buttons and insignias that symbolized the era more than weapons and military hardware.

It was generally agreed that both Sumter and Moultrie needed increased manpower, weaponry, and repair. Colonel Gardner failed to act forcefully enough to obtain them to the degree they were needed. Perhaps he tired of fighting the Washington status quo.

Captain Doubleday indicated that after applying pressure on Colonel Gardner to request workers to aid in the repair of the forts, he acquiesced and the workers were used to strengthen the defense perimeter of Fort Moultrie.

In early November, Captain Seymour was entangled in an incident that inadvertently led to the end of Colonel Gardner's command at the fort. Ironically, Captain Seymour was substituting for Lieutenant Norman Hall, who was scheduled to make the trip but overslept.

Recently, one of the troubles emerging between the commander of Fort Moultrie and the state of South Carolina was that of access to the U.S. Arsenal located on the Ashley River in the city of Charleston. As tensions mounted in Charleston as well as South Carolina, the arsenal attracted critical focus from each side. The Charleston authorities believed they were at the mercy of the forts, and after secession, the state planned to capture the arms stored in the arsenal. The military, on the other hand, wanted them for protection, and their reduction meant they could not be used against them.[37]

The fear of a mob attack on the workers hired by the engineers to repair the area forts was an immediate concern for the military, but even then the issue did not end cut-and-dried. Not all workers were loyal to the Union cause; in fact, some were brave enough to wear secessionist cockades. Colonel John Gardner referred to them as "secession propensities and foreign nativity."

The problem that emerged on November 7 had its origins in the previous month when John Foster, the captain of engineers, requested 40 old muskets for the protection of his workers. The application was approved by the secretary of war, John Floyd, upon the condition that the commander of the fort would sign on to the request, but Commander Gardner feared the consequences, and the weapons were not issued. In lieu of the muskets the commander applied for two companies of drilled recruits.[38] The order was suspended without action.

On November 7, Colonel Gardner requested from Captain F. C. Humphreys, the arsenal's storekeeper, "all fixed ammunition for small arms," and percussion caps and primers. Captain Seymour became involved the next afternoon when he manned a schooner with a detachment of soldiers dressed in civilian clothes to the city where he docked at a private wharf near the arsenal. The late afternoon was selected since, at night time, the state had troops guarding the armory. The city authorities justified this guard, believing their presence would quell a slave uprising. As Captain Seymour and storekeeper Humphreys conferred inside, the men were ordered to load the boxes on the schooner. They had about four carts loaded when a man appeared claiming he owned the wharf and would allow nothing to leave without the permission of city authorities. As the crowd grew, Captain Seymour was summoned by the corporal in charge of the detail. The alleged owner said he could wave his hand and have another one hundred men appear from a nearby factory. Thinking it best not to create a collision, the boxes were unloaded and the captain, with darkness setting in, decided to avoid further confrontation.[39]

The following day Captain Seymour was given permission by Colonel Gardner to receive an explanation for yesterday's incident. He received an apology from the mayor for the behavior of his constituents and granted permission for the removal of the arms. When Captain Seymour told Gardner of the chain of events, the commander in anger tersely replied that the city authorities had no right in any way to control the transfer of United States weapons.[40]

With all the turmoil in the area, President Buchanan and his cabinet decided it was time to get a close look at the situation at Fort Moultrie. Soon an inspection team under Major Fitz John Porter of the Adjutant General's Office arrived to inspect the discipline and condition of the fortifications and troops. War Secretary Floyd called the colonel's behavior "folly" and seemed intent on removing him. After Porter's inspection, the die was cast and thus ended the command of John Gardner at Fort Moultrie.[41]

Colonel Gardner was not the only distressed Moultrie officer. It was clear to Captain Doubleday that the inspectors came to see if they were doing their duty and then he raged about John Floyd's role of sending "seventeen thousand muskets to South Carolina when he knew that Charleston was a hot bed of sedition and that in all probability the arms would be used against the United States."[42]

VI. Anderson and His Daunting Task

Fort Moultrie's new commander would face a daunting task. The harbor garrisons were understaffed by men with little military discipline; the forts were physically deteriorating, all in an increasingly hostile atmosphere. At least workers had been assigned to Moultrie and progress was slowly being made. Sand had been removed from the scarp wall. The building of flanking devices had begun. In the guardhouses loopholes were constructed for musket fire, and the mounting of more guns was under way. Still, it was the outer defenses against a ground force that made the fort susceptible to potential invasion by Southern militia.

Tensions with the state and city continued to escalate. Since Lincoln's election, secession was now more freely and openly discussed. State militia was being activated and reorganized; judges were leaving their benches, while a troubled Buchanan administration searched for some means to control the Federal machinery and to exercise its authority.[43]

"The way to create revolution is to begin it" was a popular phrase with the Carolinians. However, Doubleday assessed their mood: "They are more bitter now but not as aggressive as they will become because they can still rely on President Buchanan on taking no decisive action against them."[44]

On November 15 the garrison received word that Major Robert Anderson, a West Point graduate, had been chosen to assume command of the United States forts in the harbor. He was coming back to Moultrie after a 15-year absence when he had served a tour of duty. With 35 years service, he was the senior major in the 1st U.S. Artillery. His past service had included a stint as instructor of artillery at West Point, where he had written the artillery manual. He had been seriously wounded in the Mexican War at Molina Del Rey. Known by his peers as a solid, reliable officer, the 5'8" Anderson always stood tall as a gentleman. Although Southern by birth and marriage, he was an antisecessionist. His brother declared him to be a man that lived by the Holy Bible, the United States Constitution, and U.S. Army regulations. Major Anderson felt he had "a hereditary right to be in here"[45] as his father had fought the British from Fort Moultrie. Ironically, he had fought side by side with some South Carolinians for independence. Everyone noticed the major's "gentlemanly manners" and a spiritual sense that sought devine guidance. He frequently wrote, "By the Blessing of God, there may be hope that no blood will be shed."[46]

On November 21 the dawn broke clearer and cooler as Anderson took command. Major Anderson posed a question to Crawford concerning the proper place of the infirmary which at present was outside the fort. The assistant surgeon explained that it would be better within the confines of the fortress. Anderson replied he would see to its removal to the interior. It was the beginning of more than a military relationship between the two officers. They would become trusting associates.

Two days later, "the engineer officer [Captain John Foster] joined Major Anderson on an inspection tour of the harbor forts."[47] The boat tour allowed Anderson to witness the physical condition of the various facilities. Castle Pinckney, a small round brick structure, stood at the mouth of the Cooper River less than a mile from Charleston. It was not garrisoned, but manned by an ordnance sergeant, his family, and a few watchmen. Despite the lack of manpower, it was clear to all that the duty sergeant spent most of his time polishing the cannons and their rounds and trimming the harbor light that gleamed from its walls at night. For all practical purposes, from a military point of view, Castle Pinckney had been abandoned even though 22 heavy guns were mounted on the parapet. Its location was a prime concern to Anderson, as was the fact that the U.S. Arsenal's powder, shot, and shell were stored there. Once Doubleday had gleefully noted that mortars could be lobbed into the city from this fort, Anderson pointed out that shells could also reach Moultrie from this position. The

Charlestonians would not attack Fort Moultrie or Fort Sumter if they knew their city was at the mercy of the commander of Castle Pinckney. Therefore Robert Anderson asked that Castle Pinckney be garrisoned immediately. The captain of engineers, through Secretary Floyd, allowed some engineer workers to be sent.[48]

The ride continued four miles to the narrowest point of the channel "to the fort on the shoal."[49] The inspection party came face to face with an unfinished large pentagon-shaped fortress of brick walls approaching 50 feet in height, Fort Sumter. Anderson had noted the structure's strategically defensive significance when he first sailed to Moultrie. Those with a "Military Eye" saw Sumter as "the key of the entrance to the harbor." Doubleday informed Anderson that the year before, the fort had been used by the U.S. to temporarily confine Negroes who had been captured by the navy in an African slaver.[50]

The accompanying engineer, John Foster, pointed out that even though the fort appeared unfinished and without its full complement of arms, there were some guns in the lower casemates. They found in the parade ground area several 10-inch Columbiads known for their fearful range. Since this fort represented the key to the control of the harbor, it was evident that needed repairs and installations should increase immediately.

Directly across the channel to the east stood Fort Moultrie. Major Anderson noted several major concerns for Moultrie's security. Its potential adversaries were certainly aware of the fort's shortcomings. First, the houses were near enough to the fort to accommodate sharpshooters who could hit his men manning guns on the parapet. Secondly, the sand piles nearby could serve as a staging area for enemy infantry who could then overrun the small garrison. In this November 23 memo, Anderson's first to the war department, he warned about problems that would become constant themes: time is short, undermanned personnel, decayed conditions, lack of weapons that are mounted, the urgency of repair and maintenance, and the hope to prevent blood shedding.[51]

Major Anderson now instituted a plan aimed at alleviating the shortcomings as pointed out by the Porter inspection report. First, he insisted on the enforcement of strict military discipline. Next, guards were placed at all essential buildings, especially at night. Finally, he placed restrictions on what had previously been an easy access policy into the fort.[52] His diplomatic approach differed from the second in command. Doubleday called for burning every house to the ground. Anderson believed to prevent bloodshed the forts must be fortified to a degree that the state would feel it "madness and folly" to attack.[53]

The new commander advised his government of the need to properly repair, garrison, and provide additional ordnance for each fort. And then in a fearful tone he looked into his crystal ball, "the clouds are threatening, and the storm may break upon us at any moment." It was the third week of November 1860 and suspicions on both sides were escalating.[54]

These changes at the forts did not escape official Charleston. The Buchanan administration suggested that the repairs had to be undertaken in case England responded to the Mexican problem. That proposition was, for the most part, suspiciously discredited by the locals. They believed the guns would be turned on them; therefore, Anderson decided to meet with the officials of Charleston to dispel their concerns.[55]

After the meeting, Major Anderson relayed his concerns about the state's attitudes to the War Department. He stressed that the Carolinians were tempted to defy the U.S. Navy and occupy Fort Sumter, thereby compelling the abandoning of Fort Moultrie. This would give them perfect command of the harbor. He also noted that "It is the romantic desire of the Carolinians to possess the works defended so nobly by their ancestors in 1776."[56]

By early December, Captain Crawford was in his fourth month as Moultrie's active assistant surgeon. During that short period, he too sensed change in the attitude and mood of the citizens, becoming more aggressive and defiant in tone. The fear of a developing coalition of Southern states seemed more menacing than in any previous periods of their history.

Each time the major requested enlisted men to garrison the forts and additional ordnance to fill the empty magazines, he faced a Federal government reluctant to act. South Carolina asked the Federal government to maintain the status quo until its decision on the question of secession was finalized—this edict the Federal government followed.

Anderson asked the War Department to be allowed to push down the sand dunes since the houses could not be burned without provocation. Anderson promised they would wait until fired upon before taking action on the houses, but the sand dunes could be leveled now. Then he pleaded that more troops and ordnance be sent. Secretary of War John Floyd countered with the Buchanan line that if the forts were stocked, the state would desire them. If nothing was done, not even pushing sand hills down, a collision was not being initiated. The noninitiating policy was in full bloom.[57]

On December 7 the Buchanan administration sent the assistant adjutant general, Don Carlos Buell, to Charleston to inspect the situation personally and deliver messages from Secretary Floyd to Robert Anderson. After Buell conducted his review, they returned to Anderson's quarters where they discussed the situation and jointly concluded that if Sumter were occupied it could be used to reduce Moultrie.

VII. Buell's Advice

Major Buell also delivered to Anderson written instructions from Floyd, "The Secretary of War wishes to avoid a collision with the state. He will not increase the forces so as to keep from exciting the public mind. Be careful to avoid every act that would provoke aggression. Take no position that would be construed as hostile. If attacked, defend yourself to the last extremity. Your small force can protect only one fort. You can put your command into the one you deem most proper to increase resistance. You are authorized to take steps when you have tangible evidence of a hostile act."[58] Buell ended his time with Anderson with a bit of his own advice, "Do not allow the opportunity to escape you."[59]

Even though Floyd had signed the report, there was no indication he thoroughly read the memorandum when President Buchanan called for it at a cabinet meeting on December 21, 1860. After that, Anderson received yet another memo from Floyd relaying the president's instructions: "it is not the president's intentions that you and your men sacrifice your lives on a mere point of honor. Exercise sound military discretion."[60]

Already heightened tensions were increased by another incident at the U.S. Arsenal in Charleston on December 17. The engineer, Captain John Foster, tried to acquire a couple of muskets for his workers to defend themselves. The military storekeeper told him that he could not have the two guns but could pick up 40 muskets that had been ordered earlier. Foster settled for the 40 weapons. After Secretary of War Floyd heard of the incident, which he was told created "intense excitement,"[61] he telegraphed instructions to Foster to return the muskets in an effort to avoid a confrontation. As he was bid to do, Captain Foster reluctantly returned the munitions on the very day that South Carolina declared its independence from the United States. Foster fumed, "our defense is keeping the gate closed and shutters fastened." Major Anderson expressed his frustration, "they make ready for a fight which must take place and insist upon us doing nothing."[62]

South Carolina's newly selected governor, Francis W. Pickens, wasted no time to jump into the fray. He prepared a letter directed to President Buchanan in which he expressed his desire for all work in the forts to cease immediately. Furthermore, he conveyed his wish that the state deploy forces to occupy Sumter so the citizens of South Carolina would feel a sense of security. Although the aggressive and bold letter was officially withdrawn, it proved to be an omen of events to come. Even on the evening of his inaugural, Pickens ordered gunboats with armed forces to patrol the Moultrie and Sumter area.[63]

Commander Anderson's most pressing concerns in those gloomy days were for both the safety of his men and how to best control the situation so as not to initiate a civil war. One evening after returning from his medical calls in Charleston, Surgeon Crawford alerted the major of a conversation that took place after treating one of his patients. As he was about to depart, the husband asked him to step into his library where the gentleman stressed what he had heard from a reliable source. In approximately fifteen days, he told the doctor, South Carolina planned to occupy Sumter and turn its guns on Fort Moultrie.[64]

VIII. Samuel Crawford and the Secessionist Sessions

Crawford was disappointed to learn that the convention considering secession would convene on December 17, 1860, in Columbia, South Carolina. He would be unable to attend the sessions. He, like Anderson, believed in the value of state powers but not secession.[65] In a highly emotional letter written to A.J. in early December he indicated that he had witnessed the operation of slavery on a plantation. While acknowledging his brother's sincerity, he implied the system may not be as horrible as abolitionists signified. In his final analysis, he questioned what system could replace it. He was still searching for answers. He had hoped to personally watch the proceedings, and then because of an unexpected event, his hopes were fulfilled.[66]

Due to an outbreak of a contagious disease, the convention was reconvened in Charleston on December 18. When the delegates returned to Charleston, the first complaint Crawford heard was that the people were disappointed and openly dissatisfied because the Ordinance of Secession had not been passed. The movement to Charleston had given Crawford the opportunity to attend most of the sessions open to the public. He sensed history was in the making and did not want to miss the opportunity to witness it. The South's attitude was that there was no hope for continuing in the Union since Lincoln's election. They scorned the idea of compromise. Secession was symbolized by replacing the Stars and Stripes with the Palmetto flag. Disunion seemed a foregone conclusion.[67]

As a member of the audience, Captain Crawford noticed with sagacity how history was being written and symbols being used. "One of the first things I noticed on the speaker's podium was the wooden gavel, with the word 'secession' carved in it in deep black characters."[68] Samuel noted the meetings were rushed since "overtures from without were feared." The leaders tried to stir the emotions and subdue reason with inflammatory rhetoric. The appeal to Georges Danton's charge was typical: "To dare! And again to dare! And without end to dare!"[69]

Samuel noticed that the convention delegates appeared to be the older and more financially secure individuals from the populace. He recognized several ex-U.S. senators, former representatives, even a prior house speaker. There were also ex-South Carolina governors, as well as members of the judiciary, clergy, and delegates from earlier secessionist conventions. This time the prevailing aura and structure mandated success. Secession was being carefully orchestrated. Crawford believed that the Southern authorities knew war would be necessary but "held out to the people that no collision would happen."[70]

The ever present tone of the meetings was to pressure the delegates not to compromise. No delays were to be tolerated. The Federal government and its Constitution were railed against. Instead, the delegates pressed the doctrine of state sovereignty and the right to continue slavery. In so doing, they sought to sever all ties with Washington and the Northern states.

On December 19, the delegates met at St. Andrew's Hall so that speakers could be better heard. A dispatch from the governor of Alabama urged the assembly to make no compromises, nor to create any delays. Most of the delegates were of the opinion that separation from the Union and the transfer of Federal property would be peaceful. At least, that was the impression the officials and delegates were trying to create. This broadened their base of support. Some of the more volatile subjects and committee reports were given in closed session. A committee of three would be sent to Washington empowered to accept the delivery of the "forts, magazines, and other real estate. Every step had been anticipated."[71]

With pressure mounting to pass the Ordinance of Secession, a meeting was set for noon December 20, 1860. Ordinary business was concluded rapidly. According to Captain Crawford, who must have appeared out of place in his United States Military uniform, "There were no visible signs that the state of South Carolina was about to take a step more momentous than at any time in her history."[72] Finally, a speaker with a loud firm voice read the following Ordinance of Secession:

> We, the people of the State of South Carolina, in convention assembled, do declare and ordain, and it is hereby declared and ordained, That the ordinance adopted by us in convention on the twenty-third day of May, in the year of our Lord one thousand seven hundred and eighty-eight, whereby the Constitution of the United States of America was ratified...and that the union now subsisting between South Carolina and other States, under the name of the "United States of America," is hereby dissolved.
>
> Done at Charleston the twentieth day of December, in the year of our Lord one thousand eight hundred and sixty.[73]

At 1:30 p.m., by a vote of 169 to 0, the ordinance was approved. The formal signing moved to Institute Hall and lasted from 7 to 9 p.m., whereupon the convention president spoke, "I proclaim the state of South Carolina an Independent Commonwealth."[74] It was five days before Christmas 1860. How would this special birthday be celebrated in Washington, D.C., or in Springfield, Illinois? Differently, no doubt. The United States was now a foreign country.

Inside the Hall, Captain Crawford saw souvenir takers shred the palmetto trees placed on either side of the speaker's chair as the audience "broke out into a storm of cheers."[75]

Outside he saw a city go wild. Cockades were displayed in every hat. Flags of all descriptions, except the national colors, were flying from every public building and most private residences. Bands played, groups gathered to sing, numerous bonfires burned, and the state militia strutted and paraded as public speakers touted the virtues of the state. Charleston's elite and aristocratic folks displayed a swagger that seemed to symbolize the public mood. The doctrine of Calhoun reigned supreme this night. At this moment in time it seemed as if Judge James Petigu's reproach was truthful and precise: "South Carolina is too small for a republic and too large for a lunatic asylum."[76] That evening as the Moultrie officers sat on the parapet, they no doubt heard the continuing drones of the festivities. Now and again they surely caught a glimpse of the flames from the many bonfires. Flames and the fort symbolized two republics within one nation.

Samuel and his brethren were of one voice in their praise and admiration for the physical beauty of the city. Man and nature had joined in a harmonious undertaking in the city of Charleston. But he and the fellow officers agreed that the wealthy, the vocal, and the powerful were the recipients of the beauty and ambience of the aristocratic lifestyles in Charleston, South Carolina. As he had walked pensively through the celebrating crowds, little did he, nor they, know that in four years neither would recognize the city of tonight's memorial celebration.

IX. Christmas Eve, 1860

On Christmas Eve, Surgeon Crawford had completed his medical duties when he encountered Major Anderson. After an exchange of pleasantries, Anderson strongly encouraged the captain to attend chapel later that evening. Despite the torrential downpour, Captain Crawford made his way to the place where he hoped his spirits would be lifted and his commander pleased.[77]

Because of his early home training, Samuel had always arrived early for a church service. One can imagine him relishing the enjoyment of quiet comfort in the intimate sanctuary. The decision to sit near the altar was an unconscious one that Father had insisted on the family members. Tonight Captain Crawford must have felt a unique connection to his loved ones at home. Once seated, he allowed his mind to drift over all that he had witnessed this past year. He had gone from the rough and tumble life of the frontier to a world where an aristocratic economic class was hell-bent on turning the world upside down. Duty in South Carolina had proved a challenge both professionally and personally.

After chapel service, Captain Crawford had been invited along with other officers to a Christmas party at the Foster's cottage. His relaxed style and manners were evident in small social gatherings such as this. He greeted Seymour's sister and expressed his gratitude to both Mary Foster and to Captain Foster himself. He and Major Anderson probably reminisced about home, events, and some trivial matters. They enjoyed each other's company. Of course Samuel, being a doctor, had slightly more liberty to discuss issues with the fort's commander. He had accumulated increased respect for Major Anderson as a military man, as a communicator, and as a man of God. He trusted him without exception and the major enjoyed Crawford's yarns of his varied experiences. The anecdotes served as a means of keeping the mind off the constant pressures, at least temporarily.[78]

Crawford noticed the major seemed distant and left the merrymaking after the children had opened their gifts. He assumed Anderson had departed because of an emptiness caused by the absence of his family. Little could Samuel appreciate the turmoil his commander was internalizing.

Chapter Seven
The Crossing, December 26, 1860

I. The Day Seemed Like Any Other Day.

Christmas night 1860 was one of the loneliest Robert Anderson had ever spent in his 35 years of army life. He had been in many perilous situations in the course of his career, but he never before felt such responsibility for his every move.

At the Christmas outing, held at the Foster's Cottage, his assistant surgeon reiterated in detail what he had heard in Charleston. "A force to attack Moultrie had been selected by a war council and the attack would come within the next two weeks."[1] Earlier Crawford had informed Anderson of "State Militia inspecting Fort Sumter." Buell had written that if he detected tangible evidence of design to proceed to a hostile act. "You may put your command with either of the other forts in your possession." Anderson felt the time had come and he needed to honorably protect his little band of troops. "The march of armed bodies to attack Moultrie was at times loudly proclaimed."[2]

A civil war seemed likely; and although he was a soldier, Anderson did not favor war against his countrymen, especially at this time in this country. He favored avoiding bloodshed that seemed sure to come. Americans should not war against Americans. For weeks, he grappled with his dilemma—assuring the safety of his men versus the blind loyalty to his government that was as far away as it was out of touch. Recalling Major Buell's admonition, "do not allow the opportunity to escape you,"[3] Anderson sought to discern the true meaning of the statement. During their conversations, they had acknowledged the fact that the hostility of the state was growing with each passing day. The safety of his command at Fort Moultrie depended upon the whimsy of South Carolina. Should the state control Sumter, he and his men would be dead in the water. They were already under constant secessionist scrutiny and surveillance.

Anderson was ever mindful that he commanded all the forts in the harbor. If a transfer could be made by boat to Sumter, his trump card would be the control of commerce into the city of Charleston. Crawford would write home, "the storm is about to break upon us." The threat was hanging over them like an ominous cloud. Spies, midnight gun boats, a U.S. arsenal, but no armaments for the Federal troops and no clear policies from Washington.[4]

In one of his letters from Moultrie, Crawford's concerns, frustrations, and anger were particularly revealing: "This state has planned and anticipated every step to leave the union. They do not want remedies for wrong, they want revolution, they are in revolution. They have been nurtured in the school of Calhoun. Even the children and women are imbued with that spirit. It is difficult to believe that such hatred could be exhibited toward the union. We are preparing for war with these mad Carolinians."[5] Doubleday's cliché seemed like a truism.

Upon awaking the morning after Christmas, Samuel sensed the stormy rain of yesterday had stopped. As he went out to meet the day, the sun warmed his face and changed his mood. Today was the day to make calls at Fort Sumter. He had risen some time before he heard reveille which sounded at 6:30 a.m. He knew the men would soon be busy at their work details, so he tried to avoid congestion by leaving for Sumter as soon as breakfast was finished.

The surgeon probably was accompanied by his hospital steward. They traveled by steamer to Fort Sumter. As they sailed across the tranquil waters to their duties, the captain noticed the lack of activity. After his medical call and while looking for a boat to go to the city, he was pulled aside by Lt. George Snyder, the engineering officer, and advised, "Go back to Moultrie and do not take your eyes off Anderson."[6]

Still puzzled by the man's cryptic remark, he and his steward returned to Fort Moultrie where they discovered there were no boats available to transport them to Charleston to complete their civilian rounds.

Captain Crawford found the major atop the parapet staring seaward through his glass. Anderson sensed Crawford's presence and pointed to a steamer of the Savannah Line near the fort. "I hope she does not attempt to come in. It would be an embarrassment for me as I intend to move to Fort Sumter tonight."[7] The surgeon, stunned by the revelation, responded in his best military manner, "Sir, shall I move the hospital?" Anderson replied, "The state will not disturb the medical supplies. Pack just your effects. I determined to leave the hospital supplies until tomorrow morning."[8]

A short time later, Crawford discovered that the commander had arranged with Lieutenant Norman Hall, an engineer officer, to provide the lighters to move the women, children and approximately four months' supplies. Boats to move the men had been stored near the rocky shore about a quarter mile from Moultrie. Anderson had sworn Hall to secrecy until he chose to reveal the escape plan. He had hoped to go at Christmas, but the storm cancelled those hopes.

After he learned of the commander's decisions, the captain walked around the fort looking for signs that the others knew of the pending move. Since everyone seemed to be routinely carrying out their duties, he concluded the secret was intact. Anderson's daring scheme, one that had the potential to change all the rules, was being hatched under the watchful eyes of the state.

At noon "two Carolinian citizens"[9] observed the loading of women, children, and four months' provisions, to be transported to Fort Johnson. Confused about what was transpiring, the two men finally questioned Lieutenant Hall about the movements. The lieutenant nonchalantly replied that they must know more than he does, and anyhow, he just did what he was told. That excuse really came in handy when the man spied a box of ammunition to be placed on board. It was taken back into the fort as "a mistake."

In fact, Lieutenant Hall's orders were to move his cargo toward Fort Johnson and wait until he heard two signal shots from Moultrie. "That was the sign the soldiers had safely arrived at Sumter and Hall was then to deliver his human cargo to their new home."[10]

In the early evening, Anderson and Crawford were approached by Captain Doubleday as they stood on the parapet. "It's a fine evening, Crawford,"[11] intoned the visitor. Preoccupied by the secret, Crawford muttered a vague response. When Doubleday then invited them both to tea, Anderson finally spoke, "You have twenty minutes to form your company, Captain, we are moving to Sumter." Abner saluted, turned, and disappeared. In his quarters he told Mary, his wife, to pack her trunk as she was moving to the chaplain's home. He carried her trunk to the main gate where they bid a sad farewell. Their personal belongings were few, as they had sent most of their personal effects to New York. Mary took comfort in the knowledge Chaplain Harris or the post sutler, Dan Sinclair, would welcome her prearranged stay. Moving toward his company, Doubleday strapped on his revolver and placed a blanket over his shoulder.[12]

The 20 minutes allotted to Captain Doubleday coincided with "retreat roll-call" at dusk. The cold, chilly fog and mist seemed to be clearing as the soldiers appeared in full gear as they had for the past few days. They were in full alert gear because they had been warned the state could attack at any moment. After Doubleday's quick inspection, his men were ordered to meet Major Anderson at the main gate. The commander then led the way to the boats. As they passed not far from Moultrieville, they encountered not a single person. The folks were settling in for an evening of family rituals and were awaiting the morrow.[13]

In his diary, Samuel noted, "The night was lovely, the moon shone brightly and the sea was calm and still." The conditions were just the opposite from the evening before.[14]

Crawford was ordered to be a member of a rear guard consisting of himself, Lieutenant Jeff Davis, Captain Foster, four sergeants, and three privates. Their duty was to protect the boats traveling to Sumter. Lieutenant George Snider, the engineer officer in charge of the workers at Fort Sumter, and Major Anderson manned the first boat with part of Doubleday's company. The major secured the flags—"the twenty by thirty-six American flag and the ten by twenty storm flag."[15] The second boat was under the control of Lieutenant Richard Meade, the engineer from Pinckney; Doubleday himself followed in the third boat with the rest of his company. Pushing off silently they had about one mile to row to Sumter. They were soon within the shadow of the fort. But as they approached, they caught sight of a steamer apparently bearing down upon them. It was recognized as the *Nina*—one of the boats used on the nightly guard. At the same time, Captain Foster and Crawford, back at Fort Moultrie, had observed the potential encounter, and they immediately went to the loaded 32-pound guns in anticipation of firing on the steamer. Samuel recounted later in a letter to A.J. how the incident played out, "Just then I noticed the steamer was towing a vessel and in a few minutes she passed by. We were all relieved!" Again he wrote, "It was a moment of suspense."[16]

After delivering the first set of troops, the boats returned for Seymour's Company H. As the men quietly took their places, Crawford placed an armful of cartridge bags into one of the two boats. At that instant he saw a state guard boat approaching. In response, the soldiers in the first boat lowered their muskets to prevent reflection. The other boat, since it had just cast off, was recalled. Unaccountably, the guard boat stopped at a long distance from the fort, permitting the halted boat to continue to Fort Sumter.

Sergeant James Chester told the story of those who landed. "It was just twilight when we left the Fort Sumter and nearly dark until we reached the boats." Doubleday reiterated that on the journey to Sumter the secession guard boat slowed to inspect them. He had the men take off their jackets and cover their muskets while he opened his jacket to conceal his buttons. He wanted to give the impression of an officer delivering workers to the fort. The guise worked.[17]

Once they reached the fort their problems had not ended; "they were met by workers, some friendly and some armed with pistols." Bayonets were used to get the workers inside. Doubleday posted sentinels immediately.[18]

Sergeant Chester also admitted the fort had to be prepared for a potential invasion as Southern artillery was not prepared to attack them. That would change.[19]

"In the following days, we took the flagstone from the parade, arranged them in two tiers making our casemates splinter proof. In the weeks to come we had immense quantities of materials to move, guns to mount, shot to distribute, and embrasures to enclose. Beyond that our hands were tied by policy and instructions."[20]

II. "It was a masterly move; militarily, strategically, and politically."[21]

Captain Crawford returned to Fort Moultrie to watch the crossing. He finished the story in a letter to Alex, "The boats disappeared in the thick shade of the fortress. As my heart pounded, I stepped beside the ordnance sergeant who fired the first signal gun, and then I seized the lanyard and detonated the second."[22]

Lieutenant Norman Hall, in charge of the lighters loaded with the women, children, and provisions, after restraining a reluctant pilot, proceeded to their new home.

Captain Crawford and the others now completed their assignment. "We spiked the guns and pulled down the flagstaff." "I took a part of the flagstaff to have a cane made."[23]

Years later Crawford would uncover the story of the other Southern gunboat. Loaded with an armed force ready to move, the boat's captain never received forwarding orders from the governor. For some unexplainable reason it dallied until Johnston Pettigrew, an aide to the governor, finally acted. When he heard the two signal shots, Colonel Pettigrew ordered the craft under way without waiting for official orders. For the South the delay proved costly; for the Union troops, a miracle. The hour had passed and the mission was accomplished. It was hoped the soldiers would be provided greater safety.[24]

By 8 p.m., all 7 officers, 76 men, 45 women and children, and the laborers were safely in Sumter. Eventually, some of the 150 workers would leave while the others remained loyal to the Union cause. Those wishing to leave immediately were kept onboard boats until morning so they would be unable to report the move to the Southern officials.[25]

As the Southern officials slept serenely and dreamed of the success of their first week of Carolina independence, they had only to await the commissioner's return from Washington with instructions to the Northern command to evacuate Fort Moultrie and the other forts with workers still in place. At that moment in history the new independent state would take command of the harbor defenses, and the relationship between the Federal and state governments would be changed forever. Dreams often differ from reality. The awakening on the second day after Christmas would indeed be as rude as the tranquility of the sleep the night before was peaceful.

As Anderson sat in the solitude of his new quarters, he completed his Official Report to Colonel Cooper, the adjutant general. Dated December 16, [sic] 1860, 8 p.m., Anderson recounted the last few hours:

> I have just completed, with the blessing of God, the removal to this fort my entire garrison, except my Surgeon, four officers, and seven men along with one year of hospital supplies. We brought four months of provisions for my command. I left orders to have all guns at Moultrie spiked, and the carriages of the 32-pounders destroyed, and the ammunition that could not be brought over destroyed. The step, which I have taken, was, in my opinion, necessary to prevent the effusion of blood.[26]

In the early morning hours of the 27th, Crawford took a boat and crew and returned to Fort Moultrie to retrieve the hospital and aid in destroying the gun carriages, "5 guns fell from their beds upon the parapet." He worked off and on all day moving it to Sumter. In addition to the medical supplies, he was able to salvage case after case of ammunition that would come in handy in the months to come.[27] For this he would receive Anderson's commendation. He reported on January 2 that the "arrangements for the hospital were made and the operating table ready."[28] To the family he wrote, "We believe the hand that protected our arrival will sustain us in the future."[29] In his diary, he was more concerned. "Seymour declares it is his conviction that we will be attacked at once."[30] A week later, "Everything foreshadows conflict and brings new indignities daily; the lines are being drawn tighter every day."[31] The state was applying the pressure quickly, probably in the hopes the government would evacuate the fort rapidly.

III. "We feel the action of the administration is to leave us to our fate. We are determined to stand by our flag to the last man."[32]

Fort Sumter symbolized the Union. It was the home of two companies of the First U.S. Artillery. Surrounded by the sea, the fort covered two and a half acres. It was a five-sided edifice with a parapet 50 feet above the water line. Along the east and west walls were the soldiers' barracks and mess hall. On the southern side were the officers' quarters and Crawford's hospital. The casemates were protected by bombproof arches. The first tier had eleven 32-pound guns already mounted and many more to be placed. In the center lay a parade ground cluttered with temporary wooden sheds used to store equipment for the workers of the engineers. The flagpole was directly above the stair tower which gave access to the barbette tier. The magazines were located on either side of the sally port and provided storage for 40,000 pounds of powder.[33] The amount of shot, shell, and powder were not the problems, but friction primers and cartridge bags were. The bags would be made of many substitutes, but there was no means of improvising a substitute for friction primers.[34] Anyone approaching the fort had to enter on the south side of the structure. As intimidating as it seemed, Captain Crawford would say, "It was in no condition for a defense."[35] It sat in a harbor of the most defiant state in the Union in 1860. The fort stood proud, pompous, and envied by both sides.

Detailing their crossing to Sumter, Crawford again expressed to his family his admiration for the fort's commander. "Our movement was a masterly one, not only in a military and strategical sense, but also from a political view. The administration is now forced to take a position on the question." But Mary Chesnut, who reflected a totally different view, wanted an answer to her unique question, "Why did that green goose, Anderson, go to Fort Sumter?[36]

For Dr. Crawford, U.S.A, the first day of line duty was over. He would now make application for a line officer in addition to his medical duties.[37]

The thoughts and memories of that night would be with him always. Surely, it was that move that solidified two peoples and two governments—albeit in different directions.

IV. The Meeting

On the morning after the crossing, the soldiers were drilled and details assigned. In his Official Report Anderson said the men mounted guns and closed some embrasures. However, since there was no plan in place, Major Anderson convened his officers for that purpose.[38]

In his small room in the officers' quarters located in the gorge, he first thanked them for all they had done to make the move possible and then solemnly reminded them that the fort might not prove to be their permanent home. His actions had stirred emotions, and he feared reaction. Anderson vowed to plead with his government to back the move, but as they were all aware, political expediency might trump his best arguments. No matter, they had to strengthen the fort. This would also keep the men busy so their minds would not so much concentrate on the potential dangers and the gnawing hunger that would be part of the Sumter experience.

As Anderson was outlining his strategy, a messenger arrived bearing a card for him. It announced the arrival of the governor's aide-de-camp and commissioner to Major Anderson, Colonel Johnston Pettigrew of the South Carolina First Rifles, seeking a meeting with the major.

Pettigrew and his compatriot, Major Ellison Capers, were shown in. Introductions and greetings were very formal, reserved, and firm. Doubleday wrote that their "looks were full of wrath." Declining an offer to sit, Colonel Pettigrew spoke first, "Can I communicate with you, Sir, with the officers here on the subject for which I am here?"[39]

Anderson sat up in his chair and looked at his officers, "Certainly, Sir, these are my officers, and I have no secrets from them." Both Pettigrew and Capers seemed uneasy but the colonel carried on, "The Governor states that he is very much surprised that you reinforced this works." Anderson's reply was quick, "I have not reinforced this works, I moved my command from Fort Moultrie as I have the right as I am commander of all forts in the harbor."[40]

The scholarly Pettigrew came to the point, "When Governor Pickens came to office, he found an understanding existing between the previous Governor and the President of the United States by which all property within the limits of the state were to remain as they were and no attempt would be made against public property. Also the Governor had hoped a peaceful solution of the difficulties could be reached and that the resort to arms and bloodshed would be averted. But your actions greatly complicate that, and the 'Governor does not see how bloodshed can now be avoided.'"[41]

Anderson understood the implied blame for any bloodshed was being placed on his shoulders, so he did not falter in deflecting such undue responsibility, "I know of no agreement between the Governor and the President of the United States. I could get no positive orders from Washington, and my position was threatened every night by the troops of the state."

Capers spoke for the first time, "How so?"[42]

Looking directly at his questioner, Anderson responded, "Sending out steamers armed with troops. We feared the occupation of the sand hills that would make manning my guns impossible." Slowly he added, "I moved solely to prevent bloodshed."

"Those steamers were sent to prevent the people from being disorderly," intoned Capers.

"I could not know the intentions of the state," was Anderson's reply.[43]

"My sympathies lie with the South. These officers know that perfectly well, but I have a sense of trust and duty as a Commander."[44]

Pettigrew stepped in at that point, "Be that as it may, the Governor directs me to say courteously but peremptorily to return to Fort Moultrie."[45]

Calling on his reserve of discipline and restraint, Anderson ended his part of the conversation, "My compliments to the Governor and say that I respectfully decline to accede to his request. I cannot and will not go back."

"Then, Sir, my business is done," returned Pettigrew, as he and Capers withdrew. Doubleday believed they may have been ready to attack them by boat, but a storm with a violent wind came up.[46]

Samuel wrote to his brother, "There has been no breech [*sic*] of faith. If there was an understanding between the President and the Governor we knew nothing of it. How could it be kept on only their side?" To emphasize his point he underlined, "no" and "we knew nothing." The penmanship strokes were bold and angry! Crawford believed that the state lulled the administration to sleep by promising they would not attack. Such chicanery! The feeling was beginning to develop that the command was safe but not secure.[47] In anguish he cried, "All communications with the city are forbidden. They have seized our mail. Each day we suffer new indignities. It is now a question as to whether they will attack us."[48] Almost two weeks later one could see his torment as he wrote, "They [Carolinians] are more like pirates and thieves than brothers of a common confederacy."[49]

Doubleday concurred, "to seize the property without a declaration of war was the first overt act against the sovereignty of the United States."[50]

V. Sumter or Oceans of Blood?

Governor Pickens immediately began confiscating Federal property. First, a militia headed by Colonel Johnston Pettigrew captured Castle Pinckney and the dominoes started to fall. Later that same evening Fort Moultrie was seized. Next, the already partly occupied United States Arsenal was captured; the Custom House fell next; Fort Johnson would be taken by the new year. Only the post office was left untouched for the time being since it was more difficult to replace. Crawford was concerned with the seizing of the Engineer's office in Charleston because of the valuable maps that included the details of construction on Fort Sumter.[51]

None of the takeovers saw the state troopers challenged. They were hollow victories in that there was no resistance, and the papers to authorize the transfers were not signed. Overseers at the various facilities simply refused to recognize the governor's authority. Furthermore, South Carolina's aggressive manner acted to strengthen the resistance of President James Buchanan. The question of whether or not to fortify Sumter was now an open topic of discussion, whereas previously the administration had not publicly supported the idea.

All of Anderson's dispatches to Adjutant General S. Cooper revealed the building and positioning of Southern batteries. We are "treated as if enemies," Anderson reported, and this statement is included in Crawford's letters also. The tensions were stretching the manners.[52]

In a letter to A.J. dated January 5, 1861, Samuel took time to acquaint his brother with recent events, "We have seen by our papers that Major Anderson has been ordered back to Moultrie. It was a sad night for us all I can assure you. I could see how deeply the Major felt the responsibility of his position. Every one of us urged him to hold our position. He has said to us that our fortunate movement was attributed to providence alone. Every day and night the steamers cruise between the forts. During the day they bring parties from town with the express object of making plans for our works. One party surveyed a suitable site for the establishment of a battery. They planned to take Sumter and drive us out of Moultrie.[53]

"We have checkmated their designs. To be sure we live on pork and have a shortage of fuel. The never ceasing vigil we keep is telling upon us but our glorious flag still floats high above us and it will sustain us when we are called to the fight.[54]

"We are doing all we can to make the fort impregnable, we are but a handful and our guns are not all in battery. There is much to do before we will feel really secure. The batteries on the first tier are established and officers specified to command them." Everyone seemed to be learning their duties and places. "Everything foreshadows conflict and we are ready."

"My arrangements for the hospital are in order. My operating table ready and the lint, and bandages, and instruments prepared. Until someone is wounded I will be on the ramparts doing my share of the fighting." Captain Crawford acknowledged in the same letter, "hostile acts are committed daily but still no declaration of war. We could destroy their batteries at any moment."[55]

VI. The Ceremony, 1860

December 27, 1860, was a busy day for Crawford. The surgeon had returned to Fort Sumter from Fort Moultrie bearing one load of hospital goods along with hidden ammunition.[56] One of his returns was concurrent with the officers' meeting with Pettigrew and Capers.

He was between runs and at Fort Moultrie, however, when the noon ceremony took place. Anderson had ordered the ceremony to celebrate the safe crossing. Captain Crawford would hear the details later from Doubleday. The men with Crawford at Moultrie heard the national anthem, saw the raising of the flag, but were unable to hear the chaplain's prayer, or to witness Major Anderson's solemnity marking the occasion. Crawford would have to wait four years to observe the reenactment.

Sergeant Chester, who watched the proceedings, wrote that "anyone who doubted Anderson's loyalty and could have had one glimpse of the scene would have doubted no longer."[57]

In a letter to Alex, Samuel recalled, "I was finishing removing the hospital at Moultrie when the flag was unfurled. We gave three cheers and ran to the guns to salute the national colors when we realized the guns had been spiked so they could not be turned against Fort Sumter."[58] This moment brought out the pride in Major Anderson. He wrote to Reverend Duane that he wished he could have seen them "throw the stars and stripes to the breeze." They settled for cheering. Sergeant Chester indicated the prayers were held and the flag raising was done among the building materials, guns, carriages, derricks, timbers, blocks, and coils of rope.[59]

Out of concern for the mental welfare of his commander, Samuel asked his brother to write Anderson as he would appreciate words from a minister. "Have no fear for us as we are strong in the right."[60] He expressed a stronger degree of confidence in their position when he wrote home as the year ended, "The glorious flag floats above us. Millions support us and we are ready to meet the storm."[61]

The year of turmoil ended in a fittingly cold rainstorm that washed wintry tides into the fort. The harbor lights were out, the inspector of the light house had been asked to leave by the state, and the other thing the two adversaries had in common was the "mutual hatred of each other."[62]

At times his diary entries, though short, revealed his innermost concerns. Such was the case on January 2, 1861. "Operating table ready. Instruments prepared. Our cause just. We will defend to the last extreme. Until someone is wounded, I will be on the ramparts doing my share of fighting."

ℰ Chapter Eight ℛ
Fort Sumter: Symbol and Prison

I. The Prison

By the end of 1860, some conclusions about Sumter were obvious to those in and out of the fort. Although the movement from Fort Moultrie had been a highly successful military operation in providing more security, it had come at the cost of unforeseen, unhealthy, and uncomfortable conditions for those involved.

Departing in haste and secrecy, the men and officers lost some essential supplies. Almost immediately the lack of fuel brought misery as that winter proved to be more damp and raw than most. In early January 1861, Surgeon Crawford bemoaned that there was "One fire in the hospital, one for the men in their quarters, and none in the officer's rooms. A sentry has been placed over the coal."[1]

Additionally, fresh provisions were no longer allowed into the fort by the state, so the garrison's diet declined significantly. Morale was further weakened by South Carolina's restrictions of either withholding or irregularly allowing the delivery of mail and newspapers.

The constant vigil and implied threats by South Carolina forced increased diligence at Sumter. The already undermanned garrison responded with amplified security and vigilance. This meant more and longer duties for the 10 officers, 64 soldiers, 8 band members, and the assistant surgeon's hospital steward.

On New Year's Day, in a melancholy and gloomy mood, Samuel wrote reflectively to members of the family, "I never felt, I never knew how much I love my country until now."[2] In the coming months and years those feelings of patriotism would be thoroughly tested.

"The state destroyed the prismatic lenses in lighthouses, warning lights, and other lights used to illuminate the harbor."[3] Additionally, they painted their gunboats black. More shore batteries were being built. When mail was processed to the men in the fort, it was delivered by suspected spies. Everything was being done each day to prevent the relief of the besieged fort and increase the misery of those within.

The surgeon tried to retain a positive attitude, "We are masters of our position."[4] Many of his brethren expressed a different sentiment, like Doubleday's view that it was difficult not to use the guns as the enemy built batteries under their noses. Despondent about the lack of action by the Federal government, Crawford wrote, "The truth is, our government rests upon the points of our swords."[5]

The problems of daily living were more immediate for the men and officers at the fort. For the next couple of months their health would be challenged. The hardships were taking a toll. As medical officer, the assistant surgeon was concerned about the improper diet, long work hours with little rest, and the depressing atmosphere of the quarters caused by a nature that was their antagonist. During the first three months of the New Year, Samuel had recorded in his diary a total of 14 days that were characterized as rainy, cold, and windy. In that same period he noted one fine day. By early spring the fort's sick list was growing; Crawford noted, "the men are showing signs of the long confinement and the effect of the climate is exacerbated by the lack of fuel." The supply of oil was used by the third week of March. A few remaining planks provided little warmth and he reported that they were considering burning the $400 gun carriages for heat.[6]

This combination of conditions also caused Dr. Crawford to become ill for the first time in his military service. At one point they had no means of lighting fires until Mrs. Doubleday brought a gross of matches. In a string of letters during the first two months of 1861 Samuel revealed his illness. First it was a sore throat. By February he wrote of a burning throat, weight loss, and the need for change. According to Doubleday, Crawford could not always perform his officer-of-the-day duties.[7] Ultimately he confided, "I must have the air of the mountains of Pennsylvania."[8]

His discouragement was evident in his messages to John Agnew. Writing his faithful sounding board he lamented, "they build batteries, they dismiss our beloved Chaplain because he prayed for the welfare of the American Government, they destroy lights in the harbor and light houses, and commit treason daily. Even our commander is depressed as he fears nothing can prevent a desperate fight." At one point he wrote that Anderson would reply, "It is in the hands of God."[9] He continued to let his toxins pour out, "North and South are alike in only one way, their hatred of each other. Can you comprehend why the south 'rises in revolution against conditions that must, in the end, sap its very foundation of existence?'"[10] And finally, "You and I will have lived to see the saddest sight that will ever be witnessed by man."[11]

Later in the first month of the year he wrote in even more depressed tones of an existence, "With pork, flour, sugar, and vinegar disappearing and soap, candles, and milk already gone. Our course is clear; we must be true to ourselves and our flag."[12] There were, however, some bright spots to help the struggling men endure.

A few days before the House of Representatives voted to sustain Major Anderson's move, Mrs. Elizabeth Anderson arrived by boat for a visit. Captain Crawford, officer of the day, met her at the landing and accompanied her to her husband's quarters where a stunned Anderson welcomed his glorious wife. She brought with her his dear friend Peter Hart, an old sidekick, now a New York policeman who volunteered to stay at Sumter. Mrs. Anderson wanted Hart to watch over Robert's spirits. But her, all too brief, visit yet raised the collective spirits of those at Sumter. The mood of the officers was heightened when they read Buchanan's quip, "If I return Anderson, I might go back to Wheatland by the light of my burning effigies."[13]

Crawford spent some of his free time learning the details of firing artillery. He made note in his diary and a letter home that they "had a great practice with our 42-pounders today and some canister."[14] Doubleday and Seymour were good teachers and Crawford found another aide in Sergeant James Chester, a knowledgeable and patient instructor. At first, Crawford merely observed, but slowly he learned to aim and calculate distances, which proved difficult for him. Convinced by his mentors that it was not an easy art to learn, Samuel's tenacity enabled him to reach a degree of mastery. Fog, smoke, and darkness were problems with which even Doubleday, who had created a complicated mechanism to deal with the elements, had difficulty.

As time passed, the drastic changes in Samuel's mood could be felt through the ink. To his brothers he relayed, "the mail brings requests from strangers asking for our autographs and all union men warmly applaud our course."[15] He did not tell the family that Talbot told them that South Carolina officials said, "We must have Sumter or oceans of blood will flow."[16] Likely he felt some things best left unspoken.

II. "The Major would not inaugurate war if he could prevent it."[17]

It was January 9 and one of the rare moments that Crawford was able to get some rest. However it was a time when Sumter's men faced their first overt crisis. Knowing the stress and strain he was under, his peers rarely interrupted his time of rest. However, Crawford had instructed his hospital steward to awaken him if he felt it important.

As the steward shook him gently, Samuel knew something was amiss. As soon as he came fully to his senses, he inquired of the problem. The Carolinians were firing on a vessel flying the Union flag. Only yesterday the engineers brought a newspaper that had announced the *Star of the West* was on its way. Since it was not an armed vessel but a $1,250 a day merchant steamer with three months' supply of subsistence and about two hundred troops on board, the officers did not credit the information. Additionally, the commander of Sumter had received no special instructions in regard to aid or to provide assistance for the craft. The prevailing attitude was that General Winfield Scott would only send troops by a vessel of war. General Scott however thought a merchant steamer would not excite suspicion.[18]

Doubleday, the officer of the day, had the drummers called and the alarm sounded as Crawford dressed uncharacteristically fast and ran to the parapet where he found Doubleday and Anderson. As Anderson looked through his glass, the major relayed what he saw. The Southern battery concealed on Morris Island, the one flying the red Palmetto flag, had already fired a shot over the ship's bow plus several shots that appeared to hit the ship but did little harm. Doubleday told Crawford that the ship had arrived before dawn, but due to the removal of the lights and buoys by the Carolinians, it had waited until daybreak before moving up the harbor. Crawford was able to observe Moultrie's guns open on the ship and the national flag on top of the mast. The long roll had called the men to their guns where they replaced the grape stored overnight with solid shot. Only the lighter guns were mounted. Later that day Samuel noted in his diary, "One gun trailed in on the ship and the gunner stood with lanyard in his hand awaiting the command to fire."[19] Crawford, watching through his glass, saw the steamer dip her flag, indicating a request for help, but as the men at the fort tried to reply, their halyards got tangled in the flagstaff and the flag remained useless. Eventually, the *Star* turned, hauled down its colors, and went back out to sea. Once the original crisis had passed, Anderson immediately requested his officers report to his quarters. A tense atmosphere prevailed as the major sought comment from his officers concerning an American flagged vessel being fired upon in their presence. More specifically the commander wanted their opinions on the idea of using the fort's guns to close the harbor.[20]

The junior officers were encouraged to give their opinions first. Lieutenant Hall reiterated the feelings of a number of the officers: "use the guns to close the harbor."[21] Doubleday felt "it was plainly our duty to do all we could to aid an American vessel flying an American flag. They grow stronger and we get weaker with each passing day."[22] Later, in pure frustration, he wrote that the South delivered the mail to them because they were "harmless people who deserved a reward for their forbearance." Lieutenant Meade countered that to close the port would be an act of war and would therefore initiate a civil war.[23]

Crawford doubted if the guns could have reached the batteries. Solemnly he felt that, since they missed the opportunity to take action at the moment the battery fired on the ship, they must now take a diplomatic approach.[24] He believed that the Buchanan administration sent an unarmed vessel for a reason. As the Southern battery was not fired upon, the best procedure would be to ask the governor for an explanation and with it a notice of their determination to close the harbor. The American embassy days in Mexico slid back into his psyche. Anderson understood the logic and the "sense."[25]

The commander preferred this kind of diplomacy and sent Lieutenant Hall with a dispatch to Governor Pickens asking the state to reply as to their reason for firing on the vessel.[26] Later back at the fort, Pickens' message was read aloud to the assembled officers. In his diary the captain remembered the clear and decided message from the governor that said, "It will suffer to say that the occupancy of that fort has been regarded by the state of South Carolina as the first act of public hostility by the troops of the United States. My act was perfectly justified."[27]

Samuel wrote home, "The iron missiles would have gone had Anderson nodded, but he would not inaugurate war if he could prevent it."[28] Pickens would not prevent it if he could encourage it. In the morning of the 11th of January, the hulks of four vessels were sunk across the entrance of the harbor. About noon, the troubles continued as a boat of Southern officials arrived demanding the surrender of the fort.

In response to the surrender demand, Anderson decided to send the information to Washington to allow his government to respond. Near sunset and carrying a white flag, Lieutenant Talbot and Captain Crawford were sent. Their arrival in Charleston was met by a hostile crowd hurling insults. Talbot was dressed in civilian clothes while Crawford donned his full military uniform. They had to shove through the throngs to get to Pickens' headquarters where they met the governor and his cabinet. Talbot was permitted to pass north and Crawford to return to Sumter with the mail that had not been delivered for some time.

Crawford wrote, "The Major decided not to open civil war. Should we use our position to deluge the country in blood? It is doubtful if our guns could have reached the enemy battery."[29] The major appealed to Governor Pickens, "in the name of a Christian, a fellow countryman, and a man, do all you can to prevent an appeal to arms."[30] It was clear that war for the moment had been averted, but the first shots had been fired. President Buchanan's new secretary of war, Joseph Holt, called it "an act of war, without the slightest provocation."[31] While one Southerner, Louis Wigfall, informed the Carolinians that since Holt succeeded Floyd, "It means war. Take Sumter as soon as possible,"[32] the *New York Tribune* called the cannonading of the *Star of the West* "a national disgrace unparalleled since the Bladensburg races."[33]

To help President Buchanan clarify his policy, Lieutenant Hall was sent to Washington to provide a detailed report of the incident. Throughout the surrender demands, Anderson's assistant surgeon advised, "The flag of this country has been fired upon. Do not surrender as long as a man of us remains."[34]

The *Star of the West* episode and the resultant threat of closing the harbor ratcheted up the already confrontational situation. The brashness of the governor of South Carolina grew proportionately with all of these acts. The garrison could only imagine that the worst was yet to come as five more states had withdrawn from the Union by the end of January 1861, and Texas followed on February 1.[35]

John Agnew frequently told Samuel of articles he had read in newspapers to try to relate to his brother's situation. Samuel tried to dismiss any misgivings. "Major Anderson is not a secessionist; he just wanted to avert beginning a civil war. He has not shot mutineers; we have some in ball and chain for sentences, but others have returned to duty. He does not retain workers who do not wish to stay, and we do not send notes to the Southern officials asking to surrender." He would then assure A.J. that there is espionage of all letters. The letter ends, "We are 82 soldiers with a band and 40 Engineer laborers."[36]

III. "My heart is sad for the condition of our country."[37]

The stalemate continued. Near the middle of January, Crawford took on additional duties of commissary and quartermaster officer.[38] Standing in for Lieutenant Hall, who was on the mission to Washington, the extra burdens took a further toll on his health. As he personally became aware of the shortages in coal, coffee, sugar, salt, candles, and soap, the letters home reflected his state of mind. In spite of the isolation and privations, he tried to convince himself, "I know we are not forgotten."[39]

"Do not believe the newspapers that say there is mutiny in the fort. They are frustrated because our flag that floats high above our fort is an insult to their sovereignty."[40] The mental and physical strains began to leak through the ink. "My heart is sad for the condition of our country."[41]

In his diary, practical matters surfaced, "We hope the Border States do not go to the South; if so, the Union is forever gone. If they stay, the tide can be arrested. Virginia is only pretending and waiting for her moment." Dr. Crawford often expressed the fear of two republics in this country.[42]

Fatigue proved the cause for many accidents among the troops. One incident demonstrated the grit and spirit of most of the soldiers at Sumter. John Doran, an Irish soldier from Connecticut, had suffered two smashed toes when a gun wheel slipped, crushing his right foot. Crawford did all he could for the gutsy 22-year-old, and for additional therapy recommended rest. The injured, limping private went back to work the next morning, only to have a similar accident a week later.[43] He was a symbol within a symbol!

Surgeon Crawford feared an epidemic of illness given the state of affairs. Dysentery was now a constantly growing concern; fresh provisions were lacking; and the men were not getting the proper amount of rest.

In an effort to distract the men from their pain, hunger, and depression, they were kept busy with numerous duties. The embrasures at the back of the fort were enclosed for security, as were the casemates. The main entrance was bricked and the second-tier embrasures were filled with a mixture of sand, stone, mortar, and bricks. Each day the men were assigned the task of sewing additional cartridge bags, but with only six available needles the process was slow.

Sergeant Chester indicated little grumbling was heard. They sang at times, they had friendly competitions, and no doubt shared concerns about their situation.

Samuel Crawford's additional commissary and quartermaster duties gave him new questions to ponder. He was now concerned with the amount of provisions in the fort. They had all heard the enemy outside trying to justify mutiny on behalf of hunger. There were no signs of any such activity, but hunger and health were major legitimate concerns for a medical officer.

Along with military personnel, the workers, women, and children had to be fed. The provisions, especially the essentials, were running terrifyingly low. Something had to be done. Rationing was applied. Later Anderson permitted the rations to be cut again. The Confederates believed that once hunger was rampant, mutiny would follow.[44]

Captain Crawford knew that his concerns were but a small part of the overall responsibilities faced by Major Anderson. Worries about security and duty assignments, as well as provisions and morale, all caused distress in Anderson's thoughts. Believing that morale was the chief cement for his band of fighters, Anderson came to the difficult decision to order the removal of the women and children to Fort Hamilton, New York. The provisions would be extended and the families would be safe. In late January, Crawford in his capacity of quartermaster began preparations for their evacuation on a lighter. Each lady was allowed one trunk and bedding. Samuel "sent a trunk to Anne in New York."[45] With each passing day, Anderson continued to struggle with what he saw as inevitable but continued to hope, "trusting in a God that He will be pleased to save us from the horrors of a civil war."[46]

At noon on February 3, the steamer *Marion* sailed past the fort with 20 women, 17 children, and 5 infants aboard. They were cheered from the parapet; the women waved hankies as a one-gun salute was fired. A source of cheerfulness and light was gone. Samuel noted in his diary that they were much relieved, but it was a sad sight. Insufficient food would have soon told a more depressing story. It obviously cost much more than the $12 for the ladies and $6 for the children as the fort was full of uncertainty and gloom. The cold, wet, heavy wind did not help. Doubleday described the fort as a deep, dark, damp, gloomy place where sunlight rarely penetrated.[47]

Samuel took time to record in his diary his views on the political situation: "President Buchanan will not surrender the fort and yet he does not want war. Collision is inevitable. South Carolina is only half out of the Union as long as we are here. The state is disgraced each day they fail to take our fort. We are to be a sacrificed to turn public opinion against those who attack us and maybe even to hold the Border States."[48] That theme continued as Samuel wrote, toward the end of February, that local papers are "trying to goad the public into action, seventy men keeping the state at bay is humiliating."[49]

As the Southerners built the circle of fire around the fort, the feeling grew among the men that a storm was imminent. It was the family that brought solace to the hearts of the men imprisoned by the 50-foot-high walls. A.J. informed his brother that his and Susie's next child would carry the name of Anderson. He received boxes of foodstuffs from his mother, Margaret, and friends from Philadelphia; coffee from Susie; a flag came from Alex; and Anne wrote of her constant prayers as did her two daughters. His family and those of others in the fort sustained them in these dark hours.[50]

Samuel answered his support system; "the prayers you offer for us are not forgotten." In one emotional plea he wrote, "Keep us in your memory, for we are the last hope of the nation."[51]

In late February, Anderson sought to enhance morale. In a communiqué to the War Department, the major wrote about his officers' unrelenting devotion to duty. He thanked Surgeon Crawford "For kindness shown and for taking his tour of officer-of-the day regularly." He also expressed his thanks to his surgeon "for the relief he provided his brother officers."[52]

March arrived with clouds and winds but milder temperatures. In Lincoln's first full day in office, he was apprised of a newly arrived letter from Anderson detailing Sumter's status of provisions that would last less than six weeks. This shocking news meant an urgent response by the Lincoln administration. Shock was also felt in Fort Sumter as it was rumored that an ill Crawford would resign his position. The fury in his words was felt in the mountains of Pennsylvania: "my disgust for people who steal forts, etc is too great to give them my sympathies much less my sword."[53] He stayed, he fought, and he found a door to fame.[54]

Surgeon Crawford reported that the *Charleston Mercury* was recommending starving the men into submission. Since his youngest brother, Mac, was the one who felt the critical nature of his situation, Samuel tried to come to terms with the overall predicament when he wrote him, "I have the singular hope that I sustain with honor the reputation of the name I bear."[55]

Still, at times, humor prevailed. On March 9, as they made preparations for possible battle and its consequences, a Confederate shell hit the wharf. Thinking this was quite possibly the beginning of the war, their fears were calmed when they learned it was Southern practice and had not meant to be a live round. Samuel wrote in his diary, "We went to breakfast, instead of war."[56]

Samuel's mood swings were more noticeable now. About a week after the practice shell hit the wharf, in his diary Crawford jotted, "I have lived years in the events that have transpired the last few months."[57] More despondently he posed the question, "do we want to initiate bloodshed for a fort that is of no use to the government? Is it worth initiating the horrors of a civil war, losing every chance of reunion by blood shed?"[58] And more poignantly in his diary, he recorded a recollection from his university days, "Go stranger to the Spartans and tell them that here, obedient to their laws, they fell." Father, the teacher of classics, would have been proud of his son's remembrance at a time like this.[59]

By the middle of March the fort's sick list unrelentingly grew and Crawford's health continued its downward spiral. Again, the surgeon would reveal in his diary that he yearned for the health, the peace, and tranquility of the Pennsylvania mountains. Sumter's officers derived some mixed pleasure when they saw the likeness that *Harper's Weekly* published. Though awful, it caused much fun as did the fact that dramas were being presented in Boston and New York based on their experiences at Sumter. In a letter to Alex, he asked him to throw away the photo of him with Talbot and Seymour as he "harily" [*sic*] had the strength to stand. By now the glands in his throat were so swollen he was almost unable to swallow and his appetite was practically nonexistent. On March 14, Samuel confided to Alex that "Sumter is impressed on my life," and the last diary entry for March reads, "Time drags heavy on us." Captain Foster wrote, "Their world seems to be at a standstill. A storm of wind is prevailing."[60]

It was at this moment the officers again spoke of mining the fort and escaping by boat. However, after the intrigue of destroying 40,000 pounds of powder and the fact the state would be deprived of such a magnificent works, they realized they were observed around the clock, and suitable boats were next to impossible to obtain. Logistically they were overwhelmed, and the idea was scuttled.[61]

In the beginning of April, the sergeant of the guard entered the mess and announced for the second time that Confederate batteries had fired on a schooner flying the national flag. They would learn later that the schooner's captain had mistaken Charleston harbor for his Savannah destination. In the fog he was confused, and believed he was delivering his cargo of ice to the more southern port.[62] The smallest spark could explode the powder keg!

Commander Anderson wrote, "Our flag runs the hourly risk of being insulted and my hands are tied by orders and if that was not the case I have not the power to protest it."[63]

IV. "The giving of bread to a few brave and hungry men."[64]

The fateful week of April 8, 1861, began with a gentle rain in Charleston. Six hundred miles to the north the relatively new Lincoln administration was trying to find a solution to the plight of those in Fort Sumter. A letter from Anderson outlining provision problems was Lincoln's first major challenge. The letter, handed to President Abraham Lincoln on the afternoon of March 5, loomed large as it concerned Anderson's forty days to empty cupboards and required a quick decision by the Lincoln administration. Later, Lincoln, his cabinet, and the elderly General Scott devised a plan to reinforce Sumter. Governor Pickens would be notified, in advance, of the move. The next move was up to the Confederate government; they could allow "safe passage of the provisions, or interfere whereas the Union would use force." Lincoln had found a way to give provisions to the starving men peacefully, if allowed, and if not, forcibly, if all else failed. The ships would depart New York on April 10. The ball would be placed in the hands of the newly established Confederacy.[65]

Meanwhile the Confederate cause was building momentum. Clandestine measures were deemed appropriate for the gathering of information: messages, documents, and public letters from Sumter. The materials were confiscated with some reluctance by Governor Pickens, who was trying to garner information to determine the fort's strengths and the mindset of those within. The momentum was pulling Jefferson Davis toward the opening shot. He felt diplomacy had failed; he had heard of the relief fleet. One of the commissioners wrote, "The sword must now preserve our independence." The words the Southern officials were now using were: "under no circumstances and if refused—reduce."[66]

The Confederates rushed more men and materiel to the region at a furious pace. The floating battery was placed at the upper end of Sullivan's Island where its guns could cover the fort's left flank. New weaponry in the form of a state-of-the-art British Blakely Gun was positioned to enhance the circle of fire. The Southern officials, political and military, inspected their batteries frequently during the last two weeks of March.

Inside Sumter, ammunition and canister were carried to the guns; battery and gun assignments were checked and finalized. As if provisions were not meager enough, it was discovered that a number of bags of rice that had been soaked with water from a high tide and placed in the officers' quarters to dry were now full of glass. Some rice that had been splashed with salt water was ventilating when an artillery explosion from a practice shot shattered a nearby window, mixing glass and rice. The damaged rice was sorted and used during the last week.[67]

Crawford reported in *The Genesis of the Civil War* that once the men heard of the coming of a relief fleet they could be seen on the parapet at all hours of night and day as they scanned the horizon to verify their hopes. Dr. Crawford had just finished his duties as watchman. The breezes and the sun brought a ruddiness to his face as this April 11 seemed like a summer's day. On duty Captain Crawford had noticed that the Confederates had also taken advantage of the mild weather. The movement of men and materials by sloops, guard boats, schooners, and even ferries created a hectic pace for them and a helpless one for those in Sumter. The unusual state activity included towing the iron clad battery of four guns to the western point of Sullivan's Island, and destroying a wooden building that unmasked another four guns that had been hidden from the garrison.[68] After being relieved, Crawford hurried below to find the major pacing and in deep contemplation. His mood, body language, and words were those of a depressed man. Later Captain Crawford wrote again that Anderson felt he had done all he could do to prevent war, but, in spite of his efforts, he felt a sense of failure. Samuel consoled him that the prevailing circumstances were much larger than the efforts of any one man. Their own government had deserted them long ago. He assured Anderson that it was he who held together this fort against all odds without initiating a civil war, whose horrors they all feared. He believed if the act of war came, it would be from the other side. They would have to live with their conscience, but everyone would have to live with the consequences. The soldiers were constantly reminded as they saw everything in the fort packed. Crawford tried to put it all in perspective: "our long and weary vigil is about to close either by our being withdrawn or by a bloody conflict."[69]

V. At 3:20 a.m. a Compromise Was Not Possible.

On April 11 a boat appeared, but it was not the hoped-for relief craft. Crawford related, "Shortly after noon a boat sailing under a white flag, was seen leaving Charleston. It arrived at 3:30 p.m. with three men astern." Later at the dock they would be identified as Colonel James Chesnut, an aide to General Pierre G. T. Beauregard, as was Captain Stephen Lee. The third member was Lieutenant Colonel Chisholm, aide-de-camp to the governor. After being escorted to the guardhouse, the trio made their mission known. They demanded the fort's surrender under terms that would allow the garrison safe passage for all, along with all property—both government and private. The fort's venerated flag could also be ceremoniously saluted, removed, and could accompany the departing troops.[70] Crawford tried to put it into historical perspective, "Was ever such terms granted to a band of starving men."[71] Anderson sought the counsel of his officers. When asked, he informed the commander that the fort could hold out for four or five days, but some would be without food. After an hour's discussion, the Southerners were informed that their proposal had been rejected. In a letter to his brother, Samuel said, "the major would not tie his hands by any special agreement."[72]

To Anderson it seemed clear that it was "a demand with which my sense of honor and my obligations to his government prevent my compliance." Then, in his gentlemanly way, he thanked the Southern officials for their fair, manly, and courteous terms. Along with his officers, Anderson accompanied the three envoys back to the dock. When the major asked if General Beauregard would notify him before opening his batteries, he was assured he would. Anderson admitted he would await the first shot, but he would be starved out in a few days anyway. Crawford, standing near, heard the major repeat his words and gave permission to the three commissioners to report his conversation to Beauregard. The party departed under a red flag. The time was 4:45 p.m.[73]

Powder kegs were placed at the ready and the garrison prepared to retire. No sooner had they done so than at one o'clock in the morning of April 12 another boat with a truce flag arrived with another proposition from Montgomery. "If you give us a time you will evacuate and will not use your guns in the meantime, we will not bomb the fort." Now a "long protracted"[74] conference between Anderson and his officers took place. The principal discussion evolved around how long they could hold out with an inefficient supply of rations. The lack of a proper diet was already evident in the men of the fort. After a three-hour discussion, Seymour, Doubleday, Crawford, and the major proposed the evacuation date of the 15th instant unless their flag was fired upon, or otherwise instructed by Washington.

Colonel Chesnut was apparently under orders not to compromise. He then served formal notice to all assembled, "We have the honor to notify you we will open the fire of our batteries on Fort Sumter in one hour." Crawford listed the time as 3:20 a.m.[75]

Anderson and his officers went through the casemates where the men had been quartered and were asleep. They aroused and informed the men of the pending attack and told them not to move until ordered to do so as they would not open their batteries until dawn. Return to sleep was now impossible, so conversation filled the tense atmosphere. As officer of the day, Crawford probably took part in the talks, which were mostly speculation of the South's first move.

Sergeant Chester thought a landing assault might be tried. Someone pointed out that an approaching vessel could be relief and to fire into them would be horrific. As time passed, silence prevailed as the men contemplated their private thoughts, fears, hopes, and prayers.[76]

Their hunger was real as the fort had long been without the needed amount of milk, salt, vinegar, vegetables, and fresh meat. Fuel to create warmth was almost nonexistent; soap and candles for personal use had disappeared long ago. Crawford's sick list reflected only a few injuries, but problems related to the lack of proper diet touched many of the soldiers. Ailments such as digestive problems, dysentery, and fevers were the old adversaries. Now the hunger pains were steady, mind-numbing, and nerve-racking. Some believe the water stored in copper lined containers caused health problems.[77]

"The sea was calm, the night still, the stars bright,"[78] just like the December evening they arrived at Sumter. About this time one of those unbelievable events occurred. "The flag that flew over Sumter split in two."[79] The Southerners felt it was a good omen for their cause, a second republic. Responding quickly, a new flag was hoisted and those inside likely saw it as a new unity. So it would go for the next four years: the same symbols, the same words, but different interpretations. Samuel thought of a remark he made earlier to his family, "I am committed heart and soul to our flag."[80]

Chester called the first mortar, which they followed by the lit fuse, "a capital one."[81] Then Captain Crawford, watching from the parapet, said the Southerners opened with their "circle of fire." Irony is the substance of history; only four days ago the garrison was packed and expecting to be evacuated.[82]

Samuel took a few minutes to finish a letter to A.J. Like everyone he was on edge, a mixture of anxiety and exhilaration. He tried to give his brother the impression that he was nonchalant as he wrote they "fire as I write." He probably wore the patriotic pin from his Philadelphia friend, thinking of it as a symbol of protection for the Union and himself. The war was about to be real and deadly, but not even the most insightful in the fort, in the nation, knew how real and how lethal.

ᛞ **Chapter Nine** ᛯ

"God Bless the Poor Noble Fellows"[1]

I. "The powder kegs were rolled in place."[2]

Finally, after threatening to starve the soldiers at Sumter, have them evacuated, and failing to negotiate a surrender, the Southern government realized that "Anderson did not need a champion, he averted civil war and held the fort together."[3] The lines were drawn. The Confederates believed that by opening the war they could blame Lincoln for aggravating this war since he had sent armed reinforcements.

Samuel Crawford stood looking at most of the seven million bricks in the walls lit by the light of a curved moon. He could see and hear the flag above. The opponent had 6,000 soldiers; they mustered 71 soldiers, including eight band members, and approximately 40 workers. They faced a circle of fire that consisted of 19 batteries with 43 guns. The Union artillery consisted of 48 guns—most of them without breech-sights—but how many they could man and use was questionable. How long would the 700 cartridges last, and how fast could they be replaced with six needles and material to create them? They had used most of the available flannel shirts and woolen socks to make the amount they possessed.[4]

Momentarily, a biting breeze hit Crawford in the face. He looked up and saw what appeared to be a "falling star"; it was indeed the lit fuse of the first mortar from Fort Johnson. The time was 4:27 a.m. The date was Friday, April 12, 1861, and the Southern artillery was beginning a hot war that the best of minds could only contemplate and wonder where and how it would end.[5]

To the seasoned officers about to breakfast it was clear their guns would soon have to respond in kind. Samuel had arranged a Friday treat for breakfast. Instead of sour pork and pieces of crackers, he replaced the fare with farina. He had reserved it for a special occasion, and it now seemed appropriate to serve. "Dr. Crawford triumphantly brought forth a little farina."[6]

"This war actually started months ago when the troops of Sumter were beleaguered by armed thousands and the subsequent seizure of federal forts, arsenals, mails, and other federal treasuries. These acts of war combined treason and robbery."[7]

For several hours, on this April morning, the Confederate guns and mortars from Fort Johnson, Cummings Point, Fort Moultrie, and the end of Sullivan's Island, where the floating battery was located, had been taking the fort's measure. The "circle of fire" continued to take its toll. The Southerners had participated, if not pleasured, in war alone. The feeling was empty as "the fort received her shot and shell in silence." Some at the Southern batteries were concerned the fort would not reply in kind. It would be such a hollow and unfulfilled victory.[8]

II. 7:03 a.m. April 12, 1861

The first shot from Sumter did not come until a few minutes past 7 a.m. as Captain Doubleday, without any feeling of "self-reproach," fired the first shot from the right gorge angle toward Cummings Point, the enfilading battery. "It was a contest whether virtue or vice should rule." According to Crawford, they only had 48 available guns, all in casemate and barbette. Confederate gunners and those civilians perched on the housetops were no doubt relieved by the return fire. They likely felt foolish firing into the shadows; had Sumter not replied, they would have garnered what surely would have been a superficial victory of war.[9]

Sergeant James Chester, with the most time in service among sergeants in Company E, marched his men to the guns directed toward the floating battery. With no officer present, Chester took the liberty to place the men at their duty stations with rammers, sponges, and handspikes. The sergeant hoped his cartridge bags would "hold out," but it was a concern. Just then Crawford arrived and informed Sergeant Chester that he would command the battery until his medical duties summoned.[10]

The surgeon's and crew's nervousness was evident as the first shell overshot the target and hit a house. Once free of the initial jitters, the crew fired accurately but failed to do much damage to the powerfully constructed and well-placed floating battery. Crawford later asked Anderson's permission to move along the casemate to the battery on the right. Those heavier guns were directed at a closer target: Fort Moultrie.[11]

The Chester/Crawford battery fired for almost four hours, achieving slightly better results against their old fort than they had against "Noah's

Ark," the nickname for the floating battery. Captain Crawford reported the crew had "hit but one gun" on that contraption. Doubleday thought some of the problem was the defective guns and Chester noted aiming problems through smoke.[12]

Near noon, Sergeant Chester's fears began to surface. The fort's 700 cartridges were nearly exhausted or not attainable as they had been stored in the magazine with a damaged "copper door."[13] With only six needles, the off-duty men and officers in another magazine were unable to sew quickly enough to keep pace with the firing. When so informed, Anderson ordered the pace to be slackened and reduced the firing to six guns, those firing on Moultrie, the floating battery, and Cummings Point. At the same time, the major made another fateful decision. Due to the potential danger from the Confederate mortars, the guns in the barbette would not be used. Consequently, the most formidable batteries in the fort would not fire, except by chicanery of Irishman John Carmody.

The Southern bombardment from Cummings Point, particularly the new Blakely—a rifled gun that just arrived from Liverpool, purchased by a South Carolinian now living in England—took an immediate toll on the fort, hitting her "with shot and shell." Those rifled shells did damage to Sumter. On three occasions the officers' quarters were set afire and then extinguished. Twice by Sergeant Hart and some volunteers and the last time by a rain shower. The last Confederate shell hit the iron cistern over the hallway and spilled its water over the flames.[14]

Surgeon Crawford in his casemate hospital officially treated four wounded. Others may have been treated and quickly released and were not recorded. The most severely wounded was Sergeant Thomas Kirnan who had contusions and had to be treated at the gun, as he refused to stop fighting. One of the workmen, John Swearer, was also injured but stayed the course after Dr. Crawford treated the shrapnel wound. At times, the men could see the flags of the relief ships offshore; the hope and spirits of the soldiers were aroused.[15]

III. The Night of the 12th

As darkness descended, Anderson decided to go to a night phase and no longer returned fire. "The night became stormy with rigid winds and tide." His men were hungry and near exhaustion, and the material to make the cartridges was almost gone. Still, the Confederate mortar fire continued at 15-minute intervals throughout the night. For the men in Sumter the war went on. The tension of war overruled the type of anxiety they had endured for months. The falling rain no doubt had both a soothing effect and added to the mental anguish.

Realizing the exhausted men had done their best and yet angered and frustrated over the results, the surgeon retrieved a bottle of brandy and gave each worn-out soldier a spoonful.[16]

Crawford agreed to accompany Lieutenant Snyder as he inspected the fort's exterior to determine the extent of damage. The wind, rain, and darkness made the chore most difficult. He would later record in his diary that the "wall of the gorge toward Moultrie had crumbled and left some small brick craters, the casemates were undamaged and the lower tier of guns remained untouched. The parapet had suffered the most but it had been undefended."[17] Some of this damage was due to the antics of a gunner that Crawford would learn later.

The officers and the men spent a night in rest, if not in total sleep, due to extreme fatigue and hunger pains. Samuel took some horrible-tasting medicinal potassium before going to sleep. For over three months the weather had been "very bad" and now the command and camp followers were crammed into the space of the officers quarters.[18]

Saturday's breakfast consisted of "rusty pork and broken glass with damaged rice as the bread ration was exhausted."[19]

The men's largest grumbling came when they had to substitute spun yarn to replace their tobacco "chaws." Enough is enough! As soldiers they expected to make sacrifices, but yarn for tobacco?[20]

Giving no respect to that fine breakfast cuisine, the Confederate fire increased early but not as intensely as the previous day. Since they anticipated naval fleet movements, the firing from Sullivan's Island slowed conceivably so the Confederate gunners could conserve ammunition.

IV. The War Began Again.

As the rain of yesterday went out to sea, leaving only the pleasant smell of April ozone, the 13th arrived in a bath of sunshine. Some South Carolinians claimed they saw a gamecock land on Calhoun's tomb to crow. They believed that was a good omen. After sunrise the Confederate bombardment increased. Sumter's guns opened about the same time as yesterday. The Confederate batteries' aim, according to Captain Foster, was better than on the first day.[21]

Later when fire eventually broke out in Sumter, the Confederate batteries increased their shelling, and Moultrie added "hot shot" to the assault in hopes of causing added problems. The Southerners said they were sending "hot rolls for breakfast." By 8:30 a.m. the barracks, the quarters, and the partitions were aflame and Anderson forbade any further attempts to extinguish them.

The next threat came from the three hundred barrels of powder in one of the magazines.

While opening the magazine door, Chester burned his hand, but they were able to remove about one hundred barrels and pack earth against the doors. Extreme caution was demanded amidst the raining cinders and smoke since the powder from the cartridge bags had sifted a natural fuse for stray sparks. Of the barrels salvaged, all but five were tossed into the sea, and they were wrapped in wet blankets. A portion of this would come back to haunt some of the men in the fort.[22]

As the powder was emptied, Anderson ordered Crawford to go to the parapet to look for signs of the naval ships on the move toward Sumter. As he made his way, an explosion eliminated the stairs and then set off the ammo stored in the tower. Foster reported it was exploding grenades. A short time later, he crawled through the rubble to the parapet where he saw no movement of the ships but many shells ripping the inside of the fort, including the main gate. He feared an infantry assault would follow.[23]

The south wind forced clouds of smoke and cinders into the casemates, and the men were practically suffocating from the burning, smoking pine. For relief some of the men lay on the floor, others covered their mouths with wet cloths, while still others rushed outside the embrasures for a lungful of fresh air. General Crawford called the scene "well nigh indescribable."[24]

About 30 minutes after noon the flagstaff was down for the seventh time, but only for an instant, as Lieutenant Norman Hall pounced on it, fashioned a makeshift replacement, and carried it to the parapet where Seymour and Hart secured it to a gun carriage. Samuel wrote to A.J., "the barracks and quarters are knocked to pieces, our buildings are on fire, and the men are worn out." Sumter's firing had practically ceased. Doubleday was able to return an occasional round, but was enraged when the enemy cheered his efforts. When Sumter's flag went back up, the war began again.[25]

Discussions on how the South should handle the delicate political and military decisions were ongoing on Sullivan's Island. Before a decision could be reached, Louis Wigfall, the former Texas senator and now a colonel, and Gourdin Young decided to seek on their own initiative an agreement with the besieged at Fort Sumter. Aboard a skiff, they headed toward Sumter, ignoring a Moultrie shot across their bow. When they reached Sumter, Colonel Wigfall, with wind-blown hair and bulging wide eyes, tied a white handkerchief to his sword and tried to enter through an embrasure guarded by a sentinel.[26] One wonders what method he would have used to kidnap President Buchanan that he proposed to Secretary of War Floyd on Christmas, 1860.[27]

Once inside the "burning palace," Wigfall cried out, "Your flag is down, you are on fire, and you are not firing your guns. General P. Beauregard wants to stop this."[28]

Confronting the colonel, Lieutenant Davis guided him to a point and said, "Our flag is not down you see it floating."[29] Louis, now completely flustered, told them to stop the firing by hoisting his surrender flag. "No Sir, if you want to display it, Do it yourself!" Wigfall waved his flag, but it had no effect.[30] A corporal grasped the banner and waved it with the same results; consequently the effort was stopped until Crawford had a bed sheet brought from the hospital and displayed on the parapet.[31] The firing then ceased.

Major Anderson assumed the colonel to be acting as an official emissary and agreed to a truce after Colonel Wigfall promised the same terms as General Beauregard had tendered. A white flag was raised as Wigfall and Young departed the fort.

Shortly thereafter at three o'clock General Beauregard's aides approached. They entered before Crawford, now officer of the day, could meet them, as was customary, at the water's edge.[32] Warning them of the mines that had been laid, the surgeon led them to Anderson who immediately asked if they had come directly from their commander, to which they answered in the affirmative.

When informed by Anderson of Colonel Wigfall's mission, the three men showed surprise and told him that he had not been seen at the headquarters for a couple of days. According to Dr. Crawford his visit was "wholly unauthorized." At this, Anderson lost his composure. He felt Colonel Wigfall had used him, and the major would restore his flag and reopen his batteries.[33] Besides being deadly, war can be frustrating and confusing.

The aides countered that if General Anderson would render his terms in writing, one of the aides would deliver them to General Beauregard. The men had been led to Crawford's hospital since it was the safest place. One of them, Roger Pryor, sat on Samuel's bed and had a drink from a brown bottle on the bed stand.

A short time later, the aide officially offered the previous General Beauregard conditions: the command would maintain ownership of regimental and personal equipment and the flag could be ceremonially saluted. By 7 p.m. on April 13, the truce had been arranged. The garrison would evacuate the next day.

Now a shambles, Sumter was barely recognizable. The main gate was gone, the magazines were smoldering, debris cluttered the interior, the cartridges were exhausted, and only four barrels of powder remained. The piney smell burned the eyes and throats so badly that many of the men sat outside long into the night.

To Crawford and others it was a cruel irony that "The fort had been carefully and artfully constructed to protect those who tried to destroy it."

It had withstood some 1,800 shells from 17 mortars and 30 heavy well-placed guns served and had been protected by 6,000 men. Fort Sumter would be "left in ruins."[34]

At nightfall, the surgeon once again distributed "small glasses of brandy"[35] to the weary soldiers. He likely spoke to them of their valiant effort as he bandaged and dressed their wounds. He would have noticed their reserve and quiet manner. As he left, he was heard to say, "God bless these poor noble fellows. They have done gallantly." Outside, small groups chatted as they took in the fresh air. Probably, the conversations centered on how best they could deal with their disappointment in surrender, but not defeat. Even now they were aware they had endured combat and acted honorably under immense adversity. Each seemed to derive a sense of personal satisfaction from his achievements. They now knew war on a personal level. Many of them would see much worse in the years to come, but this was enough for the moment. They knew they could be courageous under fire. Foster thought the weakness of the defense was lack of food and materials to make cartridge bags and lack of men to man the guns on the barbette tier.[36]

V. "I can not tell you how much it grieves me to leave this fort where every stone is impressed upon my heart."[37]

The men and officers awakened early on Sunday, April 14. The men carried equipment to the *Isabelle* amidst the still burning embers. The smoldering rubble would await Confederate extinguishing days later. Anderson insisted on formality and wanted his flag honored by the departing troops. Just before noon, the troops would witness a hundred-gun salute. The cartridges were difficult to amass but were finally completed. All seemed to go well until about the midway point when an unexpected blast took place. The officers had feared the stiff breeze blowing directly into the gun muzzles may cause problems. Crawford and his steward attended the wounded. Because a number of soldiers were severely wounded, the ceremony was ultimately shortened after 50 salutes. Doubleday promptly marched the troops out with the sergeants bearing the flag they had so nobly defended. The flags had made the trip from Fort Moultrie and would be proudly displayed in New York.[38]

The drummers beat "Yankee Doodle" as the crowd made "threatening demonstrations"[39] against Doubleday, the abolitionist, who would make the statement, "60 men against their 6,000 made a strange set of odds." The defenders were a mixed lot of Irish, Germans, Prussian, Scots, English, French, and 10 who listed their home as the United States. Most of those represented the large cities of Philadelphia, Boston, New York, and Baltimore. The eyes of the enemy watched in silence.[40]

Crawford was the last of the command to depart at 4 p.m. He and his 28-year-old German steward likely walked side by side. He would always recall the feeling of his surrealistic state of mind. He had just lost his first war patient to death, by friendly fire, and witnessed his burial.[41]

The harbor was filled with the boats of every description, the white hankies waving, and the Southerners acting "perfectly wild."[42] Because of low tide, the ship *Isabelle* could not depart until the following day, April 15. As the ship passed slowly by the Confederate troops lined along the beach, the enemy stood silent in tribute to the gallantry of those aboard the vessel. Crawford wrote, "Our enemy believes we have done our duty; we hope our countrymen will also." He felt Major Anderson had risen above the politics "by not tying his hands by any special agreement."[43]

Again he recounted with a stabbing pain that trembled up and down his mind, "I can not tell you how much it grieves me to leave this fort where every stone is impressed upon my heart."[44]

VI. The Ride Home on the Ship That Came to Relieve Them

Once out of the harbor they were transferred to the *Baltic* for the voyage home. As they steamed away, Captain Crawford first went on deck and through his glass watched the brick structure that was Fort Sumter disappear. In *Annals of the War* he wrote, "as the fort sank upon the horizon, the smoke cloud still hung heavily over the parapet."[45]

No one on the *Baltic* clearly understood the national consequences of their efforts, and unknown to them President Lincoln would call for 75,000 volunteers to put down the rebellion. Now it was a fight to restore the Union without recognizing the Confederate States of America.

As they sailed to their destination, Fort Hamilton, New York, it was a time for rest and recuperation. The men were physically worn out, but emotionally gleamed with an inner pride.

Samuel Crawford was reacquainted with Gustavus Fox, whom he had first encountered earlier at Fort Sumter. Fox had been sent by Lincoln to inspect and report back to him on the condition of Sumter's occupants. Crawford surely learned on the way home that his real mission had been the examination and on-site analysis of the Confederate naval defenses.[46]

Fox eventually reported his findings to President Lincoln, and a privately financed plan, in hopes of better secrecy, was devised to resupply and regarrison the fort. April 6 was the go date, but the scheme ran into problems from the outset. The steamers *Baltic* and *Harriet Lane* were to sail separately to avoid suspicion. They would carry most of the men and

98   Chapter Nine

supplies and would be joined, outside Charleston, by the warship *Powhatan* and from that point be tugged to Sumter. Due to a mix-up, the *Powhatan* was diverted on another mission and when it failed to arrive, another ship, the *Pawnee,* which was to rendezvous with the *Powhatan*, refused to continue. The *Pocahontas* arrived late and the tugs never made it due to heavy northeasterly gales. The heavy seas doomed the idea of sailing heavily loaded craft into the Charleston harbor. By the time Lieutenant Robert O. Tyler drilled a boat crew and volunteered to take one small boat in to drop supplies, it was too late. Sumter had capitulated. The entire naval operation had been a failure not due to any single individual or event, but it lifted the spirits of the soldiers in Sumter by providing a glimpse of hope.[47]

Now as they headed north, the men occupied their time recounting personal adventures. Samuel probably overheard the tale of one Irishman, who voiced his frustration when the powerful batteries on the barbette tier were placed off-limits by Major Anderson. The commander feared their firing would bring unnecessary danger to the men. When no officers were looking, John Carmody decided to take the situation into his own hands. He sneaked up the ramparts to the loaded and generally aimed weapons to give the Southern troops a snoot full of the big boys. The sergeant from Kerry, Ireland, quickly and deliberately discharged each gun in succession, which aroused the enemy, who responded with a heavy fire on the barbette. Carmody did not end his personal war with the enemy batteries because he was beaten and frightened, but because he could not, by himself, reload the guns. Contrary to the Southern belief that it had been a change of strategy by the major, it was merely Carmody versus the Confederacy.

Some of the exterior damage reported the night of April 12 was probably in response to the antics of Carmody's war.[48]

Surgeon Crawford felt he had earned his $170.50 per month that Uncle Sam was paying for his services. Indeed all those in the fort believed they earned their pay and, more importantly, the respect of their nation.[49]

Among those wounded in the surgeon's care were men with different degrees and types of wounds. Two were in rather severe condition: one burned and the other wounded by shrapnel. Another man had a right eye injury, which Samuel feared might affect his sight. Among those who had superficial burns and cuts was a corporal who managed to breathe through his ears. Through it all, his steward, Ed, was probably at his side to assist in whatever manner he could.

The surgeon certainly inquired about the details in the death of Private Daniel Hough during the gun salute; Sergeant Chester and Corporal F. Oakes were near the scene. Oakes had known Private Hough and knew that he originally had some problems in the army relating to his cohorts. After his adjustment, he was liked by others and certainly too young to be punished by death.[50]

As to the details of death, Surgeon Crawford learned what he could by listening to his gun mates. Hough had just inserted a cartridge when that south wind blew some burnings into the cartridge, causing a premature explosion. Body parts were seen flying—an arm, half a head, and gray hair matted with blood. But Chester, Oakes, and the others surely felt that Daniel Hough would have appreciated the one-gun salute later on his behalf.

Surgeon Crawford was probably questioned about the wounds of the others: Sergeant James Ed Galway had lost one arm and practically two, and with the loss of blood Crawford felt it would be difficult to save his life. Galway was sent to a hospital in Charleston as was George Fielding who was severely burned. Private Fielding returned north six weeks later. The other gunner who appeared badly hurt, John Irwin, was taken to Charleston; but after he created enough of a scene, the medical folks sent the 34-year-old Irish Irwin back to the fort before the ship left for New York. Private James Hays had the dubious distinction of being wounded the first and the last day. Both wounds were slight.[51]

Once the men were able to reflect about the last four or five days, they, almost to a man, felt that they could not be ashamed of their defeat any more than the South could be proud of their victory.

Assuredly Samuel could not have made the return trip home without being harassed about one of the incidents that happened during the last days at the fort. Doubleday could not have passed up the opportunity to chide him about the story of how he was a savior of a Southerner. Samuel would have had to tell his side of the story of an incident that occurred when the commissioners had visited the fort in a final attempt to resolve the Wigfall stalemate. While awaiting word from General Beauregard, one of the emissaries, Roger Pryor, sitting on Crawford's bed, helped himself to a giant swallow from what he thought was bourbon, not knowing he had consumed enough medicinal potassium to have poisoned him. The surgeon pumped his stomach and now Captain Doubleday accused Samuel of wittingly aiding and abetting the enemy. Crawford contended that he could not allow the enemy to take government property from the fort.[52]

One can almost hear the bouts of laughter at Samuel's recounting. Humor seemed a little more appropriate and welcomed than it would have a few days earlier.

With his duties performed and no officer of the day to keep him up at night, Crawford sought the refuge of his bunk for rest and time to relay his news to his brother John: "We have fought for two days and our works is quite literally knocked to pieces. The fire was so hot and accurate that the Major withdrew the men from the upper tier to save lives. My 32-pounders against Cummings rifled shells did slight damage. The fort received 1,800 shells." According to the Fort Sumter handbook it was more than 3,000 shells.[53]

"I will see you soon. We will fight the battle again with full particulars." Captain Crawford, the surgeon, had been a fighting surgeon and at present seemed without spirit. It would return, but now it was the foothills and family in Pennsylvania that were foremost in his mind.[54]

Surely his father now had a degree of pride in his middle son. He had defended his country as his father had wished, and had Samuel failed, he knew the rest of his life would have been blighted by his father's words, "he would be no son of mine." Before those words of disowning his son he wrote, "I am persuaded he will defend the stars and stripes or make them his winding sheet."[55]

Before leaving Fort Sumter, Anderson sent a note to the War Department asking that his officers, including the assistant surgeon, be brevetted for their services above and beyond the call of duty. The total of one hundred-plus daring and bold men would all be heroes of the Republic.

Governor Pickens, caught up in the moment, proclaimed, "We have defeated 20 million and humbled their flag." The fort he won carried a price tag of civil war. It would be thousands of gallons of blood, tons of flesh, and trillions of tears before Samuel Wylie Crawford would return to this fort.[56]

The town of Chambersburg had received the telegram about the bombardment at 4:27 a.m. on April 12, and many in Chambersburg were aware that one of their own had served honorably at Fort Sumter. The telegram prompted one of her citizens to announce, "The musket must be shouldered to save the Union Flag from dishonor."[57]

Officers' photo taken at Fort Sumter in March of 1861. Front row, from the left: Captain Doubleday, Major Anderson, Captain Crawford, and Captain Foster. Samuel despised this photo but said they had much fun about it. He was suffering from a constant sore throat and more. His illness seems apparent in this photo. Back row, from the left: Captain Truman Seymour, Lieutenant G. W. Snyder, Lieutenant Jeff Davis, Lieutenant R. K. Meade, and Lieutenant Theodore Talbot.

USAMHI

One of Samuel Crawford's Fort Sumter drawings that he had published in *Harper's Weekly*.
Crawford Papers, Library of Congress

Our flag flies yet high above all around us. The all important position we occupy as the key to the harbor, the absolute controller of the channel, must make our remaining here a never failing source of irritation to the Carolinians & until we are removed there can be no peace for the authorities here. You will have seen that Col. Hayne had presented the ultimatum, so called of S. C. in reference to our fort, & that he was about to leave Washington. It is said that the legislature in secret session urged this course upon the Governor as one absolutely necessary to the honor & actual position of the State. I do not credit it entirely. I believe & always have believed, that our stay here depended upon the action of the Southern Confederacy delegation to meet in Montgomery on Monday. It then becomes a serious question — several States banded together & heartily supporting each other in the demand for the several forts must precipitate the issue & my own idea is that after sending commissioners to Washington Mr. Buchanan will officially receive them & send their demand to Congress. If it is refused the sooner we are reinforced the better for the struggle must come. I told you in confidence something in reference to our plan.

A part of one of the many letters Assistant Surgeon Crawford wrote from Fort Sumter. Notice his comments on the flag and the significance of the Federal army's position.

Crawford Papers, Library of Congress

Part Five

The Decision and the Inspector General

"God was pleased to guard my little force from shot and shell."
—Major Robert Anderson

"I must have the air of the mountains of Pennsylvania before I am made well."
—S. W. Crawford, 1861

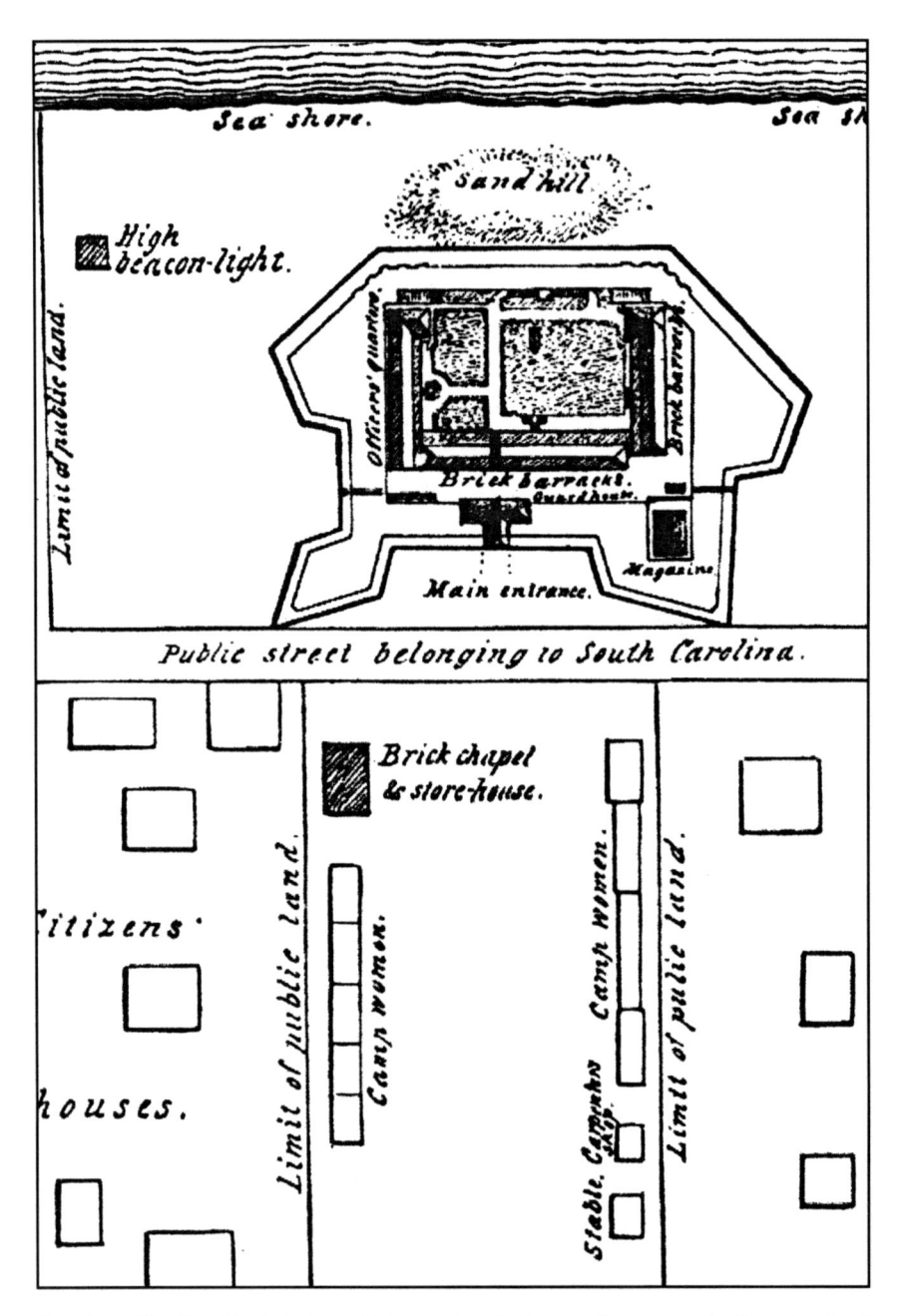

Drawing of the Fort Moultrie Area. Note the chapel where Anderson urged officers to attend services December 25, 1860.

Crawford, *Genesis of the Civil War*

೫ Chapter Ten ಞ
From Assistant Surgeon to Major, U.S. Infantry

I. "We were treated with unlimited kindness and hospitality."[1]

All of those on the *Baltic* heard the blaring whistles and chiming bells of a welcoming New York as it saluted the storied garrison and the flags furled on the masts. Friends attended the wounded so they also could revel in the glory. Men and officers were touched by the thankful recognition accorded them by what seemed to be the entire city. Samuel Crawford said they were received "with enthusiasm and demonstration seldom exceeded and wholly exceptional by the generous hearts of New York."[2] Doubleday wrote, "the men and officers were swept off their feet and lifted to and forced to ride the shoulders of the crowds. Merchants refused payment for goods, we were besieged with visitors, and many highly distinguished in all walks of life."[3]

Someone aboard the *Baltic* probably remembered that it was Patriot's Day, anniversary of the Battle of Lexington-Concord. Was the commotion on shore for those first patriots or the new ones on deck?

The steamer *Baltic* wormed its way through the narrows with Sumter's torn garrison flag at the mainstream head and at her foremast head the Moultrie flag. On April 18 the craft which was unable to aid them in the fort had transported them home to safety.

The ovation they received reminded them of the cheering Southerners who celebrated their defeat in Charleston. The city's answer was a "mighty upheaval never before seen in New York."[4] The country was uniting behind the little band whose cause they and their flags symbolized.

Dr. Gun, the medical examiner, and his assistants pulled to the side of the steamer accompanied by the Associated Press and a few city reporters. A feeble, willowy, and serious Robert Anderson met them near the gangplank. He looked exhausted and overburdened by an event he was unable to control. He did not agree with the war. Anderson had done everything in his power to prevent it and failed. At one point a nod from him and the iron missile would have raced toward the Palmetto flag. He did not make the nod. On the trip home his greatest pleasure came handing mail to his men; other than that he stayed mostly to himself in his cabin, a tired and emotionally spent gentleman.[5]

On Thursday, April 18, 1861, the human cargo found their journey at end. Whether they were veterans of nine years like the Irish American James McMahon or the French American John Laroche, who joined Company H less than two weeks before the move to Fort Sumter, all considered the ordeal a once-in-a-lifetime experience.[6]

After greetings, salutations, and words of praise, Captain Crawford took a couple of the medical assistants to the sick bay. He outlined their individual medical histories and the nature of their wounds. There were questions as well as praise for their exploits.

Dr. Gun understood that Samuel had been taking iodide of potassium for a urinary infection, in addition to his extremely sore throat. He determined the surgeon's condition was worse than he was outwardly disclosing.

A number of the reporters who boarded the *Baltic* quizzed anyone who would, or could, relate their stories for publication. Topics ranged from sheer survival of the bombardment to the fact the last biscuit had been consumed 36 hours prior to Sumter's fall. One writer wrote of a wound on Surgeon Crawford's face, even though Samuel had never mentioned it in diary or letter.[7]

In the streets of New York it was a scene of welcoming for the courageous garrison. Standing on a balcony, Anderson watched his men pass. He witnessed the outpouring of red, white, and blue by supporters who wore the colors on their hats, coats, pants, and carts and wagons. Even omnibuses were similarly hued. The Southern guns had united the North.

The wives and children of the men of Sumter who had departed on February 3 swarmed to meet their husbands and fathers. Most of them had taken sanctuary in a number of nearby churches near Fort Hamilton.

A couple of days later in a celebration to honor the first heroes, Peter Hart took the storm flag and hung it on a tree behind the grandstand and placed the garrison flag, still attached to its makeshift pole, in the arms of George Washington whose statue highlighted Union Square.[8] Hart, the old faithful sergeant who had served Anderson in Mexico and came to his aid as a volunteer, was a first class patriot and an Irishman to love. The men of Sumter spent the days and nights at Fort Hamilton in rest and recuperation. Visitors poured into the fort on a regular basis and brought with them offerings of homemade delectables hungered for by all. Trips to the city found the New Yorkers welcoming them to the point of showering them with free gifts. Those fortunate enough to be united with their loved ones were the happiest of the recipients.[9]

During these days of celebration, Samuel and his cohorts were "treated with unlimited kindness and hospitality" by his friends Mr. and Mrs. August Belmont. Samuel would pen just four years before his death thanking them "for friendship and attachment that has never changed nor diminished."[10]

In the midst of the glee, Surgeon Crawford had a number of men under his medical care. The long confinement and the emotional shock of the experience had resulted in a number of soldiers suffering from colds, sore throats, inflammations, and tonsillitis. It was now that Crawford first allowed himself to believe he might have signs of malarial infection.

Shortly after their arrival in New York, Captain Crawford likely had the unpleasant duty to inform James Chester and the men of Company E that Ed Galway had passed on in the Charleston Hospital.[11]

Robert Anderson, though fatigued and weakened, seemed to reflect an inner peace. His medical advisers suggested rest, but he took the time to press the War Department for leave for his entire command and the brevetting of his officers.

At Sandy Hook on April 18, Anderson had been too emotionally distraught to write and dictated to Gustavus Fox a message to the secretary of war. The elongated sentence summarized the facts of the bombardment, the physical consequences, and the overall plight of the members of the garrison:

> Having defended Fort Sumter for thirty-four hours, until the quarters were entirely burned, the main gates destroyed by fire, the gorge wall seriously injured, the magazine surrounded by flames, and its doors closed from the effects of heat, four barrels and three cartridges of powder being available, and no provisions remaining but pork, I accepted terms of evacuation offered by General Beauregard, being the same offered on the 11th instant, prior to the commencement of hostilities, and marched out of the fort Sunday afternoon, the 14th instant, with colors flying and drums beating, bringing away company and private property and saluting my flag with 50 guns.[12]

On April 20, Anderson received a telegram from Secretary of War Simon Cameron. Its text was relayed to the troops:

> I am directed by the President of the United States to communicate to you and through you to the officers and men in your command at Fort Moultrie and Fort Sumter, the approbation of the government of your and their judicious and gallant conduct there and to tender to you and them the thanks of the government for the same.[13]

Anderson bared his soul when he released the text of his personal memorandum penned before departing from South Carolina:

> God was pleased to guard my little force from shot and shell, which were thrown into and against my works, to Him my thanks is due that I am enabled to report that no one was seriously injured by their fire but I regret that I have to add that in consequence of some unaccountable misfortune, a man was killed, two seriously wounded and a third slightly whilst saluting our flag as it was lowered.
>
> I think I would do injustice to my command to order them to duty of any kind for some months, as both officers and men need rest and recreation of the garrison life to give them an opportunity to recover from the effects of the hardship of their three month confinement within the walls of Fort Sumter.[14]

Captain Doubleday was to remain at Fort Hamilton where he had accepted command. As they prepared to depart, Crawford sealed their farewell with salutations, not good-byes.

Bidding farewell to his comrades with whom he had shared life, death, and hunger was a most difficult task. As Samuel went through the motions, he remained convinced their paths would certainly cross again. Under the embattled conditions he saw a model for a "Christian and a warrior." This lesson would be tested in many ways during the next four years.[15]

In his message to Congress in July of 1861, it was left to Lincoln to place the affair in perspective: "the giving of bread to few brave and hungry men in the garrison was all which upon that occasion would be attempted unless they should provoke more."[16]

II. The Decision

As the days at Fort Hamilton passed, Captain Crawford's mind was most likely occupied with the nagging question of whether he should remain in medicine. For the past decade he had done his best in the medical arena, but he had also felt a sense of futility with the contributions of his profession to the war effort.

He certainly was cognizant that a full-fledged rebellion meant teeming hospitals and overworked surgeons who might be forced to do shoddy work. He was no doubt personally repulsed at the thought of being forced to accept such butchery. Those stark realizations conceivably darkened his mood. The fear of failure had always been a motivating force in his mind, while the fear of the unknown haunted him. Medicine or infantry, which would best fit Samuel Crawford?

He was not entirely naïve about the role of a line officer. Previously, he had served as volunteer line officer at Sumter, a role in which he was able to command and observe personnel. He had taken part in rear guard details where he experienced trying circumstances. In the frontier days, he accompanied expeditions of marches as well as field maneuvers. Though they now seemed trivial, they had allowed Samuel some practical military leadership. In manning a battery in the defense of Sumter, he had only tasted his first combat.

Should he stay the course, or change to infantry? His professional frustration, coupled with the certainty that the war would create a demand for staff officers, was forcing Crawford to make a decision. Undoubtedly, he was aware that infantry command offered faster advancement in rank.

Until now all the years of education and experience had been dedicated to his profession. Medicine had been the most significant part of his life for the past 15 years. He had honed his skills in his military years. Now at this critical juncture of his career, the captain felt tugs in both directions. Medicine was a noble pursuit, but the infantry had its attractions as well. The thought that his personal goals and their ego-satisfying attributes might overshadow his need to serve his divided nation gnawed at Samuel. It had to be more, much more, than an ego trip, for there was too much at stake to be that shallow. Samuel had learned long ago that living consisted of the process of choices and abiding by the consequences of those decisions.

His letters to John Agnew allow us to share his inner feelings. Once he wrote that they "will live to see the saddest sights witnessed by men"[17] and that the fragile future was more than any human could foretell. "Alas, my brother, why are we divided on this senseless issue, which will destroy many of God's children and much of His world?" Why would the Southerners rise in revolution against conditions that must in the end sap the foundation of their very existence? His mind was bombarded by the unanswered questions.[18]

Finally, Captain Crawford accepted that which was tendered. With the best wishes of his cohorts, Captain Crawford ventured to Fort Columbus, New York.

In May 1861 he received notification of promotion to major under Winfield Scott's signature. He was certain that Robert Anderson, now brigadier general, had something to do with the promotion. Anderson, too, had to thank one of his former soldiers for his upward mobility. The commander in chief, Abraham Lincoln, who boasted that his military heroism consisted of "leading a charge through an onion patch," was one of Anderson's recruits during the Black Hawk War.[19]

After the number of statements such as "I must have the air of the mountains of Pennsylvania before I am made well"[20] and the fact that he did not report to Fort Adams until September, one can conceive Samuel traveled home. Back at the "farm" the family would have noticed his gaunt appearance and troublesome cough. Surely the peaceful environment of the old homestead would help him in his rehabilitation. It always did.

He would have learned that Margaret, Ed, and the children had departed earlier for Springfield, Illinois, where Captain Edward Washington was stationed with the army's 13th U.S. Infantry. John Agnew had almost decided to go the route of chaplain. The fact Father was turned down for a chaplaincy went unspoken, but the reality was the Crawford family would have three sons and a son-in-law involved in the war.[21]

Son and father probably discussed what the odds were in going to war totally. The Union strengths were likely examined: an already established government, an industrial base, a solid banking system, greater wealth, and a larger population to build armies of fighting men.

They no doubt realized the horns of the dilemma of the Confederate style of government. If the Confederate method worked in wartime it would be a miracle because Confederacy and war are contradictions in terms. The central power they fear is the power needed in any emergency.

While Crawford agreed to the concept of States' rights, he observed in South Carolina that the few had the power and the voice. Could the few convince the many to fight and win a war? Samuel had expressed a number of times that the South had only to hold the territory they had. In most civil wars the challenger had to conquer. In this case, the insurgents constructed their government within their boundaries and needed only to protect it.[22]

The Southern economy was based on one crop that was produced by slave labor, and the profits went back into more slaves, land, and more cotton. Their social system was frozen in layers of the past. Their political clout was now nonexistent in the national government. They lost that power when they removed themselves from the Federal system. Now "the common thread is our hatred of each other."[23]

At some point Samuel would have to explain to his parents that after much deliberation he was changing to infantry. His parents, he understood, would be flabbergasted, and he would have to ask them to listen to his reasoning. But he also realized they would only respond in disbelief. He could hear them now: Hear you out? After studying medicine to heal people, now you study to kill your fellow man! Hear you out? They repeated again and again that he had been taught formally and at home to heal, not kill.[24]

Once again, Samuel would understand as he had from the Penn days that life was a series of choices with corresponding consequences framed in individual responsibility. He was prepared to accept that premise. After 34 years, he probably felt that he had made a decision that did not receive the full support of his parents, especially his mother's. He understood that he must try more now than ever to bring honor to his country and his family name.[25]

III. Nature's Obstacles

Upon his arrival at the headquarters of the 13th United States Infantry at Camp Gauley in the New River region of western Virginia, Major Crawford would meet his new commander, General William Starke Rosecrans who had recently been appointed brigadier general. He had military flowing in his veins as his father fought in the war of 1812. Having finished fifth in the West Point class of 1842, he acquired a position in the corps of engineers. He missed participation in the Mexican War because of working on a number of engineering projects. Presently, General Rosecrans commanded two brigades: one under General Robert Schenck and the second commanded by H.W. Benham. The mission of "Old Rosey" was to secure communications, dislodge, and if possible cut off Confederate General John Floyd's forces.[26]

As Rosecrans' acting inspector general, the major would have a myriad of duties. The overall concept of the job was to aid the commander in making the military machinery run as efficiently as possible. In reality he would be the eyes and ears of the commander and try to do what the commander requested. Certainly hard work and loyalty would pay dividends for both officers.

Sometimes he would be a glorified courier and other times he would participate in the operation of an important mission. Such was the case when he reacted to a call from General Rosecrans' headquarters on November 6, 1861.[27]

The fighting in the Shenandoah Valley had been volatile for some time. On the Confederate side Henry Wise and John Floyd, both ex-governors of Virginia and now commanders in Robert E. Lee's army had a tendency to bicker and antagonize each other, which prevented the Southern cause from having a united front. This area of western Virginia was particularly significant because it had voted and declared statehood as West Virginia. Additionally, the control of the Baltimore and Ohio Railroad and the Ohio River was at stake.[28]

In the beginning of November the Union army was trying to get to the rear and flank of Major Crawford's old Sumter adversary, John Floyd, the previous secretary of war, who showed his Southern partiality in carrying out his duties in 1861.

General Rosecrans assigned Major Crawford to report to General Robert Schenck commanding the Third Brigade. Crawford noted his mission: "It had been determined to throw a body of troops under General Schenck across the New River about five miles up river." Relying on information supplied to him by Sergeant Haven of the 23rd Ohio, Crawford inspected a crossing called Townsends and found the access exceedingly difficult but evidently unwatched. The challenge lay in finding a means to cross the 90 yards from one bank to the opposite.[29]

He had four skiffs sent from Camp Gauley and the rest were to be constructed by himself with items he could scrounge. Two floats were made from wagon frames secured by wedges and pins, placed on a duck paulin and all secured by ropes to hold the parts together and to be used to guide the monstrosities.[30]

On November 7 the inspector general found a path leading down the mountain but unfit for lowering the boats to the water's edge. Another search unveiled a cliff that opened on a 12-foot-high smooth rock. As the rain poured in torrents, the men lowered the skiffs and wagon beds and concealed them near the water below. It was Saturday, November 9, as a guard protected the vessels in the rain and mud and without light, fire, or loud talk. The venture had been completed in three days. However the rain had accompanied the entire project and the river was watched hourly.[31]

On Sunday morning, three Rebels attempting either to escape or spy came from the opposite side to the Union side. They launched a small, crude boat of planks which could carry only two of them. When they discovered the guard, they "delivered themselves up. The third man was fired upon." According to Major Crawford, the incident proved inconsequential to the completion of the project. The area continued to be free of the enemy. It was not mankind but nature that became the obstacle of the crossing. The recent heavy and incessant rains had swelled the river to the point it became impassable. Crawford asked three experienced oarsmen to try their hand at negotiating the water. If this could be done, a rope tether would be secured on the other side. However, once the boat was in midstream, the swift current swept it downriver. After much exertion the boat and crew were recovered safely. General Schenck determined that the risk was too great. The rain stopped but the river continued to rise, and according to a Schenck staff officer it was still too dangerous to attempt a crossing on the 12th. It was time for a new scheme.[32]

A backup plan was placed into effect. The acting inspector general now became responsible for coordinating the two brigades. The second plan lacked the surprise element of the original. General Schenck's men would cross Kanawha River below Camp Gauley and would attack Floyd's side and front. General Benham, meanwhile, would be placed to broadside General Floyd's troops if possible and, at least, cut off his retreat route. The plan had a much better probability of succeeding if two units reached their destinations quickly. The soldiers became exhausted from marching in the continuing rain, on mucky, slippery roads and on unfriendly terrain, with no blankets and their ration wagon unable to pass on the roads. This was not the key to success. The slow developing plan gave Floyd time to smell it out. The Confederate general was able to jump-start his retreat course. Ultimately the hunt was called off.[33]

Before returning to General Rosecrans' headquarters, Crawford walked to the 12-foot rock at Townsend's Ferry to judge the river's power and reassess its military value. He wrote that it was "perfectly practical for infantry to cross and still no evidence of the slightest effort made to protect it." The enemy this time was the weather.[34]

On the 15th, Major Crawford returned to Rosecrans' headquarters with dispatches from the two brigade commanders.

Rosecrans had practically driven the Confederate forces under Lee out of the area and secured western Virginia for the Union. General Rosecrans summarized the affair, "Floyd's forces, though beaten and demoralized, are not destroyed and must be watched. The country is now more nearly pacified."[35]

For Crawford's work, Rosecrans commended him not only for his reconnoitering and preparation for the crossing, but for laboring day and night in the most inclement weather to get everything in readiness. "To his exertions mainly the accomplishment of this difficult and arduous task is chiefly due."[36]

The bombardment of Fort Sumter, April 13, 1861
Those aboard one of the relief ships look on helplessly as the fort is bombarded and burns.
Mollus/USAMHI

Part Six

The Early Years of Infantry Command

"There is work for you to do up there."
—General S. W. Crawford, Antietam

"I Point to the vacant places of my Officers and the skeleton regiments of my brigade."
—Crawford Report after Cedar Mountain battle

Major Crawford's first photo after joining the U.S. Infantry. He was acting inspector general under General Rosecrans.

Nelson Collection, USAMHI

℘ Chapter Eleven ☙

Cedar Mountain or Slaughter Mountain

I. Stonewall in the Shenandoah

As the nation faced the new year of 1862, the Northern citizens felt an increased sense of fear and trepidation. Earlier optimism that the conflict would be brief and casualties light was rapidly dissipated by the stark realities of 1861.

Casualty lists were now trickling home and more local burials gave witness to the increased carnage. In the South, it was becoming clear that the Union was not going to allow the erring sisters to depart quietly. In the beginning of the year, the Confederate cause had little to celebrate. The Western campaign was going badly and the Southern ironclad had failed to break the Northern blockade. In the east, George B. McClellan's movements toward Richmond, up the Virginia peninsula, were causing concern. However, by the early summer of '62 Robert E. Lee and Thomas "Stonewall" Jackson were providing some hope and what solace the Rebels could muster.

In the North, despite criticism of Lincoln and his administration, Abraham Lincoln was becoming better acquainted with the many roles of the president. With successes in the Western Theater and the likelihood of a positive outcome by McClellan, Lincoln used the opportunities to bolster his cabinet with a secretary of agriculture and push through the Homestead Act providing land to those willing to develop it. The ordinary Southerner did not receive the same government amenities as their Northern counterparts.

To divert aid from General McClellan and to move against Pope's threat to the rail junction at Gordonsville, the South decided to go after the relatively small Yankee army in the Shenandoah Valley. In the middle of June 1862 Northern General John Pope, brought from the West, was now in charge of the newly formed Army of Virginia. During the steamy month of

July, his Second Corps under General Nathaniel Prentiss Banks in the vanguard and camped in Culpeper, Jackson was bringing his army, estimated at 25,000, north from Gordonsville, about 25 miles distant, in an effort to halt the Northern advance.

Jackson was at his best when he was able to dare, hit, run, and hit again. His deception landed him a victory at Winchester near the end of May. The North was terrorized more than necessary and the South hailed it as a victory probably larger than it was strategically; but perception is often more authoritative than reality, and so it was this time. Another reality would prove to be larger than perception; a few days after the Battle of Winchester, the commander of the Southern army, Joseph E. Johnston, was severely wounded at Seven Pines. His first replacement was G. W. Smith, and then on June 1 Robert E. Lee, Jefferson Davis' advisor, was placed in command of the Southern army.

The Shenandoah Valley was the arena for active troop movements on both sides of the conflict. From the third week of March until the end of June, Jackson's "foot cavalry" had covered an area of 675 miles, fought five battles, and managed to confuse and frustrate Northern commanders by using the mountain terrain, trickery, and tempo.

The North responded to Jackson's maneuvers by devising a plan to trap him. Crawford, assigned to the Department of the Shenandoah, under Major General N. P. Banks, came into the Shenandoah Campaign on May 8. Crawford had received kudos from F. H. Pierpont for his work in western Virginia[1] and a new promotion to brigadier general effective April 25, 1862.[2]

On May 25, at Winchester, Jackson again defeated General Banks, who had a lot of success before the war in the political arena and was now finding military success in the Shenandoah very difficult. On that same day, Banks would write in his report that General Crawford and others reported for duty, was unassigned a command, and "they all rendered me most valuable assistance by accompanying the column throughout the march." Crawford's volunteer duties consisted of scouting, reconnoitering, and interrogationg individuals.[3]

Brigadier General Crawford would experience his first infantry command in this area against that warrior, "Stonewall." Jackson. General Crawford was mounted on a beautiful, dark red, blood bay named "Blood." The animal was representative of General Rosecrans' generosity. Crawford hoped to command a brigade riding him.[4]

II. Brigade Command

When the corps reached Williamsport, Crawford was assigned the First Brigade in Alpheus Williams' First Division. Williams, a "Yale man" in the Second Corps of General Banks, with a law degree, fought in Mexico and received his generalship a year before Crawford. General Williams was known for his superior organizational skills. He and Crawford originally came to appreciate each other on a professional level. General Crawford's command consisted of the following regiments: 5th Connecticut, 10th Maine, 28th New York, 46th Pennsylvania, and Captain Joseph Knap's battery. The regiments were commanded by veteran leadership.[5]

During this transitional period, First Lieutenant Alex McLeod Crawford was selected by Crawford as his aide-de-camp. Alex likely admitted to his brother that the adventures of the army were more glorious than his medical studies. He knew he would get a lecture about the value of education, but that mattered less to him than serving his sibling. Alex had been serving in the 12th Pennsylvania Cavalry as a first lieutenant.[6]

As Crawford looked at his younger sibling he realized how he had grown. Now about the same height as Samuel, he also possessed the erect Crawford stature, and a chiseled frame that provided a stylish look in his uniform. Alex was not the first sibling to join the staff of a brother, and such arrangements had been known to create problems. Duty would seem to be more important than birthright to both men.

As his brigade was concentrating on accumulating knowledge about the enemy, General Crawford emphasized the roles of proper scouting, interrogation, and the value of being disciplined in the process. Most of July was spent trying to locate "the active and wily Jackson who was much encouraged by his successes which resulted from his own actions and our restraints..."[7] Toward the end of July, Crawford's scouting efforts had secured enough intelligence to inform Pope and Banks that "General Jackson is at Orange Court House with two brigades of infantry and 1,500 cavalry."[8] In another incident, Crawford in his excitement about some information and its rapid relay earned him a reminder from Banks: "dispatches will be more explicit if the hour is stated." The nervous energy that drove him was at work; this time negatively.[9]

Throughout July General Banks cautioned and prodded Crawford's efforts: "make reconnaissance vigorous and bold, press the enemy closely and guard against unexpected attacks. Move in different directions without cessation. That will best serve to harass our foe and show his position and plans."[10] As he was carrying out these duties he was trying to understand how to effectively lead a new brigade. He felt the necessity to instill discipline which he believed was needed for the unit to be a good fighting force. The new brigade commander struggled to find a medium between discipline and humanness. The men in his ranks felt he went overboard with too many frivolous inspections and too much insistence on being saluted. He was "very particular and when he is superseded it will be a good day for our brigade," wrote John Gould of the 10th Maine. At one point Gould raised above his anger and wrote, "if Crawford has a good general over him to control his excitement; we are in safe hands with his cautious nature. Still in all, we would like to break out and give him a ducking in the river."[11]

III. Battle of Cedar Mountain

Lee was concerned with Pope's threat to mistreat Virginia citizens. He requested Jackson to apply pressure to Pope's army. Jackson planned to strike the Union army with blows on isolated units but Banks made the first move and Jackson was forced to go on the defensive.[12]

On August 8, cavalry leader Brigadier General George D. Bayard reported the enemy advance on Culpeper. Crawford, stationed at Culpeper Court House, was ordered to support Bayard's cavalry with his four regiments of infantry and artillery. General Crawford's mission was to work with the cavalry to determine the strength and disposition of the enemy force.[13]

By midday he had his army on the move and by four o'clock he met Bayard between Colvin's Tavern and Cedar Run.

Along with an engineering officer, Major Houston of McDowell's staff, Crawford selected a suitable position. He then brought up his artillery where it was completely concealed from enemy view, and placed the infantry in a close supporting distance. He concealed them from the enemy. Strong pickets were thrown out and the command bivouacked for the night.[14]

Alpheus Williams, Crawford's division commander, arrived about noon on August 9 about the same time the enemy artillery was greeting the first brigade "which was speedily silenced by the fire of Knap's Battery." The division commander then found General Crawford near a stream called Cedar Run and about a mile from Cedar or Slaughter Mountain. In his Official Report he called the country "much wooded with intervening strips of cultivated land." After placing the infantry brigades in position, General Williams continued the story, "our cook got us up a good lunch of ham and coffee and I invited the officers of my old brigade, now Crawford's brigade, to join me. After lunch we lay down under a shade tree and talked about the last ten months that we had been together. Col. Donnelly of the 28th New York, a great joker and full of humor, was in excellent spirits. Sorrow and misfortune seemed far away." Not more than six hours later every one of them would be killed or wound.[15]

Commanding a brigade in battle was now the challenge facing General Samuel Crawford since it was the primary tactical unit of maneuver in combat. Crawford would have to use the skills of his staff and his ability to communicate orders to others. This could not be underestimated. Knowing the role of the brigade in the overall scheme was necessary for success. One important lesson he would have to grasp immediately, if he hadn't at Camp Gauley, was that after meticulous planning all could quickly fall apart upon initial impact. Adjustments in combat were almost always constant.[16]

At dawn on Saturday, August 9, General Bayard reported that the enemy was advancing to their left toward a range of elevated hills. Together Generals Bayard and Crawford determined that the movement was to conceal three pieces of artillery at the foot of the mountain slope. Bayard placed the cavalry in front of the infantry to closely monitor the movements of the Confederates. A few hours later the enemy opened their artillery against the Union lines. Crawford directed Captain Joseph Knap's battery to return the fire. This battery's accuracy was so excellent that the enemy's guns ceased firing in a short time and changed positions. After the Rebel artillery changed, a long-range artillery battle continued for some time.[17]

Initially the first brigade commander was ordered to resist any enemy advance. General Banks was on his way with support in the event it turned into more than a defensive battle.[18]

About five o'clock in the afternoon the First Brigade was ordered to move to the right of the Orange Road. As the movement was taking place, Crawford received an order to deploy the regiments in a line of battle directly opposite the left wing of the enemy. The regiments were formed in a thick belt of woods which skirted an open wheat stubble field. The field in front was opened for 300 yards before reaching a belt of woods on the opposite side. Ignorant of the terrain which seemed uneven, Crawford sent a scouting party to try to identify the goal of the assigned mission. The enemy could not be seen from the woods where the First Brigade had massed. The scouts returned in a frightened state reporting the land was uneven and the Confederate troops were secured in the woods on the flank and in the field opposite the Union position. The scouts could have been shot or captured by the enemy, but the suspicion was the Rebels were waiting for larger game. Bayonets were fixed and Crawford wrote, "I requested Napoleons from Muhlenberg's 4 U.S. battery to clear the woods in front and on my flank."

Before the guns arrived, the brigade was ordered to charge. The 10th Maine was removed from the brigade by a corps staff officer. It practically fought alone as it was a distance from the other regiments. Commanding a brigade in combat was an everchanging process![19]

The charge would now be made by three and six-tenths regiments across a 300 yard open field without the desired artillery support and with the enemy concealed in the bushes and woods, in addition to a brutal 98 degree heat. The troops climbed a log fence that skirted the woods, releasing blood-curdling screams.[20] The charge took place in the face of a fatal and murderous fire from the concealed enemy infantry in the bushes and woods in the front and flank. Against the odds, Crawford's brigade drove the enemy back and through the woods. The 28th New York, the 5th Connecticut, and part of the 46th Pennsylvania were involved in hand to hand combat. The brigade was dealing with superior numbers, even though some of Jackson's troops had fallen back. Some of Crawford's men reached a battery that was "the heart of the position." Now the troops were running low on ammunition. Crawford looked for the critically needed reinforcements, but they would not show. Some of Crawford's troops were moving toward the Crittenden gate. "The slaughter was fearful" as more enemy artillery joined in the unraveling.[21]

General Stonewall Jackson arrived near the gate looking for A. P. Hill's reinforcements. Jackson grabbed a Confederate battle flag to confront the retreating troops. Then he tried to wave his sword which was rusted to the scabbard. He was forced to remove belt and all, swinging the whole contraption and yelling, "Jackson is with you!"[22] He was able to stem the tide until order could be restored by the arrival of Hill's troops. Generals Hill and Jackson had been having one of their celebrated disagreements, but Hill arrived with the Reserves on time. For Crawford's men the story was very different. "My gallant men, broken and decimated by a fearful fire in an unequal contest fell back leaving most of their number on the field." As the Union troops arrived back at the Cedar Run Baptist Church they were met by the First Pennsylvania Cavalry who attacked the oncoming Rebels. This was one of the few times that cavalry directly attacked infantry in the Civil War. Robert Krick called it "the stuff from which legends are made."[23]

Crawford stayed on the field until midnight directing and aiding the removal of the wounded. His brigade surgeon, Helmer, remained on the field almost all night. The general later praised the surgeon's efforts and fortitude.[24]

As if enough blood had not been spilled, Crawford and his escort were in the process of finding a suitable ground for camp when they came under enemy cavalry fire that killed two of his escorts. The command was reformed near Colvin's Tavern. The troops rested and received their first rations in 30 hours. They were delivered under the direction of Lieutenant A. M. Crawford.[25]

The little brigade had retreated but took pride in the deeds of valor and bravery it had displayed. They had fought valiantly, even though they were ultimately defeated. Some of the veterans that would go on to fight in every major eastern battle would write, "Never did we fight in as hot a fight for the time it lasted." The death, destruction, and annihilation lasted just over a half hour.[26]

The one satisfaction, if any can be gained in such carnage, was that this was the first time in battle the famed Stonewall Brigade had been driven from the field. General Jackson wrote in his report, "the federal infantry fell with great vigor upon our extreme left, turned it and poured a destructive fire in the rear." In his report to Robert E. Lee he referred to the battle as Slaughter Mountain.[27]

Later General George Gordon found General Crawford in a wooded area sitting alone on Blood with a musket across his saddle. The general never heard Gordon approach as he internalized the pain of the day.

General Jackson was on the brink of disaster but neither the artillery support nor the promised troops arrived. Out of the 1,767 officers and men that the brigade commander took into battle almost 50 percent became casualties. The morning after the battle as Crawford talked to Colonel George Beal, the 10th Maine commander, the colonel sobbed as he asked rhetorically, "Where is my splendid brigade? Where are my brave fellows? Poor Donnelly, Knipe, and Blake!"[28]

IV. The Burials and the Stuart Hat

Sunday evening, after the battle, a shower cooled the air. By dawn of August 11, the heat and humidity could be felt again with the promise of another day of steamy misery. It was necessary to hurry the burials because of the intense heat that was quickly decomposing the bodies.

A Federal party, including Alex, under a flag of truce, requested permission to treat their wounded and bury their dead. Both sides agreed to a time period.

Mangled limbs, torn faces, and bloated bodies were strewn everywhere; a piece of hand, or leg, or foot, or face lay apart from the bodies. The burial details were often only able to identify their own by a piece of cotton underwear or a belt buckle.[29]

Crawford took advantage of a noon lull to rest in the shade with George Bayard. They shared a basket lunch provided by his friend. As they ate, a cavalry officer approached from the Confederate lines. Crawford noticed the rider's obvious horsemanship and his ostrich-plumed hat. As he neared, Crawford stood thinking he recognized the man. The rider dismounted, bowed, and gave a jaunty salute with his hat. It was James Ewell Brown "Jeb" Stuart.[30] Crawford asked Bayard if he knew Stuart, and he indicated that they had served in the old army. After Stuart introduced William Blackford, Samuel most likely told Jeb that his brother was his aide-de-camp. They immediately began reminiscing about times in the old army. Stuart was invited to share lunch. As he did, Jeb informed them he had arrived at Cedar Mountain early that morning and helped negotiate the burial truce now under way. Stuart's tales about the lovely ladies of Maryland, and his thanks to General McClellan's hesitancy, allowing him to ride around the Union army and win his major generalcy, helped to temporarily lighten the mood. As the conversation neared its end, Stuart mounted and said, "Well, Crawford, I suspect the northern press will call this a northern victory."[31]

Crawford replied, "No, not even the *New York Tribune* will call this a victory for us." Stuart looked slyly from under his hat and said, "I guess you wouldn't want to bet a hat on it?" "A hat it is, General Stuart."[32]

Under the cover of darkness, Jackson withdrew across the Rapidan and returned to his former camp at Gordonville. The Union army did not pursue.

Until August 14, the brigade commander was thankfully occupied. But the coming Thursday must have jolted him as he had never been hit before.

V. "With heroism hardly found in the records of war"[33]

It is not difficult to imagine Crawford sitting in his command tent with all the regimental reports on his field desk in front of him, mere paper covered with script and figures. Just black and white; stark opposites conveying to him exactly what he had tried to avoid thinking about during the past few days. How could he make sense of the overwhelming casualties?

His solitude only served to deepen the anguish of the moment. He read of the absolute carnage experienced by his brigade. Pain, bitterness, and disillusionment overcame him as he penned, "My brigade was decimated by a fearful fire of an unequal contest. The color guards are beyond all praise." Again he turned and leafed through the pages of numbers. He felt sick to his stomach as he saw the numbers: 1,767 troops in and at day's end 867 remaining, many dying daily. Colonel Chapman, Lieutenant Colonel Stone, Major Blake of the 5th Connecticut, and so many others were no more. Still the brigade soldiers brought back the colors of every regiment.[34]

"Bravery was attested" to in the report of the 5th Connecticut. When their colors fell, they were picked up, only to fall again, arise, fall, and gathered once more and handed to Crawford for safekeeping near retreat's end. Colonel Donnelly and many other officers who had enjoyed lunch and reminiscing would do neither ever again.

Throughout the slaughter "not one Union regimental color was captured by the enemy." The 10th Maine's color bearer was the original one to survive and retreat with the remnants of the regiment. That regiment was Crawford's primary source for scouts. How many could they supply now? He read of Lieutenant Sprout, the young officer that had reached the enemy battery, one of the brigade's objectives, only to fall as he touched the prize.[35]

The proud Niagara Rifles suffered as much or more than most. Sixty-three percent who entered were listed as dead, wounded, or missing.

In the end Samuel did not forget the numerous acts of gallantry displayed by his men. He scribbled, "It is customary to mention the gallant conduct of those who merit recognition, but I point to the vacant places of my officers and the skeleton regiments of my command." Those all deserved his canonization. Most of the company officers had fallen beside their men.[36]

The division commander, General Williams, said of Crawford and his men, "These men fought with a heroism hardly found in the records of war and their commanders, Crawford and Gordon, gave prompt, zealous cooperation and demand a special commendation."[37] General Pope echoed William's sentiment, "gallant and distinguished conduct and conspicuous gallantry."[38]

Later General Pope wrote of the human devastation, "dead of both armies were found mingled in masses over the whole ground of the conflict."[39] General Banks expressed his approval because Crawford, although outnumbered, struck Jackson's loosely knitted line at the gate and shattered his left in desperate hand-to-hand combat.[40] The veterans remembered the charge as unsurpassed in ferocity by any other during the war.

Nothing prepared a man for this kind of human destruction. None of his prior training had prepared him for the personal shock he was undergoing at this moment. Words were replaced by body counts. He was on the brink of understanding for the first time the emotional requirements that battle command dictated. He now emotionally understood the stark reality that he rationally understood before: individual lives were disposable. He knew it as a military axiom but this was its translation. It seemed the burial parties, the undertakers, were winning the war. He had to keep his mind on the larger goals.

The general took pride in the performance of his troops. They had fought against exceptional odds. Artillery support and reserves that had been promised never materialized, yet Jackson had been halted.

Now he had to go on and continue to test his ability as a brigade commander as the fighting now would be shifted to the Rappahannock

River area. It was imperative that he find company and regimental commanders in whom he had full confidence.

Nineteen days later Jackson and Pope would meet again at the Battle of Second Manassas. Although he would never command on his own after Cedar Mountain, Jackson would continue to plague the Union forces until a late evening in May of 1863 when those who would have given their lives for him would mistakenly take his life.[41]

On the other side, General Pope would be removed from command on September 15, 1862. The Lincoln search would continue for someone to deal effectively with General Robert Edward Lee.[42]

๛ Chapter Twelve ☙
Antietam: From a Wheatfield to a Cornfield

I. The Changing Mindsets of the War by 1862

By the autumn of 1862 nearly eighteen months had passed since the beginning of this conflict. This was longer than many citizens, north and south, had expected. The pendulum of momentum had shifted a couple of times in the year and a half. In the early years after the bombardment of Fort Sumter, the South had been successful. The Confederacy had obtained some arsenals, were able to hold the state of Virginia, essential to the Southern cause, and militarily the Southern army had been successful at Big Bethel and later at First Manassas.[1]

By the fall of 1861 and spring of 1862 the pendulum had swung back toward the Northern cause. President Lincoln's grand design was slower to show results. Realizing the incredibly large physical size of the Confederacy and the value of their rivers and railroads for trade and transport, the administration fashioned an overall concept to cut the Confederacy in half and asphyxiate the Southern economy by using a series of blockades. Isolation from the remainder of the world would place a tremendous strain on the Southern people, armies, and economy. This strangulation plan was initiated on April 19, 1861, with the Union navy patrolling parts of the Southern coastline.[2] In the following months, infantry and naval operations were implemented in the western theater. The Union began to have multiple successes: Port Royal Sound, Island number 10, Forts Henry and Donelson. The Southern defenses on the Mississippi, Cumberland, and Tennessee Rivers were under attack. Soon Shiloh, Corinth, the *Monitor*, and New Orleans became a part of the Northern lexicon of victories. These Union successes continued to apply pressure on the Southern defense of water and rail ways. Resources for industrial capacity were falling under Northern control, and a number of good harbors and ports were passing into Union hands.[3]

The Lincoln administration was also working to keep the Border States in the Union, trying to deal with the rising cost of the war which now stood at two million dollars a day, and the Union government tried to continue to provide essential services for its constituents.[4]

James McPherson called the 2nd session of the 37th Congress one of the most productive in American history because it revolutionized the nation's tax and monetary system, disposed of public property, and brought attention to higher education and the transcontinental railroad, both to be more fully developed at a later date.[5]

Then, for the Southern cause, an unexpected event started the momentum to shift once more. It happened on the first Sunday in June 1862 at the battle of Seven Pines. The commander of the Southern forces, General Joseph E. Johnston, suffered an injury, and Jefferson Davis' senior military advisor, Robert E. Lee, was waiting in the wings to take command of the soon to be named Army of Northern Virginia. The forces would begin to sway back toward the Southern cause. Lee gave chase to General George McClellan, who was, at the time, moving up the peninsula toward the Southern capital of Richmond. McClellan retreated to and remained inactive at Harrison Landing. Lee busied his other lieutenants. Thomas Jackson was sent to secure the Shenandoah Valley. As a morale booster, cavalry commander Stuart circled McClellan's Union army. General Lee's army was successful at 2nd Manassas against General John Pope.[6]

II. The Time Seemed "propitious" for General Lee to Move His Army North.

The Southern impetus gathered from defeating two Union armies in a three-month period provided the Confederacy an opportunity to take the calculated risk of an invasion north. Lee himself said it was the "propitious time." The reasons to invade the North now were manifold. By Lee's own admission his men were poorly clothed and shoed but "still we can not afford to be idle." The North, with its abundant resources, could provide the materials his soldiers needed. Arguably his native Virginia would be given a reprieve from the devastation of war and trampled crops in harvest season. Another consideration that Jefferson Davis placed much emphasis on was the possibility that the border state of Maryland would provide Lee's army with needed manpower. The hope was similar in Kentucky where the South would also invade. This thesis could be developed a step further, as with the latest Confederate victories on the battlefield and the increasing cotton shortage in England and elsewhere, European recognition seemed more probable now than at any other time since the formation of the Confederacy. The foreign powers would look favorably on a Southern victory on Northern soil. It seemed obvious to Southern officials and merchants that the threat of the "cotton hurt" or cotton famine was soon going to bring England down on the side of the Confederacy. This could be the jolt it needed.[7]

A fourth reason for the invasion formed on the horizon. Mid-term elections were around the corner, and perhaps a war weary Northern populace might force Lincoln's alliance to fragment.[8]

The positives seemed to outweigh the negatives; and therefore on September 3, Lee's army broke camp near Chantilly, Virginia, heading for the Potomac River north of Washington, D.C. The next day the camp smoke swirled in Maryland. Lee with bandaged hands from a fall from his horse some weeks ago and his ragtag army entered Frederick, Maryland, on September 6 with less than 50,000 soldiers. The die was cast. This was a significant juncture for the Southern cause for independence as their armies invaded Maryland and Kentucky while continuing to struggle for control of their river systems. To add to their enhancement, it seemed like a time when Union morale and discord seemed to be at the bottom of the well.[9]

Once in the North, General Lee knew he could employ the superior road system to do what his lieutenants did best: divide his army in enemy territory, plant rumors, and show false trails, all to deceive the larger manned Union army.

Near Frederick city on September 8, 1862, the dapper Southern commander made his formal peace proposal to the Marylanders. In part he appealed to the citizens of Maryland because of the "wrongs and outrages that have been inflicted on them. The people of the south have long wished to aid you in throwing off this foreign yoke to enable you again to enjoy the inalienable rights of freemen. Our army is prepared to assist you with the power of its arms in regaining the rights of which you have been despoiled." The response to the peace initiative was a caustic disappointment to Jefferson Davis' government and Robert E. Lee's army.[10]

III. Crawford: Trying to Replace Vacant Officers and Skeleton Regiments

For General Crawford the past month had been a busy one. He had pressed his cause via numerous requests to have the "vacant officers and skeleton regiments" reinforced. When the Pope army became the McClellan army, Crawford was provided three new large regiments from the "Pennsylvania nine month levy." After Cedar Mountain, Crawford's concern with the morale of his brigade heightened. On September 8 near Rockville, Maryland, he rode through the encampment to talk with his officers and men, and his impressions were confirmed. The complaints were not the ordinary gripes voiced by most soldiers. Instead, Crawford heard tales of inexperienced corporals leading companies of "ghost soldiers" existing only on paper. He knew immediate action was needed for the welfare of the soldiers who remained in the brigade. They had to be augmented with new soldiers to make the unit a more formidable fighting force. As of this moment the "four regiments consist of 629 effectives."[11]

Almost to the man, the brigade complained of the declining toughness in the unit's character. Samuel shared their concerns, as he talked with good men too sick or lacking in energy to keep pace. They were men who had never straggled and took pride in that fact. General Crawford took their pleas to heart and the next evening placed in writing an urgent plea to his division and corps commanders:

> Since Cedar Mountain where my brigade was well nigh destroyed, the service has been such as to threaten the reduction of its shattered state. I fear for its very existence. Every day adds to the report of the medical officers. The men suffer from exposure, the deprivation of proper food and the want of rest. The marches are long, done in the heat of the sun, and when we arrive at camp at night the men without regard to weather or hunger throw themselves on the ground to seek rest.[12]

He continued, abandoning his normally concise and thoughtful prose style, and evoking his medical training. Emotionally, he penned, "The depression of spirits adds significantly to the induction of our camp diseases."

He sought aid for a command whose "Organizational existence is threatened. The organization trembles in the balance. The men feel the want of officers and nothing keeps them together but common interest and association." Samuel went on, "I urge to have my command placed where they may do useful service and at the same time have an opportunity to reorganize and recruit the health and the spirits as well as men."[13]

His veteran regiments of Cedar Mountain were the wellspring to replenish his depleted officer corps. His twice-wounded Philadelphia cobbler, Joseph Knipe, typified the officer's attitude; he was back in command by September, after a head wound that caused unbearable pain, driving him to the brink of insanity.[14]

The men whose spirits he so admired had been given a break from the front-line fighting, but not the constant marching. Their spirits were disheartened by the past experience—the retreats, and defeats. The usual emotional support of comrades, so essential for the spirit of a fighting unit, had evaporated at Cedar Mountain and after. "The very existence of its organization is threatened."[15]

Near Rockville, Maryland, the Crawford brigade was supported by the addition of the 124th, 125th, and 128th Pennsylvania Volunteer Infantry Regiments. They were fully officered and nearly as large as brigades, but they had not seen combat. Since they were yet to be initiated into combat, military discipline had to be instilled in them, primarily while marching. This made for difficult situations for both the men and the officers. The miles of long, draining marches, followed by picket duty, combined with fatigue and hunger, all resulted in frayed nerves and occasional conflict.[16]

The marches through Maryland were representative of the problem. The new troops were not accustomed to the prodding and discipline being instilled in their marches. Stragglers were the norm. On one night march General Crawford encountered some members of the 124th Pennsylvania foraging for food. He told them to stay closed in ranks as ordered and chastised them as "Pennsylvania cattle." Though he generally admired the quality of the soldiers from his home state, Crawford had felt an overriding responsibility to teach the value of discipline. However, Sergeant Sam Potts took particular umbrage at Crawford's remark. Potts confided to some of his companions that if the "old man" got between him and the Rebel in his sights, he would not think twice about "pulling the trigger." Luckily for Crawford the opportunity never presented itself.[17]

Other moments of the march were pleasurable. At times it seemed the hardships endured were worthwhile. Fond moments of water provided by pretty ladies, tubs of lemonade, and homemade bread smothered with preserves, apple butter, or smearcase were all a part of a day's marching.[18]

General McClellan's army followed the Army of Northern Virginia into Frederick one week later; the citizens noticed the stark contrast between the ragged, dirty group of men and the neat, orderly army that followed. However, they noted that the Rebels, like their counterparts from the North, had clean weapons and full ammo boxes. The Southern newspapers reported that the Confederate recruiting "was extremely active and encouraging for the Stars and Bars." This proclamation was largely exaggerated as most of the Southern soldiers expressed disappointment in their reception and recruiting.[19]

On September 12 during mail call, Crawford received a letter from his long lost brother A.J. He now understood the reason for the delay. John Agnew had accepted a call to a church in Brooklyn, New York, and shortly thereafter, he made the decision to carry the Union torch in the chaplaincy. Now Father officially had three sons and a son-in-law in the Union army. Samuel, Sr., the old patriot, would proudly tell his neighbors of four sons saving the Union.[20]

IV. The Incident and the Mountain

It was while camped near Frederick on September 13 that a soldier in the 27th Indiana of the XII Corps made a startling find. A paper around a bundle of cigars he found proved to be more than wrapping. It was Special Order 191 dated September 9 from General Lee to his corps commanders. Incredibly, it detailed Lee's plan to fall swiftly on Harpers Ferry and cut off escape routes. Then two divisions would cross South Mountain to seize Maryland Heights and capture Martinsburg. The remainder of army and artillery reserve would hold at Boonsboro, the reassembling point for all. The next phase would be planned at that point. Execution was to begin Friday, September 12.[21]

General McClellan was suspicious. Was the "lost order" real or a plant? Was it a godsend or a trick to misdirect him? In 1874 Samuel Crawford would call it "a piece of wondrous fortune!" General McClellan had full information of the movements and intentions of the enemy. Although the order did not provide division or corps strengths as McClellan hoped, it did seem plausible. McClellan ordered reconnaissance to determine if Rebel troop movements did confirm the discovery's validity. Ebullient and confident, "Mac" notified Lincoln that "Lee would be severely punished and he would catch them in their own trap."[22]

While camping in Frederick City the XII Corps was introduced to their new commander, General Joseph King Fenno Mansfield. A West Point officer who had finished second in his class of 1822, he was assigned to engineering where he worked on coastal defenses in the Southern states for nearly twenty years. He later served with distinction in the Mexican War. Later he designed Fort Brown in Texas and served as inspector general. For forty years this veteran of the regular army had never fulfilled his desire to command a fighting unit. His promotion to corps command came when time was running out for him. The 59-year-old major general cut an imposing figure with a large frame and snow white hair. Although he was a trifle finicky and old-fashioned, the men were enthused by his energy and devotion to duty. He had a tendency to be intense. General Alpheus Williams, the senior division commander, called him "fussy but a most veteran looking officer."[23]

As the Union army moved out of Frederick and began the long trek up the Catoctin foothills and mountains, nearly all admired the view of the valley. Peering down from that height on a clear day the miniaturized town with the numerous church spires would have impressed the viewers. The tranquility of the little villages they marched through likely evoked memories of home on a Sabbath morning.

General McClellan did not move with the alacrity of one who knew his enemy's intentions. The Union general did not move for almost nineteen hours after being provided with the knowledge of his opponent's plan. On the other hand, the Southern commander acted audaciously.[24]

On the night of the 14th, Stuart sent a courier to Lee claiming unusual excitement in the Union camp. His information indicated an offensive movement. Stuart had been informed by a Frederick citizen of the possibility of McClellan finding an important document. With Stuart's information Lee considered terminating the invasion. First, however, he would have the gaps at South Mountain blocked to buy some time for decision making. The Confederate delaying action provided their commander with the time he needed. On September 15, as Lee prepared to direct his troops back across the Potomac, a courier arrived with "manna" from General Jackson: "through God's blessing, Harpers Ferry and its garrison are to be surrendered." General Jackson would join the army as quickly as possible and General A. P. Hill's command would follow. Lee was reborn as he invited Generals Stuart and Longstreet to meet at Sharpsburg. Generals Jackson and A. P. Hill would soon be in attendance.[25]

The Union high command made the decision not to attack Lee's army on September 16. At the time the Southern army was about one-third the size of Union command, but positioned in a relatively good defensive posture. McClellan sent two corps across the Antietam Creek. Initially, Hooker's I Corps led the way. An evening fire fight between Hooker's corps and the Confederates possibly gave the Southerners insight as to the Union overall plan for the morrow. The Union battle plan was for Hooker's I Corps and Mansfield's XII Corps to attack in unison against the Confederate left.[26]

V. The Night Before the Battle

On the evening of September 16, General Crawford's first brigade was positioned on the western side of Antietam Creek. Ammunition trains had been brought forward and the soldiers' cartridge boxes filled. The veterans were cognizant of the meaning of numerous troop movements and couriers dispatching orders in urgency, but the untested youths had a lot of questions about the activity.

It was late at night when the orders arrived to move to the area near General Joseph Hooker's I Corps.

Crawford's First Brigade led the division. Frederick Crouse of the 128th Pennsylvania, one of the new brigades, later wrote an account of the battle that provides much insight into the military movements and the human aspects of the battle. "We was [sic] aroused at 11 o'clock from tired natures sweet repose. Our officers ordered us to fall in and make no noise. We were even warned not to let our canteens or tin cups rattle."[27]

Crawford sent a staff officer to locate the position. During the march it is probable that the division commander was informed that the southern line extended from the Potomac River at their backs along a ridge that ran north and south to the village of Sharpsburg. It was the right end of the northern line that would be anchored on the Hagerstown Pike facing south. In his Official Report Crawford wrote that Hooker had engaged with the enemy.[28]

The rain and darkness were pervasive as they crossed the Hitt Bridge. Night marches were exasperating under normal conditions, but for the new troops with their large numbers it was extremely difficult. One soldier of the 124th Pennsylvania complained about being ordered to conduct "a noiseless march in the silence of night." Again, Private Crouse provides insight, "we march in the terrible darkness. We went groping through the bushes, over fences, across ditches, fields, creeks and through a woods." The brigade finally settled on farms owned by the Line and Hoffman families. It was nearly 2 a.m. before they made camp. To add to the misery they bivouacked haphazardly on a "freshly plowed and manured field." Many jokes were made of their situation but exhaustion prevailed more than the smell of unadulterated cow manure. General Williams reported that they were about a mile and half behind Hooker's corps.[29]

This war never failed to instill a sense of both awe and oddity in General Crawford. After Fort Sumter Crawford had bid farewell to Captain Abner Doubleday and Truman Seymour, both now brigadier generals assigned to General Hooker's corps. Another Sumter cohort, Norman Hall, was a colonel in General John Sedgwick's division of the II Corps. On the ridge on the other side of the Hagerstown Pike, members of the opposing armies consisted of his Cedar Mountain nemeses, Stonewall Jackson and Jeb Stuart, and his prewar acquaintance, James Longstreet. On another part of the field, Roger Pryor, whose life he had saved at Fort Sumter, bivouacked with his brigade. The ironies of this war accumulated.[30]

The night of the 16th was a restless one for all. The two armies had been glaring at each other for a couple of days and then earlier in the evening the armies had been engaged in a fire fight of sorts. Now both sides sensed that everything was in place for something larger. The fear of the unknown and the noise of troop and artillery movement made all but the heaviest of sleepers uneasy. Stephen Sears called it "an undercurrent of nervous energy." Private Crouse wrote, "the constant firing of the pickets kept us from sleeping but at the break of day everything became as still as death. It was only the calm that proceeds [sic] a terrible storm."[31]

For some unaccountable reason this night was different. The men seemed to drift in and out of a trance. It was a surreal-like dream state. Alpheus Williams wrote, "The night was so dark, so obscure, so mysterious, so uncertain; with the occasional rapid volleys of pickets and outposts, the low, solemn sounds of the command as troops came into position."[32]

No matter how the troops passed the night, they agreed on one thing: it was short. General George Gordon, the Third Brigade commander in the First Division, wrote, "we were aroused after a short slumber." Private Crouse wrote that "it was hardly light when we got up to look at our surroundings."[33]

A few minutes after dawn Crawford rode out to scout the area. He rode to a farm he was told was owned by Joseph Poffenberger. The woodlot to his front was the North Woods. The Hagerstown Pike was off to his right and a short distance down from it was the D. R. Miller farm with a large cornfield. Off to his left was another wood area, the Miller or East Woods. In his front down the Hagerstown Pike on a rise he could see another wood lot with a white building that appeared to be a church. When he returned twelve years later, he would recall "the shady woods, ripening grain fields, and the pleasant slopes," but that was through the eyes of the poet. Today he saw the terrain as a warrior.[34]

VI. "There is work to do up there."[35]

As nature attempted to lift her eyelids through the predawn of a September mist, the readied I Corps under Hooker prepared to move south down the Hagerstown Pike toward the high ground over a half mile away. The men could see the ghostly shape of the plain white building that seemed to be beckoning from a patch of woods. The Union artillery broke the silence of the morning air. The shaking ground was enough to let all know this was not a normal morning awakening. After both sides had their way with the artillery, Hooker's men would leave a wooded area, press forward into a cornfield of a farmer named D. R. Miller and on toward the white building. From his experiences of yesterday, the I Corps commander was relatively certain that the enemy was clustered in or near the cornfield. More Confederates than he had bargained for rose up. The enemy artillery turned up the intensity as the air filled with the screams and hissing of missiles. It was a "most galling fire."[36]

Over an hour had passed and the first wave of the battle was beginning to fade. General Hooker looked for help. The XII Corps of General Mansfield was beginning to show near the area where the I Corps' men had departed. Mansfield's corps had bivouacked only a short distance from the I Corps, but they had not been ordered to go simultaneously with Hooker's corps. It seemed they would lead the second wave. The piecemeal tactics were not the original plan but would set the tone for the day. "Never during that long, bloody day from dawn to dusk did McClellan get more than 20,000 into the action at the same time; 20,000 of his soldiers did not fire a shot." General Lee was given the luxury of moving troops to meet each new emergency.[37]

The XII Corps was relatively small for a Union command in 1862, a few hundred over 7,000 men. In preparing to leave camp, one soldier recalled General Mansfield ride by with his hat at an angle and his grey locks flowing. At this moment, he extolled confidence.[38]

The soldiers of the XII, old or new, were not pleased with the way they were being managed. They could tolerate a short night, as that was rather normal, but they had been ordered to rest on their arms—not a comfortable way to sleep. No time for breakfast, or worse, coffee, meant a lot of unhappy campers on this "misty, moisty, morning." Frederick Crouse jotted disgustingly, "breakfast was not to be thought of, although we had really scarsly [sic] eating [sic] anything for the last two days. Sitting on a stump I took out my pocket Bible and read the 91st Psalm." Next as the troops moved it was "deploy—don't deploy—deploy," but worse, their new corps commander had ordered them to continue to stay in "columns of companies" like massed cattle. He feared the new regiments might panic because the enemy artillery was beginning to get the range.[39]

Crawford told the men, "There is work to do up there." Crouse said they had been given 40 rounds and now each one was given 20 more.[40]

The veterans of the 10th Maine, the 46th Pennsylvania, and the 28th New York, who had been ravaged by the fighting at Slaughter Mountain (Cedar Mountain), understood what was about to happen. They had been this way before. They knew the sounds, the sights, the aura, but the soldiers selected from the "nine month levy and had seen no field service," and whose regiments looked like the size of brigades, were bewildered by it all. They would need leadership. At least they were afforded strength in numbers. It was good to know that your comrades would be "seeing the elephant," a term used by soldiers who were about to face live battle for the first time, with buddies of the same stripe. Hopefully they could garner strength from each other. After this morning, that "elephant" label would never be applied to them again. Frederick Crouse wrote that they "presented a fine picture. We had over 1,000 men in line in new uniforms, bright new arms, beautiful new flags and marching to the inspiring music of the fife and drum corps."[41]

General Mansfield continually insisted on keeping the men en masse. First Division commander General Williams argued vehemently against the formation. In his mind it senselessly endangered the men's lives. He wrote home, "I begged to be allowed to deploy in two rows, not twenty. I could not move him." Finally, after deploying and then going back to formation, Crawford reported, "the third time an officer from division staff ordered the deployment of my men." Deploy they did. The veteran units of Crawford's brigade moved quickly almost on their own. Pleasantly surprising were the actions of the new troops. Although "wholly undrilled," they moved with "promptness and coolness." During this deployment Williams took the 124th Pennsylvania "past the farm house of Mr. Miller, across the pike in the woods beyond and ordered them to hold the ridge as long as practical." When the Crawford brigade was finally into battle position, it formed a semi-circle from the Hagerstown Pike around to the north and back to the East Woods, sometimes referred to as Miller's Woods.[42]

Crawford's troops would fight on all parts of this sanguine field this Wednesday morning. Each regiment played a slightly different role in aiding the Union cause.

If the plan was to use the veteran units in reserve, Colonel Knipe indicated in his Official Report they soon realized "that was not to be so."[43]

Crawford reported that prior to their initial movement Hooker made an appearance to examine the line and ordered him "to hold the Miller's [East] woods at all hazards. Otherwise the right of the army would be seriously imperiled."[44]

The 10th Maine played a significant role in this endeavor. Mansfield was aiding in the deployment of the troops. Having placed the 10th Maine, the veterans situated themselves into a regimental front as Mansfield went for another unit. In this process Colonel George Beal lost his horse and another musket ball penetrated both its legs. To add to the regiment's problems, Colonel Beal's horse, before being wounded, kicked the next healthy commander, Lieutenant Colonel J. Fillebrown in the stomach, disabling him for a few days. In spite of these adversities they fought with "personal courage."[45]

When the corps commander reappeared, he noticed the 10th Maine was firing into an area where he thought Union troops were located. Mentioning this fact to the men from Maine, they responded, "They shot at us first." Mansfield, after a more careful look, said, "Yes! Yes! You are right." At this moment, Mansfield slumped forward and his horse seemed to reel. As the general turned his stead and gave the command to jump a fence, the animal was unable to do so. Mansfield had been shot in the chest-stomach area. The horse and the general staggered back toward the rear where he dismounted. When a gust of wind blew open his coat, he saw his wound.

Men from the 125th Pennsylvania formed a seat with their weapons and carried him to a tree where they gently positioned him. The concern for the Confederates in the East Woods took priority over further aid for the general. He would sit there until men from the 10th Maine later arrived with a blanket and placed him in an ambulance. Surgeon Flood of the 107th New York recalled stopping the bleeding and having him taken to the nearby Line home. The surgeon later wrote Mansfield's wife that he knew after inspecting the wound that it was fatal, "a small portion of his lung was protruding." Mansfield died the morning of September 18. His two-day command was over, as was his life. On March 12, 1863, he was "promoted posthumously" to major general of volunteers.[46]

General Alpheus Williams, General Samuel Crawford, and Colonel Joseph Knipe of the 46th Pennsylvania were notified of their promotions to corps, division, and brigade command, respectively.

Crawford's other veteran regiments who had experienced devastation at Cedar Mountain, the 46th Pennsylvania and the 28th New York, had a bout in Miller's cornfield. Near the 46th Pennsylvania was the 128th Pennsylvania, which had been in existence only five weeks. Frederick Crouse of the 128th claimed, as they waited to go in, they detailed two men from each company to carry off the wounded, and a detachment of the pioneer corps came with axes and leveled the fences in front as if by magic. The order to advance was given. As they moved forward, toward the woods were the Rebels were "we heard the whistle of the Minnie ball and we all began to duck and I got a little weak in the knees." They had no sooner begun to return the fire when they lost their commander, Colonel Samuel Croasdale. He was shot in the head and killed almost immediately. His replacement, Lieutenant Colonel William Hammersly, was wounded soon thereafter. Command fell on Major Joel Wanner who relied on veteran Joseph Knipe of the 46th Pennsylvania in this nearly impossible situation. Colonel Knipe suggested a charge. Major Wanner recorded the consequence of the charge: "I ordered the regiment to charge into the cornfield. They started in a gallant style cheering as they moved and penetrated the cornfield, but because of overpowering numbers of concealed enemy we were compelled to fall back." Crouse admitted firing as fast as he could trying to remember to fire low but "we would load raise up and bang away." Knipe reported the 46th Pennsylvania made the same charge with the same results. The 28th New York with their 60 men fought alongside these two units. Later the regiments were ordered by General Williams to the rear to reform.[47]

The 124th Pennsylvania still in the North Woods awaiting orders, after almost an hour were called on to shed blood in the cornfield also.

They had gone about 20 paces without being able to see when their commander, Colonel Joseph Hawley, was wounded. They advanced in spite of receiving a raking fire. The commander, Major Haldeman, reported, "We advanced through the cornfield making many successful charges on the enemy, until ordered back to the support of the battery."[48]

The men of the 125th Pennsylvania also displayed unbelievable bravery in the course of the morning. They had fought on Crawford's orders to push the foe from the East Woods. This being accomplished, they kept moving down the Smokestown Road toward the West Woods. Now it was General Hooker who ordered them to "advance and hold the woods." Colonel Jacob Higgins in command of the unit noted to Hooker that his horse had been shot. He replied, "Yes I see and turned and went away." A little later the enemy would miss the horse and hit the general in the left foot. The time was about 8:45 a.m. Mansfield was gone, as was Hooker. The Union army in the area was without a directing officer.[49]

About 9 a.m. an eerie silence settled over the field as series of troops moved from place to place. These reinforcements would be used in the next phase. That stage came with the advance of Major General Edwin Sumner's II Corps. McClellan was still feeding the units piecemeal as General Sumner was ordered to move with only a part of his corps as the rest was held in reserve. It was held in reserve at a time that the XII Corps seemed to have lost much of its aggressive force. It also provided Lee the ability to move troops to meet the advance.[50]

The XII Corps had driven the enemy from Miller's woods (East Woods) across the fields into the woods beyond the Dunkard Church and Hagerstown Road. "A fine wooden fence which skirted the road proved a very serious obstacle." General Williams referred to it as "a high post and rail fence on each side of the public road" that proved a problem to the soldiers' pursuit. None-the-less the "regiments of Crawford's division had done some credible fighting and accomplished results."[51]

John Sedgwick's division of Sumner's corps came through the East Woods to the "hearty cheers of our men." The third wave of the morning was about to begin. The Confederates rolled in reserves and the cheering was replaced with Southern fire power on Sedgwick's exposed left flank. In half an hour they lost almost 2,000 troops. James McPherson wrote that Sedgwick was "ambushed by two fresh enemy divisions." In 1874 Crawford tried to put the best spin on the charge by saying, "Sedgwick retook the ground, secured the road, and the area around the church until two confederate divisions withdrawn from the right exposed his flank."[52]

Now the 125th Pennsylvania Infantry was fighting for its very existence. Colonel Jacob Higgins' 125th was holding the edge of the West Woods when Sedgwick made his charge. Some of his men were shot down from only 50 yards. Higgins sent his brother, Lieutenant Joseph Higgins, with his own horse to find General Crawford for aid. Either he did not find him or there were no available reserves.[53] Crawford wrote that Higgins' men "pushed into the woods beyond our line and was seriously engaged while much exposed but returned in good order but with great loss."[54]

Crawford was ordered to remove his troops to the woods held in the morning for rest and replenishment of ammunition. It is understandable why Crawford would write that the regiments composing his command did their "duty nobly." With a break in the action for the 128th Pennsylvania, Frederick Crouse tried to put in words what he was observing. "I can only say it was awfully grand and teriable [sic]. The sun was shinning through the sulphorous smoke of the battle, the ground was thickly strewn with dead and wounded. The crash and rattle of musketry, the roar and thunder of the artillery that shook the ground under our feet the cries and groans of the wounded and dying made up a scene never to be forgotten."[55]

The color sergeant of the 125th Pennsylvania was emblematic of the regimental tribulations. He was hit a number of times before handing the flag to a corporal with the admonishment, "don't let it fall." They retreated in order through mangled bodies, and screaming, wounded, pleading soldiers crying for water or relief or home or pleading to be shot. Only a few hours before, the most these men had witnessed was an artillery gunner with both legs shot.

Higgins wrote that "had I remained in my position for two minutes longer I would have lost my whole command." He lauded his troops, "the men behaved in splendid style."[56]

VII. The Wound

When General Sedgwick's force began to retreat, Corps Commander Williams called for Crawford's aid and the assistance of the Third Brigade to plug some gaps. Crawford wrote that the Third Brigade moved gallantly forward but under severe fire had to fall back. As the new division commander tried to rally some broken units, amidst the smoke and confusion, he felt a sledgehammerlike blow on his right thigh. His pant leg moistened with blood. He explored the wound with his fingers to determine the extent of the damage. The pain, though annoying, was not intolerable and he could and would continue on the field until toward evening. The fact he continued formed the impression that his wound was slight. In reality it would still demand a physician's care thirty years later.[57]

After the gunshot wound in the leg, Crawford went to aid a section of battery under Lieutenant Thomas and Captain Knap's battery. They were stationed at a point on a road "across toward the Dunkard Church. At noon the enemy advanced infantry to take possession of the batteries. I sent staff officer, Captain d' Hauteville, to find infantry support. He found Major General William Smith's Division of William Franklin's Corps. They arrived and along with Gordon's Brigade both supported by effective fire of the artillery, the enemy met with bloody punishment. The south made no further attempts on the right of the union line."[58]

But the hours of fighting were not nearly complete. More desperate hours of fighting at Bloody Lane and Burnside Bridge were yet to come. More daring, pain, death, and agony were on the docket. Historians would record it as the bloodiest day of the Civil War. A day that would see 23,000 fewer soldiers; soldiers, depending on their station in life, that were fathers or husbands, boyfriends, sons, or cousins, but all humans. The humanity, inhumanity, the sweat, the blood, the cries would spread to almost every village and hearthstone in the country. The pain would last a lifetime and more.

It was not the same landscape Crawford had viewed earlier that morning. It had changed vividly. General Gordon put it in perspective, "from sunrise to sunset the waves of battle ebbed and flowed. The fields of corn were trampled into shreds, forest were battered and scathed, grape and canister mingled their hissing scream in this hellish carnival…yet through it all the patriots of the north wrestled with hearts strong and nerve unshaken….then with one mighty bound throwing themselves upon their foe driving them into their protective forest. We slept on the bloody field of our victory."[59]

The armies still had the same nomenclature, but almost 2,000 men per hour were casualties in the course of the day. During the five hours of vicious and hideous violence of the morning 12,000 men were taken to hospitals, ready to be placed in graves or prisons. The regiments that began the day under brigade commander Crawford were also counting losses. The old veterans of the 10th Maine lost the most of the old regiments—seventy less soldiers for them and nearly thirty in the two other Cedar Mountain regiments. The new units seeing real live action for the first time lost heavily. The 124th and 128th Pennsylvania lost just fewer than 200 casualties, while the 125th was hardest hit with losses in the 225 range. The First Division lost 25 percent of their number in casualties.[60]

The Union did not receive a clear-cut victory as it hoped, but Lee and his army, two days later, "Left under the cover of night" back across the Potomac, back home to Virginia.[61]

Many of the participants tried to give the slaughter a vision. Twenty-seven-year-old Frederick Crouse, who had seen paintings of battle scenes as he was growing up, tried his hand comparing fantasy and reality. In his young heart, he swelled with patriotic pride and longed to participate in such an event. Now he had just participated in one of the greatest battles ever fought on the American continent. The real experience overwhelmed the imagined. "The air seemed filled with messengers of death, the batteries belched thunderbolts of death and destruction from their red throats and their vivid lightning flashes showed ten or twelve men torn and bleeding in the agonies of death." Frederick would not only see but feel the effects of war as a minié ball smashed into and through his left shoulder. The wound ultimately was responsible for his discharge in 1863 as it rendered his left arm useless. His granddaughter later wrote that the same bullet that wounded Frederick hit and killed his brother-in-law. Hopefully the new Union that would be created would be worth the spilled blood.[62]

Five days later it was the pen once again of General Gordon to garner the gratitude of this entire country: "every soldier deserves a nation's thanks."[63]

President Abraham Lincoln used this "victory" to issue a document that would change the course of the war. His first goal of preserving the Union had been written in stone from the beginning. On September 22, five days after Antietam, he took the opportunity to issue the preliminary Emancipation Proclamation. By using his war powers as commander in chief, he served notice that come the first of January 1863 "all persons held as slaves within any state or designated part of a state then in rebellion against the United States shall be...forever free."[64]

The character of the war would change. The North was now fighting for both the preservation of the Union and the freeing of slaves in any state in rebellion. Those two ideas would now be "inseparable." How could England or any civilized nation oppose a country that was fighting for freedom and to free slaves? Perhaps the most important aspect was to invite the slaves' help to win the war and to aid themselves in gaining their long-yearned freedom.[65]

The fall campaign finished with the Confederate invasion of Kentucky thrown back. Lee's army was back in Virginia, European recognition was delayed, Lincoln's party would retain control of the House of Representatives, and the scope and purpose of the war was enlarged by the Emancipation Proclamation.[66]

Would the pendulum swing back toward building momentum for the Northern cause? That would remain a mystery for some time to come, but what was not an enigma was the cleanup process that had to begin immediately in the Antietam area. Bloated bodies releasing malodorous gases had to be buried as quickly as possible. The mutilated bodies of horses and mules had to be disposed of, as disease was a major concern. Contaminated water also caused illnesses. Trampled crops could not be used for winter's reign. The second battle would be fought by humanitarians and would take more than twenty-four hours. The sanitary commission would distribute almost 29,000 shirts, towels, and pillows; 30 barrels of linen for dressing wounds; 3,200 pounds of farina; 4,000 sets of hospital clothing; several tons of citrus fruit; chloroform, opiates, surgical equipment, and the lists go on.[67]

VIII. To Alandale for a Different Reason

Samuel Crawford's feelings were the same as those of a North Carolina soldier, who wrote, "The sun seemed to go backwards and night was set aside."[68] Finally, at the cessation of hostilities, Crawford, weak and exhausted because of the loss of blood and the nature of the wound, made his way to the field hospital where he was examined. The wound appeared to be inflicted by a gunshot. Entry had been made on the lateral side of his right thigh approximately six inches above the knee. Part of the ball was extracted, the wound dressed, and the general was assured he could return to his command after a brief recuperation, barring complications.[69]

By the beginning of the fourth week of September, Samuel was permitted to travel home. Surely the trip home was one of the most depressing of the war as he tried to deal with the reality of personal injury and the continuing pain of war. Every barn, public building, and many homes were filled with the wounded and dying. The *New York Times* had called the battle "The most stupendous struggle of modern times."[70]

At home, Samuel and Alex found their father, Margaret's two sons, Reade and Samuel, the hired man, a cook, and a housemaid. Their mother had wearied of the constant warning that the Rebels were coming, taking the horses to the woods, hiding the silverware and carpets, and being terrified of physical abuse. She had taken the smallest child and Jenny in a spring wagon driven by the hired man to Shippensburg. From there they traveled to New York City by rail and then to her daughter Anne's in Orange County, New York.[71]

Considering the closeness of neighbors in a small town, it is likely that the Crawfords heard of Jacob Hoke's description of his experiences at South Mountain, especially since Samuel had been a participant. Jacob Hoke, Colonel A. K. McClure, and others had gone over by carriage to inspect the field of battle. In the Crawford Papers the men were listed as visitors to his headquarters' tent.[72]

Mr. Hoke admitted that though they were first struck by the obvious loss of equipment, it was nothing compared to the human cost. They had seen "half-live men with brain matter pushing out of their heads, countless flies on immobile bodies laying eggs that would produce maggots, dead with blackened faces and protruding tongues. They saw human decomposition at every stage, and blood that had trickled from a soldier's ear and the path was followed into the ear cavity by a stream of ants—and the stench, God Almighty, the stench! It often caused onlookers to vomit."[73]

Merchant Hoke, turned historian, told of a wounded soldier, "I found a Confederate soldier in a garden, behind a cabin and wrapped in a blanket with a tree branch stuck in the ground to provide a degree of shade from the scorching sun. He had been shot in the leg and had to be taken out of the sun and potential rain. He needed a shelter, but I was unable to find a place for him. I made the medical people in a nearby home aware of his plight, but they had no hope for him as his wound was in the body proper. The gentleman was from South Carolina, and he told me he had done what his wife had asked and he then requested I write to Mary—Mary Cotton—and tell her he had kept his promise to her to pray daily and that if he did not see her on earth he would see her in heaven. She was to do the best she could without him."[74]

Days later, Samuel anticipated a call from Dr. Abraham Senseny. After the initial pleasantries about the weather and family, Dr. Senseny began his examination. He probed gently and warily. Given the fact that it was a shotgun wound and healing slowly, he probably acknowledged that there was the potential of bone damage.[75]

IX. Jeb and Sallie Pulling in Opposite Directions

In early October, Lee contemplated another venture into enemy territory, this time into Pennsylvania. Stuart was the man for the job. Stuart would lead a raid into Pennsylvania to create transportation problems for the Union army. He would not touch Maryland property, but Pennsylvania constituted an open season. Stuart, in addition to Lee's orders, admonished his men to not impede the progress of, nor seize the horses of, female travelers.

With that, "Beau" Stuart was off with approximately 1,800 horsemen accompanied by four pieces of horse artillery. It was October 10. A blanket of heavy fog greeted them as they crossed the Mason-Dixon Line and rode into Franklin County near Mercersburg, Pennsylvania. They camped there to conduct "pantry inspections." Stuart headquartered on a porch of a magnificent stone edifice a short distance from the center of town. He and his staff supped on a fine meal provided by the hostess of the house, Mrs. Steiger, who "was invited south after the war to share her bread baking skills."[76]

The weather took a turn for the worse as Stuart and his men with prisoners, livestock, and goods purchased with Confederate money, headed east with a stop in Markes and then to the larger town of Saint Thomas. Along the way, they made routine searches of farms, storehouses, or stores.[77]

Meanwhile, in Chambersburg, events were anything but routine. Mr. Hoke, attending his dry goods store, had a visit from a soldier wearing a blue overcoat over a butternut uniform and wearing a cavalry saber. The man surveyed everything in the store carefully, and the store owner supposed that a number of such spies had been sent to check out the supplies and the defense of the town.[78]

His suspicions were later confirmed when another patron informed him that an invasion was a fact. Earlier, two citizens from Saint Thomas had visited the local chambers of Judge Kimmel to warn of Stuart's coming. Hearing of the Rebel approach, Jacob Hoke hid some valued items, closed his store, and went to the upstairs window to await the invaders. In the square, the flag was quickly lowered and the rope cut so the Confederates could not raise their "hated rag." Stuart sent General Wade Hampton to demand the surrender of the town.[79]

As Samuel relaxed on the front porch in the evening of October 10, admiring the sky of light and darkened clouds that tantalized his imagination, he noticed a slight cloud of dust near the lane entrance. The pounding of horse hooves soon was audible. It was a lady rider who identified herself as a neighbor from Fayetteville. She knew of General Crawford, his wound, and she had an important message for him concerning his safety. Before Samuel was able to assist her, she was off her horse and heading toward him.[80]

She introduced herself as "Sallie Horner, a Fayetteville native" who came to repay him in some small way for all he had done in keeping her family and friends in the valley safe. The sun was beginning to move toward the Tuscarora Mountains in the west as Samuel invited her to sit. She obliged in spite of her visibly fidgety manner. Even as she started to sit she was talking. Did he know that General Stuart was conducting a cavalry raid in the area? The telegraph office in Chambersburg had received information about noon that the Rebels had arrived in Mercersburg. The rough count of horse soldiers was 1,800 to 2,000. They were organized and looking for "horses, grub, and you." Since then, they had passed through Saint Thomas. This was not rumor; the news was delivered to Mr. Hoke this afternoon, and the soldiers were expected in Chambersburg at any moment. Sallie didn't seem to pause for breath as she told her story. Samuel no doubt quizzed her, almost to the point of interrogation, to determine the veracity of her story, but all points in her story seemed valid.[81]

Crawford could not thank her enough. She informed him she was going to ride to all the neighbors in the area to warn them to take their horses to safer areas. In so doing, she dodged Stuart's horsemen and arrived home about midnight.

The Crawford family was so intrigued with her manner and patriotic purpose, they could not help asking about her family. She had six sisters, but they were all ladies, and she was her father's "longed for boy."[82]

Crawford knew that his old nemesis, Jeb Stuart, would like nothing better than to capture a Union brigadier general. As he contemplated his fate, it was decided it would be best to leave without delay. In a painful ride he made his way east toward the Gettysburg Railroad. Ultimately, he traveled to Anne's in New York where he could see his mother again. Here Samuel sent his first telegraph to the War Department informing them he would not be able to obey his orders to report in the near future.[83]

When he arrived back at the homestead, he no doubt heard that Sallie had kept her promise to reenact Paul Revere. One peculiar man would not heed her advice to scatter his horses in the mountains. He said he would hide his horses in a sink hole. Stuart's men found and confiscated all of the animals including one that the man had refused to sell a few days before for $800.[84]

Samuel would later hear of Sallie's exploits. She told about the Rebel detachment assigned to capture General Crawford. They stopped a man on the streets of Fayetteville and asked if he could tell them where he could find the general. The man "feigned idiocy" and told the Rebel leader that Crawford had passed through the day before yesterday about the dinner hour. When asked how many men Crawford had, the leader was told, "Oh gosh, I guess about 75,000." The Rebels rode away in a cloud of dust looking for the entire rear guard."[85]

Sallie said about a dozen Rebels came to their gate asking for something to eat. Her sisters made peanut butter sandwiches and Sallie played hostess. "I do not give you this food because I agree with your cause, because I do not. I do not give them to you because I am afraid of you, because I am not, but because I would feed, even, a hungry dog."[86]

The men laughed and all tipped their hats. She was told they respected her for speaking her sentiments. The leader assured her that "the damn northern copperhead was no good to north or south." Before ending the parley, the men told her how they admired the beauty of the valley. It reminded some of the "Garden of Eden."

Before finishing his lunch, the leader presented Sallie with some sage advice. He advised her not to associate with the rear of the army as they are the ragtags and not trustworthy.[87]

At home Crawford finished his Antietam Official Report and sent it to General Alpheus Williams on October 21. It was signed "S. W. Crawford, late commanding the First Division, 12th Corps."

As Crawford placed the number "1076 killed wounded missing," again he must have agonized over the fact that the number represented human faces, human lives that had hopes and dreams, and loves and memories. They were future doctors, teachers, lawyers, and ministers. They were not just numbers in a report. Napoleon's maxim certainly applied: "in war life means nothing but in the end nothing is as important as life."[88]

The Chambersburg town folk told how prisoners were used as hostages and the troops divided into three equal segments: one was used as an advance force; a second, to collect horses, etc.; and the remaining protected the rear. Machine shops, all ammunition, and military stores were destroyed. Merchants suffered the loss of goods, especially bakeries. However, the Rebels were unable to loot the bank's currency due to Mr. G. Messersmith's foresight to have the assets removed prior to Stuart's arrival. The Rebels were further frustrated when they were unable to destroy the designated bridge because of its formidable structure. The heavy rains created muddy conditions and even more frustration on the trip home.[89]

Samuel Crawford had often been cantankerous even before the wound. Now, however, Alex, staff members, and soldiers would notice a more permanently ill-tempered and surly man.

A month later Samuel would go see Anne and her family in New York, contact Alex, and report for duty. Each time he departed Alandale he left more of himself, and each time it seemed less likely he would return.

ෲ Chapter Thirteen ☙
Gettysburg, on a Rocky Ridge and Beyond

I. The Pendulum Had Swung Both Ways; It Was Time for a Reckoning.

In 1861, at the beginning of this national turmoil, people could not even agree on what to call this disagreement. Whether it was labeled the War of Northern Aggression, the War for Southern Independence, the War for the Preservation of the Union, Mr. Lincoln's War, or the War of the Southern Planters, mattered little. Most agreed the conflict would be brief and that their side would prevail. It was now two years and almost two thousand battles later. Some of those engagements had been so small that they were practically lost to historical records; others seemed to have changed history. Both sides had obviously miscalculated. Neither side had prevailed nor was the strife's end in sight.[1]

The fighting had wrought dramatic change for the average soldier who was being shot, often wounded or killed. If he survived, he would write of his experiences. His war was very private in that sense, but it was the public war, the war of the strategists and tacticians, that bore so heavily on the individual soldier's survival.[2]

After General Lee completed his Maryland campaign, the Perryville Battle also forced the Confederates under General Braxton Bragg to withdraw from Kentucky. However, in December of 1862 the Rebels prevailed at Fredericksburg and again in early May of 1863 at Chancellorsville. The pendulum appeared to swing again toward the Confederate side.[3]

Early 1863 saw the Lincoln administration and its policies under attack from many directions. Still the president remained steadfast and kept the nation focused on the key issues of reunification and the abolition of slavery.[4]

By political acumen he had managed, so far, to hold together most of the contrasting interests in the Northern coalition such as: pro-Unionist, those distrustful of Federal government, abolitionists, racists, some Democrats, skeptics, capitalists, and those who harbored anti-capitalist sentiments. President Lincoln tried to interweave their beliefs into the administration's policies to some degree, and all the while he was playing a major role in the conduct of the war as an active commander in chief.[5]

On the nonmilitary side of the war ledger the Union was in relatively good condition. Foreign allies still stood by her side and the war time economy was fairly stable. Lincoln followed and worked with Congress and party leaders to adopt the National Banking Bill and the National Currency Act. They stabilized the greenback and centralized the credit system.[6]

Conscription, though dreaded, had finally been adopted when its necessity could be evaded no longer. It came about a year after the South had instituted its draft. In the North, males between the ages of 20 and 45 became eligible; not unlike its Southern counterpart, it contained provisions for substitutes and exemptions. The government believed that such legislation would prove beneficial by encouraging more men to volunteer, and fewer draftees would be required.[7]

Militarily, the administration continued its search for a competent and aggressive commander. The lack of such a commander frustrated Lincoln and his War Department, as well as the officers and soldiers of the Army of the Potomac, where the dissatisfaction was most prevalent. Most Northern soldiers held the belief they were rarely outfought on the field of battle, just outgeneraled.

From the time of the Crawford wound at Antietam until the Battle at Gettysburg, a period of approximately nine months, the Army of the Potomac had been led by four different army commanders. After a disaster at Fredericksburg in late December of 1862 and an infamous mud march the next month, General Ambrose Burnside, who had replaced General McClellan, was succeeded by Joseph Hooker. Just three days before Gettysburg, President Lincoln turned to General George Gordon Meade of Pennsylvania as his new military leader.[8]

In the spring of '63, optimism ruled in the military for a period of time as General Hooker used his organizational skills to improve the life of the average soldier. Hooker, a West Point graduate ranking in the middle of the Class 1837, exuded self-confidence. In his braggadocio way he felt a Devine being should watch over "Bobby Lee" since he, "Fighting Joe Hooker," would be busy routing him and his army. It was this type of bashing, when used against his fellow generals that concerned Lincoln. The verbosity against

Robert E. Lee and his army was released before the Chancellorsville campaign. However, as Colonel Charles Wainwright said, "Hooker certainly talks a lot about what he can do and should he fail, great will be his fall."[9]

Confident that he had the Rebel army exactly where he wanted them, he would not only overrun the foe but travel to the gates of Richmond. What a surprise for General Hooker when Generals Lee and Jackson chose to slap normal military protocol in the face, once more, and divide their smaller army to attempt a risky flanking maneuver. They confused Hooker who responded by withdrawing his troops after the initial engagement. Hooker would say later he lost confidence in Joe Hooker.[10]

For Lee and the Southern cause, Hooker's defeat provided them with a Pyrrhic victory. Stonewall Jackson had been accidentally shot by his own men on a late evening inspection ride and days later, on a Sunday, May 10, 1863, succumbed to the resultant complications of pneumonia. When word of Jackson's death arrived, General Lee knew he had lost his alter ego. The crucial loss of Jackson forced Lee to be the one to search for an aggressive commander. This process was not unlike that which prevailed in the North. He now had to reorganize his command and reshuffle his commanders.[11]

As Lee prepared for his second foray into the North, the loss of experienced commanders from the regimental to corps level forced him to give larger commands to men with no or little experience in those capacities. That created a potential weakness, but Lee remained unswerving in his belief and confidence in his army. Since Antietam, recruiting had been going rather well.

In Richmond, President Jefferson Davis was constantly sensing the inherent contradictions within the Confederate governmental structure. As the war demands grew, he realized the conduct of the war required increased centralized power. Davis had to delete some individual state influence and make more decisions from his power base. This was creating enemies within his cabinet and the Confederacy.[12]

In the West the Confederates were fighting a defensive war against the onslaught of General Ulysses Grant and others. General Lee convinced Jefferson Davis that the time was ripe for another thrust northward. It might relieve some pressure from the western front. Additionally, a successful campaign into the Union would give the Virginia planters a break from the turmoil when they needed it most—spring and summer. Lee saw his troops as being physically and mentally prepared for the adventure. Hopefully, they could create unrest in the Northern populace and take advantage of the growing resentment against the war. Once again the European powers would look more kindly on the Southern cause if they could win a battle on "foreign soil." A victory might place the Northern capital in jeopardy—a psychological victory, if no more. Finally, there were the obvious benefits to be gathered in the form of foodstuffs, supplies, fodder, and overall increased morale. Once more the positives accumulated in the eyes of Southern leadership.[13]

One month after the victory of Chancellorsville, General Robert E. Lee was again in the "cat bird's seat." His army would leave the Fredericksburg area, move up the Shenandoah Valley, cross into the Cumberland Valley, and toward a hopeful destiny—a coup de grâce to end the conflict.

Had we been in Chambersburg at this time, we would have witnessed the Union recruiting process. Samuel, as he headed for the train station, would have seen the perplexed looks on the men's faces who were trying to make the momentous personal decision as to whether they should enlist. For some the decision to enlist held enticing possibilities: adventure, independence, a new life, being a soldier in a brand-new uniform, to be with friends and acquaintances who were already doing their part. Of course, if they enlisted in the army, they would have to leave their homes, the love therein, and travel to distant places where a variety of dangers awaited them.[14]

Given his experiences and flair, it is difficult to imagine Crawford not taking advantage of the occasion by offering a few words of encouragement. To those gathered he likely emphasized the significance of the American flag. It flies proudly and freely because brave, young men have sustained it with honor. The thought Samuel likely expressed now remained a part of his thinking until the end of his days. He believed that the influence of soldiers resonated through time. The heroic deeds of the soldier would not perish but remain an untainted and shining light to lead a nation to a loftier patriotism and a higher endeavor. This concept of the role of the soldier in American society was expressed by Crawford in a Decoration Day speech at Antietam National Cemetery in 1874.[15]

Those in the audience could see the outline of the dressed wound under his right pants leg and still he stood before them willing to fight for the way of life in which he believed. They could tell by the words and the demeanor that he was a believer in the system of government for which he fought. After all, he had seen firsthand the evils of the Confederates' system. They defiantly fired first on the flag, causing the Union to defend its ideals. The North had no choice! Those who died in the American Revolution did not do so for two republics or for the freedom for the few. "May the patriot blood flow in your veins with enthusiastic support for the cause of this country."[16]

II. The Return to Duty February 1863

The journey to New York was likely more uncomfortable than past train rides. Samuel would have had to move and shuffle his position constantly in a futile effort to relieve the pressure caused by the wound. Arriving in Orange County, New York, and seeing Anne and the two eldest girls certainly helped lift his spirits. Meeting Andrew, his brother-in-law, would have brought more delight to Samuel, especially when Andrew told him of Anne playing the role of farmer's wife and of the support for the Union cause in the area.[17]

By the middle of December, Samuel made the decision that he would be unable to go back to duty at this time. He wired the War Department; the last two words were, "excessively painful!" These words indicated the healing process was not only slower than hoped, but considerably more serious and painful than he was able to hide.[18]

General Crawford's message prompted a response from the War Department inquiring as to when he would be able to return to duty. This questioning procedure could mean that the War Department was contemplating the possibility of an indoor administrative position. Crawford went through an uncharacteristically depressed mode. When he returned to duty the fearful suspicions were confirmed. He was assigned to a court-martial board. Even though his heart was not in the assignment, his superiors noted his work as being "energetic, courageous and discreet."[19]

According to a War Department memo "on the 19th of May, Crawford was relieved from General James Ricketts' board and reassigned to duty with Major General Samuel Heintzelman in defense of Washington, D.C." On June 3 the world of General Crawford went from emotional turmoil to ecstasy when he was given command of the First and Third Brigades of the prestigious Pennsylvania Reserves. He would have the opportunity to follow in the footsteps of Pennsylvanians such as George Meade, John Reynolds, and other respected fellow officers.

The position assured that he would be under intense scrutiny in this high-profile command, especially since his previous experience had consisted of leading a division for less than a day at Antietam and having only about a year's experience in line command.[20]

III. The Beginning of the Relations with the Pennsylvania Reserves

The Pennsylvania Reserves had originally consisted of 15 regiments of infantry, cavalry, and artillery, who volunteered for service in 1861. Since the numbers exceeded Pennsylvania's quota set by the Federal government, these extra soldiers were refused recognition. Not discouraged, the government of Pennsylvania stepped in to organize, equip, and train them at the state's expense, for state protection. They were mustered into Federal service in July of 1861. By 1863 they were an established and respected group of veterans, having distinguished themselves in a number of battles and with special distinction at Gaines' Mill and Fredericksburg.[21]

Several of their commanders had moved to greater distinction. They also had solid leadership at the regimental and brigade levels. Coupled with this able command structure, the Pennsylvanians were well equipped with primarily .69 and .58 caliber rifles, a few smoothbores, and even some Sharpe repeaters by the time of the Gettysburg campaign.[22]

Upon learning that Lee was moving toward their home state, the Reserves immediately applied for assignment to the Army of the Potomac. Colonel William McCandless, commander of the First Brigade, made the request in mid-June. He, too, was a Pennsylvanian who had earned the respect of his men through his service, especially since he had worked his way through the ranks. After starting his military career as a private he was special in the eyes of those he commanded. He was also admired for his bravery. In 1864 he would decline promotion to brigadier general.[23]

Toward the middle of June, Crawford paid a visit to General Hooker to add his voice to that of Colonel McCandless and others to have the Reserves attached to the Army of the Potomac. Soon thereafter it became a reality. The Second Brigade would be retained in Washington, D.C., for continued garrison duty while the First and Third would join the Army of the Potomac. In late June General Crawford tried to have the Second Brigade placed in his command. On the 25th of the month he was informed that General in Chief Henry W. Halleck refused the request. The Third Brigade leader was another Quaker state native and Reserve original, Colonel Joseph Fisher. General Crawford would lean heavily on these two experienced commanders in the upcoming engagements.[24]

Of all the companies of the Reserves, the most elated about the prospect of returning to their home state were the men of Company K of the 1st Reserves. Comprised of men from in and around the Gettysburg area, they looked forward to the prospect of a brief visit with friends or relatives. They knew they could rely on then-company commander Captain Henry Minnigh to do his best for them. They certainly were a different looking group from those early days when they wore white pants, blue shirts, and grey jackets.[25]

Before setting foot on home territory these troops had much work to do. The transition from the relatively easy garrison duty in Washington to that of a disciplined, tough marching unit had to be accomplished in a relatively short period of time. The hardships of physical conditioning would be accompanied by dirt, rain, mud, unbearable heat and humidity, typical of the mid-Atlantic area in the summertime, not to mention the blisters from the lack of shoes or ill-fitting ones. The march of one day promised only the right to do it again tomorrow, and the next day.

When they finally started on their northward trek, the Keystone troops were full of esprit de corps. Although the terrain was challenging, they pushed on as the landmarks came and passed. Up the Leesburg Pike, over the rolling hills of Maryland, and in the mist of June 27 they had crossed the Potomac and marched into Frederick, Maryland. There they joined the V Corps. Their resolve was summed up by their prized slogan: "We shall not rest until the invaders are driven from our beloved state."[26]

IV. The Hometown Folk Suffer Yet Another Invasion.

Back in Chambersburg a growing sense of anxiety prevailed. The townspeople felt threatened, uncomfortable, and terribly angry. For the third time during this war, the invaders of the South had paid them a visit. First, it was General Jeb Stuart; next, cavalry General Albert G. Jenkins; and now, Robert E. Lee with his reorganized mass would trudge through. Chambers-burg merchant Jacob Hoke made the count from his second story window, "47,000 souls, plus artillery, wagons, and ambulances rolling through the town for hours and hours." They foraged for food, cattle, horses, and goods that had not been removed. They paid in Confederate money for the confiscated goods as Commander Lee's directive specified. However, the directive's abuse was obvious in the treatment of the free Negroes who were carried away almost at will. However, the Southerners were generally an orderly and mannerly group. Many were impressed by the beauty of the town and valley. One young Georgian compared the town to Atlanta and confessed it was as nice and fine a town as he had ever seen.[27]

Despite outward appearances of serenity and seclusion from the invading army's reach, Alandale was also touched by the events. After conferring with General Lee on Chambersburg's town square, General A. P. Hill moved his corps east and set up his headquarters in a house across the field from the Crawford homestead.[28]

With little time to spare before Hill's staff paid visits to the neighborhood, Reverend Samuel, wife Jane, and Margaret's children tried to protect their most important personal belongings. Ma and Jennie took silver items to hide in the woods. Later the silverware and china were planted in different buildings. Jane protected the everyday utensils by placing them in a muslin bag which she tied to the hoops inside her dress. Two servant girls took the carpet from the house along with some perishable goods and secreted them in the forest. Their greatest fear was that the house would be torched. The boys took livestock to Chambers' Woods.[29]

When the Rebel cavalry finally appeared, they came to the back door demanding to be fed. Father, remaining calm, told the girls to provide them with food. In spite of the Christian-based charity, the Southern soldiers left with the family's cache of smoked hams, cured meats, and most of the chickens. The elder Crawford was determined to turn the other cheek, until the Rebels had done too much damage. He finally lost his resolve and headed across the field toward Font Hill to have a manly chat with Little Powell Hill. Before long, he reappeared on horseback accompanied by several grey-clad soldiers who were to act, forthwith, as household guards.[30]

One day during the occupation by those guards, Alex, a servant in the Crawford employ, had an encounter with one of the Rebel house guards. The black servant had been hiding in the upstairs garret as he feared being sold into slavery. One afternoon due to the intense heat, he sought a breath of fresh air at a window. Just then, one of the Confederate guards was taking a drink of water from the pump below when he looked up and saw the black man. Nearly apoplectic with fear, Alex froze. His fears were somewhat allayed as the soldier merely reacted by telling him to stay out of sight if he wanted to avoid capture. Even after the soldiers left, Alex's fear of their return compelled him to spend most of his time in his self-imposed prison.[31]

Treatment at the hands of the Southerners was less severe for those at Alandale than at many other places in the valley. United States Senator Thaddeus Stevens, an outspoken proponent of arming the South's slaves and confiscating Southern property, owned the Caledonia Iron Works, where Samuel Crawford had gone with his father on a number of occasions to have broken parts fixed or purchase new ones. General Jubal Early on his trip across the mountains to Gettysburg in late June of 1863 applied harsh and immediate revenge for the views of its owner. When told by the manager that the iron works did not make a profit, General Early replied that Yankees don't do business that way. The buildings were burned, equipment destroyed, and animals confiscated. "The total damage was in the range of $50,000" according to Mr. Sweeny, the manager.[32]

June 28, 1863, would prove memorable for the Southern army in Chambersburg, Pennsylvania, and the Northern army in Frederick, Maryland. The Sabbath weather in both places was clear and pleasant, but the commotion taking place in the two command centers was not clear nor pleasant.

The V Corps of the Northern army had bivouacked that night under the command of General George Meade near Frederick, Maryland. Meade had gained the soldiers' respect and appreciation during his time as commander of the Pennsylvania Reserves. They had also witnessed the quick temper and the sharp tongue. Having fought under the command of this Philadelphian, they knew his inner strength and mettle. In the early morning hours of June 28 he was awakened and informed that he was the newly appointed commander of the Army of the Potomac. His focus and determination was evident in a letter to his wife the next day, "I will move against General Lee now." He sensed a battle was near. He would not back down, but find the parts of his scattered army and move them in a way that each corps could find support in another. He had witnessed firsthand the problems of Joseph Hooker and others. Meade would try not to repeat those obviously unworkable approaches.[33]

Upon hearing of General Meade's selection, a number of fellow officers visited his headquarters. Prominent among them Generals Reynolds and Oliver Howard offered their congratulations and support. General Meade understood how crucial their aid would be in the test ahead, but little did he know how much he would ask nor how much they would give.[34]

When reveille called the corps members to duty on the morning of the 29th, scuttlebutt had it that George Meade was now commander of the Army of the Potomac, and the new V Corps commander was General George Sykes, a career regular who commanded by the book. He was considered a first class, brave, and professional officer. He was a stickler for detail, which at times slowed his pace and gained him the nickname "Tardy George." However, when his men entered battle, they were, for the most part, a well-disciplined unit prepared to play their role. His superiors would be watching his performance since this was his first corps command. Sykes was Crawford's elder by a number of years. When Crawford was entering Penn, Sykes was beginning his military career. Sykes preferred regulars for fighters and officers trained at West Point. Neither Crawford nor his men fit the desired categories. From Sykes, Samuel would learn the value of being a steady, well-prepared commander. From the Third Division of the V Corps, General Sykes would attain the fighting spirit of the volunteer soldier.[35]

The Pennsylvania Reserves were headed into the unknown with new corps and division commanders. Those closest by their side, however, were trusted, reliable, and experienced commissioned and noncommissioned officers.

As the flurry of command events unfolded in Frederick, across the South Mountains to the west, a tranquil forest setting, Messersmith's Woods near Chambersburg, belied the nervous churnings of the Southern commander. Generals Lee and Longstreet camped in this peaceful grove. An anxious Lee quizzed each new arrival in the same manner. James Powers

Smith, who arrived back from escorting Mrs. Jackson home after the death of her husband, was asked, "What have you heard of Stuart?"[36]

General James Ewell Brown Stuart had not arrived back from his cavalry excursion which began after the Battle of Brandy Station, and he had always provided Lee with trusty eyes and ears. Commander Lee needed to plan the next stage of the campaign confidently, and to do it accurately, he needed Stuart to tell him the location of his opponent. Stuart, who had been caught off guard at Brandy Station where he had held splendid reviews and dances that lasted long into the early morning hours, was searching for a way to heal a bruised ego. He and his cavaliers could gather some headlines if he could find a way to interpret his orders to guard Lee's right and perhaps circle the Union army as he had done in previous years.[37]

On the Union side much of the credit for improving the cavalry that had surprised Stuart and his men at Brandy Station had to be given to a tough and reliable horseman from Kentucky. John Buford was as modest and unassuming as Stuart was pretentious and pompous. He demanded much from himself, his men, and his fellow officers in cavalry and infantry.[38]

As Stuart attempted to get to the flank of Ewell and consequently to Lee's position, he found passes blocked by crossing Yankees. Because of the extra distances, his horses needed longer to graze and recoup; his men were exhausted, and he was dealing with more than one hundred captured wagons from near Rockville, Maryland. In war as in life nothing goes as planned, Stuart was behind schedule and in the fore of his commander's mind.[39]

With tents on either side of the Chambersburg Pike, the Confederate camp was nestled in a wood lot that had been used for picnics, and reunions; now its acres were covered with tents, wagons, and a multitude of horses. The military camp was easily detected by friend and foe. On the night of June 28, most of Lee's and Longstreet's staff had settled down for the night. The fires were moving toward glowing embers and death, and guards had been posted inside the picket.[40]

Before the adventure north, General James Longstreet had paid a man in gold to be a "scout" for him. This man, Harrison, was to report any information he felt essential to the Southern cause. This night the guards practically dragged the dirty, mud-strewn man to Longstreet's aide, Moxey Sorrel, who listened to his story and then awakened Longstreet. After hearing his tale, the First Corps Commander had Harrison taken to Lee. Ever skeptic of scouts, Lee listened inattentively as the grimy man told the general that the Union army had crossed the Potomac and much of it was in the Frederick area. Harrison relayed some unofficial gossip that he had heard. General George Meade had replaced Joseph Hooker as the Army of the Potomac commander. It was after 10 p.m., June 28, 1863.[41]

So far, Lee's objective of pulling the Union army away from Virginia appeared to be working. However, he was still concerned with the whereabouts of Stuart's cavalry. He had not received a word from him since June 22. Stuart had Lee's ear and confidence like no other cavalry officer, and Lee was sorely in need of confirmation about the Federal army. Lee had only the remnants of cavalry that Stuart had left him and they were of little use in this moment of quandary in the Southern commander's mind.[42]

Lee's dilemma was evident. He could not totally discount Harrison's information; nor could he rely unquestionably on its veracity. The general's internal turmoil was not lessened by the fact he was now in Pennsylvania, not friendly Virginia. After processing and analyzing the information, Lee made his decision. He told his aide, Lieutenant Colonel Charles Marshall, he wanted to keep the Federals east of South Mountain and he would move his army to the east side of the Blue Ridge to threaten Washington and Baltimore. The troops to the north approaching Harrisburg would be redirected, and the rest of the army would continue eastward through the South Mountain gaps.[43]

Meade would show no timidity in assembling his forces. He marshaled his troops northward in search of the invading force. The two armies used the roads that led to the active, carriage-building town of Gettysburg, Pennsylvania. June 30 dawned misty and still at Gettysburg. One of the commanders Meade would lean on arrived in Gettysburg that morning. John Buford, the observant and reliable cavalry leader, was already at work screening, guarding flanks, and reconnoitering, all of which he did flawlessly. With his keen eye, he had spotted a reconnaissance force most likely in search of supplies. He noticed red North Carolina flags. The Southern leader, unbeknown to Buford, was Johnston Pettigrew, who since the meeting in Sumter in 1861 had offered his services to his native state of North Carolina.[44]

On June 30, under orders not to engage the enemy, Colonel Johnston Pettigrew, upon detecting Buford's patrol, obeyed, and upon his return to camp near Cashtown, Pennsylvania, relayed his discovery immediately to his superiors. He warned them but they were reluctant to take seriously the advice of a scholarly, "high-strung" and non-West Point trained officer. Also General A. P. Hill, the commander in the area, believed the main Union army was not in the vicinity.[45]

V. A Kentuckian and a Pennsylvanian at a Crossroads

General Buford's reactions were similar to Pettigrew's. He began formulating plans and relayed the information to his superiors. Those supporting John Buford would listen and act. His alert staff captured a pass signed by Lee just this morning in Chambersburg.[46]

General Meade was doubly fortunate to have another fine officer near the scene that morning. General John F. Reynolds, of nearby Lancaster, a 20-year regular with an excellent military record and credentials and "widely admired" was a few miles south in Gettysburg in a meadow with trees and a running stream. The I Corps commander, Reynolds, liked his men to have all the comforts humanly possible. His men knew that if they stopped on a march they would not leave before they had time to make their morning canteen of coffee. In early June, Lincoln had offered the overall command of the Army of the Potomac to Reynolds only to be turned down because he feared political interference. Gentleman John recommended General Meade for the position. Reynolds was regarded as a strong, resolute leader. His troops were as good as any in the Union army.[47]

The actions of Generals Buford and Reynolds would set the stage for the initial portion of the battle. Also, their choices would prove to form the foundation for later decisions and the ultimate Union victory at Gettysburg.[48]

Buford had an uncanny sense that a large portion of the Rebel army was near, and promised his commanders the enemy would come "booming in the morning and the devil will have to be paid." Accordingly, he set up outposts, a skirmish line, and a battle line. Reynolds, the commander of the left wing, was only four or five miles south along Marsh Creek with the I Corps. He notified Meade and the XI Corps commander, General Oliver Howard, of the circumstances. This type of informative staff work would be typical of the Union army for the next few days.[49]

Wednesday, July 1, promised another hot, humid, sticky day as the sun rose across the horizon. The Southern forces emerged from the Cashtown area early in the morning to bump into Buford's dismounted troopers. Some of the troopers with repeaters, and all in advantageous defensive postures, gave ground grudgingly. Buford and Reynolds decided to delay the Rebel push in order to give the remainder of the Union army time to assemble. Reynolds had his tough, hard-fighting First Division going to aid Buford and had some artillery in place by about ten o'clock in the morning. Soon after this the Union's first disaster occurred: Reynolds was mortally wounded. Crawford's old Sumter cohort, Abner Doubleday, now a major general, was catapulted into the I Corps command position of the deceased John Reynolds.[50]

The men of the I Corps paid in blood as they bought precious time. Quaker Solomon Meredith's Iron Brigade, Lysander Cutler and his Second Brigade, and the charge at the railroad cut directed by Rufus Dawes all led to the slowing of the Confederate advance throughout the morning.

General Doubleday did not have the confidence of all his superiors, and Meade replaced him at the end of the day with General John Newton.[51]

About noon there was a lull in the action, except for artillery exchanges. By early afternoon the Confederates were on the field in force as the Southern reinforcements were arriving from the west and north. The afternoon belonged to the Confederates, who were able to overwhelm the I and XI Corps. The Union objective had been accomplished at a horrible price. The I and XI Corps suffered casualties approaching 10,000. After the first day's fighting, the "black hatters" of the Iron Brigade and other units were mere remnants of their former selves. The Army of the Potomac would manage to converge on the hills just south of town where, throughout the day, some of the arriving Union troops created a strong defensive position for the rest of the retreating army. Many believe the planning of the first morning and the falling back to the high ground in the afternoon created the basis for the Union victory at Gettysburg. The in-depth defense strategy had placed the Union forces in a position to fight on their terms.[52]

VI. Crawford's Reserves and Pennsylvania

A day prior, Crawford was shepherding his nearly 3,000 Reserves toward their home state. On June 30 the Reserves mustered for pay with a disturbing doubt that they may never receive the compensation.[53]

In later years they would call it "a time for memory and for tears." On July 1, as they rested near the imaginary Mason-Dixon Line that separated the mythical North and South and the real Maryland and Pennsylvania, Crawford had the flags unfurled, and the band played national and sentimental airs. It was one happy time for the soldiers of the Pennsylvania Reserves as they were home, really home.[54]

The members of Colonel Fisher's Third Brigade heard a rousing speech because, said one pundit, the brigade commander was "always anxious for an opportunity to make a speech."[55]

"We are Pennsylvanians and we have come to stay." They remembered it as one of the happiest days of their lives as the bands and regimental drum corps poured forth their soul-inspiring airs. About three o'clock they were drawn up to hear a patriotic address from General Crawford.[56]

Like his men, 36-year-old Samuel Crawford was nearly home. He took advantage of the moments to address his men. Sitting upright on his horse, Blood, he spoke from his heart:

> You have once more been called to the field. A rapid and fatiguing suffering on many hard fought fields. If you would hail the prospects of active service, at any time, with delight, how much more now. Our

native state is invaded by the ruthless horde of plunderers and who desire to spoil our rich valleys, our homes are desolated, and our fields laid waste, our property destroyed! We shall in a few hours tread the soil of the Keystone. The eyes of all will be upon us. To us, they will look with anxious hearts for relief. Let the sight of the mountains and our native plains free your hearts and nerve your arms in the hour of battle. We strike for all that is dear to man. Remember you are Pennsylvanians. Let no breach of discipline mar the glory of the past but let us pledge to each other never to cease until we drive the foe from our country.[57]

Their spirits were high going into Pennsylvania. "With flags fluttering and the bands playing, their steps lightened and their spirits lifted as they crossed the Pennsylvania line, and the cheers rang out from the regiments and rolled over the hills and through the valley."[58] They made their way through the darkness and after a march of over 25 miles, finally halted for rest and a little sleep near McSherrystown, a couple of miles west of Hanover, Pennsylvania. The Reserves rolled on to the good old Pennsylvania soil feeling somewhat satisfied with their marching accomplishments. They had made a serious threat of catching the rest of the V Corps. Inevitably, however, the wagon trains either prevented them from leaving on schedule or significantly slowed their pace. They had paid a price to get home, "tired, footsore, cross and ready to sleep—some for the last time on this earth." The extreme heat had made many of them ill and some were so tired they were unable to sleep. At daylight, after two hours of relative rest, Crawford was aroused by a staff officer who informed him that orders had come from General Sykes to march immediately to Gettysburg. Crawford ordered reveille sounded and ammunition issued. The men saw the hazy moon disappearing and shook the heavy mist from their blankets or clothes as they readied for the march. The soldiers were not given time to make coffee, only rations and ammunitions were distributed. One wit said, "Rations for ourselves and 60 rounds for our friends the 'Johnnies.'" One weary trooper saw the sun was beginning to crimson the eastern sky as they headed for Gettysburg about fifteen miles distant. Troop morale was improved when, after marching a few miles, they stopped long enough to make a fast cup of coffee.[59]

Crawford's strict discipline, coupled with his aloof manner, made him unpopular with some of the men. However, most would grudgingly credit him for conducting the whole march with good judgment. His finicky style and nervous anxieties were usually evident, but now the Third Division troops detected a greater degree of enthusiasm; he too was close to home. During this ride to the battlefield Crawford told Colonel Samuel Jackson that General John Reynolds had been killed. Reynolds had once commanded these troops and Crawford felt it would be best for the troops' morale if the men were not told for the time being. So strong were their feelings for General Reynolds that a ceremonial sword for him was being carried in the First Brigade ambulance.[60]

As they began to move, some of the troops encountered familiar faces among the civilian populace. In Company K one boy's uncle yelled, "Why did you let the Rebs get this far?" Came the answer, "Uncle Sam, it was all planned so I could see my Mammy."[61]

Sometime before noon on July 2, the First Reserves arrived in the Gettysburg area. Crawford rested the Reserves near an assembly area west of Rock Creek. They used the time and place to fulfill a variety of activities: fill canteens, have their first really good meal since June 28 while in Frederick, Maryland, examine and clean their weapons, relax, and write home; and some in Company K wandered to Culp's Hill to see their homes or the houses of relatives and friends. Most, however, "were soon wrapped in restful slumber."[62]

Colonel William McCandless wrote that it had been "a week of continuous marching." The Reserves had marched over 75 miles since June 28, 42 of those miles on three hours of sleep on the first two days of July. Many of the men wrote of the severe rains, slippery conditions, roads filled with wagon trains, and the burning sun. In spite of it all, they were soldiers from Pennsylvania ready to carry out their duty.[63]

Crawford and his staff went to alert Sykes of their arrival and location. The division had brought up the rear of the V Corps. From the information he garnered, he learned that the Union army had created a defensive position on Cemetery Ridge, an elevated north-south ridge with a group of hills on either end. On the north was Culp's Hill, and to the south the ridge terminated in two round tops, one larger than the other. The Union line gave the appearance of a large inverted fishhook. The Confederate line to the north and west paralleled. The compactness of the Union line would make communication and troop movements easier and faster.[64]

VII. The Rocky Citadel

At 2 p.m. on July 2, Crawford received orders to form his command and proceed toward the Union left flank. The men fell in marching formation quickly as they were anxious to protect the soil of their mother state. Since Crawford had not been provided a staff member to guide the troops into position, he ordered Colonel Fisher's brigade to follow General Romeyn Ayres' Regulars. When they reached a crossroads, Crawford believed Ayres headed in the wrong direction. While still in a quandary, he was approached by one of Daniel E. Sickles' staff officers, Captain Alexander Moore, in search of reinforcements. Crawford took him to be a member of Meade's staff and committed his troops to follow after confirmation from General Henry Slocum, the wing commander. The Reserves advanced on a road that probably reminded them of a farm lane. It was corduroyed with a fence on one side and brush on the other and woods on both sides. This path led to the smaller of the two round tops. As they neared their destination, Crawford and his troops began to encounter the wounded and ambulances moving to the rear. Colonel Martin Hardin of the 12th Reserves indicated the ambulance traffic was so heavy the troops had to walk to the side of the road. When Captain Alexander Moore learned that Sickles had been injured, he rushed off and left Crawford to fend for himself. Fortunately, at this moment General George Sykes, the V Corps commander, rode up and told the division commander to hold his men on the northeast slope of the round top. They held their position for only 20 minutes, as they carefully observed the developments to their front. Sykes then ordered Crawford to take his division across the road to a position on the little round top, or as Crawford would refer to it, "the rocky ridge."[65]

Both Crawford and his First Brigade commander, William McCandless, saw the position as a naturally strong one. They described what Crawford called the "rocky ridge" in detail. It was wooded at the top and along the sides and descended down a slope, across a plain toward a small stream. The ground the stream traversed was low and marshy. In front of that area was a wheatfield between two thick masses of timber. Skirting the timber was a low stone wall approximately 700 yards away.[66]

It was remembered as a hot afternoon. The time was about 6 p.m. One soldier noted, "the sun was a dull red ball of fire wrapped in drifts of lurid smoke."[67]

While General Sykes' original deployment order was being carried out, he ordered Crawford to send a brigade to support Colonel Strong Vincent's brigade. Retaining Colonel Samuel Jackson's 11th Regiment, the other four regiments of Colonel Joseph Fisher's brigade filed left toward the larger of the two round tops. Before they left, Franklin Horner of Fisher's brigade expressed the hope of the Reserves, "the boys are determined to drive the rebels out of the state."[68]

The area to the front of McCandless and Crawford was now emerging as a major concern as Ayres' regulars, after a gritty struggle, were falling back. One Pennsylvanian defined the situation as "not a reassuring sight." Crawford called the firing "heavy and incessant." Colonel Jackson saw it as "discouraging but sublime." Evan Woodward called the moment "Most Critical," and Pfanz labeled the Reserves, "Sykes' ace in the hole."[69]

Chapter Thirteen

The Reserves were brought into place and laid down for protection. From that vantage point they painted a picture with words, "it was not a cheering scene given the roar of cannons, the screaming exploding shells, the continuous crash of musket fire, the whole atmosphere thick and heavy with sulphurous smoke of battle."[70]

Crawford had requested further orders from Sykes, but the corps commander was occupied trying to rally Generals Barnes and Ayres on the right. Crawford was told to do what he felt best since he was on the scene. He watched through his glasses. "The plain in my front was covered with fugitives; fragments of regiments came through in disorder and without weapons." He decided "not a moment was to be lost." He and "Buck" McCandless prepared for a charge. Bayonets were ordered fixed. The troops ran into most resistance once they reached Plum Run but the fire from Devil's Den bedeviled them.[71]

Before moving, the Reserves hesitated, waiting for Gibbs' canister and the retreating regulars to clear the front. During this period Colonel Jackson requested permission to charge as he was being hit by a "galling fire from Devil's Den."[72]

Earlier in the day Captain Gibbs of the First Light Ohio Battery had to get his pieces into position by unhitching the horses and placing the guns by hand. Always anxious to protect their artillery pieces, this was especially important now because of the circumstances. A story later developed and, while it might be just a yarn, it is worth spinning. He supposedly came to the Reserves and said, "dunder and blixen, don't let dem repels took my batteries." The Reserves told him to stand by his guns and they would stand by him. The next day he saw some of the men and said, "the Pennsylvania reserves saved mine pattery, by —— I gets you fellers all drunk mit beer."[73]

After Gibbs hit the oncoming Rebels with canister, the Reserves delivered two solid volleys into them. The effect was immediate as the Rebels seemed momentarily stunned and slowed. Now the Pennsylvania Reserves were ready for the moment they had anticipated.[74]

Crawford, proudly astride Blood, led the charge. He cheered his men to stem the disaster with the words "make Pennsylvania your watch word and quail not upon its soil. Forward Reserves!" They "screamed their special Reserve yell." Crawford would later say, this yell was the loudest he ever heard from them. Evan Woodward would write that there was a "simultaneous shriek from every throat that sounded as if it were coming from a thousand demons." The troops had about 700 yards to go to the stone wall. Forward they went! "The timing for Pennsylvanians was perfect."[75]

Crawford seized the flag of the First Reserves regiment. It was the flag that instilled special pride and deep emotion. It combined the Pennsylvania flag with the state symbol, set in a field of stars, along with the red and white stripes of the national colors. The red stripes contained the Pennsylvania Volunteer identification. The entire flag was embroidered with a gold fringe. Another flag carried to the charge designated the Third Division of the V Corps. It was emblazoned with a blue Maltese cross on a white background.[76]

As the Reserves were about to charge, Crawford rushed to the flag, waved it, and held it high for all to see and follow. One of his staff wrote that he "rode out into the swamp with the 1400 following and cheering." The color bearer, Corporal Bertless Slott, hesitated to yield the flag, not recognizing the general, and therefore stayed by Crawford's side possibly grabbing his pant leg so he did not lose the presence of the flag. This was the attitude of a Civil War flagbearer. At one point an enemy bullet destroyed the finial. When they neared the wall, the general returned the banner to the anxious corporal.[77]

The men in Company K swept down into the valley, across the stream and to the stone wall and were amused that they had been over this land before as "boys chasing rabbits, gathering berries and playing hide and seek." At the stone wall the enemy put up a short but determined resistance with bayonet and rifle butts that at times "turned desperate." Crawford wrote, "It was short but determined."[78]

Meanwhile, in the sweep to the left, the Bucktails, led by Colonel Charles Taylor, had cornered some Confederates who were ordered to surrender; some did and others refused. From the back of the group came the comment, "I will not surrender to a corporal's guard." Those who were going to surrender picked up their weapons and fired. One story told of the Bucktails jumping behind trees, but Taylor was a step late and a shot pierced his heart, causing instant death. Crawford would mourn the loss with the words: "No braver soldier and patriot gave his life to the cause." Later the sobriquet "Valley of Death" would be applied to the area the Reserves contested.[79]

Near the stone wall an elated Crawford, with hat in hand, told the commander of the 11th Reserves, Colonel Samuel Jackson, "You have saved the day. Your regiment is worth its weight in gold, sir."[80]

In the action on the south side of the smaller round top, Fisher's brigade, sent by Crawford to aid the Vincent brigade, arrived about the time the initial fighting on that front was ending. The fighting had caused "organizational fragmentation" and Fisher had refused to move until given permission by a higher authority. "He and Rice were unable to locate General

Chapter Thirteen

Sykes and both realized the need to seize and occupy the big round top." So Colonel Fisher called for General Crawford to ask permission for his and Rice's troops to occupy the larger hill since the enemy, still present, could use it as a catalyst for a counterattack. "I directed Colonel Fisher to occupy it at once." He assured Fisher and Rice they could cooperate as long as the movement was done quickly. By the time the troops were deployed, darkness had descended. The terrain was exceptionally difficult to climb, let alone maneuver. The Reserves tried to follow the 20th Maine. In a short time, bewilderment was the key component of the maneuver. At this point, Colonel Fisher ordered the Reserves back to the starting point. Most of the 550 Reserves came back and prepared for another go.[81] When Chamberlain requested help, the 83rd Pennsylvania was sent to support the Maine troops near the summit. Realizing the hill was held by Union troops, the Reserves moved up the hill and took positions at different places on the slope "to merely support those in place." Franklin Horner, of the 12th Reserves, wrote that "they charged Sugar Loaf Mountain and took possession without firing a shot."[82]

Crawford had returned to establish his headquarters on a rock near the wall east of the Wheatfield and made arrangements for the care of the wounded, friend and foe. It would be surgeon Major Louis Read who ably and promptly cared for the wounded. "The bright full moon looked calmly down on the trodden wheat, scattered arms, dead and wounded."[83]

The morning of the third promised one sure thing, even more humidity. As the unrelenting sun began its upward arc, Crawford's men rallied from their sleep and as they came to life around the wall, they could hear the fighting off to their right and rear. They assumed correctly that the Rebels were trying to turn the northern flank. Crawford's men endured intermittent picket fire in their immediate area.

A soldier who was given access to a stray horse broke the monotony as he jumped on the animal and rode in the front of the brigade line imitating "Buck" McCandless, "Now boys remember your pappies and your mammies and your best gal and never desert the Old Flag as long as there are rations." The horse then "bucked" him off and ran to the Rebels as both sides cheered.[84]

The fighting to their backs quieted before noon as an uneasy truce prevailed and mimicked the sultry day in a tedious stillness. The veterans sporadically glanced at the sky, and by experience could tell the time was nearing one o'clock. Instantly, the firing of two signal guns near the Peach Orchard broke the weary spell. Some of the men, gazing in that direction, saw signal shots explode; others just heard them. In either case, they were alerted to a possible bombardment, but few, if any, were prepared for the extent of what was to follow. Southern guns opened at intervals to be answered by Yankee guns returning fire.

For the next two hours they would hear the noisiest event ever staged in the United States. Later from other Union troops the Reserves would learn that the cannon fire had been a prelude to Lee's final attempt to break the Union line. Lee had tried to roll the left, then the right wing of the Yankee line, and now the center would be challenged with more than an 11,000-man assault force under Pickett, Pettigrew, and Trimble. Shortly after 4 p.m. the cheering from the Union side of Cemetery Hill told the Reserves behind the "stone wall" that the center had held. In that area another Sumter officer that Crawford had known well there made his leadership and his brigade's presence felt. Colonel Norman Hall, the kid at Sumter, fought heroically.[85]

On the night of July 2 the Union command, upon Crawford's request, sent divisional support under the command of Brigadier General Joseph Bartlett. Also the Southern command placed a battery between the Trostle and Rose Woods. The Southern command was moving units, and toward morning, General Henry Benning understood orders from General Evander Law that he was to take the place of General Lafayette McLaws who had retreated. Just as this was being done, Benning received another order to move back to the ridge where they had started the day before. The first communication was unclear and misinterpreted. One of the units moved was the 15th Georgia under the command of Colonel Dudley M. DuBose. He never mentions receiving orders to retreat but later does acknowledge that he had received a communiqué that General McLaws would support his left. DuBose had his troops in a wooded area to the left of McCandless and at a right angle to the Reserves.[86]

Friday morning and afternoon the newly placed battery and sharpshooters "greatly annoyed" the Reserves around the wall. About 5 p.m. on July 3, Sykes ordered Crawford to enter the woods on his front and left and, "if possible, drive out the remaining enemy." "It was supposed the enemy had evacuated the position." McCandless was given the honors to carry out the reconnaissance. The First Brigade commander judged the battery to be about 450 yards from his position. As his men prepared to make the charge, the battery opened on them. The men lay down, stood, moved another direction, and repeated the maneuver.[87]

The 6th Pennsylvania Reserves under Lieutenant Colonel Wellington Ent and Lieutenant Colonel David Nevin's 139th Pennsylvania went through the Trostle Woods on the right and drove the enemy skirmishers. The story had a number of endings. McCandless wrote that the skirmishers "annoyed the gunners"; another wrote that when they neared the Rebel gunners, the Confederates abandoned their guns; another story relayed that when the enemy discovered the Union movement they limbered up and fled. And they "captured one gun and two caissons."[88]

With the remaining regiments of the brigade the colonel of the First Brigade cleared the woods to his front, then moved diagonally 800 yards across the wheatfield. He found the enemy in the woods on his left and at right angles. "I faced my command by the rear rank and charged the enemy directly on the left flank." Evan Woodward wrote that "they ran like hounds and yelped like devils." Others said they "fought stubbornly."[89]

General Benning reported that Colonel DuBose wrote, "found myself in the immediate presence of two long lines of enemy, one almost at right angles to the other," and "the enemy came rapidly and in heavy force, turning my left entirely and advancing in front and moving upon my right. I fought until I realized I was flanked, I secured my men behind rocks and trees."[90]

McCandless wrote that it was a rout of the Georgians who were behind rails. He listed in the Official Report the capture of 200 prisoners, including a lieutenant colonel, 2,000 to 3,000 small arms, most of which had been piled on brush heaps, ready to burn, and a stand of colors. The colors were those of the 15th Georgia flag, captured by Sergeant John Thompson of the Bucktails. Some of those captured included men who were butchering and engaging in skinning beeves and a detail burying their dead.[91]

Those Confederate soldiers who had not evacuated were a willing foe. A disappointed DuBose wrote that he had fought a desperate fight but "seeing no reinforcements coming to my relief and looking for expected support which did not come, I retired." From the Union perspective, General Robert McCoy later called it "one of the brilliant dashes of the war."[92] This was the last organized charge of the battle of Gettysburg.

Two days later Crawford received a note from his sister Margaret. It informed him that she had just returned from Cincinnati. Sadly, she was now convinced her husband had been killed at Vicksburg. With all the death, dying, killing, and maiming that occurred around him, it was a death miles away that had a profound impact on him. The death of the husband of his eldest sister, the father of four, encouraged reflection. The routine of post army battle was a standard order to dig trenches, bury or cover bodies, and list the casualties in the Official Report. He tried to always remember to concentrate on the living and not dwell on the dead, but death was associated with parents, a wife, a child or children, an aunt, or a close relative. Samuel Crawford was suffering vicariously. For his gallantry and meritorious service on this slope and at Antietam he would later be awarded a brevet colonel of the United States Army and, in the winter, his lieutenant colonel rank.[93]

Soon after the battle a reporter from the *Franklin Repository* came to talk with Samuel. The reporter wanted a participant's view. After Crawford provided a general analysis of the battle, they walked the fields, and later the reporter filed this article for his paper:

> It is not a morbid curiosity, but a feeling more akin to a reverence that we draw nigh to the broad and bloody altar on which thousands of our fellow beings have so freely laid down their lives for our redemption. The sun was just setting as we began to walk, and the silence of the coming night seemed best calculated to impress the scene. The rising fogs of evening were not unlike the smoke of battle. It is difficult to arrive at truth, each soldier claims for the point where he stood as having special importance. But some points tell their own story: the deep ruts made by artillery, the broken fragments of shells, the shrubbery cut down as with the scythe, the trampled caps and haversacks and the graves, thick as if sown broadcast on the hillside, these need no interpreter. Bravery was met with equal bravery.
>
> In order to obtain a correct conception of the sanguinary character of the battle one must visit the hospital sites, and there are acres of them. Men bleed and groan and die. Pity turns away to weep.
>
> The rebel wounded had been left by friends, under a tree, in a shed. The gnawing hunger soon added to the pains of their neglected wounds while drenching rains increased their discomfort.
>
> The debt the north owes the Army of the Potomac is one we can never repay but the story of how they fought at Gettysburg needs repeating. History shall record it on her pages and this story will not grow old. Generations yet unborn, shall read it and bring their tribute to the memory of those who bled and died for their country's redemption.
>
> General Crawford displayed the utmost concern for the care of the wounded. He sent at once for litter bearers and ambulances. The hospitals are filled with wounded Union and Rebel soldiers.
>
> I have written this in haste as I had to find shelter from the dashing rain.[94]

Many of the 2,000 folks who called Gettysburg home now had to fight another battle—the results of the first battle. More than 20,000 wounded humans needed some form of aid; many of the 7,000 who had been killed needed buried, as did thousands of animals. The folks of the little crossroads town could never "go home" again.

The days following the Battle of Gettysburg were a time of preparing the Pennsylvania Reserves for more marches as General Meade "looked to drive from our soil every vestige of the presence of the invader." Prior to departure most were read the commandant's General Order 68, which took the opportunity to note that

The commanding general, in behalf of the country, thanks the Army of the Potomac for the glorious result of the recent operations. An enemy superior in numbers and flushed with the pride of a successful invasion, attempted to overcome and destroy this army.

Utterly baffled and defeated, he has now withdrawn from the contest the privation and fatigue the Army has endured, and the heroic courage and gallantry it has displayed will be matters of history to be remembered. Then came the warning they knew but were reluctant to hear, "Our task is not yet complete."[95]

Post battle meant mounds of paperwork requiring completion. General Crawford, as all regimental, divisional, and corps leaders, wrote his Official Report. On July 6 he petitioned the War Department for permission to have the Second Brigade of Reserves join his command. The next day in the *Philadelphia Inquirer* their hometown scholar was noted as having "surpassed, if possible, the accustomed gallantry of the youthful commander of the Pennsylvania Reserves."[96]

When the V Corps finally started to move in a southwesterly direction, they headed toward Williamsport, Maryland. Their effort to catch the retreating Army of Northern Virginia was a tiring and taxing one. The V Corps, after a rainy and disagreeable day, spent all of the night of July 13 in a muddy field. The following day a charge was to be made to prevent the Army of Northern Virginia from going back to Virginia, but by daylight it was found the enemy had left. As the Reserves walked over the formidable rifle pits three layers thick, they were relieved they did not have to make the charge.[97]

VIII. The Death of a Sumter Adversary

As the Southern army retreated, another dagger was thrust into the Southern cause. On July 14 at Falling Waters, General Johnston Pettigrew was fatally wounded when Union cavalry was mistaken for Confederate riders.

Word of Pettigrew's death reached the Pennsylvania Reserve headquarters soon after the fact. Samuel would no doubt have shared with his staff the story of Castle Pinckney during the Southern takeover of Federal property on December 27, 1860.[98]

At that time Colonel Johnston Pettigrew was an aide to Governor Francis Pickens and was ordered to seize Fort Pinckney in Charleston Harbor. Crawford had met Pettigrew earlier that day as he requested Major Anderson to go back to Moultrie. Having lost that skirmish, his next assignment was Castle Pinckney, about six or seven hours later. Crawford replied belatedly that while Pettigrew lost his argument to have the Federals return across the water, his manner was polite and his reasoning befitting that of the exceptional University of North Carolina scholar he had been.[99]

As Samuel's mind drifted back to that time, he probably smiled to himself. Pettigrew had arrived at Pinckney with a force consisting of, as he remembered, Washington Light Infantry, Carolina Light Infantry, and the Meager Guards. He certainly had enough infantry as Lieutenant Richard K. Meade, the engineering officer, garrisoned the fort with a few workers and an elderly ordnance sergeant with his family. The militia found the gate locked and called for scaling ladders. Colonel Pettigrew led the troops up the ladders to the parapet. The moment he landed, he ran into Lieutenant Meade who awaited his arrival. Pettigrew demanded to talk with the officer in charge and Meade informed him he was that person. All the while the gate had been unlocked and the soldiers were pouring into the fort—hundreds of them. Quickly and proudly Pettigrew produced his orders and began to read them when Meade interrupted and told him he did not acknowledge the authority of the governor, but since he had no means of resistance he could only enter his protest against the proceedings. Pettigrew replied that the governor would give a receipt for the property, but again Meade indicated since he did not acknowledge the governor he would decline to accept the receipts.[100]

Lieutenant Meade asked if the colonel would give consideration to the ordnance sergeant and his family until they could be removed. Colonel Pettigrew gave his consent. Meade, not considering himself a prisoner since he did not recognize the proceedings, left for Fort Sumter. Crawford remembered that the state did seize a month's provisions, the armaments of the fort, and considerable powder.[101]

IX. The Good, the Bad, and the Ugly

Later the reality of the present situation reasserted itself. The men had been marching, countermarching, going on picket duty, digging sinks, sleeping, marching, and beginning the same routine the next day. Near the end of July they made camp near Warrenton, Virginia. Now, given a slight break from marching, their mood turned to protest as they turned their collective complaints to the lack of adequate rations. For the past few days the men had been eating ripe berries and what they could procure from generous civilians. Their anger came to a head as Crawford rode among them. At first their chant was not discernible, but as the volume increased with more dissatisfied soldiers joining in, the sound of "Crackers! Crackers!" became clear.[102]

General Crawford was so annoyed he rode directly to Meade's headquarters and confronted the commander on the matter. Meade replied, somewhat flippantly, "Well my dear General you should not let that bother you. One night at White Plains, I marched the boys a few miles on a night march and they called me 'a four eyed son of a b——h' and upon my soul I could not get angry at them." The rations appeared a few days later.[103]

By the end of August the lot of the Reserves was improving. They had settled into a camp where they could bathe routinely for the first time in nearly a month. Now the structure of camp life near the Rappahannock prevailed. Discipline was reinstilled and reinforced during this time. The men carried out orders no matter how seemingly wrong-headed they might appear. The next battle would probably be on enemy soil away from the homes of family, friends, and relatives.[104]

An event was scheduled for August 28 in which the troops looked forward to participating. Earlier, Crawford's staff and the men of the Reserves had expressed a desire to honor General Meade. A ceremonial sword, made in Philadelphia, was to be presented to him that day. Another sword, from the same source, had been requested earlier for a similar presentation to the now deceased John Reynolds. This sword would be delivered to the sister of their beloved general, who resided in Lancaster, Pennsylvania.[105]

In spite of the extra duties, the preparations for the Meade sword ceremony brought an air of anticipation and excitement. The Reserves had heard of the sash and gold spurs that would accompany the "dress blade." Invitations had been sent to many military and civic leaders and this provided them an opportunity to show off their pride through their camp and dress. After all, it wasn't every day the governor, a representative of the president, and other assorted "brass" paid a visit. For 10 days the Reserves decorated their camp by building green arbors and arches, creating wildflower wreaths, and displaying national pride everywhere.[106]

When the time finally arrived, God in the heaven presented a beautiful day. About five o'clock in the afternoon, the assembled, including Robert Lincoln, standing in for his father whom Crawford had invited, Governor Andrew Curtin, and other dignitaries as well as the full division in dress uniform, accompanied the Pennsylvania Reserve officers in full dress uniforms, sashes, and belts but no swords.

From the platform General Crawford noticed many of the officers from his past, notably General Alpheus Williams, his First Division commander. When the ceremony began, Crawford asked General Meade to step forward. Crawford, somewhat nervous due to the gravity of the event, presented the dress blade sword along with the accompanying sash and gold spurs. Wainwright reported that the sash, spurs, and sword cost $1,000. In what one soldier called "an appropriate little speech," Crawford marked the event:

General: I stand before you today, sir, the representative of the officers and men of this division who once called you its chief. Impelled by a desire to perpetuate the memory of your connection with them; desirous also to manifest to you the affection and esteem they bear to you. They ask that you accept this day, sir, from them, not as a reward, but as the exponent of their heartfelt thanks whose values cannot be expressed in words. Transmit it to those who bear your name, and let it ever express to you and them that devoted attachment and regard that the officers of the Pennsylvania Reserve Corps shall never cease to feel for you.[107]

In accepting, General Meade received the tumultuous cheers from the men of the Pennsylvania Reserves. "General Crawford and officers of the division of the Pennsylvania Reserves Corps, I accept this sword with profound gratitude." He went on to thank the division for its gallantry and bravery.[108]

After Governor Curtin's patriotic and soul-searching speech, the ceremony concluded. Everyone retired to the banquet hall to partake of any delicacies the palate could suggest. Wainwright alleged there must have been 500 officers present and of these perhaps 30 were gentlemen. His reasoning was the result of some of the officers pilfering knives, forks, and plates. Other officers stormed the table and Wainwright was without food until one of Crawford's staff brought him some boned turkey and a bottle of champagne.[109]

Numerous toasts, accompanied by Meade's favorite beverage, champagne, were given. "The whiskey and the champagne soon began to tell" until the merriment finished about ten o'clock.[110]

X. The Man was Going to his Own Interment.

The event of the next day was the antithesis of the day before. On August 29, 1863, the Union troops still stationed along the Rappahannock River would be forced to witness multiple executions. Some soldiers deemed it a waste of life and others felt it was a necessary evil. It seemed essential to the general who commanded the Army of the Potomac. Public execution was a technique that Meade believed was necessary to internalize discipline. Attendance was mandatory for such occasions and was, almost to a man, abhorrent to all. Many means of deceptions were used so one did not have to watch. The soldiers closed their eyes or focused on a living flower or tree. While they understood that something had to be done to reduce or stop the hemorrhaging of desertion, these ceremonies were distasteful and dehumanizing. Many had never witnessed such a spectacle; numerous others too often:[111]

> The condemned men were all foreign born, who had limited use of the English language, had been assigned to the Fifth Corps for judicial cognizance and were without friends or associates. They had petitioned General Meade, through an interpreter, for clemency or more time to prepare for death. Given the fact that two were Roman Catholic and one was Jewish, they had difficulty locating spiritual advisers. Meade was first able to locate a Roman Catholic Priest, and not until the morning of the execution did he find a Jewish Rabbi who arrived at noon on execution day.[112]

On the afternoon of the execution, the V Corps was marched "to witness their end." The soldiers marched about one and one-half miles to a serene area that appeared suitable for picnics and family gatherings. The area gave the impression of a valley amphitheater. The men formed on three sides of the hill on gently sloping ground. The five freshly dug gravesites were about one hundred yards away. Beside each grave a common board coffin had been placed. "The silence was not broken by a single sound until the death dirge could be detected in the distance."[113]

> The strains of funeral music were soon heard as the band slowly led the way from the guard tent. After the band, came the surgeons, followed by a provost guard with neat clean uniforms and shiny weapons and then the victims came in single file with their hands tied behind them. They all wore blue pants and white shirts. The convicts were paraded in front of our line, four of the five walked with rather steady steps. At the gravesite each man was seated on his coffin and accompanied by a chaplain. The bugle sounded to recall the chaplains and the eyes of the convicts were covered. The allotment of time was running low and some officers feared if the deed was not done immediately a murder charge would be brought against those in charge of the proceedings.
>
> The firing squad took their positions at 12 to 15 yards in front of the prisoners. The Rabbi, still beside his trembling man, performed a Hebrew religious ceremony, and then quickly departed. The entire amphitheater was breathlessly quiet. On the command of "fire," the guns fired in one voice. Four of the men fell over and the fifth leaped forward still standing. An officer moved toward him with pistol in hand and then slowly the victim sank. The surgeons pronounced them dead.[114]

As they marched back to camp, the men could not help but react to what they had just witnessed. Their reactions would have surely varied; some would have believed it served them right as they also had to face a hail of iron and lead while another might have indicated that they should all face the music together as their security was interwoven with everyone's. Others felt that it was better to die a patriot's death on the battlefield than in that manner. One veteran expressed the feelings of many of his colleagues by voicing the belief that soldiers who sell their blood for money and then desert deserve no sympathy.[115]

One can suspect that some of the men looked back, still transfixed by the day's events and its aftermath. They could see the chaplain reading the funeral service. As the soldiers quietly neared camp, a soldier, known for his sensitive, insightful, and reflective attitude, selected this quiet time to present his views concerning the execution they had just witnessed. He expressed the belief that these men could have aided the army in other ways and at least they would be doing something constructive in the war effort. Now they just turned to dust and made the division less in number and weakened the cause. That opinion likely resonated among those who heard the comment.

Although Crawford's service was recognized and rewarded, other able officers were not so fortunate. His old friend Alpheus Williams was such a case. Williams looked upon self-promotion and political self-aggrandizement as degrading and unworthy of his character. Perhaps that was a factor in his not progressing. Resentment and frustration led him to lash out in a letter to his daughter, "A fellow such as Crawford will be promoted before I am because he knows the Secretary of War, is from Pennsylvania, and gives great dinners he never pays for." Williams then claimed, "At Antietam he got a small puncture—self inflicted, I think. He recently got assigned to the Pennsylvania Reserves and had a big time presenting a sword to General Meade." In this moment of anger and frustration, he listed other officers who had been undeservedly promoted. He was insulted that "there were twenty such men on the last list that were promoted over him." The War Department's search for West Point-trained regular army officers left General Williams embittered and envious of those chosen. As a non-West Pointer, General Crawford would find himself facing some of the same problems when it came to selecting a V Corps commander.[116]

Colonel Joseph Knipe, who was a brigade commander, also disliked Crawford, and hoped he would not return after his wound had healed. Williams and Knipe, both Mexican War veterans, were good friends; Knipe's one child was named Alpheus Williams Knipe. They were of the belief that the old school officer was more capable of leadership. Jealousies stemmed from many sources, were banal, and to a degree predictable. Given Crawford's aloofness, almost to the point of arrogance, he was an easy target for such disdain.[117]

XI. More Physical and Emotional Pain

In late August, in addition to the chronic pain suffered from the thigh wound, Samuel fell victim to the return of malaria. He experienced frequent bloody bowel movements. Initially, he passed it off as the "soldier's complaint" or perhaps hemorrhoids. When the problem failed to subside, he sought the advice of the division surgeon. Stomach cramps, a dry cough, chills, and fever resulted in a diagnosis of malaria, possibly contracted during the Moultrie-Sumter assignment from contaminated water from a cistern. Surgeons had warned him that the illness may recur.[118]

He stayed in command until after a conflict with the Rebels at Bristoe Station, where General A. P. Hill advised General Henry Heth to make a charge that ended in a devastating trap for the Southern soldiers. In a matter of minutes over 1,400 troops were killed, wounded, or captured. The results caused Lee to say to Hill, "General, bury these poor men and say no more about it."[119]

After the Bristoe battle, Crawford was on medical leave and back to Franklin County by late October. Most probably he was plagued by a recurring attack of malaria. His health always seemed to be aided by the mountains of Pennsylvania.[120]

Sister Maggie would have had time to talk to her brother about her husband's end. For months she thought Ed had been wounded and would return.

Samuel no doubt thought of the many times his oldest sister had been there for him and now he probably felt woefully inadequate when she most needed his emotional support. He had not one single answer. Reasoning was useless. Silence probably prevailed for seconds in what seemed like an eternity. He then conveyed the idea that there was no rhyme nor reason nor sense to it all. Sometimes just being at the wrong place at the wrong time meant death. How do you explain a man marching and riding hundreds of miles to a battlefield where a bullet's trajectory crosses his path at that very instant, and sometimes missing by inches?

Margaret began to tell him the details of Edward's death. Crawford would have understood his sister's discussion as cathartic.

> A Lieutenant Clark had brought his pocketbook and diary and told her that the Captain had been wounded on May 19th and carried to a wagon shed for protection. Before being able to move him and a couple of comrades to a military hospital, a shell hit the shed, set it on fire, and the wounded could not be retrieved.[121]

Margaret's husband had burned to death and at that moment she hated the war. She likely asked her brother what it was like to burn to death. Margaret's son, Reade, accompanied by a growing Samuel, had walked to and from the battle site at Gettysburg, roughly 33 miles. They no doubt relived much with Uncle Samuel.[122]

Samuel would have told his father about the practical aspects of "the soldier's trot"—the excruciating pain on the marches, and the long, agonizing hours on his horse Blood. The conversation soon turned, at the son's direction, to another topic. In an effort to deflect the talk from himself, Samuel mentioned that he had heard of servant Alex's tragic death, but did not understand the strange circumstance of the hired man's end. The family found the tragedy unbelievable. After the Rebels left in the summer of 1863, Alex continued to hide in the garret and no amount of coaxing could get him out for very long. The family cajoled, threatened, pleaded, and did anything they could think of, but he was positive he was going to be captured, taken south, and sold into slavery. One day a hired girl went to take him a meal, and he didn't respond; her scream told all. According to the doctor, apparently he died from fright. His mind had stopped his heart. Samuel had witnessed similar incidences during his times in battle.[123]

Ever so slowly the days passed and Samuel's recuperation occupied much of the time. His days were filled with the constant changing of the thigh bandages. There were also moments of seclusion when he felt the onset of the shakes, which were followed by an intense fever, and then profuse sweating. Rest and quinine were accompanied by numerous trips to the out back privy.

Samuel would have surely read in the *Repository* some of the local ramifications stemming from the Battle of Gettysburg. During the Southern retreat, a number of Rebel wounded had been diverted to Chambersburg. The people of Chambersburg saw a dejected lot. It was natural for the wounded to be discouraged by their current plight, but the Rebels were disheartened by the number of young men they saw in the North still available to fight. The thoughts of home created more melancholy, as they knew, through letters, that back home there was a shortage of everything. They realized their family members were fraught with death and disease as they served their cause. They feared returning to graves, instead of the live and vibrant humans they left. They further despaired that after all of this misery they might fail to obtain their independence. The townsfolk might have disdained the anonymous Southerner, but they sympathized with the individual human.[124]

One light moment the family shared was Father's story about the confrontation he and General A. P. Hill had at Font Hill, the cottage across the fields.

> First, the Rebs took those two beautiful black horses I used on the Sabbath and special occasions and hitched them to Hill's carriage. When those same men asked for food, we fed them; and still those confounded

Rebels confiscated all the smoked meats and the live chickens, but when they shot "Bea," my pet peacock, I lost my sense of self. I went across those fields lickety-split and told General Hill what I thought of him and his whole Rebel army. I must say he listened closely, and then apologized for the action of his men. In his soft voice he told me not to repeat those same things outside, or he could not be responsible for the actions of his men.

Before leaving, the reverend also told "Little Powell" Hill that his son was in the Union army, and would fight him, and he was lucky the War Department did not allow him to go because he would have been beside his son. "He impressed me as a real gentleman though because at the end of my tirade, he had two of his men take me home and act as protectors of our home and family."[125]

By late fall, the early frosts crystallized the morning grounds. Samuel had mended enough to have the maladies under control, but his surgeons assured him they would most likely recur. He said his goodbyes and was off to rejoin the V Corps in Virginia.

XII. The Fall and Winter of '63

General Crawford was back in command about mid-November, and at the first chance of division review he congratulated the men on their fine appearance following the long severe marches after Gettysburg. He ended the review with some words of encouragement for the troops, "The people I visited in Pennsylvania told me that they look on you with pride, and their thoughts are with you. The governor has promised me he is trying to have the transportation of food improved." As a bonus, he informed the troops that he had requisitioned cigarettes for them from the Sanitary Commission.[126]

Another bit of welcomed news arrived shortly after his return to duty. Brother Alex would be assigned to him as an aide once again. Besides being a good steady staff member, he was Samuel's security blanket.[127]

His father probably relayed with pride the story of Mr. and Mrs. Hoke who had been to Gettysburg to hear the president of the United States help dedicate the National Cemetery. The Hokes had a great position near the platform because they had left the hotel early in the morning and were practically carried to the cemetery by the crowd. Mr. Hoke said, "the President spoke after Mr. Everett's address." Many in the crowd did not hear the words, but he and his wife were among the lucky ones. He said that he "had never heard such words in only a few minutes." After the speech, as the president mounted his horse, Mr. Hoke asked if "Mr. Lincoln would shake the hand of a strong Union lady, his wife." Lincoln said "he would gladly if only his horse would cooperate." Lincoln shook her hand as she repeated a number of times, "God bless you Mr. Lincoln and God bless you Mr. President."[128]

The Chambersburg merchant also reported Gettysburg conditions as he and his wife saw them in the days following the president's speech. "Inside the cemetery were 3,500 freshly dug graves. Over 1,600 bodies were unidentified." He noted that "the stench greeted all who neared the town. The sources of the smell were numerous: sinks, latrines for 165,000 men, manure from 90,000 horses and mules, piles of amputated parts, shallowly buried bodies that now had exposed limbs sticking through the soil due to heavy rains, additionally there were the bodies of humans and horses who had simply not been buried. A common sight was the citizen who carried camphor oil or peppermint oil to offset the smell, but they could do little about the related diseases." It was an image worthy of Dante.[129]

For the most part, the war news from the rest of the Union army was encouraging. In Charleston and the island fortress, the tables had been turned. Since April of 1861 when Samuel Crawford and his brethren struggled to bring dignity to the national flag, the Confederate flag was being bombarded daily by the Union. In another area of the war, the Union victory of Chattanooga would provide a base and opportunity to invade Georgia. In addition, Knoxville was under a Union siege.

In Virginia, Meade had continued to try to penetrate Lee's line at different places. He decided on one more offensive threat. November 30 looked bleak for the Reserves who faced an alley of cannon and the icy waters of the Rapidan. In a humanitarian move Meade called it off and by December 2 the almost frozen men began to walk or were carried to the rear.

However, more of a threat than Lee's army, Crawford and his men recorded the cold weather. The men were forbidden to build fires, and even tough, veteran soldiers suffered in the bitter cold. The Reserves had already seen some of their buddies "freeze to death" and suffer varying degrees of frostbite.[130]

By December 5 the entire division had recrossed the Rapidan and Rappahannock Rivers and set up winter camp at Brandy Station two days after Christmas. Some relief was finally achieved when they moved into huts built and previously occupied by the 149th Pennsylvania soldiers. They were sturdy men who built sturdy huts, and in the case of any needed refurbishments, a Southern ghost town located a few miles away, provided a ready and convenient source for repairs. Doors, windows, and various structural components were available for the taking. Even occasional stray dogs or cats were commandeered and served as different mess mascots. It was a winter without hardtack as they often received baked bread and a winter with some opportunities for furloughs.[131]

Constant harassment by roving guerrillas was an irritant all winter long. One such attack on December 13 was recorded by Crawford. "A party of 6 guerrillas dressed in Union overcoats attacked Colonel M. Hardin at Catlett's Station. The attack came along the railroad track within sight of our pickets. Both colonels, who were at the time examining ways to tighten defenses against the guerrillas, had their horses shot from under them and were wounded, one in the arm and the other in the hand. Our cavalry is in pursuit." Crawford, at one point indicated they feared traps being set against the pursuing cavalry.[132]

As the year drew to a close, the first hints of disagreement about the importance of the role the Pennsylvania Reserves played in the Battle of Gettysburg surfaced. General Crawford had received a letter from Professor Jacobs of Gettysburg College who had published an account of the battle, asking him to confirm the details of the Reserves' charge, as Colonel James Rice, who had assumed command of Vincent's brigade after the former's death, had challenged the Jacobs version. Rice placed his objections in the form of a published letter to the *New York Times*. It seemed in the article that Colonel Rice was indicating that the Reserves did not participate in the charge.

General Crawford twice corresponded with General J. Rice and wrote a reply to the professor. Crawford tried to identify and clarify the mistake he believed the colonel had made in his assessment. No one had ever claimed that the Pennsylvania Reserves were present at that struggle between Vincent's brigade and Rebel General Hood. "At this time we were drawn up in reserve. The extreme left had been partially repulsed." The charge that he wrote about, he reiterated, was the one under his immediate command. That charge began "near the foot of little round top driving the enemy across the stone wall."[133]

Crawford wrote that he regretted that anyone at this late date question the role of the Pennsylvania Reserves at Gettysburg. The charge was between the two round tops.[134]

Crawford closed, "You can now judge, my Dear Sir, whether the praise you have awarded the gallant men of our state is more than justified."[135]

XIII. The Charge, the Reserves, the Leaders, and History

Samuel Wylie Crawford and the Pennsylvania Reserves became welded to the rocky citadel. They never missed a chance, within their powers, to extol that early evening charge.

The situational background gives some insight into why they were enthralled with the event. A few weeks before July 2 they were on guard duty in Washington, D.C. General Crawford was serving on a court-martial board. Then he was given a command of Keystone state soldiers with a reputation of being a "gun powder" unit. When General Lee invaded the North toward Pennsylvania, the Reserves pleaded with Colonel William McCandless: "having learned our mother state has been invaded, we respectfully ask, if it is within your power, to have us ordered within the border of our state to fight for her defense. We have more than once met and fought the enemy when he was home; now we wish to meet him where he threatens our homes, our families our firesides. We feel confident that we could do service to the state and hopefully increase the luster that attaches to our name." So it was done.[136]

On the march to Gettysburg they paused near the Pennsylvania state line where they were urged by their commander to "Remember you are Pennsylvanians. Pledge to each other never to cease until the foe is driven from the country." Both the officers and the men were feeling the urgency of the call they had implored.[137]

On the evening of July 2, the Union left was being challenged when Crawford and the Reserves arrived on the battlefield "at the right place at the right time." From their immediate vantage point they saw a battle raging, Union troops fragmenting in front, some with weapons and many without, an artillery commander fearing the loss of his battery, Union troops "rushing through with the enemy following closely behind." In the eyes of McCandless and Crawford, no time was to be lost. McCandless reflected in his Official Report, "the enemy advanced in a disordered mass driving our forces back on our position."[138]

In their mind, they "arrived at the supreme moment of a terrible crisis." Crawford's assistant adjutant general wrote that as the Confederates approached "a sheet of flame swept the regulars who were falling back in a disorderly mob followed by the rebels yelling like demons."[139]

Crawford showed his energy and zeal when he grabbed the Reserves' flag and led the charge on horseback. The charge that followed was enthusiastic and rewarding for those participating in the ranks. The normally high strung Crawford in his first charge as a divisional commander exulted in the achievement as he told Jackson that "his regiment was worth its weight in gold."[140]

The divisional commander would later write, "but for that charge on Thursday evening the key to our position would have been taken." The rocky citadel became a "watchword to every patriotic heart." Without a doubt, it was exaggerated.[141]

In the eyes of the Reserves and their leaders, they had seized the moment that had grown out of the situation of the past month, the circumstances of the last few days, the stimulus of the moment of the charge, the place of the battle, the mental state of the participating troops, and the psyche of the leaders.

To those analyzing the situation today, it does not seem to have been that crucial. To many Gettysburg pundits the Reserves did make a successful charge that did stall the enemy advance; and the enemy would make no further charges whatever the conditions.

Some of the claims of Crawford and his officers were "gross exaggerations" and in some way Crawford "self-aggrandized": the opponent was wearing down, "our little band was thinned and exhausted by three and a half hours of fighting and made a gallant attempt to take the battery." The Reserves did not run into significant resistance until they were near Plum Run. They did however receive fire from the Devil's Den area. Longstreet because of troop exhaustion and the late hour said he commanded his troops to retreat, and a large body of Union troops were in place to challenge a countercharge.[142]

When July 2 was over, the V Corps held the round top areas. The Reserves had helped to reject the Confederate advances. General Sykes would write, "the key of the battlefield was entrusted to my keeping." His V Corps was larger than any of its parts, but its achievements were a part of the whole.[143]

Part Seven

The Spring and Summer of 1864

"More desperate fighting has not been witnessed on this continent."
—General Ulysses S. Grant

"We stood side by side as the storm of death swept by— it was the parting of brothers."
—The Pennsylvania Reserves

Colonel William McCandless
The First Brigade under McCandless led Crawford's troops down the slope of Little Round Top late in the afternoon of July 2.

Gil Barrett Collection, USAMHI

✥ Chapter Fourteen ✥
Spring in the Wilderness and Spotsylvania

I. This land would become "the bloodiest swath ever cut through the globe."[1]

The Army of Northern Virginia was back in its homeland again, among friends, on terrain they knew like the back of their hand. The two large Confederate moves into the North had opened with a multitude of hopes and finished with less than the desired results. The conclusions sought were unresolved, and now the two armies were mere miles from where it had all begun three springs ago. Being on their home turf was a factor in the Confederates' favor, but in this fourth year they had other problems: Georgia was the only part of the West the Confederacy could call their own. The Tennessee and the mighty Mississippi Rivers were in the hands of the Union.

The officials, civil and military, on both sides, were searching for solutions to make 1864 the year to end this bloody rebellion. There was no magic button to be pushed; the strategies for victory were as difficult and complicated to find as the reasons for this bloody conflict. Too much blood had been spilled to quit, and the prospect of spilling even more blood was repulsive.

At the end of '63, the Confederate military had slipped slightly. The year began with glorious victories at Fredericksburg and Chancellorsville, but on July 4 when Northern victories at Gettysburg and Vicksburg were realized, conditions had to be more delicately scrutinized by President Davis and his top military leaders. That magnifying glass would lead them to detect some familiar and other not so recognizable problems. Lack of manpower was the omnipresent issue that once again came to the fore. To encourage greater numbers, the South gave its veterans furloughs to recruit new able bodies; the Confederate Congress did its part by eliminating the substitute clause, allowed fewer occupational deferments, and extended the age so the recruits could be younger and older. Lee added able manpower as Longstreet was brought back from the Western Theater with his two divisions of infantry and two battalions of artillery. That part of the formula encouraged Davis and Lee and his lieutenants. However, other additional manpower did not measure up in either quantity or quality. Early on, some Southerners hired a substitute but now they themselves could be employed by the Confederacy. For those who were already serving, the Confederate Congress extended their time "for the duration."[2]

While these procedures increased the numbers of soldiers, another plague continued to drain manpower. By the spring of '64 desertion had become a problem for both armies and a colossal one for Lee and Jefferson Davis. Communications between the Confederate president and his military chieftain on the subject of desertion were now frequent and intense. Often it was the families of the men who had served "more than their fair share" that urged them to come home to their helpless, starving wives and children. They could be of more value to their loved ones than dying in battle for a cause that looked, at best, hopeless. Lee, whose personal life was in agony, tried his hand at fairness. When a case was brought before him, Lee searched for a rational means to avoid the death sentence. The dead were of no value to his army; the living might be of some aid. Perhaps by granting life, appreciation would be shown by loyalty to his army.[3]

The greatest morale and confidence booster to the Southern soldier in the Eastern Theater was, indeed, General Robert E. Lee. His soldiers felt he knew what had to be done to win this terrible conflict. With all its turns and twists "Marse" Robert would remain the one constant. But Lee, in the pri-vacy of his mind, realized that replacing the corps, division, brigade, and regimental commanders lost in the past three years was an exceptionally challenging task. They were the heart of an army's strength, reliability, and progress because they managed and touched the lives of the soldiers.[4]

As the war slid into 1864, many Southern soldiers had heard about Ulysses S. Grant, but they felt that Lee would be dealing with just another Yank commander.

To President Lincoln, General Grant was the missing link for whom he had been searching these past 48 months. The president believed Grant, as a fighting general, could and would turn Northern fortunes.

The Union army faced some of the same problems as its counterpart, but in most cases to a lesser degree. Mr. Lincoln, in this election year, knew that the role of the military would determine, to a large extent, his political fate as well as that of the nation. The commander in chief decided to bring Ulysses Simpson Grant and his aggressive manner to the Eastern Theater. Providing him with a lieutenant general rank and by selecting him as the supreme commander of the Union forces, Lincoln believed that an overall strategy under one individual was essential to unify the armies and bring that elusive Union victory. By March 9, 1864, the strategy was on paper and ready to be executed. General Grant's overall concept was more than capturing a capital. Richmond was more of a symbol than military substance. Grant's plan was to "concentrate all the forces possible against the Confederate armies in the field." War as it had been known would change incalculably. Grant, the strategist, would have his subordinates generate the tactics into reality. General Crawford and the other Union officers faced the haunting question: Could they fight the way General Grant would expect—relentlessly and continuously? It would certainly help if success and war's end came quickly. To make the army more mobile, Grant reduced the corps to three in the Army of the Potomac. That alone placed extra strain on corps leaders. As the four armies moved in concert, the pot would be stirred and boiled non-stop in every military theater. As Lincoln so succinctly put it, "Those not skinning can hold a leg."[5]

General S. W. Crawford, promoted to colonel in the United States infantry, would continue to serve as brevetted brigadier general in the volunteer army. He remained Third Division commander in the V Corps, but under a new corps commander. General Gouverneur Warren had been a New York-appointed West Point engineering graduate who had the honor of placing second in his 1850 class. Being proficient in mathematics, he went back to teach the subject at his alma mater. He would bring intellect to his new post, which often translated into cautious detail. At 34 years of age he would be the youngest major general in the Union army. In the spring of 1863, he opted for chief engineer in the Army of the Potomac. Warren refused General Meade's offer as chief of staff because he felt he would be of more value in his engineering capacity. July 2, 1863, would confirm that belief as he stood on Little Round Top and selected that part of the battlefield to be refortified. Crawford's division would be a part of that defense, and both men would look at that time as their moment of shining grandeur.[6]

After the Battle of Gettysburg, some believed that General Warren sided with Lincoln in the belief that Meade had "lost the opportunity to destroy Lee's army." Meade would live with that criticism and offer his resignation to General Grant only to have the idea quickly rejected by the new Union commander. Warren and Meade would know the stringent, lifelong pain created by blame from superiors.[7]

II. Fighting with Malaria in No Man's Land

In early March, the *Franklin Repository* reported that General Crawford "was North under medical treatment for his Antietam wound. He looks well, but suffers much." That was followed in late April with another bout with malaria. Samuel knew of a doctor in his home city of Philadelphia that might provide some relief. Regardless of the expertise of the doctors, he was assured that he suffered from malaria, and he would continually be plagued with intermittent fevers and attacks of dysentery.[8]

On his return to camp, the fever had subsided but the toll on Samuel's system was becoming more evident. He tried to adjust his duties of command as best he could. However, most of the daily chores could not be delegated. The workload of brother Alex was extended as together they tried to maintain the general's energy. With his medical training, his younger brother was the ideal aide to treat his brother's health complications.[9]

The division commander immersed himself in the preparations for the coming campaign. A cold, damp rain blew in on May 2, reminding him of the days he experienced at Sumter; he loathed the wet chill more now than ever. These early days of May were filled with nonstop duties and orders. On May 3, each soldier was issued 50 rounds of ammunition, rations for their haversacks, and bread for the knapsacks. Of special importance, the officers readied the medical wagons, the ammunition transporters, the carriers of subsistence, and forage. Some beef was taken on the hoof.[10]

The logistics of the coming campaign were gargantuan. No one felt that responsibility more than General Rufus Ingalls, chief quartermaster of the Army of the Potomac. The means of transportation provided in his Official Report on May 3, 1864, consisted of 3,500 wagons, 590 two-horse ambulances, 29,650 horses, 20,184 mules, 4,000 private horses, 1,600 cavalry horses, 5,000 artillery horses, and 1,400 ambulance horses. Artillery Colonel Wainwright wrote that there was "so much to be done at the last minute: 50 rounds of ammunition, 3 full days of rations, and 3 partial rations. 99,438 were equipped and ready for battle; of these 73,000 were infantry, 12,000 cavalry and 10,000 artillery. Last minute drilling and target practice for the infantry and artillery" were also on the busy agenda.[11]

It seemed the men and officers sensed that the next part of this conflict might be different from any other in their military careers. One soldier characterized the Union army as "healthy, well fed, and full of enthusiasm." They had fought in the junglelike conditions in the past years and knew war's potential horror, but they had not fought under a commander whom both soldiers and civilians considered unremitting and merciless. A war of attrition would affect the enemy as well as the soldiers fighting it. In light of coming events General Meade told the soldiers of the Army of the Potomac, "the eyes of the whole country are looking with anxious hope to the blow you are about to strike in the most sacred cause that ever called men to arms. Remember your homes, your wives, and your children."[12]

As Crawford was riding to meet with his brigade commanders, he likely sensed a quiet tension among the men. A huge number were probably writing home and bringing their diaries up to date. It was obvious that memories of home and loved ones were uppermost in their minds. The veterans were able to predict when they were going to "strike tents." Of course, they could not help but notice the activity around them: troops moving or preparing to move, the crunching noises of wagons and guns, and the turmoil created by the itinerant cavalry. All the activity in the Union camps was noticed by Southern commander Robert E. Lee on Clark Mountain where he indicated to his commanders on May 2, 1864, "I believe the enemy will cross by the fords below us, at Germanna or Elys." The next day proved his prophesy.[13]

During a cold, damp spring storm that was creating discomfort and mud, General Crawford informed his brigade commanders that the time had come to open the 1864 Campaign. It was hoped the misery caused by the weather was not an omen for the coming campaign. General Crawford's division would depart Culpeper around "midnight the 3rd–4th of May." The wagon trains would follow the three brigades of infantry. Crawford ordered his First Brigade commander to send a staff officer to the divisional adjutant general at midnight with a report of its position and condition. Each soldier would carry "fifty rounds and six days of rations with Bucktails in the lead." The tides of war were ready to roll.[14]

Grant's objective was to maneuver Lee from the Rapidan River into the open and defeat the Army of Northern Virginia with a decisive contest, or force his army to Richmond. If the Southern commander could not be flushed into the open, the Union superior numbers, its cavalry and artillery, would be of less value. The plan and the hope was to move the army rapidly through the dense wilderness and into the more open spaces.[15]

By the time the First Brigade arrived at Germanna Ford, the orange-red morning sun throwing slivering heat waves to either side slid gracefully into a bright blue sky. One officer recalled this Wednesday as clear and warm. After a wait that allowed the troops to make "Java," they were bouncing on the pontoon bridges crossing the Rapidan and into the other side called the "Wilderness of Virginia." Those that lived would shudder every time they heard the words "the wilderness." "Stretching 10 or 15 miles in each direction, it was an area of secondary growth, thick underbrush, deep ravines, swamps, stunted pines, and dwarf oaks, all with only three main roads which now, more often than not, were either muddy or crowded." Soldiers' letters often used the line that "the dense undergrowth is almost impenetrable." Just before he entered the wilderness, Ted Lyman of General Meade's staff noticed a different sight, "green grass, wild flowers and little green leaves opening and purple violets, in great plenty along the roadside." He also had a more macabre impression when he considered how strange it would seem if each man, destined to fall, would have worn a large badge.[16] The men were relieved that the prevailing scuttlebutt proved wrong about General Lee attacking them as they crossed the river. Perhaps he was, as reported, entrenched on the other side of Mine Run. On the Germanna Plank Road moving toward the Wilderness Tavern they noticed or remembered from past years the entangled undergrowth. The green hell![17]

Ted Gerrish would write that "man thought himself to be the noblest work of the creator, but he is the one out of harmony. In the midst of peace and joy, he prepares for strife and sorrow." John Vautier of the 88th Pennsylvania wrote in his diary that the "woods were so thick they were dark," and other times, "snakes made you jump and the exposure gave the enemy a target." The poisonous serpents were a dreaded lot. One private from Maine wrote, "man is not in love with death even in the most seductive form, but to die from snakebite must be one of the most repulsive."[18]

Before one o'clock in the afternoon on May 4, Crawford conducted his exhausted men through Wilderness Tavern to the other side where they encamped near a rough, dirt road toward Parker's Store. The men hastily threw up some tents and settled down. William Ray felt they had traveled 24 miles that day. Crawford made his headquarters in a field near the Lacy house where General Warren located his headquarters. Here was the site of the grave where Stonewall Jackson's arm was buried. He probably thought of Cedar Mountain where they first met. Everything was in place to open the Overland campaign.[19]

Crawford met Warren near his headquarters. The V Corps commander noticed the men were washing their feet and believed that the men after a good night's rest would be fine. Observing the flat landscape, Warren and Crawford discussed using flags to communicate. The division commander was given orders to march his men to Parker's Store on the Orange Plank Road the next morning, May 5. Much of the march would be through dense undergrowth and quagmire. Crawford was warned that it was imperative to use skirmish line deployment. The word was caution even though the command officers were confident that Lee's army was miles away. To assure the V Corps of safety, the Federal cavalry was near. It was a state of watchfulness but not one of anxiety.[20]

III. A Different War in a Similar Place

Each day brought different meaning to different soldiers and officers. Artillery commander Charles Wainwright reflected the personal meaning of the day for him, "This is my second anniversary of my first battle in the army; the first I went into the battle of Williamsburg; the second at Chancellorsville, and today we've been at it for the third time and the smell of gunpowder again." Crawford celebrated by rising at the usual 3:00 a.m., reveille, which came quickly on this Thursday morning, May 5, 1864. First item on the agenda each morning was Alex tending and bandaging Samuel's oozing and painful thigh. Additionally, having just returned to duty because of another attack of malaria, all precautions were deemed advisable under the conditions.[21]

S. W. Crawford's Third Division of Warren's V Corps was in the lead as it moved before 5:30 a.m. For the most part the troops felt relatively secure as it had been reported that Lee was somewhere behind the Mine Run entrenchments, a safe distance away with Union cavalry between. The marching conditions were torturous as promised. The Parker's Store path was rough and laden with entangled vegetation with the store five miles away. Samuel Crawford's division emerged from the confining undergrowth into the fields of William Chewning's farm a couple of hours later. On the march, Charles Wainwright spoke of a "kind of weird excitement and senses that seemed doubly awake to every impression."[22]

At this time Crawford still had his sights set on Parker's Store when he received orders to suspend the movement. Griffin's division on the Orange Turnpike was to guard the rear and he reported Confederates moving up the turnpike. General Grant permitted Meade to place the Union army on the turnpike, but at the time the commanders did not know how many Confederates were involved or exactly where they were located. Fred Locke, Assistant Adjutant General, informed Crawford to "halt, face Mine Run, and connect with General Wadsworth on your right." Warren needed the scattered divisions of Generals Crawford, Griffin, and Wadsworth to create a solid line of battle.[23]

From Crawford's location the battle scene did not appear in such clear-cut, simple terms. He had selected a knoll where both Parker's Store and the Orange Plank Road were visible. Both were seemingly important elements since this was the left flank of the V Corps. According to Thomson and Rauch, the Bucktails were sent out with their newly issued repeating Spencers to support the Union cavalry on the Plank Road. They were told to conceal themselves behind trees, logs, and rocks. At one point a Southern officer tried to encourage his men to charge as the enemy was only cavalry. One Rebel who had made contact yelled, "Cavalry hell, cavalry don't wear knapsacks and bucktails."[24]

About this time Crawford alerted V Corps headquarters that he had advanced to within one mile of Parker's Store. He acknowledged that "the general's order is received." He added a brief sentence that would remain a problem for him and the V Corps for the rest of the morning, "I am halted in a good position." Additionally he wrote, "There is brisk skirmishing at the Store between our and the enemy's cavalry." With cavalry in the area it was possible General Lee's forces neared the Orange Plank Road in addition to the Orange Turnpike.[25]

Lee had not played the game as expected. He was applying the hurting stick to Grant's flanks before his army was able to get into an open area or formidable line of attack. With his inferior numbers, Lee could not pause and allow the machine of destruction to smash his army. He knew the terrain, and how to use it to his advantage against a two to one manpower superiority. The Southern commander would try to maneuver his smaller, quicker army to defuse Grant's slower more cumbersome one.

The wheels were wobbling. General Charles Griffin had his division on the Orange Turnpike. General Wadsworth was working his way through the disheveled conditions to get to the left of Griffin. It seemed now that Meade intended to make a unified attack against the enemy down the Orange Turnpike. At this moment, however, nothing was fused.[26]

At 10:15 a.m. Crawford sent more disturbing news: the Rebel movement up the Orange Plank Road was not just Confederate cavalry but infantry. "The enemy are working around to get up the Plank Road." The left flank of the Union army now became Crawford's albatross. Warren was in the Orange Turnpike area working with Griffin since it was believed this would be the focus of the Rebel army advance. An hour later the Third Division commander was intensely searching. "Shall I abandon this position I now hold to connect with General Wadsworth? The Fifth Cavalry has not yet joined the fight." Crawford could not control or fight on two fronts.[27]

Warren was trying to fairly appraise the importance of the Crawford flank position. To provide better insight he decided to send his personal aide, Major Washington Roebling, to confirm the danger. Warren was being pressured by the higher command to have the Third Division hook up with Wadsworth who was over a half mile to his right and through snarled underbrush. Warren had sent a number of dispatches telling Crawford to "move as quickly as possible." After a quick glance, it did not take the trained engineer, Major Roebling, long to comprehend the importance of Crawford's flank position. He would later write, "It was the best fighting ground in the neighborhood." He reported to his boss, "our whole line of battle is turned if the enemy gets possession of it. He cannot hold the line against an attack." More troops would not be sent, but more dispatches called on Crawford to "connect, cover and protect" General Wadsworth's left as he advances.[28]

The time was nearing noon and the Third Division commander, torn between protecting the left flank and following orders from superiors, tried to do both. At noon he sent the long awaited message his corps commander wanted: "the connection with Wadsworth is being made." He obstinately finished with "the enemy hold the Plank Road and are passing up."[29]

To obey his orders, Crawford, instead of sending the entire division to Wadsworth's aid, sent First Brigade troops under Colonel William McCandless. The approximate mile march was tedious and wearisome. When the First Brigade arrived in that area, Wadsworth's front was dissolving from General Richard Ewell's right flank's pressure. "The First Brigade provided some assistance to Wadsworth's troops, but in the end the Pennsylvanians were practically surrounded and had to fight their way out. Their commander was almost captured but 'Old Buck' as the men called McCandless escaped by running a gauntlet of Rebel fire, hat in hand, ultimately unscathed."[30]

Crawford's troops were also in danger of being isolated. A messenger from the Lacy house told his staff that the enemy was moving against his advanced position. Time was limited. The troops made a left half wheel to the rear, and doubled back around a hill while under fire. The rear guard action allowed them to establish their line near the Lacy farm.[31]

The unified attack that Meade had hoped for early in the day never really fully developed. It ran out of steam by 3 p.m. The fear of losing the heights on Chewnings, which had caused anxious moments for Crawford and Washington Roebling, soon became reality. By the end of the day the estate would be in the hands of General A. P. Hill's troops and would be used later to aid the Confederate defense.[32]

Warren reported that his force attacked impetuously but was outflanked by an entire division of the enemy and was compelled to fall back to the original position. The V Corps commander felt the operation failed because General Wright's division of the VI Corps was unable to get up to protect the right flank due to the terrain.[33]

Late that night after the brigades and regiments were cared for and settled, Crawford went to receive orders for the morning of May 6. The best judgment at V Corps headquarters was that Lee would attempt to turn the Union left. It was believed that Longstreet was coming to add strength to Lee's troops. The Union V Corps was to secure a line across the Orange Turnpike with Crawford on the left and Griffin on the right. Warren told Crawford, "Replenish your ammunition tonight. When you march forward keep your line of battle perpendicular to the turnpike, keep Griffin on your right and double back your left to prevent a flank movement. You must attack at 5 a.m."[34]

When Crawford arrived back at his headquarters' tent, Sergeant Henry Minnigh of Company K, who had made a reconnaissance for the division earlier in the day, found it necessary to return through the burning woods. He awaited the general to file his report. Due to the severity of the fires, he was covered with grime, stain, and smoke. Initially Crawford did not recognize him. Once he realized who it was, Crawford told him, "We never expected to see you again." Minnigh won the gallant and meritorious service award for his efforts and was commissioned as brevet major.[35]

Back at Grant's headquarters, Ted Lyman was changing his perception about the wilderness and the nice wild flowers. Now he described it as "a thick growth of small saplings 15 to 30 feet high seldom larger than one's arm. The half grown leaves add to the obscurity, many places it is difficult to see a line of troops at fifty yards."[36]

Crawford made the last contact with his brigadiers, McCandless and Fisher, after midnight. This long day was over, but the long days were only beginning. As he lay down to rest before the three-bell wake-up call, he could hear the shrieks of the wounded. The moans, cries, and screams of men and the grating sounds of wounded beasts were a heartrending experience. At times, night pickets whose nerves were almost completely shattered shot at noises or shadows. "The smell of burning and burnt flesh was sickening." Everything was a foggy obscurity.[37]

Bruce Catton summarized the first day's fighting, "nobody could do anything right this day." It was however a "fight of invisibles against invisibles." Warren did not want to attack piecemeal but he felt pushed by Grant and Meade. Crawford and Roebling were disenchanted because they did not receive support to hold the flank or to attack A. P. Hill's troops coming up the Plank Road. Crawford hesitated at a time when the unsuspecting enemy was moving toward the Plank Road and vulnerable for attack. Even the soldiers were learning about fighting in an almost impregnable area. Private Haley wrote in his diary, "nothing could be seen but trees and bushes, except the flash of their guns and that was guide enough." The most positive outlook was given by a Bucktail, "since most soldiers die from diseases, fewer will die from illness since the casualty lists will be higher."[38]

Both armies planned to be aggressive on May 6. Lee had planned a dawn assault which included Longstreet's corps. Grant's plan had Warren and Sedgwick move from the North to overpower Ewell's troops in the South; Hancock and Wadsworth would try to destroy A. P. Hill and be cognizant of Longstreet. Burnside was to charge the area between the two Confederate flanks to support, if necessary, the most exposed flank.[39]

On the morning of May 6, between 7:00 and 7:15 a.m., Crawford's 2,000-member division moved through the woods south of Saunders' field. From just below the Orange Turnpike, the V Corps battle zone, Crawford soon informed the V Corps commander, "The enemy has a long line of entrenchment in our front. My left is strongly felt by the enemy." General Warren told him to throw back his left to strengthen it. Warren reported, "the enemy was found to be entrenched and but little impression could be made." Until he could fight as a unit, Warren was not going to attack piecemeal.[40]

Later Crawford was to join Burnside's IX Corps, but Major Roebling pointed out because of the lay of the land and roads if Crawford made the move to connect with Burnside, he would be taken away from his designated area. Roebling saw it as the wasting of precious time.[41]

The remainder of the day the Reserves spent strengthening their breastworks and firing at the enemy. In these types of conditions, this was a noxious business for Rebels and Yankees. A couple of unproductive exploratory charges attempting to find a weakness in the enemy front proved fruitless. Woodward reported that "General Crawford would not warrant the heavy sacrifice it would require. When General Warren reconnoitered, he ordered us to fall back to Lacys."[42]

On the other end of the line, the Grant plan seemed as though it was working, as Hancock and Wadsworth initially made progress. However, Wadsworth was riding his third horse when it became uncontrollable and darted toward the Confederate lines; as he tried to turn, he was shot in the back of the head. Again, after the loss of a leader, the charge slowed and ultimately ceased. The II Corps was overrun by Longstreet's countercharge. At a decisive moment in this charge, visions of déjà vu for the Confederacy raised their ugly head as James Longstreet was wounded by his own men only a few miles from where Stonewall Jackson had been shot by his men almost exactly a year earlier. The wound, darkness, and exhaustion all stopped the Longstreet charge. While propped against a tree and choking on his own blood, he tried to get out the command, "tell Major Fields to go straight on." Just what Robert Lee did not need, another reliable Southern commander to try to replace. The throat wound of Longstreet was reported as "serious but not fatal." These were the words spoken to the commanding general concerning Jackson's injury. "The old workhorse" would live and be back by early autumn. He would remain by General Lee's side for the duration.[43]

As twilight was passing, Crawford's Reserves were ordered to give aid to John Sedgwick, who had been attacked and was struggling to keep his line from breaking. Warren reported that Crawford went on the "double quick" and succeeded in helping Sedgwick secure his line. Crawford's men arrived back in their old camp at 2 a.m., ending another long and weary day.[44]

Chapter Fourteen

The end of the day's fighting "remained indecisive." Artillery Brigade Commander Charles Wainwright wrote in his journal: "Warren failed to shake Ewell's Corps and at night both sides dug entrenchments."[45]

Again the screams of the wounded persisted, and the smell of men and horses who could not crawl or stumble quickly enough to escape the burning flames permeated the air. Even burying one's nose in blankets or Mother Earth could not alleviate the smell of the burning, charred flesh. The men listening to the desperate cries hoped they would not receive a leg wound that would prevent them from escaping the inferno. The high Union command realized that in this environment, under these conditions, victory was too elusive and would come at a higher cost than expected or desired. Tactically the Union arrangement was partially going as planned. Lee's army was diminishing, but the price was very high. The job now was to find another battlefield that provided an opportunity to do more than be involved in a stalemate with the loss of approximately 17 percent casualties. Grant confided in his aide Horace Porter that he could not hope to gain an advantage in "this forest." The horrors could not be described nor could they be forgotten.[46]

General Meade in his Official Report for May 6 reported, "the attacks were made without any particular success on the part of the Fifth or Sixth Corps." Later he added, "the Lieutenant General Commanding directed a further movement [on the 7th] toward Spotsylvania court house…" The Battle of the Wilderness terminated this phase of Operation Overland. It had been difficult at all levels of command. The enlarged divisions made command more difficult to employ, move, and logistically maintain. They were fighting a foe who knew how to use the terrain to their advantage. As one historian said, "It was a case of on the job training."[47]

On May 7 the cruel, unforgiving fighting in the Wilderness ended after just two long, exasperating, and bloody days. There were 17,500 fewer Union soldiers traveling toward the road center and Spotsylvania. Confederate casualties were estimated in the 12,000 range. The commander understood what had happened, "more desperate fighting has not been witnessed on this continent. At present we can claim no victory over the enemy, neither have they gained a single advantage."[48]

Wainwright wrote that he had seen Warren's orders commanding the whole army to move during the night to Lee's right. He took advantage of the inside knowledge and had his troops prepare early as he was going to lead the troops as soon as it was dark. The entire mass was to unite around Spotsylvania. Now the soldiers fought war in the form of a foot race. If the Union army could get to Spotsylvania, about 12 miles south, it would be between General Lee and Richmond. The Southern commander would be forced to attack or retreat. On the other hand, if the Confederates won the race, and they had a decided advantage with the inside track, it meant more fighting for road possession or moving farther to the right.[49]

Before the night march, Crawford's men had to fight a reconnaissance mission before preparing to march. On the morning of May 7, artillery fire was heard in front of the V Corps; it was feared Ewell was going to attack. Warren ordered Crawford to "probe and strike" the enemy to determine Lee's intentions. Colonel McCandless took some men with their dirty, mud-stained, sort-of-blue uniforms to track down the enemy. After driving skirmishers from rifle pits back to the main line, they judged Lee had not withdrawn and that the "Enemy is in considerable force."[50]

The V Corps passed in Hancock's rear, passed Lacy's place and leaving Lacy's they contacted the Brock Road. The men had fought hard all day and then marched almost all night, at least those that could walk; others rode in ambulances and wagons. Many that walked slept as they marched. First the route led east, as in a retreat, and then they turned south toward Lee's right and the promise of more fighting near a little village with a number of key roads.

Some time before Ted Gerrish had written, "We had expected so much from General Grant and now he was defeated like the other generals before him." Then patience and trust would be rewarded. As the commanding general made the turn south, all was forgiven. "Many of the brave men wept like school boys over our grave situation." The bull dog would keep ripping and tearing. The tenacious Grant would not retreat, nor would he allow the adversary to catch his breath. As he and his staff rode past the troops, he received his first applause from the Army of the Potomac.[51]

Not retreating was exhilarating news but, while the darkness was used as a screen, it was a 12- to15-mile march filled with the extreme hazards of night marching. The men marched "one step at a time." Wainwright wrote about the misery of that night: "the night was so dark every lighted pipe could be seen distinctively. My horse could not see where he was stepping and once he went up a bank and fell backwards. Some places on the road the water was an inch deep. The night was dark; the march was painful."[52]

General Warren complained of two delays that cost his corps over four hours due to Meade's cavalry escort blocking their way. After marching most of the night, the troops stopped two and one-half miles from their intended destination.[53]

Of course, the strategy of unrelenting pursuit would be carried out by humans made of flesh, blood, and nerves. They slept while walking and tried to ignore the stench of rotting animal and human flesh.

John Vautier had "tripped over unseen dead bodies, fell into pools of blood, slept on wet ground in the rain, marched in mud and through swamps, saw the dying being read the Bible, and saw veterans fire at imaginary foes."[54]

General Lee did not fully comprehend the Union movement immediately, but when he realized what was happening he knew he could get to Spotsylvania with haste. He did.

As the morn of the eighth slid into day, the heat and dust of the march replaced the blackness. The residue smoke of the forest fires was still suffocating. Straggling became a problem. In spite of all the adversity, by 8 a.m. the Yankees were on a hill three miles from Spotsylvania, so close yet so far away originally. Lee had not guessed correctly, but he reacted quickly in getting his men into position. He maintained the inner circle and refused to fall back to Richmond. General Grant had not yet forced him into the open. The opposing policies of genius and hammering continued.[55]

Ted Gerrish remembered that day's Sabbath was especially "sacred in that it had been the resurrection of the Prince of Peace and those he died to save were engaged in deadly war."[56]

On Sunday, May 8, as Warren's corps reached an area around Todd's Tavern, the men heard rifle fire, which turned out to be the charge by the V Corps, First and Second Divisions. Crawford reined in his horse, Blood, on a field on the Alsop farm at about 11 a.m. Ahead, almost a quarter mile away, was an extension of this field and then a rise, later called Laurel Hill, on the Spindle farm. Crawford was given the assignment to push his men into a void created in an earlier charge by General John Robinson and Griffin's division in the battle for Laurel Hill. From the outset the omens were harsh; finally Crawford had all in readiness to charge when a noise of a cracking tree limb came from above. Neither he nor Blood were able to react quickly enough, and he was hit in the head by a top of a tree which had been cut off by cannon fire. Only a short time earlier a couple of Reserves had been killed in a similar accident. Alex came to his side immediately. The blood appeared to be coming from the ears and mouth, but upon closer examination a large gash was discovered in his head. The division commander wanted to continue, but was finally convinced the wound should be cared for. Crawford handed the division command to William McCandless and more bad luck as the First Brigade commander then suffered a severe hand wound while approaching a second line of trenches. The wound forced McCandless to leave the field. Colonel Fisher was absent due to illness, therefore command fell on Colonel William Talley. Confusion reigned supreme. His men fought in knee-deep mud, in a swamp, while being raked by artillery fire.[57]

General Warren placed himself in jeopardy by trying to rally his men at the Spindle farm, but even the hands-on leadership did not work.[58]

When Crawford returned, his division made a charge but was forced to retreat. About the only thing they had to show for the day's march and the evening fight was the 12th Alabama colors and many prisoners. The Sabbath ended with very little success but much frustration.[59]

The time after midnight found Warren in a melancholy mood. "We have not gained the junction of the Catharpin road. The men straggle back into the woods fatigued and wounded. I have done my best but with the force I have I cannot attack unless I see a great weakness on the enemy's left flank. Colonel Locke is badly wounded in the face, Colonel Ryan is killed, my staff is tired out, I have lost my old white horse, I am out of ammunition and what ambulances can be spared? Ultimately, I cannot gain Spotsylvania with what force I have." The commander had done what he could against the Confederate forces, but nature had been cruel again. His negative thinking was obvious when he indicated to a staff member the day before that if anything happened to him, General Crawford was the next in command. The infantry men also understood the frustration and pain. "We fought all afternoon, gained nothing, lost nothing but men."[60]

A few days ago the V Corps commander wanted to await troop arrivals and he was overruled; now he put them into battle line as they arrived, and both resulted in negative consequences. At Laurel Hill Warren had worn out himself and his troops and the results were negligent.[61]

With Spotsylvania only a tantalizing few miles away, the commanding generals, Meade and Grant, were resolute in their mindset to clear the road and move into the village. As the clock neared seven in the evening, Crawford, with units from the VI Corps, was ordered to turn Richard Anderson's right flank. Darkness neared and the troops were tangled "in the jungle." And before they could obtain a formidable fighting formation, the Anderson Rebels, with an enormous lift from the newly arrived Ewell Corps, swept the flank. In the melee Colonel William Talley was taken prisoner, the Reserve line crumbled, and the Spotsylvania area remained in Southern hands. General Warren's comments in his Official Report showed the strain continued to take its toll: "I am so sleepy I can hardly write intelligently, badly whipped and very tired. The Rebels are as tired as we are."[62]

The collapse of the charge ended the Sabbath in the minds of the Reserves. At least they could now eat a warm meal, something they had not done for some time. When they arrived back at camp tired, hungry, and "down right miserable," they looked forward first to a steaming cup of coffee and then some food for growling stomachs, only to discover someone had stolen their provisions. They vowed that if the perpetrators were found, they would be relieved of at least one week's rations. Furthermore, they asserted it shook their confidence in the theory that only "blue coats and pretty ladies go to heaven," but now they could not vouch for the honesty of bluecoats. "We said our prayers a little and forgave them, but if we find out the regiment, they will have nothing to eat for a week."[63]

Fatigue and battle conditions were fraying nerves at all levels. Grant had unnerved Meade. Meade had a verbal exchange with Sheridan, who lashed out at Warren, while Griffin had words in Grant's presence on May 5. Warren placed some of the blame on Griffin and Crawford and then lambasted Grant and Meade for the senseless fighting. A victory would aid morale and soothe nerves as would a day without combat. For the army, the prayer would be answered to a large extent on May 9. In the executive mansion President Abraham Lincoln asked "the friends of the Union and Liberty to unite in common thanksgiving and prayer to almighty God for previous guidance of army operations and for what remains undone."[64]

The intense labor of commanding a division with an open, seeping, wound, which at times was extremely painful, especially when riding his horse, Blood, created a more irritable Crawford. The staff surely noticed how he took careful means to mount and dismount. The fear of the return of malaria was always present.[65]

At this moment the soldiers who had fought since early May were feeling like nothing more than a pure unadulterated number, a body to be sacrificed in rain, mud, heat, and hell. Even their faith was being challenged as one trooper spewed out, "God brought us here, created this hell, closed his eyes, and turned his head." And the worse was yet to come.[66]

The Pennsylvania Reserves had additional issues. The First Brigade had lost the one commander they trusted above all others, and they could not forget that their three-year enlistments finished in a few weeks. They had pride in their accomplishments and their fighting unit, but some were looking forward to May 15 while the remainder heard that the officers were working on a plan that would request that they stay until the end of May. They were torn in many directions by their pride, patriotism and the hope to live a little longer than May 31. They wanted to leave remembered as brave soldiers, but they wanted to leave. Meade, Humphreys, and Crawford worked on the formula for release.[67]

During the afternoon and evening of May 9, the V Corps received the news that they had lost two of the fine patriots of their cause. Dying in a Confederate hospital without regaining consciousness, General James Wadsworth succumbed to a bullet that had entered his brain on May 6. The distinguished, gray-haired gentleman from New York had given his life and fortune for his country, and as a respected loyal Unionist. Wainwright wrote that the "confederates trampled his lifeless body." To honor him the Union provided him with a "major generalship posthumously."[68]

"Uncle John," as his men called General Sedgwick, had a jovial manner and unique smile. He had just finished chiding his troops about Confederate sharpshooters not being able to hit an elephant at that distance. One of those sharpshooters proved him wrong as he placed a ball in his chest. Sedgwick died on May 9, 1864, the second significant loss of Union officers that day. One Reserve would speak for many of the Union soldiers when he indicated that the death of General Sedgwick would be felt by the entire Union army. General Andrew Humphreys eulogized him as "highly esteemed an honest hearted man and courageous." Soldiers expressed their respect for some of their officers in different ways. One soldier went to view Sedgwick's embalmed body. Proving he scanned the general, he wrote, "he looked natural; the bullet entered an inch below the eye and near the nose."[69] His headquarter's flag covered his body.

For much of the V Corps May 9 was used in preparation for the next day, ammunition and rations were distributed, and for the most part the men relaxed. The exception was an order given to Crawford's Reserves who were to make a charge to determine the strength of the foe in their front. They made a forceful advance at the Southern entrenchments and soon returned, finding the Rebels very securely guarded by enfilading artillery. The Reserves were unable to determine for certain if any Confederates had been dispersed.[70]

Crawford received orders from Warren for Tuesday, May 10. The Union forces would try to clear the entire southern line of entrenchments. For some reason, it was the normally cautious Warren who now informed Meade he thought he could break the Confederate center with some help from the II Corps. "Both sides were preparing for a life and death grapple tomorrow."[71]

IV. A Day You Wished to Forget and Could Not

Today the V Corps would make an all-out attack on the Laurel Hill trenches. One soldier would characterize this day, Tuesday, May 10, as one of "hard fighting and heavy losses without a commensurate gain." Warren opened the ball on the 10th with artillery bombardment. The artillery played freely upon the enemy position but to not much avail. The divisions of the V Corps under Generals Griffin, Cutler, and Crawford waited in entrenchments for orders to charge.[72]

When the Reserves were ordered to move, they were still hit by Rebel artillery even as they prepared to get into position to make a charge. Warren called for another response from his artillery and when he believed the

Southern guns had been silenced, the Reserves were ordered toward the Rebel trenches on Laurel Hill once more. The Third Division commander slipped skirmishers into the area to determine the effect of the Union guns. About 8:30 in the morning he reported "steadily advancing as you desire." An hour later Crawford informed his corps commander that his right wing was within grasp of the Confederates and his left pushing through the woods. "When the lines are connected, I shall feel strongly for the enemy."[73] Warren responded, "form your line close and don't assault until we get the others up." When General Cutler came to Crawford's left, Warren, again, had the Rebel line shelled, but the gun emplacements positioned by the Rebel artillery leader, General Porter Alexander, were secure and his guns pinned the two divisions with grape and canister. The Confederate position behind earthworks on Laurel Hill did not seem to be a weak spot in Lee's line. Warren called off the offense as he had lost 400 men and gained nothing. The V Corps was being torn apart "bit by bit" by secluded assaults.[74] The breastworks were welcomed security after the charges. Many of the soldiers disagreed with Company K's theory that "they were d——d beautiful works for somebody else to fight behind."[75]

The day was not over however, as the higher command was convinced that there was a weakness in Lee's line. Beginning at 4 p.m. the Union line would charge the Southern stronghold in three separate attacks lasting until after 7 p.m.[76]

By 3:30 p.m. everything was in preparedness in spite of the fact the Reserves had fought most of the day. The men could see that an open field had to be traversed and then a ravine, thickly covered with heavy timber and underbrush. Most of the area could be scraped by Southern artillery. The veteran troops did not like what they saw.[77]

About 5 p.m. the next charge was to be initiated, but Warren convinced Meade it should be made now. With help, Warren now believed that Laurel Hill could be taken. General John Gibbon, with the II Corps, was to join in the charge. He inspected the line with Warren and agreed with Warren's men that a charge under these conditions was folly. In his words, "it was a dense piece of woods where dead cedar trees were spread about, their stiff ragged arms standing out like so many bayonets in such a way that any movement by a line of battle was entirely out of question. Beyond this were the enemy trenches we could not see and could judge location only by the sound of musketry from it." In Gibbon's eyes a charge could not be made, but Warren disagreed, and they were forced to explain their differences to General Meade. After listening to the two men, he sided with Warren. Gibbon wrote, "I rode to a place where I could exercise no control over my division. They made a feasible effort to get through the woods and stem the storm of bullets, and then gave it up."[78]

The Reserves had been ordered to give a Union "hurrah" as they stepped out to alert the troops on both sides to charge at the same time. It was called a "mournful cheer." None of the troops really made an all-out charge. "The deadly and rapid fire decimated the Reserves."[79]

Sharp-pronged cedar branches caused the men to scatter, and those who tried to crawl through had their flesh torn and were slowed considerably. The Rebels hit them first with double canister and then with musket fire from behind the gun placements. Pine needles caught on fire and the men were choked by the smoke and some caught on fire. Several Reserves got to within 300 feet of the entrenchments. They returned from the killing fields in disorder and panic.[80]

General Hancock was sent to conduct a charge which never got off the ground until after 7 p.m. In his intense mood Crawford became highly anguished, "This is sheer madness and can end only in wanton destruction and certain repulse." In most cases the men of the V Corps had had enough. "The highest ranked officer to examine the vicinity was a brigade commander."[81]

With almost no aid on either side, Griffin's troops did not leave their entrenchments; Crawford's men left but stumbled back quickly, stunned and disheartened. Even Warren tried to rally the men, but it was to no avail, their spirits were broken. In his report, Warren would say, "made an assault toward dark but not very vigorously made and no result." From the soldier's point of view, "We feared being led to slaughter." The weather was frightful—water, blood, dirt, more rain, pain and blood, but it was blood that would finally run dry.[82]

The contests were most furious, indecisive in results and ceased by mutual consent, according to Woodward. Colonel Wainwright, a distant observer, wrote, Crawford's troops "behaved badly, suffered much and did nothing. Cutler did little better. General Rice was killed. I hope that Warren will not repeat his stay at home order." Grant reported, "Warren was repulsed with heavy loss."[83]

The exhaustion caused by the fighting on the 10th brought a much deserved day of rest on May 11. That morning and afternoon a blessed and cursed rain fell, feeling cold and miserable to some while bringing relief to others. At night it turned to a mist, like God was covering the scene from the eyes of humanity.

The Reserves likely were told that Jeb Stuart had been mortally wounded by Sheridan's troops. This news was counted only as a rumor as Stuart had been reported captured or killed so frequently that they thought it was a "cry of wolf." He seemed like a romantic figure that would live on forever. Samuel Crawford could recall a lot of stories about James Ewell Brown Stuart because they had served on the frontier together in his early years and were opponents more times than Crawford wanted to recall. The death was later confirmed, and they thought now he would sing "Jine the cavalry" to the person in the white robe at the Pearly Gates. Would he be wearing a hat provided by a Pennsylvania general? The South had lost their "fabled cavalier." Richmond and much of the Southern army mourned and "southern morale was damaged."[84]

May 12 began in a funeral silence shrouded by fog for the Union troops, who would later charge a Confederate salient in a driving rain. They could not know what lay ahead nor would they have wished such knowledge. The Union troops under the direction of General Hancock carried the salient, the center of Lee's line and with it, according to General Meade, 20 guns and 3,000 prisoners. Hancock's men came close to cutting Lee's army in half, but the Rebels fought furiously to regain some ground and prevent their army from being divided.[85]

The human side was nearly unbearable. One soldier wrote of the sickening sight, "horses and men were chopped into hash and appeared like piles of jelly." Rufus Dawes said it was "the most terrible 24 hours of service in the war. The frightful scenes of the last week make my heart almost like stone."[86]

The role of the V Corps was to occupy the trenches that Hancock had abandoned. Crawford's men were the only original division left with Warren when he received orders to make a charge to relieve the pressure from Hancock. Early in the morning, Crawford sent out skirmishers as ordered. The V Corps commander shelled the enemy with a long-range bombardment, but he was reluctant to commit his infantry. As he received notes from Meade to make the charge, he intensified the artillery fire. Warren knew the strength of Laurel Hill, and he was concerned that his flank would be turned if he moved forward. By 8:30 a.m. Warren could no longer convince Meade the attack would be a nonproductive entity, so he sent part of his corps toward Laurel Hill to probe one more time. Crawford was ordered, "charge the entrenchments with all your force. Do it." As Meade's temper rose, he added, "Do it regardless of the consequences." Warren reiterated the order verbatim. The men charged the Confederate stronghold a number of times before being forced back. General Warren believed that they had lost all spirit for that kind of work. Woodward reported, "we went to their breast works, planted our banner, but a terrible fire and their stubborn resistance drove us back." Crawford took charge of the picket line only to witness the Confederates placing more artillery. During a pause in the action, John Vautier had an opportunity to watch the Bucktails perform one of their favorite stunts. "Two would lay on the ground facing the enemy with weapons in ready position. Another 'Tail' would run from tree to tree until one of the enemy stood up to shoot him. The two would then blast the unexpecting Reb." Later Cutler's men moved beside Crawford's but neither charged with much fervor.[87]

When May 12 was over, the maneuvers had accomplished nothing, except, as one soldier wrote, "To add more names to the long list of disabled." Warren wrote, "The enemy direct and flank fire were too destructive."[88]

Warren's assessment that Laurel Hill was unassailable had been, to say the least, accurate. The weak point the powers-that-be searched for was not in the vicinity of the V Corps. There had been little reason to doubt Warren and the judgment of his men and officers.

The Union had fought 22 hours for a piece of land not a quarter mile across. The rain continued to fall as Dawes wrote his wife, "I am with hope to pass safely and the battle must soon be renewed."

On May 11 Grant telegraphed Major General Halleck that the army had lost 11 general officers as casualties and probably 20,000 men. That was after six days of fighting and did not include the losses of the 12th.[89]

General Gibbon, analyzing May 12, noted, "the success of our assault formed an era in the operations of the campaign." He then noted that "the foresight of the enemy to construct interior breastworks and their persistent valor prevented our complete success."[90]

General Meade was preparing a statement to the troops to be issued on Friday the 13th. He would be cheerleader and commander.

> For eight days and nights, almost without intermission, in rain and sunshine, you have been gallantly fighting a desperate foe, in positions naturally strong and rendered doubly so by intrenchments... Your heroic deeds and noble endurance of fatigue and privation will ever be memorable. The foe has suffered the loss of 18 guns, 22 colors, and 8,000 prisoners, including 2 general officers.[91]

General Meade finished his thoughts by focusing the attention of the Union troops on the future, "Soldiers! Your work is not over, the enemy must be pursued and if possible, overcome.... While we mourn the loss of many gallant comrades, let us remember the enemy has suffered equal, if not greater losses. We shall soon receive re-enforcements which he cannot expect. Let us determine, then, to continue vigorously the work so well begun, and, under God's blessing, in a short time the object of our labors will be accomplished."[92]

ஒ **Chapter Fifteen** ௧

The Summer of 1864

I. "The floor is covered with an inch of mud, the roof leaks, there are signs of blood, but it seems like a blessing."[1]

On Friday, May 13, the rains continued; some soldiers rested; the surgeons did not. General Crawford, in the absence of cavalry, was sent into the Spindle farm to determine if Lee had moved. A row of fire was visible and the picket line strengthened. This was the second day of exploration. The musket fire that was returned was proof that the Rebels were still rooted. Many of the Union men constructed breastworks all day and marched all night. Grant noted, "we must get by the right flank of the enemy for the next fight."[2]

The soldiers marched before the rations arrived. With no campfires and as little noise as possible, Warren moved his corps from the right past the rear to the left of Burnside to become the Union left flank. The Third Division was held in reserve; they would be the last out of their "homes" at midnight. The roads were slippery and the mist made the darkness "pitch black." At one point, the Reserves reported mud knee-deep. After crossing the waist-deep Ni River, guides met the V Corps and told the leaders to follow the fires they had built to lead to the Beverly house. However, the rain doused some of the fires, making the march even more difficult. Some men were carrying their shoes as the deep mud and suction could strip them from their owners. A number of times when someone fell in the mud their fellow marchers reported it sounded much like an old log falling. Ted Gerrish in General Charles Griffin's First Division wrote, "we marched all night in the mud and rain. Those events are burned upon our life's experiences, and can never be forgotten." Artillery Colonel Charles Wainwright added, "the whole country is a sea of mud."[3]

The attack scheduled for 4 a.m. on the 14th had only a few men in position to carry it out, and so was cancelled for now. However, Grant would not give up so easily. He sincerely believed Lee's army was ready to crack as soon as a way was found to get the Rebels out of their entrenchments.[4]

The ledgers of the casualties were complete. In less than 10 days of fighting and marching the Northern army had lost an average of 370 casualties a day and Lee's army was still a force, but the new rules of warfare were reducing his numbers as planned. William Ray of the Iron Brigade wrote, "This has been an awful battle or it will be when finished." Another soldier wrote, "the slaughter was so sickening that the heart heaves at the details."[5] The old adage was holding true: In war a man is nothing and he is everything.

On Sunday, the 15th, Crawford said farewell to the 75 members of the undermanned 8th Pennsylvania. They had decided not to honor the request to serve until a later date. In early May, Crawford had notified Warren that he had a sense they would not remain with the others. Those that remained in their units to do more fighting were thinking of home in another way. Oliver Wendell Holmes wrote his parents, "Immense has been the butcher's bill." On the Southern side Lieutenant Colonel Charles Veneable wrote, "My God send us peace and stop this fearful carnage."[6]

May 17 found God smiling in the form of a warm spring day: "It was a clear and pleasant day." It broke the gloom and doom of days of cold rain and desolation. Crawford and the Reserves were camped along the Fredericksburg Pike on the Beverly farm on the army's left flank when the attention of the army turned toward the Mule Shoe in "hell's half acre." Tomorrow another try to unseat Lee's army would occur there. To accomplish the mission, the troops would have to cross open fields, descend down ravines, traverse a marsh, and mount a long slope—all the while being hit with Ewell's artillery and infantry. Grant now believed that this was Lee's weak spot, but for the II and VI Corps it was too much artillery, too strong breastworks, and no weakness. It would be the same devastating frontal assault story reenacted one more time. Afterward Grant would realize he had to "seek more promising fields." He would try again to get Lee out of the entrenchments and fight the Union army in the open.[7]

On the 18th, the II and VI Corps were to charge as Warren unlocked the artillery. Smoke from the friendly cannon fire gave obscurity to the Bucktails who dug entrenchments with bayonets. A Southern artillery battery was their objective. Soon the two sides fraternized and before firing would give verbal warning to "watch out thar yank." They also traded coffee and newspapers. However, the Rebels sent a newspaper with everything of note clipped out. General Griffin caught them and ordered them to have an artillery battery fire on the enemy. The men did so reluctantly.[8]

The day of the 19th passed in "unusual quietness" until near dark. Sharp musket fire alerted the Union troops that the Confederates were attempting to turn their right flank. Crawford was ordered to attack the Confederates in a way to get between the Confederate commander and the Ni River to prevent the escape of his corps. Colonel Martin Hardin, new commander of Crawford's First Brigade, sent the Bucktails across as skirmishers; they pushed north along the river. After capturing a handful of Southern troops and their leader, darkness set in and Ewell's escape route remained intact. Grant expressed his disappointment at Ewell's escape.[9]

On the 20th, a day of beauty around the Beverly house, the Reserves wrote letters, read, and picked farm berries. Some details were assigned to bury the fallen. The evening of May 20 Crawford was given orders for the following morning to move the army toward the James River. The Third Division would move to Massaponax Church and turn south on Telegram Road. If Hancock was attacked, the V Corps was to support him, if not, the troops should continue south toward North Anna River, located near Hanover Junction, "a stop on the Richmond, Fredericksburg, and Potomac Railroad." Winfield Hancock's corps was being used as bait to pull Lee out of the trenches by showing a move toward Richmond.[10]

The soldiers in Warren's corps had to crawl out of their trenches so as not to be detected. Regardless, they were just glad to leave and begin anew somewhere else. It would be the North Anna. For two weeks a series of battles had been fought and thousands died to hold this land. After all the spilled blood they were sneaking away. Wainwright wrote in his journal, "properly speaking Spotsylvania was one battle, but it bore the likeness of an irregular siege since all engagements were actual assaults on works."[11]

After a number of changes in orders, the V Corps followed the II Corps toward Guinea Station on the Fredericksburg Pike. Sweat, dust, dirt, and grunge caked on their faces, in their noses, and ears. They would arrive at the Station in the early evening of the 21st.[12]

Hardin's brigade was leading the division, and by the time they arrived there was a fight for Guinea Station. Hardin sent the 6th and 13th Reserves into the tussle. The cheers from the Union troops, "go in Bucktails and give 'em fits," livened their step. Soon the battle with Confederate cavalry was finished and Guinea was in the hands of the men in blue.[13]

A special place for bivouac was selected for the V Corps. They camped between the two main roads into the town, near water. A number wrote of the clover fields, and they scoured the fence rows for berries and game.

Crawford made his headquarters in Mud Tavern near Telegraph Road. During the night a number of units heard wagons, but never assumed they were enemy as they thought their cavalry was patrolling the roads. Such was not the case, as it was later realized; the enemy had used the road as a retreat route. At 2 a.m. on the 22nd, Warren ordered Crawford to "send a patrol to try to locate the enemy." In a half mile they ran into enemy skirmishers and in another half mile they ran into many more Rebels. In the process, Vautier reported, "We built breastworks twice and then fell back."[14]

Grant's army would move south, around the rear of the Rebels' right flank again. The big slow-moving tortoise with its long lines of troops, guns, and trains was on its way to the North Anna. Once Lee and his staff knew it was not a ploy, the "Rebel quick rabbit" sprinted to the river to await the adversary again. Perhaps George G. Meade said what many were thinking, "I am afraid the rebellion cannot be crushed this summer."[15]

II. On the Road to Jericho

At one point on the march, the V Corps was close to being ambushed and so afterward each and every home and barn was searched. Some of the stragglers were taken prisoner. The Confederates had an advantage of about three and a half hours. Lee was on his way to the North Anna. The river intersected the Rebel capital and the Union army.

On May 23 Crawford and his men left their bivouac area about 5 a.m. and strolled a rather leisurely six miles, rested, and then went to an area where they built fires, and "perked" coffee. Dawes lamented that he had not changed clothes since May 3 nor had a good night's sleep since taking regimental command (May 7). They then headed for Jericho Mills where many versions of the biblical story were told and on one occasion acted out before crossing of the North Anna. The body of water presented a number of problems; the banks were about 100 feet high on either side with a 150-foot crossing in about four feet of water. The men forded the swift current with their shoes and stockings on their bayonets, as the artillery and other infantry crossed on the pontoon bridges. Lee, not expecting a crossing at this point, had left it unprotected.[16]

Once across, Crawford managed to keep to the river's edge until they reached the fields of the Fontaine farm where the men dug entrenchments.

The Rebels were able to pull cannons to the south of Crawford's men and unloaded chaos. The bombardment made a number of the soldiers recall Gettysburg. Woodward noted the fight, "We crossed and found the enemy in force. After some shelling they advanced their infantry but were repulsed." In his journal, Wainwright wrote that his artillery had saved the day. That night Meade wrote a congratulatory note to General Warren and his gallant corps for "the handsome manner in which you repulsed the enemy's attack."[17]

One of Crawford's virtues had always been that of personal bravery. As a brigade and division leader, he tried to make himself visible to calm the fears of his men. For some reason, never mentioned anywhere, it was here that he momentarily lost that virtue and set the poorest example as he and his staff were reported by some Pennsylvania Reserves as riding away, "spurring his horse and never wishing us the best." It is the only recorded time that he lost his nerve; it had not happened before nor would it happen again. The reason for the black mark on his behavior will always remain a mystery. Was it the wound, was it too much wilderness, or was it momentary uncontrollable fear? He never revealed his reasons for his behavior nor did any of his staff. John Vautier in his diary indicated that some officers' horses that were grazing stampeded and perhaps the general and his staff left because of that threat.[18]

A. P. Hill fought a back and forth battle with the Union troops. On the 24th the Reserves were ordered to Oxford, Lee's primary defense, to disperse some Rebels to allow General Burnside's troops to cross. About halfway to their destination was a mill called Quarles. Here the 1st Regiment clashed with the enemy. Wainwright reported that "Crawford got pretty roughly handled." The Reserves made a couple of unsuccessful charges. The division commander then had a horseshoe-type defense built to protect the ford for Crittenden's Northern troops who were about to cross. General Hancock also sent help. After a number of attacks from different positions failed, the Union command realized Lee was determined to hold his strengthened position.[19]

To Lee's amazement, he faced a Union army that was split. His ideal plan was developing as he hoped. He had only to decide the most advantageous point to attack to create disaster. Then fate, not Lee, took command. Night and day, for more than a month, Lee had been physically and emotionally challenged and drained. Finally it all caught up with him in the form of cramps and diarrhea. This day in which he normally would have exerted his leadership ability to take advantage of the fragile Union situation, Lee remained in his tent with debilitating pain. The "strong hand at the tiller" was not present. His army, without their leader, ended in Rebel charges that were uncoordinated and repulsed.[20]

The Army of the Potomac evacuated the southern bank of the North Anna in phases. The Union army would go back across the river again, headed toward Richmond. Ted Gerrish understood the progression. "We secretly recrossed the North Anna and began another flanking movement. A renewal of an old experience, fight all day and march all night."[21]

III. Bethesda Church

In the third week of May, General S. W. Crawford had to use his negotiating skills learned at the U.S. Embassy in Mexico. The three-year term of most of the Pennsylvania Reserves ended at different times. The general appealed to the men to accept the May 31 departure calculated by General Meade so the men could go home as a unit. They made the decision "to see the old division through." Crawford and his brigade commanders expressed their gratitude for their loyalty and dedication. As an expression of thanks for their devotion they marched to the Virginia Central Railroad where groups of the men would lift and turn the rails while another group stacked the ties and created a bonfire; the rails were piled in the middle of the flames, bent double, or if a tree was handy, they created a "bow tie." Lee had used this set of rails to receive a large portion of supplies and reinforcements.[22]

"On the 29th two guards were sent to protect a home in the area. When the Confederate pickets drove the Union away, the southern soldiers shot both men without intercession by the owners. After the Yanks recaptured the area the men were so angry and uncontrollable that they went into the home and smashed almost every valuable." John Vautier, however, was not into the trashing but did find some molasses and salted fish in the cellar.[23]

After marching and countermarching for a few days, sometimes extensively, the Pennsylvania Reserves neared Bethesda Church on May 30, 1864.

Lee, after losing the opportunity to split Grant's army, was searching for a soft spot in the Union lines.

Aware that their service time had almost cleared the hour glass and that this would probably be their last fight, the Reserves wanted to make it memorable. They busied themselves creating breastworks and were then ordered to charge the Rebels who were in nearby woods—a charge that failed. The Confederate countercharge hit the Reserves' exposed flanks.[24] Reinforcements had failed to show. The Rebel charge was achieving its objective, but for some unexplained reason the Rebels ceased their attack. The Reserves used the time to rebuild rifle pits with stones, fence rails, and soil. Crawford used the unusual tactic of placing a man in a tree to report the enemy movements. The reinforcements with cannon and infantry arrived on the flanks and the new breastworks were concealed by a fence and bushes. It was nearly 6 p.m. when the Rebel skirmishers made their way in front of the leading elements of General Jubal Early's corps. The strongly enforced 2,400 Reserves rested quietly until the enemy reached a fence, a hundred yards distant, then they opened with grape, canister, and musket fire that devastated the oncoming Rebels. They came "three times and three times their flag was shot down."[25]

After the Confederates realized what awaited them, they became Rebels without a yell. The Reserves remembered that they came in silence. As the charge died, Crawford jumped on the breastworks and led a counterassault that faded with the darkness. He was later given the sword of an officer from North Carolina who had been killed in the charge. "The only enemy we found was torn and shapeless." Most of the men recalled a color bearer who came to the fence only to be torn to pieces by a cannon ball. Showing the guile of the Confederate soldiers, another cohort secured the flag briefly, and then fell. The day belonged to the proven courageous Pennsylvania Reserves. "It was a proper ending," boosted one Reserve. Woodward remembered, "throw down your arms come in and be spared." Four hundred did.[26]

John Vautier's company was sent on skirmish line duty. Many dead enemies lay in the front, one rather close, so he crawled to the body and "got a watch, a pipe and some other articles and admitted to shooting 65 rounds that day." Dawes hit a nerve when he wrote, "this battle breathed the inspiration of victory, a tonic needed to a weary soldier."[27]

The Reserves would always recall the slaughter of a corps of Rebels by their force numbering only a third of the enemy. "The next morning, 31 May, we buried our fallen comrades and those of the enemy on a field of honor. They sleep peacefully their last sleep side by side." A few days later in the *Philadelphia Inquirer* they recalled it was one time the Rebels ran in silence without their famous yell, almost as though they knew their fate.[28]

IV. Saying Good-bye

It finally happened, the day the Reserves could say their good-byes and travel back to their loved ones in Pennsylvania. They were thinner, as were their ranks, but they held their heads high in light of their accomplishments. General Warren wrote the Reserves, "The General Commanding begs leave to express to you his great satisfaction at your heroic conduct in this arduous campaign."[29]

The light in the divisional headquarters' tent probably burned long into the night and was lit early each morning for the past few days. Samuel would have wanted to express to his Pennsylvania Reserves his appreciation for their significant contribution to this war, to their state, and his deep appreciation for their efforts. He wrote and rewrote, and Robert McCoy, assistant adjutant, placed notes in the margins and along the sides of his paper; at times, Samuel tore paper and the quill and scratched again his thoughts. He must emphasize their accomplishments and sacrifices, of the flags that waved in front or beside him. Of course, his desire to accompany them could only be in heart and mind. Now duty called louder than all other things, even pain.

> Soldiers of the Pennsylvania Reserves. June 1, 1864.
>
> Today the connection which has so long existed between us is to be severed forever. I have no power to express to you the feeling of gratitude and the affection that I bear to you, nor the deep regret with which I now part from you.
>
> As a division you have been faithful and devoted soldiers and you have nobly sustained me in many trying scenes through which we have passed with an unwavering fidelity.
>
> The record of your service terminates gloriously and the Wilderness, Spotsylvania, and Bethesda Church, have been added to the long list of battles and triumphs that have marked your career.
>
> Go home to the great state that sent you forth three years ago to battle for her honor and to strike for her in the great cause of the country.

Anxious to be homeward bound, their minds likely drifted in and out as the words about their flags and their comrades flowed from their commander. Their world was home, not speeches.

> Take back those banners scarred from glorious associations that surrounded them, sacred with the memory of our fallen comrades who gave their lives to defend them, and give them again to your state.
>
> The duties of the hour prevent me from accompanying you, but my heart will follow you long after you return, and it shall ever be my pride that I was once your commander and that side by side we fought and suffered through campaigns which will stand unexampled in history. Farewell S. W. Crawford.[30]

After the speech, the orders for those whose terms were not expired and those that reenlisted were to report to headquarters.

The next morning they came to bid farewell. "It was one of the saddest and most trying hours of our lives. Our strong attachment was never realized until separation. It was the parting of those who shared a last cracker, slept under the same cover for warmth, and stood side by side when the storm of death was sweeping by." Crawford had asked a band to play. As it played "Home Sweet Home," the general made his way to his two brigade commanders. As he said his last farewells to Fisher and "Mac," a soldier standing near said, "Not an eye was dry from the general down. The tears gushed in spite of strife to conceal them."[31]

They would take with them almost four thousand men, many of whom knew war at its worst. The band was asked to change to patriotic tunes. Loud cheers broke out as the men boarded the cars and made their way to Harrisburg.

A few weeks later he heard of the reception the Reserves received in the capital: church bells pealed, throngs threw flowers, stores closed, and the state guns thundered a salute. "A hot dinner was offered but refused. We wanted to get home where the welcome comes from the heart alone."[32]

Colonel Fisher asked them to give three cheers as they had at Bethesda Church. Colonel McCandless told the gathering: "The Reserves in their consciences felt they had done their whole duty. As long as blood flows in our veins, we will support the old flag which we have carried in triumph in many an engagement."[33]

Rufus Dawes had that ability to reflect on the past and perceive the future. In a letter to his wife on June 3, 1864, he wrote, "thirty one days today this terrible campaign has dragged along. Would that God grant it soon be over, but until then we can only do our duty and hope that all is well."[34]

V. Crawford Behaved Handsomely.

While Crawford and the Reserves were having their last farewell, one of Warren's officers, Brigadier General Henry Lockwood, was catching Gouverneur's infamous wrath, as many had this first of June. Wainwright said Warren was in one of his pets, "as ugly and cross ground as he could be." He "cursed his staff officers" as if he were taking his problems with Meade out on his own. In any case, General Lockwood was dismissed, and on June 2 Samuel Crawford was named by General Warren to head the Second Division.[35]

As happened so frequently in this campaign, the problems of Lockwood were exacerbated by unfamiliar ground and without a guide. Incongruously, within a year an incensed leader, Philip Sheridan, would lash out at another junior officer named General G. Warren.[36]

In late May, in a memo to Meade, Warren wrote an evaluation of his officers, and noted, "I think General C. Griffin or Ayres is most competent but Crawford and Cutler behaved handsomely with me."[37]

On June 5 the V Corps was again reorganized. Crawford's Third Division consisted of a brigade of the Pennsylvania Reserves who remained and two other brigades commanded by Colonels Peter Lyle and James Bates. It was a time of marching, countermarching, and receiving newly organized units. John Vautier in his diary entry of June 3 told of the hazards of marching. He had taken canteens to get some fresh water as until then they had found only slimy water. Just as he was doing this friendly deed, a bullet cut a limb off a tree and smashed his hand. His next stop was a field hospital, then a corps hospital, and soon sweet Philadelphia, to recuperate.[38]

New units were formed and placed in diverse divisions almost weekly. Crawford's Third Division was fortunate in that the most of his replacements were good veteran units with reliable soldiers who had seen much combat. The 107th Pennsylvania became a part of the Third Division V Corps on June 6. When Crawford did receive "greenhorns," the veterans were his greatest asset. His utmost task was, with their service time relatively short, to provide the leadership that ensured them they would not be led to useless slaughter.[39]

Grant had made the decision to try to seize Petersburg before Lee and his army could react. If the Union army did not win the battle of the feet, the railroad center of Petersburg offered opportunities to disrupt the Southern supply route. Additionally, by squeezing the life out of Petersburg, Richmond would become vulnerable.

In light of this grandiose plan, the Northern army departed Cold Harbor unnoticed, marched an army of just under 95,000 to the James River and then miraculously found a way to cross. Crawford would now be a part of one of the great military troop movements in this war. It probably made him recall the other on December 26, 1860. With the use of brilliant organization, speed, and deception, the entire army "headed for the hub." Grant used different locations, boats, and pontoon bridges to make the move as efficiently as possible. Robert E. Lee would be slightly mystified for a few days as the decoy operations convinced him the Yankees would attack on the north side of the river.[40]

Crawford's division would be a part of the feint to keep Lee off balance. About supper time on June 12, the V Corps guarded the right and rear of the army as it moved toward the Chickahominy River. After crossing on pontoons, the division turned west along the southern limits of the White Oak Swamp. Breastworks were constructed to give the impression they were a vanguard that would make a stand. Along with Wilson's cavalry, they skirmished, fought, and repulsed the enemy. The intermittent battles took place all through the hot and humid Virginia summer days. After dark, the infantry and cavalry made their way to St. Mary's Church where they bedded for the night. The casualty list for the day neared 300.[41]

During the morning hours of the 14th, the rest of the Union army began the trek across the James River. Much of the army, along with 3,500 beef cattle, wagons and artillery that covered 35 miles, crossed on a 2,000-foot-long pontoon bridge that was constructed in a matter of 10 hours. The army crossed to the south side in about two days. "We stood on the opposite side of the James and it all seemed more like a nightmare than reality." The river was 2,000 feet wide, the depth in mid-channel 12 feet, and was crossed on June 16 on 101 pontoons. Grant's army was in "fighting trim."[42]

Crawford, his men, and the cavalry that reached Charles City "pleasured silently" by bathing in half barrels and slipping into clean clothes.

The paymaster was still an absentee but the troops were shined and ready to go to the "back door of Richmond."[43]

Initially, it appeared, the Union army's chances to capture Petersburg seemed rather good. On June 15 a corps of troops from Bermuda Hundred and Hancock's troops were to attack Petersburg held by only a few thousand of General Beauregard's troops who fought successfully on defense. Many of the same things that had plagued the Union army in the Overland campaign continued to haunt them. Unknown terrain and out-of-date maps led to the confusion of orders and slowed the Union attack. Consequently, the soldiers and civilians were introduced to what would be a nine-month siege that would change their lives and the war. The idea was to press, lengthen, isolate, starve, and destroy the spirit of the Rebel army as the Union army destroyed the Southern lifelines.[44]

Meanwhile on a positive note, by noon on June 17 the "miracle of the crossing" had been accomplished. The forty gory and demoralizing days of the Overland campaign were history. In some ways it accomplished what the leaders hoped, but for the soldiers who saw death everywhere, the means were difficult to justify in their minds.[45]

During the war days of July, the Third Division soldier's time was consumed in hours of fortification building, endless fatigue, and picket duty. Now and then a skirmish erupted, but mostly days were spent trying to stay clear of the fire of Southern sharpshooters. The officers of the men were not always bored. Wainwright went to a dinner party given by General Crawford. The artillery captain reported that the food was delectable, and the general entertained with "punch and champagne" and he and other officers were found to be "tight" by evening's end and his friends "decidedly boozy."[46]

At times the two opposing groups of men exchanged tobacco or news and generally acknowledged each other as humans. On July 4, as the two sides were conferring, Crawford rode up, mounted a parapet, and used his spy glass to check the Rebels. One of the Johnnies sent a note, "Tell the guy with the glass to knock it off or we will have to shoot him." The general replaced his glass and rode away hurriedly and unharmed. At a later time Crawford came back to check on his pickets when two Rebels were standing on the Union side. Crawford explained there was no official truce and they could be spies and he would have to treat them as such. They were added to the prisoner of war list.[47]

During this month, the general was inadvertently involved in a dispute between Meade and Warren. On July 19, Meade and Warren had a serious, animated, and explosive disagreement. Consequently on the 22nd, Meade informed Warren that he had seen a newspaper article that stated he had preferred charges against Warren for disobedience and tardy execution of orders. While that was entirely without foundation, Meade admitted to being irritated and deeply wounded by his tone and at that moment did plan on relieving Warren. "I did speak to General Grant as I have frequently about you and I did write a letter giving my reasons for your dismissal but in the hopes this type of thing does not happen again, I took no action. I have always endeavored to advance your interests, but I cannot shut my eyes to what I think is wrong. It is my desire to have harmony with my subordinate officers but I cannot yield my judgment to theirs. I make these remarks only so you know I talked to General Grant about you. Truly yours, George G Meade."

Crawford was present and other officers were just outside the headquarters' tent when the incident occurred. Meade stated, "This precluded the possibility of its being kept private."[48]

In light of future events between Crawford and Warren, it seemed Warren might have thought it was Crawford who informed the press. No found evidence indicates that, and more likely it was a display of the uncontrolled Warren temper, with which Crawford was destined to be involved.

VI. Chambersburg Burns. The Town Was Selected as a Target.[49]

As Alex dressed the wound for Samuel and they prepared for further military duty on July 30, 1864, little did they know that two fires would dominate conversation for the coming days. One fire began with kerosene, rags, papers, and drapes and built to a crescendo; the other, in a mine, used dynamite, fuses, and wires that set in motion a monumental explosion, then burned gradually. Both created pain, one for civilians and the other for soldiers.

The news of the mine explosion reached V Corps quickly as it was but a few miles distant that the Federal army, after weeks of preparation, exploded a mine, blowing a gap in the Confederate defenses. After the initial explosion, the rest of the planned adventure deteriorated as the Union troops failed in trying to break through the Petersburg defenses. Now the trench warfare would continue for another two-thirds of a year.

The other fire, geographically distant, was emotionally closer, in the hearts of General Crawford, Alex, and the Pennsylvania Reserves. Sometimes the body breaks; sometimes it is the heart that breaks; but the most pain is bred when the heart creates the ache. The end of July brought Samuel and Alex the sad news that their hometown was laid in ashes.[50]

The citizens of Samuel's hometown had seen Rebel invasions on three separate occasions, and each time their hearts broke a little more.

The destruction of factories and railroads, the pillaging of stores and homes, the sight of captured free blacks being carted away into slavery, or worse, the homes of the citizens being threatened with fire, all created mental anguish and weakened their spirits temporarily. Those invasions had occurred a number of months, even years ago. Since then the minds had healed and the spirits regained their strength, and they went on with their lives. During the spring and summer, the local newspapers, the *Franklin Repository* and the *Valley Spirit*, informed the citizens that the Army of the Potomac was besieging Petersburg and placing the Confederate capital in jeopardy. Atlanta was under siege. Closer to home, borders were safer than ever, they were assured; consequently, their minds were at relative ease. On July 27, the *Repository* reported, "No Rebel demonstrations had been made on the Potomac River for a number of weeks," and "The borders are picketed and the fords are guarded." All seemed secure until only three days later. The Rebels were back in town—Southerners who were angrier this time and with retaliation on their minds and in their hearts. Rebels who had heard or seen wanton Yankee destruction in their hometowns in the Shenandoah Valley were apart of the cadre.[51]

In the early morning hours that Saturday, a few shells were lobbed into the sleeping village of Chambersburg to assure the town that artillery accompanied the horse soldiers. A detachment of 900 soldiers then rode into town with Brigadiers Bradley Johnson and John McCausland. They dismounted at the Franklin Hotel and approached the clerk, who seemed extremely nervous. Although he was dressed in civilian clothes, it was a disguise as he was a local militia home on leave working at the hotel. Later, when the Confederates looted the hotel, his uniform was discovered; he was detained as a prisoner of war in a nearby building. During the confusion of the fire he made good his escape.[52]

The Confederates inquired of the location of the town's leaders. The courthouse bell was rung, but none of the town fathers emerged. Therefore, the clerk was sent in search of the fathers. When he returned with a few of the town leaders, the order for the destruction of the town was read. The deed was to be in retaliation for the Yankee atrocities committed in the Shenandoah Valley against Southerners. After the failure to produce the seemingly unreasonable ransom—$100,000 in gold or $500,000 in U.S. currency—the torch was applied.[53]

The diary of Jennie Washington Wiestling provided the specifics for those who suffered through yet another war ordeal as members of the home front. Seeing a large part of a city burn, even from a distance, was a terrifying experience. The knowledge that the family provided three men for the Union cause was a source of fear that the enemy may retaliate. When humans lose their homes, they lose more than its contents, they have lost their life's memories and in some cases, their meaning of life.

> Sadness and sorrow prevail here. Everything is in confusion. On Saturday we saw smoke from the Chambersburg area and we ran to the garret to watch [as] Chambersburg burned. We expected them to come burn us out every minute. We hid things in the woods as before and the hired girls dragged the carpet out and hid it in the hills. Union General Averil [sic Averell] drew up a line of battle across the field beyond the barn. Of course they had time to come to relieve us of some poultry. Better our boys than the Rebs. It is said Union General W. Averell chased the Rebs back into Maryland, Oh, if he would have done it sooner![54]

Later Samuel probably heard of the attacks from his friends in town. The Rebels fired the courthouse with kerosene from a nearby store, and then put the torch to the drapes, closets, or broken pieces of furniture in house after house. Crawford, Sr., had seen firsthand how the center of the town had been destroyed—its heart had been burned out.[55]

Some people saved a few valuables, clothing, and pieces of furniture, but, for the most part, even the sick and elderly were granted no favors. Estimates, according to Mr. Hoke and McClure, indicated that about 3,000 were homeless. Some drunken soldiers looted and robbed in addition to the arson. Several soldiers said they did not wish to participate, but had to follow orders. Others delighted in paying back the Yankees. Samuel heard later they made a special effort to set the McClures' home on fire. He still had under his command some of the Pennsylvania Reserves that had stayed with the Army of the Potomac.[56]

This soldier spoke for those from Pennsylvania:

> If you are a Pennsylvanian, you are aware of the fact that General McCausland burned the beautiful city of Chambersburg, Pennsylvania.
>
> Many have been turned homeless. They were turned into the streets because they could not raise the cash he demanded. Some of the Reserves that you once called brothers may have loved ones that are now homeless.
>
> The Rebel gloried in his destruction, as we will in our hour of triumph. The destruction of that southern cavalry exceeded one million dollars. The folks of Chambersburg have not forgotten us; now let us repay some kindness by providing our homeless brethren with money to begin life over again.[57]

General Crawford in an unusual mood of retaliation issued an order "calling in all guards" that were graciously guarding Virginia homes and property. If Chambersburg is to be robbed and burned, why should Virginia property escape? In Samuel's mind, the citizens of his hometown had done nothing to deserve such treatment.[58]

A couple of weeks later a rider would bring more than $1,000 to give to the broken and bleeding hearts of his hometown. For that deed his neighbors would not forget the aid and the contributions of his men. In the years after the war when he frequented Chambersburg, he would, no doubt, be told of incidents of the downtrodden in the community who were able to begin anew because of his men's generosity.

For years he saw blackened reminders, empty spaces or scars on charred wood from some of the 550 buildings burned that July 30 in 1864. In the days, weeks, months, and years that followed, the resilience of the spirits slowly repaired and the community rebuilt.[59]

VII. Weldon Railroad or Globe Tavern

As July conceded its humidity to an even more disagreeable August, the wool-uniformed soldiers became more aware of the heat. John Vautier's diary mentioned some combination of hot, sultry, and dusty on 16 July days and 23 August days.[60]

The war duties of Crawford were unrelenting because of the reorganization due to the departure of most of the Reserves and the constant transferring of units. On August 18 Crawford, in his Official Report, noted his location at the yellow house or Globe Tavern. The battle would also be called Weldon Railroad. He massed his command near the railroad as ordered. His three brigades were held in readiness after a six-hour march in the miserable heat. Later he recorded, "We met the enemy on the right and center and drove him back past his rifle pits to his entrenchments in front of a thicket of woods. The undergrowth was so dense, tangled, and interspersed with swamps that it was almost impossible to stay connected or see more than 20 feet in front." From Warren, "You have done well getting through the difficult country so far. Make yourself as strong as possible and hold on. I will try to reinforce you by Bragg's Brigade in the morning. We are going to hold here." "I am gratified you are satisfied!"

Crawford replied, "It was very hard work." Henry Matrau wrote that his sergeant major was killed. This death must have reminded Crawford of his narrow escape at Spotsylvania as Sergeant Babcock died when a tree limb struck him on the head.[61]

"General Bragg was sent by Warren at 4 a.m. on the 19th." Confused by the terrain Edward Bragg placed his troops about a mile in the rear of the desired position. A short time later, the enemy attacked on three fronts and broke through Bragg's thin line. "The Rebels passed freely on either side of Crawford and he was once in their hands, but escaped almost miraculously."

Crawford picked up the action in his report. "Now the Union artillery fired into the woods and some shells hit the back of the breastworks. The men jumped over and took position on the other side." The Confederates captured a number of men trying to escape the friendly fire. Thankfully a division from the IX Corps sent aid and the territory was regained, but Samuel Crawford anguished over the "loss of so many brave veterans who fought gallantly, especially since no dishonor could be attached to them." He may have lost more had General John Hartranft not brought his men to aid and provide a degree of stability as little Billy Mahone was providing a "stiff pounding to Crawford's troops."[62]

In the process of this fire, Crawford raised in his saddle to view the happenings to his front when he felt a thump like he had been hit by a hammer. He immediately looked for blood, but found nothing but a giant bruise on his chest. He had been hit in the breast by a spent bullet. That night after the breast wound was examined, the division surgeon noticed that once again the thigh wound had reopened due to inflammation and was discharging foreign materials that included India rubber cloth.[63]

The division commander wasn't always involved in food and ammunition distribution, and battle formations and tactics. Infrequently a situation happened like the one at the battle of Weldon Railroad. Truth was difficult to identify, so he and his staff acknowledged two truths.

During the fighting on the afternoon of August 19 a North Carolina flag was handed to the division commander in the thick of fighting. In the confusion Crawford did not get a good look at the soldier who provided the prize. Later he had his staff search for and locate the hero. He was identified as Private George Reed of the 11th Pennsylvania. A medal of honor was ordered from the War Department and orders were issued for the presentation. Commander of the Army of the Potomac, General George Meade, would perform the honors. Before the dust could settle on the affair, a group of soldiers representing the 107th Pennsylvania arrived at Crawford's Headquarters demanding that Private Solomon Hottenstein be given that medal. Sol, as his buddies called him, was grilled by the staff and they heard a story that deserved a reward. He had been captured along with a large number of his buddies by some North Carolinian Rebels. Being a quick thinker and actor, he, while the guards were disorganized, demanded their surrender. To make his point, the private grappled their colors from the color bearer and headed toward the Union lines with its bearer in tow. His newly released cohorts, more interested in saving themselves than receiving any glory, left him on his own. As his support slipped away so did his prisoners except the one he held on to, the flag bearer. The man and his flag were presented to Crawford during the heat of battle. After hearing Sol's story, Crawford promised his clique that Solomon Hottenstein would receive his medal, and so it was done on June 2, 1865.[64]

A number of Reed's friends approached Crawford claiming they had honored the wrong man for the capture of the flag. Crawford had his staff investigate the incidents. In the end each man was awarded the Medal of Honor; one for the capture of enemy soldiers and heroism and the other for the capture of the flag.

Because of the battle action, the Union would control the important Jerusalem Plank Road, used by Lee to move supplies south. On August 23 Crawford wrote in his Official Report: "the railroad has been destroyed to a point 250 yards beyond our picket-line. The ties have been burned and the rails bent."[65]

On August 24, the old 7th Wisconsin was assigned to Crawford's Third Division. In a note in his diary, William Ray indicated he was glad they were being transferred to a unit with "the old Pennsylvania Reserves and the Bucktails. They are good troops."[66]

Crawford was distraught that among the more than 1,900 casualties of his division many came at the hands of the Union artillery which was trying diligently to provide aid to Crawford's infantry. Death by friendly fire probably provoked images from the Fort Sumter ceremony in the spring of 1861.

A single line in his Official Report stated, "My personal servant was shot in the breast." Maybe it was Alex who continued to serve his brother until early October. A November 22 *Franklin Repository* announced the honorable discharge of "Captain Alex Crawford, aide to his brother, Samuel Crawford, of nearby Fayetteville." He and Alex had bonded in a way few other brothers could have imagined.[67] Alex had been his guide, his mentor, and his beloved brother. He transferred to the Veteran Corps in February of 1865.

For the remainder of the month the Third Division built breastworks, facing south. In September the V Corps was again reorganized.

Crawford was pleased when he learned that Bragg was assigned permanently to his division with his First Brigade. General Henry Baxter and Colonel William Hoffman rounded out the list of his competent brigade commanders.

Not all the commanders and men were particularly pleased to be transferred to Crawford's division, as he was still a stickler for drills and inspections on the company, regimental, and brigade levels. The general scheduled these activities on a regular basis. The "spit and polish discipline" caused grumblings in the ranks.[68]

Some time later, Meade wanted to send some of the old "Iron" Regiments to Baltimore to supervise recruitment camps. Crawford fought the idea as he believed in building esprit de corps in many ways; in Crawford's eyes, unnecessary change created internal problems. However, in the eyes of a member of a Pennsylvania regiment, he had no esprit de corps as they found Crawford "unpopular, aristocratic, vindictive and a tyrant. He annoys the commanding general and the subordinates of the brigade. Measures are on foot to cause him trouble. We have no confidence in him."[69]

Warren went on leave early in October and Crawford, the senior division leader, was assigned to command the V Corps. The "Old Pointers," Ayres and Griffin, did not appreciate the kid with the golden ticket from Sumter being their corps commander. Brigadier General, soon to be brevetted Major General, Crawford was in command of the V Corps for the second time.[70]

VIII. The Second Battle of Squirrel Level Road

On October 7 just before midnight, V Corps Commander Crawford received an order stating that Andrew A. Humphreys, major general commanding, "desires a demonstration made tomorrow that will prevent enemy from sending any additional forces north of James. Begin reconnaissance at 7:30 a.m. General [John G.] Parke, commanding 9th Corps received the same orders." The area indicated was the same place where a skirmish had broken out a few days previously.[71]

Crawford recognized the propinquity of the orders. He had seven hours to notify his brigade commanders with specifics, notify his quartermaster and ordnance chiefs, and give them time to have the troops prepare.[72]

Grant's visit to Washington, D.C., did not slow the entrenching process and the maneuvering of armies around Petersburg. In early October the Northern octopus was wrapping its tentacles tighter around the city. The overall commander was not ready to pause, and even from his Washington hotel he wanted to keep the pressure on Robert E. Lee and his army. Concerned that Lee might make a tricky maneuver, Grant ordered Meade to establish a reconnaissance in force to indicate if any Southern troops had left the Petersburg area. Grant had no information that movement was taking place, nor had Meade who was on the scene and alert about such things. Even though Meade deemed the move pointless, he decided to comply with orders but with the least possible involvement of troops and energy.[73]

Interestingly, this nondescript episode would prove a first for S. W. Crawford who would guide a corps in battle. Major General Parke's IX Corps and Hancock's II would hold the flanks as Crawford's V Corps manned the middle.[74]

It was an unusually chilly night for this area of Virginia. Staff members left Crawford's headquarters at Globe Tavern, which was on loan from General Warren.

Crawford was instructed to move with skirmishers toward the Rebel lines. Four brigades, two on left of the Weldon Railroad and two on the right, would support the 1,200 skirmishers from the railroad to Squirrel Level Road. This line would ease them toward the primary Rebel defenses of the city. The center slowed early and then picked up as the Southerners relinquished their forward pits and fell back to the main defense lines.[75]

Meade was soon satisfied that the enemy was secure in their defenses. Sometime after noon, Meade informed Crawford and Parke to advance as far as safety allowed. Before the war Parke had attended Samuel Crawford, Sr.'s academy and then attended the University of Pennsylvania. Some of his and Samuel, Jr.'s years overlapped. Crawford believed he could fight up the Squirrel Road and leave the permanent picket line in the forward position. Romeyn Ayres and Griffin suggested their reasons for disagreeing and, respecting their views, "Crawford followed their advice."[76]

Crawford's subordinates agreed on attacking a farm house where sharpshooters had been giving Union troops problems for some time. Artillery was called in and the place was burned. The 190th Pennsylvania, some of Crawford's old Pennsylvania Reserves, were called to chase the Rebels out of their rifle pits. This could not be done; therefore, General Meade and his staff were content to pull back, having followed Grant's orders.

The Southerners under General A. P. Hill were not about to end the affair and commenced a series of counterstrikes. Now it was becoming more involved than Meade had hoped. Charges and countercharges were evident everywhere. Crawford and the IX Corps commander decided to fall back in late afternoon. It had been a day of jabs and counterjabs that proved little that either side did not know. In his Official Report, the V Corps commander wrote that the object of the reconnaissance had been attained. The Southerners were still in their defenses at Petersburg and the Northerners were watching closely. It cost the two sides fewer than 100 soldiers, but the 75 Northern and 25 Southern casualties proved that a larger battle was superfluous. Perhaps Crawford's only battle as a corps commander, the Second Battle of Squirrel Level Road, had saved lives in the overall scheme of circumstances.[77]

IX. The Winter of '64

During the autumn and early winter of 1864 the Union army continued the encircling of Petersburg. The two major concerns were the destruction of the Southern supply lines and, if an Achilles heel was discovered, attempt to infiltrate. The Southside Railroad was the desired prize since it was the last key rail link to the South. The bitter, damp winter was approaching and the decision was made to make an end-of-the-battle season effort to control the railroad.

The movement was rolled into action on October 27. Ted Lyman called it "a grand reconnaissance in force whose success depended upon the enemy not having certain advantages of position. They were found to have all the advantages."[78]

Before daylight on that rainy October morning, Meade sent three corps to attack the earthworks along Hatcher's Run. If his troops broke through they would turn north and head for the Southside Railroad less than five miles away. If the soldiers could not break through, the corps would support each other. The IX Corps was placed on the right flank with the II Corps of General Hancock and the V Corps of General Warren trying to remain together. But they began to separate. Hancock was moving steadily along and the V Corps encountered more difficult terrain. Crawford was ordered to fill the gap between the two corps. The division was soon entangled in a mile of twisting, snakelike, dense thicket which prevented them from immediately joining Hancock on the other side. Crawford wrote that the thicket was so dense "it is impossible to proceed without a compass." He stopped and restructured the alignment as best he could. A number of Southern soldiers were lost while trying to find their units. They walked into the Third Division lines and were captured. William Ray wrote that "Crawford interrogated the two but they refused to tell the general anything." When Crawford arrived near Hancock's flank it was nearly dark. Meade decided to renew the battle in the morning but the foe would allow no such happening and attacked immediately. Hancock reorganized and used artillery to drive the Confederates back. Colonel Lyman was amused by a few dignitaries who had come to visit General Grant. When the artillery barrage got serious, "they giggled, jumped behind trees, and wished themselves at City Point." The Union troops had found no weaknesses and had gained no ground. The next day they moved back to the entrenchments around Petersburg.[79]

Grant wondered why Crawford did not arrive on time. Meade answered Grant's inquiry into Crawford's seemingly sluggish maneuver. "The terrain was worse than the wilderness and Crawford came under fire while trying to move. I sent Ayres on the original road but darkness set in. I trust this will relieve your mind of impressions unfavorable of Crawford, he was disposed to do all in his power."[80]

The second month into the new year the same two Union corps would do the yeoman's work. The II Corps, now under the command of General Andrew Humphreys, led the attack on February 6, 1865. He had very light resistance and was suspicious of a trap. General Meade ordered the V Corps to test the strength of the Confederates toward Dabney's Mill. The encounter was substantial. Warren ordered Crawford to explore with his division on another road toward the mill. The Third Division drove the pickets and the Rebels back into the Dabney entrenchments; Lyman was impressed with the "good engineers of the Confederates who threw up dirt scientifically." The Southern forces were reinforced and pushed Crawford's men who were then supported by General Ayres' Second Division. After pushing the Confederates back once more, the Confederates made a countereffort until darkness ended the fighting. One soldier wrote, "It was back and forth until we ran out of ammunition and the Rebs got in our rear causing us to fall back." The Union troops used the night in spite of it being "cold, rainy, sleeting, and disagreeable" to reorganize. In the morning the Yankee troopers gained the ground around Dabney's Mill. The Union line now extended to the Vaughn Road to the point it intersected with Hatcher's Run. "We did not move back, we dug more trenches, and extended our line," wrote Matrau. Private Haley wrote that sleep was out of the question. "We lay in the mud and slosh and smoke from the fires of green wet pine. It nearly smothered us and nearly converted us into hams." Adversity aside the Southside Railroad was being drawn closer toward the Union web.[81]

Corps badges had been designed by Daniel Butterfield as chief of staff of the Army of the Potomac in 1863. Some military men envisioned them to be used to increase unit pride, but practically they aided in getting stragglers, lost soldiers, or confused groups after combat back to their designated unit.

Increasingly in 1864, units were constantly being reorganized and morale problems became a problem for the troops that remained. The dilemma became evident to Crawford in his division. The I Corps had been consolidated into Crawford's Third Division and by orders from Headquarters of the Army of Potomac they were allowed to retain their flags and badges of identification. This caused confusion in the ranks of the Third Division. On November 3, 1864, Generals Crawford and Warren tried to resolve some of the problems. The division commander appealed for modification of the order. He noted that "it would be injurious to deprive them of the right to display the badges" that, to him, afforded esprit de corps. He requested that the discs of the old I Corps be retained but the blue Maltese cross be quartered on the discs, or that the I Corps insignia be worn on the outside of the arm. Warren approved of the suggestion except he wanted no part of the badge on the arm. This badge is "no mark of honor; their object is to prevent straggling." The corps commander desired that the badges only be worn on the hat. The compromise must have worked as there is no further discussion concerning the problem.[82]

Most of December was spent destroying more railroad tracks, bridges, and infrastructure, and dealing with Confederate deserters who were now making nightly runs. The rails and bridges were being destroyed southward. Weldon Railroad was ripped for 18 miles and all bridges destroyed to that point. Most of the demolition was done in cold, wet days and nights. On December 14, Generals Griffin, Ayres, and Crawford received kudos for making forced marches during six days and nights in the most inclement weather.[83]

The men worked on their shanties in spare time, but much of the drudgery of winter meant policing the grounds, the parade field, and the areas around the camp; guard duty was a constant assignment, as was picket duty. Drills from company to division were conducted at somewhat regular intervals. Inspections, when good, gave the troops a sense of pride. This was especially true if the praise came from the top leaders. Crawford did just that for the Iron Brigade. "The General praised us for our tidy camp."[84]

William Ray noted that the ration of whiskey was issued almost daily with a good portion of quinine for the health of the men. The monotony was broken when brigade bands played the "good and sweet air around the camp."[85]

At times, after his staff interrogated the Confederate prisoners, Crawford sent them to Humphreys' headquarters to present information to the chief of staff. Once he said the man seemed to be of "more than ordinary intelligence." At one point in the middle of the month a Confederate regiment in front of Crawford's men had disappeared. As the deserters came in greater numbers, Crawford and his staff realized almost the entire regiment had deserted the Southern army. Many of them had been enticed to go home, but most were just plain famished.[86]

The signal that the year's military maneuvers were coming to a halt came about December 12 when the men were permitted to construct winter huts, thereby, as Crawford said, "overall making themselves comfortable." Henry Matrau in a letter to his parents bragged, "we build more houses for winter than any other corps because we are the best builders." At one point the division was forced to move to tents, and Crawford found a way to move his hut except for the kitchen. One VI Corps officer moved into the kitchen and indicated that the "luxurious Crawford relocated but left his kitchen which is good enough for me to use as sleeping quarters."[87]

A couple of days before the end of the year Crawford was called to Meade's headquarters where he was read an announcement from the Adjutant General's Office. "By direction of the President of the United States the following officers are hereby assigned to duty according to their brevetted rank: Samuel W. Crawford, Brevet Major General, U.S. Volunteers." The *Franklin Repository* in his little hometown of Chambersburg, Pennsylvania, noted the promotion and praised him for his efforts.[88]

General S. W. Crawford. The soldiers called this the "turn out the guard look."
USAMHI

In this 1865 photo of Major General Crawford he wears his Loyal Legion pin. This and his commander's pin would adorn his burial dress.
Library of Congress, Photo by Gutekunst of Philadelphia

❧ Part Eight ☙

A Military End, but an Abiding Relationship

*"Go back to the great state that sent you
three years ago to battle for her honor."*
—Crawford speech to Pennsylvania Reserves, June 1, 1864

"There is Crawford neat and trim as usual."
—Morris Schaff

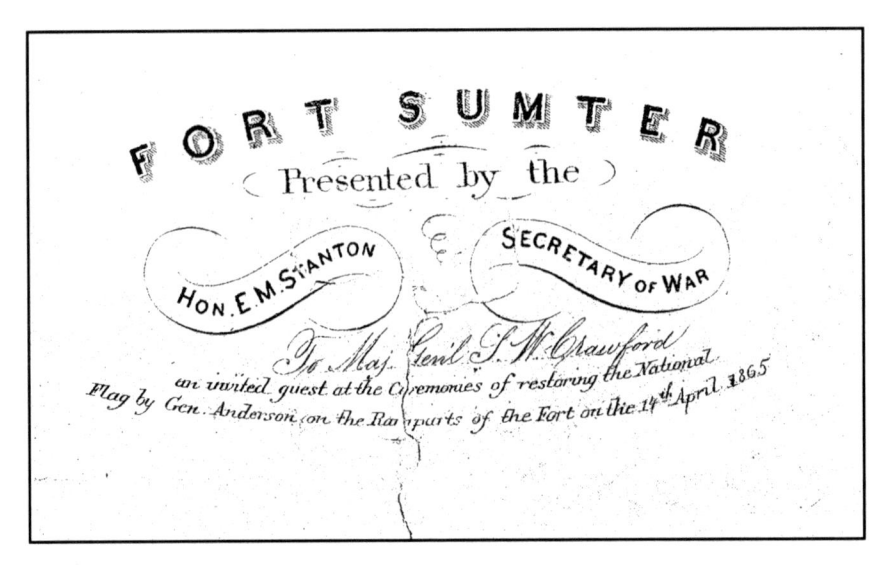

> FORT SUMTER
>
> Presented by the
>
> HON. E.M. STANTON SECRETARY OF WAR
>
> To Maj. Gen'l S. W. Crawford an invited guest at the Ceremonies of restoring the National Flag by Gen. Anderson on the Ramparts of the Fort on the 14th April 1865.

The official invitation from Secretary of War Edwin M. Stanton to Major General S. W. Crawford to attend the national flag restoration ceremonies at Fort Sumter, April 14, 1865.

Library of Congress

Major General S. W. Crawford. The photo probably was taken just after the Civil War.

USAMHI

℘ Chapter Sixteen ℘

An End and a Beginning

I. 1865, the War Year That Was Not to Be

It was 1865, a year best described in the words uttered six years earlier by one of Dickens' fictional characters who also lived in perilous times and summarized them as the best of times also being the worst of times. That philosophy seemed to fit this country in 1865.

Sherman had waded through Savannah and was on his way to Atlanta and eventually to the coast. In spite of their staggering losses, the South could not accept the offered peace terms during the famous shipboard negotiations with Lincoln and others. The integrity of the Union and the abolition of slavery continued to be the rocks upon which the talks floundered. The vision, an American one, was never out of Lincoln's mind. There were those Confederate soldiers who hoped for a "peace president." After the results were known, one wrote, "the election decided the fate of the southern confederacy."[1]

Militarily, the anaconda strategy of Lincoln, Grant, and military aides was slowly smothering Southern hopes. With the "Christmas gift of Savannah" Lincoln's fortunes turned and he was reelected with slightly fewer than 55 percent of the popular vote. Adversely, the solid support for his policies had practically doomed the probability for an independent Southern Confederacy.[2]

Lee's ragtag army had been "in a fix" for over nine months in Petersburg. The Confederate capital and the hub of the remaining Southern rail system were on the brink of being overrun. The siege was sapping the Southern strength just as Lee had feared and Grant had hoped.

Samuel Wylie Crawford, now a brevetted major general in the regular and volunteer army, faced problems not unlike many other senior officers in the Army of the Potomac. His physical impairments, the thigh wound and malaria, added to the daily distress of command. The wound in his thigh would not heal and the mental anguish about it continued to grow. Only rest and relaxation would provide a degree of healing, but this was not the time for such luxuries of respite.[3]

Now he and his men were increasingly confronted by guerrilla warfare. It mattered little if you fell to an infection, or in a massed charge, or shot by the unseen sniper, you died nonetheless. If you suffered some grotesque wound, life with pain was not noble or honorable.[4]

In January General Crawford took command of the V Corps when General Warren acquired leave to attend the wedding of his sister to his staff officer, General Washington Roebling. In correspondence to Warren in mid-month, Crawford relayed information about the troops and the assurance that all was fine except that the men did not wish to relieve the IX Corps. "We have already taken the field to give our tents to the VI Corps and twice erected stables for the animals and had to leave them as they were completed." He ended his letter wishing Roebling "the entire measure of all earthly happiness in your married life."[5]

Back in winter camp, meanwhile, soldiers had a way of creating morale boosters and one was to "pull the wool" over their officers' eyes. One soldier bragged in his letters how the men were having a great deal of fun over his reported marriage, "If Crawford only knew! I don't think it will come to light." Another soldier was not as easy on Samuel. "We don't think too much of Crawford. He habitually wears a turn out the guard expression which is fairly indicative of his military character."[6]

A constant topic of discussion in many letters was the number of Confederate deserters. On March 3 William Ray wrote they "average 125 daily into the Army Of The Potomac," and Private Haley noted, "another lot of deserters landed in our midst."[7]

March was a month devoted to the routine of drill and inspections. The V Corps was visited by celebrities and inspected by superior officers such as Generals Meade and Grant and the secretary of war. They were most honored by a visit from the president. According to one soldier in the V Corps, "Abe looks bad just like his pictures."[8]

Lee, in his last massive, offensive attempt to break out of the siege, attacked Fort Stedman. After initial success, the advantage could not be sustained and it remained under the Union colors.

The winter months of January through February and early March were furlough months. Some Union soldiers had to try for furloughs harder than others and for different reasons. Henry Matrau asked his family to send a letter saying he needed a furlough because his wife "Sally, Polly, Mary or

Jane was very sick." General Meade went on leave for a totally different reason. He had the duty of burying his son. Ted Lyman met Meade on his return. "The general still managed a wit, I had returned early from furlough and he said playfully that he would have me court martialed for returning to duty early."[9]

Before the army began another active campaign, Crawford had been told of a sculptor in camp who was doing the likenesses of a number of the officers. Proud of his physique and overall appearance, he did not want to be left out. He went to see the artist, only to find him asleep. Not using discretion, he awakened the man and asked if he would carve a statuette of him. Though irritated, the artist agreed, but set the price at three times the going rate, $400. Crawford agreed. When the story got out, the officers would see Samuel and ask if he had seen the artist around camp. Samuel replied, "Seen him, my good man, he follows me everywhere just boring me to do a statue." It is not known if the figure was ever carved, but his admiration for his physique was fully exposed and became an object of humor among his associates. "Crawford possesses a decided admiration for his looks and figure."[10]

II. A Tongue-lashing and a Quiet Response

By the end of March the Union army nearly surrounded Petersburg. The rainy season was in full swing, hampering military movements. However, Grant chose this time to benefit from Lee's most recent offensive failure at Fort Stedman. Seeking to prevent Lee from teaming with General Joseph E. Johnston's troops in neighboring North Carolina, Grant decided to attack the Rebels' thin, outstretched, and weakened right flank. This would also force the Southern commander to abandon the Petersburg trenches. Included in the area were the two remaining supply lines to Petersburg and beyond: the Boydton Plank Road and the village of Five Forks that controlled the prized Southside Railroad.

On March 29 the V Corps led the advance. Warren had ordered 50 rounds of ammo per soldier and 20 more rounds for each in the division ammo wagons. No musicians would be taken to maintain secrecy. Private Haley wrote that they left winter camp after going through the motions of eating breakfast. The extra ammo would soon come in handy as the V Corps met stiff resistance on Quaker Road near the crossing of Gravelly Run. Major General Griffin ordered his First Brigade of the First Division under General Joshua Chamberlain into the fight on Quaker Road. As the energetic Chamberlain was fighting full force on the road, Warren noticed a farm lane which he thought might be a shortcut to Boydton Plank Road. Such a road might allow him to turn the enemy's right flank and block the wagon supply route of the Rebels. He sent cavalry under General Nelson Miles ahead and they ran into Confederate soldiers. In the raid, Crawford was ordered to send one brigade to support the cavalry. The troops initially reached the Plank Road, proving Warren's geographical expertise.[11]

Once more the Virginia terrain reared its ugly head for the Union. The woods that lay on either side of the Quaker Road prevented the cavalry and Crawford's troops from keeping up with Griffin's men. The contemplated evening attack was cancelled as the units could not be aligned into a solid battle line. However, the Union troops still managed to block the Boydton Plank Road.[12]

During the night, in a heavy rain, the V Corps refortified and secured its position as ordered by Meade. Crawford and his men occupied the Boydton Plank Road with their left flank extended as far as Gravelly Run, a welcomed source of water supply and a natural barrier. General Philip Sheridan, now the commander of the campaign, set about immediately to implement Grant's overall strategy. The decision was made for the II and V Corps to advance on the village of Five Forks. General Grant hoped that infantry and cavalry would work in unison, but it didn't work that way.

During the 30th, Humphreys' II Corps and Warren's V Corps moved toward the village in the rain that turned the roads into a quagmire. As they moved toward the White Oak Road they heard reports that the Confederates were building breastworks around Five Forks. During the night the divisions of Crawford and Griffin moved within supporting distance of General Ayres' Second Division.[13]

On Friday morning, March 31, at 7 a.m., with three days of issued rations, the Third Division concentrated around the Holiday residence after marching through slushy, slippery, muddy conditions. Crawford was to support Ayres of the Second Division, but the steady rain which had been creating havoc, now forced Grant to call off any troop changes. However, with Meade's support, Warren sent Ayres to determine the strength of the enemy in his front. Instead the Confederates attacked him as they had been planning to attack Warren's left flank. They would also attack General Sheridan with General Pickett's troops. In the ensuing clash, Crawford's division was called to support General Ayres. Coulter's brigade of Crawford's division would be sent first while Crawford formed his remaining two brigades. As Brigade Commander Richard Coulter deployed, the left of Ayres' troops collapsed and as they fell back they fought a series of brief stands. Crawford's troops failed to hold as Ayres' men broke through their ranks unnerving them and causing them to fire into their own men. Crawford called on the iron veterans of Wisconsin, but even they failed to heed his reprimand to stand fast. It was only after they crossed Gravelly Run that the men could be reorganized.[14]

General Warren was ordered to stay near the telegraph center and was unable to superintend Ayres' movement. He arrived at the front to witness the troops' fragmenting. At one point he grabbed the flag and tried to rally the men. It was to no avail.[15]

While Crawford and his staff were trying to reform and renew the attack, Warren rode up and spared little kindness. He lashed out at Crawford, berating him in front of his men. Crawford did not respond to the verbal attack, but simply sat astride his mount. Colonel Wainwright had noticed General Warren's demeanor on the 29th. "The devil within him seemed to be stirring all day. These awful fits of passion are a disease with Warren."[16]

That afternoon Griffin, with artillery support and the reformed Crawford and Ayres troops, regained what had been lost and occupied the White Oak Road. Triumph had grown out of adversity again. Later, Meade asked the V Corps commander to send some men to Five Forks immediately. Warren did not want to split his men and argued with Meade that such a move would be detrimental to morale.[17]

Warren then received orders from Grant to move the V Corps to support Sheridan. The V Corps commander felt that neither Generals Grant nor Meade understood his situation. In order to move, a bridge had to be constructed over Gravelly Run. Warren sent Ayres forward and held Crawford and Griffin until the bridge was completed. Finally, in the early hours of April 1, the two divisions were quietly moved out of their entrenchments.

In a discussion between Sheridan and Grant around noon on April 1, Sheridan was given permission by Ulysses Grant to replace Warren if he deemed it necessary. Sheridan indicated he hoped it would not come to that.

Warren finally met with Sheridan personally and was informed of the planned attack. The V Corps was to be positioned by Warren to provide support to Sheridan. "Within three hours the 5th corps commander had the battle line formed."[18]

It was just after 4 p.m. when Warren directed his Second Division under Ayres to the left. Griffin was to follow Crawford, but both divisions went awry due to a "faulty reconnaissance that reflected in the map used." According to Chris Calkins, the terrain was "rough and wooded and cut by numerous ravines with the confederate works out of sight." Warren went to find and redirect the divisions. The V Corps commander found Griffin, placed him on track, and next found Colonel Kellogg's brigade of Crawford's division and instructed him to hold until he located the rest of the division. In the interim, a member of Sheridan's staff procured Kellogg's brigade for his use.[19]

When Warren found the rest of Crawford's brigades, they were in Pickett's rear in a position to prevent his escape. In the charge, the Southern line was decimated with the aid of General Warren who encouraged the troops at one point by grabbing the flag and leading the men into battle. In his memoirs, Ulysses Grant wrote that "General Crawford had backed off and was late in arriving. Once up he gave great service."[20]

The engagement produced a number of unforeseen results. For Crawford and others it meant a commendation from Sheridan for "gallantry that merits the thanks of their country and reward of the government." However, Crawford was passed over for the V Corps command when Sheridan gave the honor to Griffin. Wainwright wrote that Crawford complained somewhat about Griffin being put in over him but "not so much as I expected."[21]

Conversely, Warren was relieved of his command by Sheridan, who accused him of not being in the fight, when in truth Warren was providing hands-on corps leadership. The Southside Railroad was now under the control of the Union army. It was a matter of time until the Confederate commander ordered the evacuation of Petersburg-Richmond defenses. The capital was evacuated on April 3, 1865.

Henry Matrau asked, "Has it not been a glorious month?" The *Philadelphia Inquirer* reported, "Babylon has fallen." Richmond was in the hands of the Union at long last. Colonel Wainwright declared: "The rebellion is certainly on its last legs... The heart and spirit are gone."[22]

III. "Even the enemy cheered."[23]

Crawford received some additional good news to offset the unsettling events surrounding General Warren's dismissal. He was notified by Secretary of War Stanton that he was invited to attend a ceremony at Fort Sumter in which General Anderson was to restore the national colors. This was a chance to see Anderson, and others, four years to the day, April 14, after they had departed Fort Sumter.[24]

After the fall of Richmond, it was clear that the conflict was nearing its end. Lee's army was backpedaling and straggling through a series of small towns and villages in the attempt to secure nutrition and to escape entrapment by the Union cavalry and infantry. Even a series of night marches failed in the attempt to get to General Johnston in North Carolina. Henry

Matrau a few days earlier noted, "I did not notice the swagger. Southern conceit had collapsed."[25]

On April 6 at Saylers Creek 6,000 Confederates, General Richard Ewell, and other officers surrendered. Alex Haley was also experiencing adversity. "Nothing in the world gives me joy. I am so weak I could not carry my blanket, my ammunition goes next." Ted Gerrish wrote that the men were so exhausted and hungry, "if an artillery horse came close they hit the animal on the head with their rifles causing a warfare of oaths, words, and threats between the infantrymen and the artillerymen."[26]

The men of the Third Division had their last forced march the night of April 8. They sensed the end was near and complaining was held to a minimum.

Just before it was known that General Lee was in the process of surrendering his army, the 20th Maine thought they had to charge a battery. "Pull your hat down as far as possible, stay with the group, and pretend to be brave." As they moved toward the skirmish line they saw a white flag. "The joy of that hour will never be forgotten."[27]

Lee also recognized the situation; when Grant's offers to end the conflict were made in a few letters, he decided, reluctantly, to meet with the Union commander to discuss the terms of capitulation. The humane terms were an excellent postscript for a war between brothers who had brawled, scrapped, scuffled, wrestled, and now just wanted to go home. This sentiment was so eloquently and simply stated by a soldier in Crawford's division, "It's all over. We are going home." The news was expressed in many ways, "We acted as though we had taken leave of our senses. We shouted, sang, danced and wept." Crawford's associate, Holman Melcher, called it "the day of jubilee!" It was April 9, 1865, and Matrau would summarize, "Has not April been to us a glorious month?"[28]

Appomattox Court House was not unlike the other villages where the soldiers had camped on the retreat, and yet it had a special flavor of its own. Since it was a county seat it included a courthouse and additionally a tavern, a three-story jail, a law office, and a store that served as a social center. Near the edge of town sat a fine house that was described by some as a mansion. Its graceful facade was further enhanced by a surrounding white fence as well as a number of rather large shade trees in the front and side yards. Its appearance and tranquility reminded Samuel of Alandale. The owner, Wilmer McLean, reluctantly gave his consent to allow Generals Lee and Grant to meet in his parlor to discuss the terms ending the conflict with the Army of Northern Virginia. The McLean family had moved here from Manassas where the war began. It was said that the war began in Wilmer McLean's front yard and ended in his parlor.[29]

Crawford escorted a newsman from the *New York Herald*. "We spent several hours in the Rebel camp with General Crawford. We went to a number of headquarters, as Crawford knew the officers from the old army. We visited with General Lee. The southern leader's headquarters were simple. I suppose his office was an eight by nine foot wall tent while his staff slept under fly tents. It was located at the edge of a piece of woods with surroundings of the plainest kind. The officers, in particular James Longstreet, told Crawford to visit again, but to bring his own rations if he expected to eat."[30]

IV. "I am here to perform an act of Honor to my Country."[31]

After the reporter departed, Crawford went to his tent to examine his invitation to Sumter. "Ceremonies will be conducted to restore the national flag on the ramparts of Fort Sumter by General Robert Anderson at noon on April 14, 1865." No one in Samuel's life had more of an impact than Major Anderson. He likely left after duties on April 11.[32]

Crawford probably used military transport to arrive in Charleston a day before the ceremony. He would relish reacquainting himself with the old city he visited so frequently four years before. No doubt the city looked quite different from his first trip there in September 1860. Was it four years ago or a decade? In the interim he had advanced from a captain of cavalry to brevetted major general of infantry, and he had commanded brigades and divisions in many of the large land battles in the Eastern Theater. For a short time he commanded a corps. He had witnessed acts both of heroism and of cowardice.

He had seen more violence than any man should see in a lifetime. Though he walked with a cane due to the omnipresent thigh wound, Samuel recognized his good fortune at being able to return in spite of a series of additional minor wounds and his physical discomfort. Setting his personal adversities aside, he had returned to Charleston to celebrate and glorify that same flag that, years earlier, Chaplain Harris eloquently prayed would "fly over a whole country, a peaceful and prosperous nation."[33]

He first revisited Moultrie. Alone, he had a chance to pause at the location where they had torn down the flagstaff. His cane was a reminder of that moment; indeed, it was a part of that moment in history. Fort Moultrie and Charleston would always have a claim in his memory. The physical changes were present everywhere, but still the memories filtered through the aroma of the seaside fort. Though bittersweet, his recollections of joy, pain, sorrow, honor, pride, and humility washed over him here and in the city of Charleston.[34]

He would have noticed that the landscape of 1865 Charleston bore scant resemblance to that time just after the signing of the Declaration of Secession. Now deserted streets were flanked by decimated mansions, most now used as hospitals, that were hemmed in by twisted and distorted gates and fences enclosing cemeteries. The odor of gangrene prevailed. Gone were the bonfires, parades, and palmetto banners shown by throngs of joyous souls about to express their own "constitutional rights" and not those of a dictatorial Federal government. Though he could probably detect some of the remnants of Charleston's proud past, they were few. He likely came upon horses with protruding ribs as they labored in a decrepit state down cluttered streets and past empty mansions. Charleston now was devoid of beauty and without spirit.

Barely recognizable, the former business district would have suffered from fire and plunder. Yet he noticed that God had not entirely turned his back on the place. Natural beauty was still evident in the form of flowering magnolias, lilacs, hawthorns, and even several orange trees. Songbirds still trilled oblivious to the destruction by human hands.[35]

Once the gem of the Confederacy, Charleston now wore the cloak of four tempestuous years of warfare. Abandoned by those wealthy enough to leave, it was now home mostly to poor elderly men and women and ex-slaves. Streets were without pavements; houses had lost their former character.

These circumstances had been created by those willing to pay the price for freedom on their terms. The tab however was often paid by others, and the result at this moment was difficult to fathom.

Friday, April 14, 1865, dawned clear and cool after evening and early morning showers. Ozone perfumed the air. Crawford probably met Chaplain Harris and General Anderson at Sumter a few hours before the ceremony. On the ride to the "old brick home," he passed by the growth of pines interspersed with a scattering of straggly palmetto trees. Though less stately, the palmettos jolted his memory of the ones destroyed at the Secessionist Convention. Each delegate wanted a souvenir to mark the historical occasion, and the trees beside the speaker's table had fallen prey. Where were the proud symbols now?[36]

Atop the lighthouse surrounding Castle Pinckney, Samuel could see the large banner of red, white, and blue waving in the breeze. One can assume his mind drifted to Pettigrew and his scaling ladders on December 27, 1860. What of the men who climbed them?[37]

When they passed Cummings Point, folks thought the Iron Battery appeared as a disabled, almost shapeless monster. Crawford probably remembered it as neither disabled nor shapeless.[38]

He would have certainly dreaded the thought of viewing the remains of Fort Sumter. He had heard of the tons of shot and shell that had been thrown her way. He feared being unable to locate any area that was significant to his past. Staring intently at the old fort as it came into view, he was certainly unprepared for the degree of its destruction. Despite now being adorned with flags and bunting, the old fortress looked like a broken warrior whose clothes had been shredded, but whose flag was still held with pride in triumph.

If the outside of the fort startled him, the inside must have overwhelmed him. One can imagine him climbing the steps at the harbor entrance, and resting several times to ease the pain. When he reached the top, he would be able to survey the interior. It brought him face to face with irregular heaps and piles of sand, earth, and broken bricks. Near the walls unrecognizable debris littered what was formerly the parade ground in the structure's center.

The reunion must have been glorious as Crawford, in his full dress regalia, met those heroes of the past: General Anderson; his son, Robert Junior; Chaplain Matthias Harris; and Sergeant Peter Hart. One source indicated his old adversary, Abner Doubleday, was also present.

Emotions undoubtedly ran high as they relived the earlier years. His mentor had retired due to the mental torture of the command. General Anderson's son was now a grown man. Peter Hart, Anderson's right-hand man, was carrying a mail bag, and the chaplain held the 1861 Bible. Sergeant Hart had taken the flag down during the cannon salute four years earlier.[39]

As Anderson, Harris, and Hart made their way to the dais, Samuel could not have helped but notice that Anderson, dressed in a new uniform with a dark blue military cap, his five foot eight inch frame now slightly bent and his hair thin and gray, showed all of his sixty years.

Among those in audience were members of Reverend Henry Ward Beecher's church in New York. The church had invited Unionists to journey to Sumter on the liner *Oceanus*. Each passenger had paid $100 for the four-day voyage. Upon catching first sight of the fortress, they began singing "Praise God from whom all blessings flow." They had created a Fort Sumter Club, and deemed it a sign of "patriotism at its best."[40]

The crowd of 5,000 inside the fort to witness the event on this day was larger than expected. At midday, the initial speaker, a minister, rose to read from Psalms 47 and 126. General Townsend then stood to read Anderson's April 18, 1861, dispatch:

Having defended Fort Sumter for thirty-four hours, until the quarters were burned, the main gates destroyed by fire, the gorge wall seriously injured, the magazine surrounded by flames, and its door closed from the effects of heat, four barrels and three cartridges of powder only being available, and no provisions remaining but pork, I accepted the terms of evacuation offered by General Beauregard, being the same offer by him on the 11th instant, prior to the commencement of hostilities, and marched out of the fort Sunday afternoon, the 14th instant, with colors flying and drums beating, bringing away company and private property, and saluting my flag with fifty guns.[41]

Hearing his own words for the first time since that day, Anderson recalled his state of emotional and physical exhaustion. His state was such that he was unable to write the telegram dispatch. Instead, he dictated it to Gustavus Fox for transmission as they headed north toward New York aboard the steamship *Baltic*.

Samuel was jarred back to the present by the quivering invocation of Chaplain Harris praying for the blessing that the current American flag would fly over a whole country. It was the same prayer of four years ago.

As Anderson and Hart moved toward the flagstaff, and pulled from the mailbag the same soiled, smoke-blemished, and tattered flag that flew over Sumter, Anderson grasped the lanyard and helped raise the colors slowly to the top of the flagstaff. "It was a signal for the most tumultuous cheer."[42]

Amidst the scene of physical wreckage symbolized by the still half-buried guns, splintered carriages, and smashed bricks, Anderson maintained his stoic composure despite the intense emotion on his face. He finally spoke to the gathering. "I am here, my fellow friends, fellow citizens, and fellow soldiers to perform an act of duty to my country, dear to my heart. I wished to do it in silence, but the Honorable Secretary of War requested I make a few remarks. After four long years of war, I restore to its proper place this flag which floated here during peace, before the first act of this cruel rebellion. I thank God I have lived to see this day and to be here to perform this, perhaps the last act of my life, of duty to my country." He finished with what he had always hoped, "and on earth, peace and good will towards men."[43]

The parapet guns were fired. Their salute was followed immediately by a shot from every battery that had fired on Sumter in 1861. The one hundred-gun salute continued uninterrupted for 30 minutes.

When the firing finally ceased, a cheer arose from those in attendance. Laughter and tears combined as people embraced and the national anthem was sung. The words were at this moment more than mere words—

"land of the free and home of the brave." It was noticed that not one star had been shot out or torn away from the old, soiled flag. That seemed a good omen.[44]

Henry Ward Beecher gave the oration of the day. In the style typical of the period, the speech was both lengthy and embroidered with eloquent passages and vivid imagery. Samuel would have been moved by the phrase "No more disunion, no more secession, and no more slavery," as he also was enthralled by the hour-long delivery.[45]

April 1861 had been Samuel's first encounter with death by friendly fire. Today brought back the emptiness he had felt on that April 14 afternoon; he would write sparingly of the incident and talk even less about it. The officers and men had served their flag with honor, and with honor they would salute it.

Harkening back to April 1861, Samuel understood that Robert Anderson felt that only a one hundred-gun salute would do justice to the men who had struggled here. Back then Lieutenant Norman Hall commanded the salute, and accomplished artillerist Captain Doubleday understood there was no truly safe place to store the powder. The concern was that sparks from prior shots would be driven by the constant breezes and ignite the remaining cartridges. Their worst fears were realized near the middle of the salute when a double explosion occurred. An ignited fragment had blown back into "the cartridges and exploded."[46]

"Several men were blown into the air by the explosion." The surgeon had reacted impulsively and recognized the immediate risk of further danger. He had the injured men carried to the parade ground. Daniel Hough, a 12-year army veteran, had perished almost immediately; Private Ed Galway lost his right arm and had been severely burned by ignited clothing. He, along with George Fielding, another burn victim, was rushed to Charleston hospitals. John Irwin was sent to Charleston for treatment of a thigh wound. The other more slightly burned victims were cared for by Dr. Crawford and his steward at the makeshift hospital and on the trip home.[47]

Now four years later, with over 600,000 men killed or mortally wounded, those still alive had seen many suffer, but those first Sumter dead had served their Union and flag for the briefest of a shining moment.

The ceremonies and the memories were a part of history.

V. The Last Review was Grand.

Crawford joined his division on the march toward Washington. The marches were rather long and tiresome for men eager to arrive at their campsite. Many took time to write at the end of the day. An incident that was mentioned in nearly every letter was the loss of President Lincoln.

Henry Matrau seemed to express the feelings of many of his fellow soldiers. On April 19 he alluded to the fact that he and his mates had heard the president was murdered. "Isn't it a burning shame they didn't want him to enjoy the glory of having crushed the rebellion."

Once in camp they knew it was only a brief time until they completed the paperwork and mustered out of the service. Then home!

Crawford's division camped with the V Corps on the hills near the former Robert E. Lee home. The numerous night campfires caused Crawford to reflect and recall the inspiration that evoked the words to the "Battle Hymn of the Republic": "I have seen Him in the watch-fires of a hundred circling camps."[48]

Tuesday, May 23, 1865, was a busy day of preparations. Officers were hurriedly prepping their men to look their best. Accouterments were shined, white gloves issued, and a final inspection of uniforms and weaponry took place prior to stepping off. The proud unspoken goal was to have this army look better than Sherman's Westerners who would march tomorrow.

Last-minute details were passed from the corps to the division and brigade command. Crawford alerted his brigadiers that their V Corps, since it received the surrender, would be given the honor of following General Meade, his staff, and a few dignitaries.

Samuel Crawford, ever aware of physical appearance, tried to look his best in his military uniform with sash, belt, and sword. One individual noticed, there "stands Crawford neat and trim as usual."[49]

Reveille had been at 2 a.m. The division started across the Potomac from the Virginia side at 4 a.m. The men were relaxed and in the best of spirits. Colonel Wainwright wrote that they were in line by 6 a.m. along Pennsylvania Avenue with the head of the column at First Street East.

"At precisely 9 a.m. at the report of the cannon," the files of 20 soldiers en route step began the parade in a proud manner. The bugles in the V Corps sounded and the color bearer strode forward with the blue Maltese cross on the white flag. When they reached the State Department, cadence was called.[50]

The principal reviewers as well as the general public watched from the streets and from numerous platforms and stands. A separate stand for disabled veterans was provided with funds granted by Mr. John Forbes. President Andrew Johnson, Generals U. S. Grant, and W. T. Sherman, as well as governors, legislators, and foreign diplomats, would watch from a post in front of the executive mansion.

As they filed past the crowds of three or four persons deep which included school children, they were greeted with the singing of patriotic tunes, the tossing of flowers, and cheers such as "Gettysburg," and "the heroes of the Republic." The 2,500 school students sang national airs including the ever recognizable "Battle Cry of Freedom."[51]

Samuel, ever fastidious, was exceptionally tidy and dapper for this affair. He sported a new uniform with sash and his gold ceremonial sword recently presented to him by his staff. Once in a while as he looked down, he saw the battles engraved on its side. Astride his horse Blood, whom he hoped would be on his best behavior, like other mounted officers he saluted as they marched by the reviewing stands.[52]

As New Englander Joshua Chamberlain recorded his impressions, he stated, "Here comes the Third Division with Crawford of Sumter fame, a high gentleman, punctilious, and conscientious soldier; familiar to us all." In the heat of battle a few months before he had used another description for Crawford, "a pet of his state, not of iron fiber nor spring of steel." But now they were comrades in victory far from the pressures of battle.[53]

Washington had surpassed itself to show appreciation to these warriors and the ghosts of the fallen they represented. It was as if the legendary Camelot had arisen, for the previous night the rain had settled the dust and now the mild day was perfect for ending the army life. Even the Treasury Department flag, on which John Wilkes Booth caught his spur jumping the 12 feet to the stage after shooting President Lincoln, was draped over the front of the Treasury Department.[54]

In a little more than six hours the Army of the Potomac was finished.

The following day General Crawford, along with a number of Army of the Potomac officers, witnessed Sherman's march. It was a stark contrast. The spit and polish of Meade's men was replaced with dirty and mud-caked uniforms, unkempt beards, and slouched hats. Dirty boots completed the Western attire. That night guards were placed between the two armies as the Westerners, still looking for a fight, were ready to give the Army of the Potomac men a black eye or two.

After dinner that evening, the fires and embers burned well into the night as the old soldiers regaled each other with tales, stories of delight, humor, sorrow, and fond reminiscences of what they had endured—about what they had given!

By the time summer was seven days old, the Union Army of the Grand Review was no more.

ಸ Chapter Seventeen ಲ

The Years of Passing Flags, Friends, and Career

I. "Take your soiled and war torn banners, your thin and shattered ranks and let them know how you performed your trust."[1]

After receiving an invitation to take part in the flag ceremony in Philadelphia, Samuel decided to make the journey in spite of his troublesome thigh.

When "Sam received the invitation from Talley [Colonel William Talley, formerly of the Pennsylvania Reserves],"[2] he could only think of how he would be able to maneuver. He tried to remind himself constantly that he had only a little gimp compared to many who wished a cane would be enough assistance to walk or wished for a hand to hold their medals, or eyes to see the regimental and American flags, or ears to hear their fellow soldier's voice. He still had the health and mental capacity to take part in and recall those special events.

He had been visiting Alandale, and Sammy, his namesake, likely drove the carriage to take the general to the railroad station; he never tired of hearing the stories his uncle told of meeting Robert E. Lee. He told Sammy often that, yes, Lee was a gentleman, and, yes, his uncle had told Lee that the Northern people would not be as hard on him as he expected, and Lee had responded, "I suppose those in the north look upon me as a traitor."[3] He showed his great depth of emotions when he used the word *traitor*.

Once aboard the train on his way to Philly, as it rambled through the foothills of the valley, Crawford had time to think of the reason he was going to Philadelphia. Recently he read that the Pennsylvania legislature had made provision in 1861 to have Pennsylvania's flags formally returned to the state at war's end. July 4, 1866, was the date chosen to ceremonially retire the flags.[4]

Chapter Seventeen

Samuel arrived in the familiar city of Philadelphia a few days before the big celebration. He was to lead a division in the closing flag ceremony. Regimental flags issued by the state of Pennsylvania were now being brought home to be stored for posterity. The Pennsylvania regimental commander, Colonel William Talley, had represented the Reserves in the prior meetings.

The old soldier relied on his cane now to walk. Any movement, even the simplest maneuver, was painful, difficult, and slow. This slow pace demanded he plan far ahead for appointments. That evening at the Gievard Hotel he was able to swap and exaggerate stories with Winfield Hancock, John Geary, and George Meade, among others. Talley promised to aid him on the morrow.

Crawford's delayed and fretful sleep was interrupted the next morning by Talley's knock on the door. Again, it was time to put on his ceremonial sword. Each time he wore it he admired its workmanship. The top of the handle was fashioned in the shape of a medieval knight dressed in full armor; a gold chain connected the knight's mask at the handle, the chain extended to the eagle, separating it from the blade. The blade was engraved with the names of his division's battles. General Crawford was forever grateful to his staff for their gracious gesture.

As they finally made their way to the ceremonial site, they could tell even at that early hour that it was going to be a steamy day in Philadelphia. It was typical of those summer days he remembered from his youth.

General Crawford and some of his former staff managed to find seats in the shade of a large maple tree. They passed the time retelling old war tales, some of which were highly exaggerated, tolerated, and enjoyed.

One can only imagine the meeting between the Pennsylvania Reserves and their group of old officers. One story told of an old warrior inquiring if they remembered their last battle at Bethesda Church where "we probably killed more Rebs in one hour than in any one battle."[5] Both sides would have remembered that their military obligations had technically finished and it would be noted that Warren and Crawford thought they had the Reserves in a position that would be relatively safe, but it certainly didn't happen that way. It had been a difficult day to serve with the old brigade.

Their minds likely would have drifted to that last charge. It is a strange thing about charges; sometimes they are too successful and that is what happened to Jubal "Old Jube" Early and his boys. They had to slow down to get untangled, and the Reserves used that time to refortify their line and bring in the artillery. Crawford could not remember seeing soldiers build breastworks so fast; as fast as if their service time was finished. That fateful evening they were quite ready for Johnny Reb.

One question still persisted: Were the Reserves trustworthy in those final days of service? They were there; they felt they knew the truth. Their time to serve the country had been up a few days earlier, but they stayed on. It was never easy to have lives sacrificed, and these circumstances made it even more difficult. Originally, in this battle at Bethesda Church, they had been overwhelmed by many times their number; then, they had to cross a swamp, causing many to end their careers or lives in Southern prisons. But they had done what was expected. They bought time at the cost of over 400 casualties.

Everyone began gathering in Penn Square around 9 a.m. for the scheduled 10 a.m. ceremony. Alex, who had arrived a few hours earlier, helped his brother into the saddle. At Samuel's request Alex stayed by his side throughout the ceremony.

As the Reserves saw their flags again, they remembered many of the words their general had spoken on that first day of June 1865. "Go back to the great state that sent you three years ago to battle for her honor. Take back your soiled and war torn banners, your thin and shattered ranks and let them know how you performed your trust. Take back the glorious associations that surround them. You have made them sacred as has the memory of our fallen comrades who gave their lives to defend them." Now his voice swelled to reflect his pride, "Give your banners again to the keeping of the state, forever."[6]

One cannon boomed and 10 church bells rang as General Winfield Hancock started the parade. Crawford and his brother Alex, who arrived from New York, rode down the streets they knew so well; going on Broad Street they passed Chestnut and Walnut Streets heading toward Independence Square.[7] The streets were lined with enthusiastic viewers. As the parade turned into the area where the ceremony would be held, more than five thousand patriots waved red, white, and blue tickets. The generals were cheered with Meade appearing to garner the loudest acclaim.

"The often tattered and torn flags"[8] drew loud applause and cheering as they passed. The crowd's deepest passion seemed reserved for these passing tokens. Some flags were so fragmented that they could only be conveyed in their cases. Others were marked on empty flag poles with a commemorative tag to identify the regiment. The First Brigade's Reserve Flag was noticed for its absence of a flag top; all the others were identified with the embroidered Pennsylvania Reserves lettering.[9]

The Handel-Haydn Musical Society opened the festivities with the singing of the National Anthem, followed by a prayer thankful for victory and hopeful for continued peace. Messengers W. S. Hancock, J. W. Geary,

G. G. Meade, and Governor Andrew Curtin delivered speeches, and the mass sang "Old Hundred" to end the activities around 5 p.m.[10]

II. "Blood" Disappeared.

With the end of the war, an era came to a close. Crawford's career had already been a diverse one. After the Grand Review and the mustering out of the volunteers, the United States Army was downsized and reorganized.[11] General Crawford was given an honorable discharge from the volunteer army in 1866 and shortly thereafter given the assignment as commandant of the 16th Infantry and eventually the 2nd Infantry after the two were consolidated. Huntsville, Alabama, served as home during the last years.

The general had his beloved horse Blood in the beginning of his command, but sometime during his tenure in Huntsville, he was either forced to give him to a new owner since he could no longer ride and care for him, or the horse died. In any case, Blood's loss would have been painful for his owner, perhaps so much so that the ailing man could not write of it.

It was during the early seventies that Crawford was beginning to realize that his painful and debilitating wound was preventing him from being the commander he should be. His visits to the camp surgeon were daily; he had been ordered to remain in his room for days. He came to the stark realization that it was time to leave the army. "The certificate of disability" was processed and sent to the United States War Department toward the end of 1871.[12]

III. October 27, 1871, Nice, France

As Samuel continued the nightmare of paperwork and appointments for his retirement from the United States Army in late 1871, he saw an announcement in a War Department Bulletin by the A.G.O. Office: "The death of General Robert Anderson, 27th October 1871 in Nice, France, was announced here on Friday last. His body will be returned to West Point for interment." The article called him a loyal and highly respected soldier whose career ended in 1863.[13]

As precise and accurate as the article was, Samuel knew there was so much more to this man. He knew the devotion and patriotism of Robert Anderson from a personal sense that few others did. The crumpled piece of paper announcing his demise seemed woefully inadequate, but it remained with Crawford's personal papers and was found after his own death.

This indicated the special place Robert Anderson held in Samuel's heart. He had seen the man under constant duress for months and only for the briefest of moments had he seen him lose his demeanor. The Union was his country, the military was his life, and God was his guide. He did not waver in defense or reliance on any of them.

Crawford could not think of the major without thinking about those moments on December 26, 1860, when the world of those in Fort Moultrie was falling apart. Anderson, standing on the "parapet looking seaward,"[14] unemotionally and unpretentiously told Captain Crawford they would cross to Sumter that evening. With state spies and guard boats all around he had planned to make the move secretly to a place where his men would be safer. It had originally been planned for Christmas evening but the weather prevented the movement. It was a maneuver that shocked his closest cohorts. In the end, it molded the focus of the Union, gave the Lincoln administration its first lesson in confidently dealing with a most oppressive situation, and gave the country, North and South, a glimpse into the mind of an honest man who never blinked.

IV. Silence Prevailed.

In early November of 1872, Samuel traveled to the Carlisle Barracks in Pennsylvania for a scheduled examination by the army medical doctors. From there he would proceed to New York City to be judged by the retirement board directed by his old, wounded comrade, General Winfield S. Hancock.[15]

The doctors at Carlisle found the leg in a slightly worse condition than the medical doctors at Huntsville had noted. The swelling was now accompanied by a second opening which was also discharging bone fragments and other contaminants. In addition to the physical impairment, the doctors noted constitutional disturbances. As a surgeon, he was aware of psychosomatic relationships between the condition of his injury and his mental state.[16]

In addition to his medical problems, he heard disturbing news that struck a nerve and momentarily stunned him. General George G. Meade was dead. His old friend and brother-in-arms was to be buried on November 11, 1872, from Saint Mark's Church in Philadelphia.[17] Samuel made hurried arrangements to complete his business at the barracks and journeyed for a last visit with his noble Philadelphia associate.

Meade's stature as an American could have been measured by those in attendance at the solemn service. As the coffin was removed from the church, it was followed by the family and then a host of friends and dignitaries including the president of the United States, Ulysses Grant.

An honor guard carried the coffin through soldiers who fired volleys to honor the deceased hero. Though he had not reached his 57th year, George

Gordon Meade had made an impact on his state and nation as well as his native city, Philadelphia.

The requiem began with the Pennsylvania Reserves marching in body, with Samuel following in a carriage, as they made their way through the city. Public buildings had been closed and many private residences were draped in black. "Silence prevailed."[18] Someone observed that quietness was the password for the day. The procession moved slowly toward East Fairmont Park where the casket was to be placed aboard a barge bound for Laurel Hill Cemetery. These scenes were happening too frequently for these two Philadelphia families. Samuel heard that George Meade had lost a son only a few years ago.

The man in the carriage, who had just celebrated his 45th birthday, took time to reflect on his own life. This trip allowed him to reconnect with a city pivotal to his life. He had revisited his father's former church, and gloried in the grandeur and beauty of the city.

Meade's body had been taken from the barge, placed on a caisson, and was being drawn to the cemetery. During this leg of the journey, Meade's horse, Baldy, draped with a black blanket, followed the body carrying a riderless saddle; he plodded along at his peculiar gait. He had been left for dead at Gettysburg, but ironically the servant outlived the master.[19]

Here rested an American who had done so much for the country he loved. He surveyed much of it, he built lighthouses, he fought on behalf of its values, and he worked to heal a devastated South and even members of his family who fought for the Southern cause. Much of this lifestyle probably led to a weakened condition and pneumonia that took his life.

As Samuel stood near the gravesite, his thoughts certainly harkened back to 1863 when he had the honor of presenting Meade a ceremonial sword on behalf of the men and officers of the Pennsylvania Reserves. Meade took great pride in the special sword made of Damascus steel.

Mrs. Meade later wrote of her husband's admiration for the gift as he recognized the skill and artistry required to fabricate such a magnificent piece. Mrs. Meade went on to say George had often pondered its cost to those who donated it. He came to relish and value even more the significance of the men's gesture as time passed.

Samuel Crawford clearly recalled Meade's response to the men for their gift. He could almost hear George's words that August day at "the station" as he called General John Reynolds "friend, even a brother"[20] and reflectively remembered other officers, a number of whom he named, and the deep expression of sympathy for those compatriots who had gone to "sleep their last sleep."[21] He lamented also for those that returned home crippled and maimed for life.

General Crawford recalled the moment the general posed the question of why a country as bountiful and blessed as ours would find it necessary to send brother against brother in armed conflict. Then, thoughtfully, he provided his answer, "This great country cannot have two governments or two flags. We cannot consent to that."[22]

Unforgettably, General Meade had reflected on the significance of the role of the Pennsylvania Reserves at Gettysburg. He praised them for "deeds worthy of their reputation, daring, and that they could be relied on in the hour and post of danger."[23] This he said he heard confirmed by their "immediate commander." Again Samuel was filled with a sense of pride.

At the closing of the ceremony, Samuel likely moved at a snail's pace, turned toward the river, cautiously easing his way toward his family plot less than a hundred yards away. The autumn beauty was still evident in a backdrop of this calm, cloudy day. As Samuel peered down, his own mortality passed through his thoughts, a common occurrence under these conditions. He felt a sense of heightened comfort and succor at this time and in this place.

Upon returning from Meade's funeral, the reports from Carlisle had reached Huntsville. They confirmed the increasing deterioration of his condition, and the New York Retirement Board solidly established his disabled state of health. Retirement due to physical disability was recommended.

V. "I hoped I could perform my duties as a soldier."[24]

In January of 1873, he wrote one of the most difficult passages this proud man ever had to pen: "I perform only the lightest of duties. I hoped I could perform my duties as a soldier."[25] Attached to that note was a Declaration of Health by Ned Taylor, surgeon at Huntsville, who confirmed the problem and then went on, "The coldness in the leg indicates severe nerve and circulation damage. It disrupts sleep and only the rubbing of the surface or applied heat alleviates the pain. He is totally disqualified for active duty and there is little or no prospect for improvement under these conditions."[26]

"On the 19th of February 1873" the military career of Colonel S. W. Crawford ended after almost 23 years. The general hoped he had been, as described, a "faithful and loyal servant."[27] He was leaving the military, but the military would never leave him.

He had applied to retire a brigadier general. In 1875 after the secretary of war spoke on behalf of the recent retirees he was upgraded from colonel to the desired rank.[28]

Major Robert Anderson, Commander of Fort Moultrie and Fort Sumter, 1860–1861

Anderson was Crawford's mentor in the difficult times prior to, during, and after the bombardment of Fort Sumter.
Michael Klinepeter Collection, USAMHI

General George G. Meade, Commander of the Army of the Potomac

Crawford served under his command 1863–1865.

AHEC, USAMHI

❧ Part Nine ☙

The Adventures of a Gentleman Bachelor

"Those stones represented the material foundation of cultures thousands of years old."
—Samuel W. Crawford

"That tiny stick grew to be a magnificent willow of beauty."
—Jane Wiestling and Janet Sharpe

Crawford's Commands

Department of the Shenandoah
II Corps Major General Nathaniel Banks
First Division Alpheus Williams

First Brigade General Samuel Crawford
5th Conn., 10th Me., 28th N.Y., 46th Pa.

Army of the Potomac
Major General George McClellan
XII Corps Major General Joseph Mansfield
First Division Alpheus Williams

First Brigade General Samuel Crawford
5th Conn., 10th Me., 28th N.Y., 46th Pa.
124th Pa., 125th Pa., 128th Pa.

Army of the Potomac
Major General George Meade
V Corps General George Sykes
Third Division Brigadier General Samuel Crawford

First Brigade Colonel William McCandless
1st Pa. Reserves, 2nd Pa. Reserves,
6th Pa. Reserves, 13th Pa. Reserves

Third Brigade Colonel Joseph Fisher
5th Pa. Reserves, 9th Pa. Reserves,
10th Pa. Reserves, 11th Pa. Reserves,
12th Pa. Reserves

Artillery Capt. Augustus Martin

Army of the Potomac
General George Meade
V Corps Major General Gouverneur Warren
Third Division General Samuel Crawford

First Brigade Colonel William McCandless
1st Pa. Reserves, 2nd Pa. Reserves,
6th Pa. Reserves, 7th Pa. Reserves,
11th Pa. Reserves, 13th Pa. Reserves

Third Brigade Colonel Joseph Fisher
5th Pa. Reserves, 8th Pa. Reserves,
10th Pa. Reserves, 12th Pa. Reserves

Army of the Potomac
General George Meade
V Corps Major General Gouverneur Warren
Third Division General Samuel Crawford

First Brigade
16th Me., 107th Pa. Vol., 104th N.Y.,
90th Pa., 39th Mass.

Second Brigade
11th Pa. Vol., 88th Pa. Vol., 94th N.Y., 97th N.Y.

Third Brigade
190th Pa. Vol., 191st Pa. Vol.

Army of the Potomac
General George Meade
V Corps Major General Gouverneur Warren
Third Division General Samuel Crawford

First Brigade General Edward Bragg
24th Mich., 143rd Pa., 150th Pa.,
6th Wisc., 7th Wisc.

Second Brigade General Henry Baxter
16th Me., 39th Mass., 97 N.Y.,
11th Pa., 88th Pa., 107th Pa.

Third Brigade General William Hoffman
76th N.Y., 94th N.Y., 95th N.Y. 147th N.Y.,
56th, 121st, and 142nd N.Y.

Artillery General Charles Wainwright

Army of the Potomac
General George Meade
V Corps Major General Gouverneur Warren
Third Division General Samuel Crawford

First Brigade
6th Wisc., 7th Wisc., 91th N.Y.

Second Brigade
16th Me., 39th Mass., 97th N.Y.,
11th Pa., 107th Pa.

Third Brigade
94th N.Y., 95th N.Y., 147th N.Y., 56th Pa.,
88th Pa.,121st Pa.,142nd Pa.

Artillery General Charles Wainwright

ಬಿ Chapter Eighteen ಲ್ಲಿ
The World Traveler

I. A Good Mother, A Great Human

The year 1867 had been bittersweet for Samuel Crawford. On the ides of March his loving and caring mother, who had time for all, could buy no more time for herself against what she called God's will.[1]

On Saturday, March 16, along with his father and his siblings, he made the winding loop into Section L at Laurel Hill Cemetery. It was 3:30 p.m., Ma's favorite time. Her most difficult chores were done, the sun would soon be setting, and she took a few minutes to read her Bible.[2]

The spring was beginning to put on its new dress; the daffodils, forsythia, tulips, and crocuses spewed their awakening colors. They all agreed, this would have pleased her, and they could not but notice that her wishes were fulfilled in that it was a tranquil day in which the earth seemed to live in harmony with nature. They all prayed for the good wife, the good mother, who was "well beloved and affectionately remembered."[3] Could she "hear" the gentle rippling of the river as she had mentioned previously?

Later in the summer of 1867, the University of Pennsylvania honored its former scholar with an honorary law degree because of his diversified pursuits and for upholding his promise as a Philomathean to make an impact on the wider world. It was a moment of pure, unadulterated self-satisfaction for Dr. Samuel W. Crawford II, LL.D.[4]

II. "Mr. Crawford is a gentleman in high standing with his government and has rendered distinguished service in the Army."[5]

After retirement, in the late 1870s and into the 1880s Samuel's life was redirected. He became a world traveler.[6] Travel seemed to revitalize him.

One wonders if he used the European spa methods to aid the healing process. Most of his trips were undertaken for reasons of health. Bermuda and some areas in Europe were especially comforting due to their moderately warm climates.

In 1879 he was named a fellow in the Royal Geographical Society of Great Britain. He was also issued "a special passport" by the War Department, and a letter of introduction reading: "Mr. Crawford is a gentleman in high standing with his government, and has rendered distinguished service in the army."[7] Samuel delivered official papers to foreign governments, a flashback to the early years with the American Embassy in Mexico. At different times he represented the Academy of Sciences, Historical or Geographical Societies from New York, Pennsylvania, Great Britain, France, or Mexico. "He was handsomely received in various countries."[8]

On one occasion as a member of the Royal Geographical Society, he and another fellow society member traveled to the Middle East to observe and research biblical heritage. In articles to the *Franklin Repository*, Samuel recorded his impressions of the Holy Land. "One is amazed at stone foundations, present in the time of Jesus and thousands of years before."[9] His recollections recounted temples, places, and individuals mentioned in the Bible. It was during this trip he witnessed Simon Stilites' pillar where he had preached from its perch many years about the vices of the world.

The acquisition of knowledge and a more robust physical body were benefits of travel for Samuel. On his returns he seemed energized, as were his discussions with John Agnew. He adhered to Lincoln's admonition that "we cannot escape history." Samuel Crawford embraced it with uncharacteristic vigor; additionally, it provided him with a greater appreciation of the Greek and Roman foundations of western culture, and an admiration for the development of religious ideals.

His old self, sometimes feisty and then mild mannered, was evident in the increasing amount of correspondence after a return trip. In the *Franklin Repository* and the Philadelphia papers he replied to a South Carolina historian who implied the only reason Anderson had gone to Fort Sumter was due to his young and excitable officers. Samuel Crawford's reply, filled with daggers, covered most of the editorial page. In an extensive letter to his old Chambersburg compatriot, Mr. McClure, he expressed his gratitude for including him in his articles on "Representatives of Man."[10]

III. "A memorial service will be held at his estate at Alandale and Falling Spring Presbyterian Church."[11]

Samuel had been overseas in 1876 and when he arrived back in New York, he was greeted by the desk clerk at the Union club with the news his father had passed away on June 7. He would be on his way home tomorrow. His arrival was greeted by a subdued A.J. He told Sam that Pa had a slight cold that developed into pneumonia. He passed away at his beloved homestead. The children planned a funeral service at his much-loved home for the close friends and a larger service at Falling Spring Presbyterian Church. Temporarily, they had him interred either in that cemetery or at Alandale.[12] The children then made plans for eventual reinterment in the family plot at Laurel Hill in Philadelphia.[13]

The February wind, cold and blustery, blew across the river and shook the carriage carrying the four Crawford siblings. It was the 19th of February in the year of our Lord 1879 as the hour neared 11 a.m. It is comprehensible that the siblings focused on the hearse directly ahead of them. Immersed in their own thoughts and feelings, the riders of the carriage, three brothers and a sister, emerged from their private thoughts as the carriage turned to pass into the ornate entrance of Laurel Hill Cemetery. They had made the trip so often they knew the gravesite was just to the left of the first circle and they slipped on their gloves and pulled their warm hats a little tighter. As they emerged from the carriage, pallbearers, who represented Presbyterian churches of Philadelphia and academicians from the University of Pennsylvania, removed the coffin from the hearse.[14]

The short graveside service was performed by a friend of the deceased. As the snow blew across the freshly dug grave, the words lauded his relationship with his God and his earthly roles of father, husband, teacher, minister, administrator, and friend to those in need. Humankind had truly lost a friend.

The small gathering expressed their condolences to the four children and moved quickly to the shelter of their carriages. The noon sun's attempt to penetrate the chill was but partially successful and provided little comfort to those who stood by their father's grave. The isolated group of siblings, all in their fifties, understood the mortality of the human body and the respect due. Death could be put off no more than the pervasive chill on that day.

The children, still looking at the grave through the snow flurries, likely felt that Ma was pleased to have her partner beside her again, even if it had been nine years.[15] After all, they had been married nearly 48 years before her death. Samuel, leaning on his cane, looked at the graves of Jane Elizabeth and Cornelius, which were just a few feet away.[16]

By now the gusty winds reminded them to get back to the comfort of the carriage. Samuel was the last to arrive as he had tarried for a few moments at a headstone to his right. That his friend Meade had been gone for seven years was difficult to imagine. After the four were settled in the carriage, they pulled the wool blankets about them and had an opportunity to share reminiscences about their father.

Margaret certainly expressed her thanks for the graciousness of Father providing her with the homestead.[17] Even the way he handled the transfer of the home by selling much of the land separately was a matter of comfort to her. She remembered the time Father jammed a tiny stick into the ground by the stream promising that one day it would be a giant willow of beauty and provide a gift of shade. She remembered the laughter it created. As usual, Father's claim proved correct. It became the magnificent willow—the one they played under, where they sneaked their first kisses, and cried during heartbreak and troubled times. Margaret also recalled Father's insistence that "we girls memorize scripture and read the Bible from cover to cover five times."[18] The "we girls" comment reminded the siblings of another loss, that of sister Anne. She always remained in their hearts. Even though she was gone after only 52 years with them, her memory seemed perpetual.[19]

Samuel could not help but regret being in Europe at the time of his father's death. He recalled Father's philosophy of supporting the downtrodden. All men are indeed created equal in the eyes of God; act accordingly. Wrong should be openly addressed and opposed.[20]

John would have remembered how their father had schooled him in the beauty and glory of nature. Their father saw such eloquence in ferns, wild flowers, and particularly those special maidenhair posies.

The horses' hooves were the only sound to be heard as a peaceful silence overtook them. The still falling snow muffled the sound of the carriage wheels. It was a perfect palette for their emotions. All in the carriage seemed to share an unspoken satisfying solace with how they had worked things out, but most of all, their parents were side by side once again and this time for a very long while.

IV. "He must have been a wag."[21]

A few weeks later, Samuel came across the letter he had written Pa when he had finished a family search for his father's relatives. The son knew his father wanted to make a trip back to his roots in South Carolina to search for relatives, living and dead. But his father's health had been declining for the last few years, so Samuel accepted the responsibility of being his father's eyes and ears.

The quest took place in 1871 while he commanded the 2nd United States Infantry in Huntsville, Alabama. Knowing the search would challenge his own health, he planned the journey accordingly. In the summer he contacted Dr. A. P. Wylie, a relative, and Daniel Stinson, an area historian. Each agreed to a few days in late November; one to provide the carriage and be the intermediary with living family members, and the other to be the guide to different cemeteries that might provide some clues as to the whereabouts of Pa's family. Most of the houses and graveyards were established before the American Revolution and reading the stones had become difficult.

Samuel carried the letter to the library, pulled a plush chair near a large window, and unfolded the parchment. As he began to read its contents, he could almost see his father's countenance. He had been excited about the findings and expressed his thanks to his son many times.

> My dear Pa,
>
> Some of the folks accepted me as a Crawford or Wylie even though my home was in the north. Others shunned me with a stony silence; after all I am a Yankee officer visiting the nest of the southern rebellion. When I informed them I was writing a book about my experiences at Fort Sumter in 1861, they were not interested since I was on the wrong side of the dispute. I was assured I would not tell the truth. I tried to be polite and went about my search in earnest.
>
> One day it happened, suddenly I came upon an old bent soapstone tablet and, judge my emotions, when I found beneath my feet Rosanna Gray Wylie Strait, the kind aunt who sheltered your sister Margaret during the early years of her orphanage. On the bottom of her stone was the inscription: "I'm going unto the happy shore where pain and death are no more."
>
> One cold, rainy, windy day, the two gentlemen took me to visit some Crawfords. A Mrs. Crawford, very old and hard of hearing, could tell us little information except she thought me to be "a cute Boston Yankee." Perhaps her eyesight also failed her.
>
> Some folks remembered Aunt Margaret as having a sweet voice and spoke of her songs. Near Rocky Creek County, we stopped to talk to a lady I guessed to be in her 80s, and she would not communicate with us thinking we represented the Ku Klux Klan. She said she didn't know how old she was and "she never kept no writing's and she didn't remember nothing."
>
> We found your home site. The foundation of the old house is now grown over.
>
> I am enclosing a drawing of the well and spring house. Three old trees stand near and one is a large Kentucky coffee tree which is very old.
>
> Martin, it is said, was a fighting parson and fond of whiskey.

This is his epitaph: What man is he that liveth here
And death shall never see [?]

In an adjacent cemetery, I mused over the virtues of the departed as we located one of your men relatives who had married three times and the one wife had inscribed on her stone not to put him next to her. He must have been a wag!

"My day has come, my glass was run
My resting place is here:
This stone has got to show the spot
Less men might dig too near"

Keep this for I shall want to refer to it again. Affect'ly, your son- Wylie[22]

V. He Did Understand the Spirit of the Orders Given Him.

Samuel Crawford had been retired from the United States Army nearly seven years. He had spent the time in travel, often to attend reunions and meetings with other fellow warriors. He had even purchased land in Gettysburg with the idea of honoring the Pennsylvania Reserves. Aside from the physical distress, the years had been relatively pleasurable.

It is easy to picture Samuel with his head laid back swaying to the rocking train, thinking of the early spring of 1865. In reality it was June 1880, and he was bound for a hearing related to his old compatriot, General Gouverneur K. Warren. He was to testify before a Court of Inquiry.

Warren was finally getting a chance to present his side of the events at Five Forks 15 years earlier. Warren's removal by Sheridan had wreaked havoc on his life since he had been unable to put his dismissal, which he considered unfair, out of his mind or life.

Those were the days when the corps commanders were under more duress and strain than any other leaders. Grant's strategy of enemy destruction at any cost wore on the psyches of them all. Terrain, troop movements, weather, nothing mattered but the mission. In that light, the means justified the end. Life was a mere biological entity. The soldiers saw themselves as exhausted and expendable fodder. The judgments in wartime were not fair; those who gave their men consideration were most harshly judged. Just follow orders! Just charge! Professional jealously, for all kinds of reasons, surfaced. Do not be concerned even with injustice; it is an inescapable part of military life at war, especially this kind of war.

Mesmerized by the sound and beat of the train on the track, his mind coasted back to March 31, 1865. The scenes came so easily. The mind not only retained the events, but the corresponding emotions. The pain of Warren's treatment made him feel the shame. Warren lashed out publicly for what he believed was Samuel's responsibility for a Confederate breakthrough.

The scene occurred in Virginia near Laurel Hill. General Warren had arrived in time only to see Crawford's men fall back in retreat. He could not know the cause. Crawford's men had followed orders as given, but the Rebels had sprung the surprise attack and the unit in front of Crawford, who were just getting into position, came tumbling back on them. Conditions and fear set in and Crawford's men also broke. The division commander managed to get reinforcements, but even they did not hold.

As Crawford and his staff tried to reorganize his men, Warren came up to him and "without allowing any explanation, commenced the most abusive tirade that mortal ever listened to.[23] He used every vile word in his vocabulary against him and when the group thought he was finished, he started another tirade." "He totally forgot what was due to his self-respect as an officer and gentleman."[24] Samuel knew that Warren had vented his spleen against other officers such as Meade, Sheridan, Griffin, and even Grant. His temper was common knowledge.[25]

To Samuel, the one self-satisfying feeling he could remember was that as he was being "taken apart," he sat on Blood without reply. He tried to understand Warren's sensitive nature and the extreme pressure he and the others had been under. Crawford happened to be the closest officer against whom the general could release his pent up emotions. No matter how much he understood the situation and the person, the pain from that tongue lashing probably never washed away. The men of his division heard of it, his peers would hear of it, and certainly his superiors heard of it.[26] Some believe Crawford was deserving of the attack.[27]

The following day the V Corps worked to enforce Sheridan's plan at Five Forks. Griffin and Crawford were to swing west and north and turn left on a road to hit the side of General Pickett's division. Generals Crawford and Griffin, in the confusion of the ravines and enemy fire, had not made the left wheel at the proper time. Warren was finally able to collar Crawford and together they organized two of Crawford's brigades to come into the right and rear of Pickett and partially destroy his men as a fighting unit. The glorious victory was marred by Sheridan blaming Warren for not being in the fight. Warren had organized the three divisions, moved them into a battle position, and went to aid Griffin and Crawford as every good hands-on commander would do. The Yankee breakthrough was complete, and the Southside Railroad would begin to lose its rails tomorrow. General Lee would have to evacuate Petersburg and the capital of Richmond. The rain would stop, the sun would shine, and in eight days it would all be over.

At this point in his life, Samuel realized the anvil of war had forged his character, and failures happened for a multitude of reasons. Life is too fleeting to spend your time in spite and holding grudges. It was in this spirit that Samuel gave his testimony to the court. He and General Warren had been on relatively good terms for a number of years. He had written Warren in 1872 that his "name should be forever connected with saving our left because of his foresight."[28] Warren would say of Crawford that while "He was not highly respected by the military, he had always been friendly to him, and he is not weak if he is shown just consideration for what he has done."[29] General Warren thought Crawford would be a significant witness and he would not do damage to his compatriot from Newport.

On June 15, 1880, Crawford took the stand. Speaking softly, he affirmed and reaffirmed that he did understand the spirit of the orders given him. When asked why he did not follow them to the letter, he exclaimed, "his men were deterred by enemy fire and terrain not by poor orders. Warren had given a good account of himself."[30]

In the end, none of the charges proved to have substance and Warren was found not guilty. In a cruel irony, the court's findings were released after Warren had been placed in his grave, dressed in civilian garb, and without the benefit of military honors. Samuel Crawford likely stood at Gouverneur's gravesite thinking of the emotional pain that had been inflicted on the man and the role he had played. The greater the injustice perceived, real or imagined, the greater the reality of pain.[31]

In 1874 Samuel was invited to Antietam to deliver a Decoration Day speech. It was vintage Crawford. "We are met today to honor the dead. We have come while all nature is springing to life again to bring her first flowers as a tribute and offering to the memory of this hallowed ground. They died for you and me and it is fitting we come together to render homage to their memory, to scatter fresh flowers upon their graves. The fragrance of their deeds and sacrifice is ever fresh on our lives and immortal in our hearts.... Heroic deeds cannot perish; their influence echoes to us through all time and are a shining light to lead us to a loftier patriotism....

"Bring your children to this field and teach them its lessons.... Tell them that the truest and highest glory is in the sacrifice for principle."[32]

Part Ten

The Final Years

"I deem it my duty to my men and for historic truth."
—Crawford to A. K. McClure, June 27, 1886

*"We must stand by our flag and our dreams,
I am committed heart and soul."*
—Crawford letter, March 15, 1861

THE

GENESIS OF THE CIVIL WAR

THE STORY OF SUMTER

1860–1861

BY

SAMUEL WYLIE CRAWFORD

BREVET MAJOR-GENERAL, U. S. A., A. M., M. D., LL. D.

NEW YORK
CHARLES L. WEBSTER & COMPANY
1887

Title page of Crawford's book about his experiences at Fort Sumter.

ᔡ Chapter Nineteen ᔢ
A Life's Commitment

I. "The very name is the watchword of every patriotic heart."[1]

If it was possible for a veteran of the war to have a "favorite" battlefield, Samuel Crawford would have selected Gettysburg. In his postwar life he made his way back on innumerable occasions. Whether it was for a reunion, or just to give a tour, he firmly believed in promoting the memory of those who served honorably on this hallowed ground.

II. Back to Gettysburg Again and Again

One of Samuel's most delightful experiences as tour guide took place in June 1867. General John W. Geary, now Pennsylvania's governor, "Sam" Grant, and Horace Porter arrived on the 20th for a two-day tour—the evening of the first day and the morning of the 21st. Geary guided the men around Culp's Hill; Samuel Crawford pointed out the role of the Reserves on Little Round Top.[2] The questions from Grant were probably poignant and sharp. His military mind was active and inquisitive.

Crawford likely did not miss an opportunity to explain the exploits of his Reserves. He wrote to Professor Stover at Gettysburg College concerning the role of the Reserves on Little Round Top. He lauded, "It is a watchword of every patriotic heart."[3]

From the Union Club in New York City he wrote to Mr. A. K. McClure asking him to be his proxy at a lecture by Daniel E. Sickles. He felt his place was with his Reserves on that 4th of July, 1886. "I am not very well able but I deem it my duty to my men to be at Gettysburg with them this 4th of July. My cane is a steady companion."[4] A companion and a reminder, always, of that evening in December watching the men steal away to Fort Sumter to create history.

The 1888 journey from his residence in the Union Club on Fifth Avenue, New York City, to the battlefield, his last, occasioned by the 25th

Anniversary, a grand and fitting affair, was perhaps the most provocative. The Pickett men came back to be greeted by Philadelphia troops as they departed the train in Gettysburg. They spent time in the coming days at "the angle" where they had fought so valiantly and courageously.

III. Three Egos in a Carriage

Samuel Crawford could not forget sitting tall and erect along with James Longstreet and Daniel Sickles in a carriage being drawn through the Gettysburg battlefield by two fine steeds. It was a trio that represented both sides of the conflict.[5] However, two of them had a history that reached back to frontier duty where Crawford and Longstreet originally met. After the outbreak of the war, they would not meet socially again until Appomattox. Unlike the other two, "Old Pete" Longstreet was a West Point officer. He had been, until the bitter end, a confidant of General Robert E. Lee.

Daniel Sickles, like Crawford, had served under General Meade in the Army of the Potomac. He had moved his division of men about a half mile in front of the Union line on July 2, 1863. It was said, mostly by Daniel, it was due to misinterpretation of orders. By the time the potentially disastrous implications of this maneuver were understood, he was under attack by Longstreet's forces.

The controversy that dogged Sickles for his actions was symbolic of the questions that were probably raised about both Crawford and Longstreet on their performances at Gettysburg. Crawford came under attack for giving his Reserves more credit than they were due and from one source questioning if they were located where they claimed. Longstreet had been accused of sulking on day two by not getting into position as quickly as expected and then arguing for a defensive fight the third day. In the end, Longstreet obeyed Lee's orders to assault.

No matter how others judged the three, they probably stood steadfast in their beliefs of the validity of their ideas and decisions in light of the data available at those moments. They had known the pain of battle wounds. Longstreet had been the victim of friendly fire in the Wilderness campaign, being shot in the throat by his own men. His hearing was severely affected by the wound; consequently, today he carried a hearing horn. Samuel's wound was still evident in his limp. Sickles suffered the most obvious as he had received a wound in Gettysburg that eventually required amputation of his right leg. An artificial limb now aided his mobility, but Dan carried his red badge of courage beside him, first to speaking engagements, and later he sent the amputated leg to the Smithsonian where he visited it on the anniversary of the wound until late in his life.

They were three proud men with egos to match. As the conveyance moved around the battlefield, each man likely took his turn at defending his position. At the Peach Orchard James Longstreet presented his analysis which ignited sparks and comments from Sickles. Near the Wheatfield, Crawford likely showed the movement of his troops the third day—how Colonel McCandless cleared the woods, turned and came back through, and in the process captured the "15th Georgia flag," prisoners, many stacks of arms prepared to be burned, and a Confederate cannon.[6] Longstreet did not believe it happened as he had withdrawn his troops. But how could Crawford have captured prisoners if that had happened? The only reply was that they missed the withdrawal orders.

In a speech a few days earlier Sickles had defended the role of the Reserves. One of Longstreet's division commanders, Lafayette McLaws, indicated that Crawford had not made it to the wall, which occasioned Crawford to show them the rock where he established his headquarters. Each knew that time clouded memories and during battle perception could be wildly challenged by smoke, noise, bullets, and nerves. The three men finished it all in a mood of self-satisfaction.

IV. Crawford Park

In addition to his role in the nation's history, Samuel's other legacy stems from something he was unable to fully realize in his lifetime. The acreage he purchased on the battlefield in 1872 was meant to contain an elaborate memorial to the Pennsylvania Reserves.[7] The almost 47 acres touched the area behind Devil's Den, continued through the land drained by Plum Run, and terminated in the area where the Reserves had conducted their charge. Later, it would be called the Valley of Death.[8]

"In February of 1891, Sam deeded almost two of the acres to the Gettysburg electric railroad for $1."[9] This gesture aided in the development of the railroad to carry tourists around the battlefield. On February 5, 1894, John, Alex, Margaret, and Anne's siblings met to sign the deed for $700 in "good U.S. money."[10]

As he worked to honor his Reserves, his brother John was working to provide a chapel for the Falling Spring Presbyterian Church. Both brothers achieved the goals of their pursuits. John Agnew would see his chapel, and two years after Samuel's passing, the family, as instructed, transferred the ownership of Crawford Park to the National Park Service with the acknowledgment that appropriate monuments would be placed according to Park regulations.[11] Both stand as crowning achievements of the Crawford brothers.

The state had provided money to honor its Civil War officers, but the allotted $55,000 ran out before monuments to Generals John Gibbon and S. W. Crawford could be constructed. In some ways, General Crawford did much to benefit the remembrance of the battlefield that he held in such high admiration. However, in 1988 people from Chambersburg, Fayetteville, and other villages collected money to honor their fellow countian with a statue in "Crawford Park."[12]

The monument was dedicated at the 125th Anniversary of the Battle of Gettysburg. One member of the family remained and along with friends, Reserve reenactors, and citizens, came to honor Franklin County's forgotten Civil War hero. Samuel Crawford was remembered as having "displayed the highest qualities of an officer, good generalship, and heroic courage."[13]

No doubt he would have been pleased to be so honored. It is certain that he would have beamed with pride at the bronze silicon statue. It was simplicity displayed eloquently.

"The likeness was placed on an Alandale boulder facing Fayetteville"[14] and the mountains he adored. The love of the bullet-torn American flag is shown magnificently as he holds it with a gentle firmness. Of course, the finial is missing to show the severity of the fight for the cause. The wound, protected by a bent pants leg is a reminder of the price paid for the freedom for his fellow countrymen. His eyes scan the fields where his Reserves spilled their blood and gave their lives. The foothills that he termed "the Rocky Citadel" surround him. Little Round Top is situated to his back as he focuses on the Wheatfield ahead. He stands with that customary straightness and pride that symbolized and reflected honor, flag, and family.

As proud as Samuel would be of the simply eloquent statue, he would have gloried in what Professor Jacobs wrote in the *Lutheran* in 1913 when he said, "As the Confederates advanced, the Pennsylvania Reserves under General Crawford made a most remarkable charge down the hill pushing back the enemy not only from the foot of the hill, but from the ravine ahead."[15]

After burying his mother and namesake, Margaret's son, Sammy, Wylie's delicate and raw emotions came to the fore as his own mortality weighed heavily. After a visit to "the celebrated field" he wrote Professor Stover:

> It is impossible for me to visit it without expressing what it means to me. It is much more than a field of strife . . . when I recall what was at stake to the country and world. The rocky citadel has become a monument for a rescued Christian civilization . . . its success is written in my dying character, the Providence of God.[16]

A few months before his death Samuel was corresponding with a Colonel Wilson concerning "the 50 acres where the reserves fought."[17] The site could be used for any monument to the reserves.

On February 5, 1894, another family reunion of sorts took place as John Agnew, wife Susan, sister Maggie, Alex McLeod, and a son and daughter of Annie's met in the Adams County Courthouse to witness the transfer of their brother's land to the United States government. The family received $700 for his beloved land purchased to honor the Pennsylvania Reserves.[18] The national military park service would now decide how to use the area of the "Valley of Death."

ᗧ **Chapter Twenty** ᗩ
The End Is Near

I. "I hope to use my notes someday to tell the whole story."[1]

It was the winter of 1886–87 and Samuel was back in New York City. On a typical Gotham day, he made his way to his waiting carriage. He had to brave the conditions this day as he had an appointment with his publisher in relation to his book.

One can see Samuel, accompanied by his man servant, laboriously working his way out of the carriage where it had stopped in front of the New York City offices of Charles Webster and Company. Of course, the best known person in the business was the man who started it, Samuel Clemens. He had given the publishing company life two years earlier with the publication of *The Memoirs of Ulysses S. Grant*.[2] Sustaining that level was found to be extremely difficult.

Samuel's relationship with the Webster Publishers was for the most part a cordial one. Typically, he surely had editorial differences, but both parties were insistent on the accuracy of details in this work on Crawford's tenure at Fort Sumter. More than two decades of research and writing had gone into the book and he had been poring over drawings, maps, engravings before gleaning them down to the ones chosen to support his text. He had told only A.J. that he was taking detailed notes so he could one day tell the Sumter story. Off and on over that decade he had been deciphering, interviewing, and formatting his notes. For Samuel factual text was important for accurately recording the deeds of the players for posterity.

"April 12, 1887," the 26th Anniversary of the Fort Sumter story, had been the target date to publish *Genesis of the Civil War: The Story of Fort Sumter 1860–61*.[3] The book needed a proper cover and Samuel's business this day was the selection of that item. He had been given the privilege to suggest the cover and had considered many ideas, but he remained undecided until one evening it came to him. While reviewing his notes in his room at the Union Club in New York, Samuel uncovered the medal awarded him and his Sumter colleagues by the New York City Chamber of Commerce in May 1861.

During what was billed as the largest ever gathering in the country until then, the soldiers, noncoms, and officers were awarded three different commemoratives. He and his fellow officers were remembered with an 18-ounce medal with a likeness of Anderson on one side and on the obverse the inscription "The Chamber of Commerce of New York honors the defenders of Sumter, the first to defend freedom."[4]

As he scrutinized the award in his solitude, the matter became crystal clear. He would use Anderson's image on the front cover, the title would adorn the front, and on the spine an epaulet with two stars. As the reader opened the book, the preface actually written during a visit to his alma mater, the University of Pennsylvania, appeared.

> A tragic story is easily told. Battle pictures are not hard to paint with words or brush. It is more difficult to trace with accuracy the beginning of revolutionary movements, for these are from the very nature secret, and hidden from the common view...It was been my pleasure and my purpose to seek into these hidden things...
>
> University of Pennsylvania
> April 12, 1887.[5]

After the 449-page text, Samuel added a biographical section of tribute to those officers who went through the dark days of 1860-61. He sketched the highlights of the war years of his old friend Abner Doubleday and Truman Seymour. Most of all he wanted to inspire others. All these men needed to be honored for the cause they aspired to in 1860. It was still a part of their inner fiber 30 years later in one country, one flag. Mr. August Belmont, Sr., was one of the patriots that welcomed "with unlimited hospitality"[6] those who defended the forts. Samuel's note of thanks and friendship accompanied one of the earliest copies of the book to his faithful friend.

II. "From first shot to last he did his duty to his country."[7]

Toward the middle of May 1892, Samuel decided to leave the Washington, D.C., Army-Navy Club.[8] He was fond of the facilities including library, reading room, and dining room which cost him $20 a week to board and each meal about $3. However, he enjoyed winter in Philadelphia or New York. The trip was arduous this year, but the apartment at the Colonnade Hotel in Philadelphia was spacious for him, and the cuisine was excellent.

His days were spent letter writing, replying to invitations, and receiving visitors—old warriors who wished him well and Godspeed. Typical of those friends was a philosophy professor at Penn who had a new trial drug from Italy delivered to him with a note, "trusting your health is not suffering from the extreme heat."[9] A number of the writers encouraged him to "keep up your courageous attitude."[10] With the end of summer and the fresh transfer to Philly, he managed to develop a daily routine. The night of November 2, 1892, was typical. At 6 p.m. his servant helped him prepare for his doctor's daily visit. Dr. Pepper had made the call each day since he had been back.[11] He had been suffering from other ailments in addition to the thigh wound. The swelling in the leg made movement nearly impossible. A weakening bladder prevented him from leaving his domicile even when his leg would have allowed it. A large part of the leg bone needed excised, Dr. Pepper had informed him.

His old black servant, with a gentleman's demeanor and wise in his ways, inquired of his boss to share memories.[12] It can be imagined Samuel looking at his Loyal Legion medallion as he told of the 25th Anniversary, a two-night affair held in this city. The first evening he had been reunited with a number of old soldiers, and the second night they were entertained with a magnificent musical gala.[13]

The old soldier recounted the tale with seemingly added pleasure and smiled peacefully as he delivered his reminiscence. He spoke of his good life in spite of the injuries and pain; he remembered the experiences at Fort Sumter and Gettysburg and his proud association with the V Corps.

Samuel's mind seemed clearest and his body most relaxed when he spoke of the past. He was reminiscing more recently. When his servant told the doctor about this, the doctor attributed it to his overall physical condition.

The next day, November 3, began as a typically frosty Pennsylvania morning. The morning in the city was slightly different from one at Alandale but there was no doubt it was early November. Since it was usual for Samuel to sleep later these days, the servant usually came about mid-morning. The gentleman servant was not surprised that the old soldier had not met the call to reveille, but he was struck by the quietness, as the silence was only interrupted by the ticking of the grandfather clock in the foyer. Suspicious and yet not wanting to startle Samuel, he crossed the bedroom threshold quietly. Nothing seemed amiss, and the general was in the usual back position which allowed him most comfort; he walked to the bedside and gently tried to evoke a response from Crawford. When he could not move him to consciousness, he alerted Dr. Pepper. The doctor reported that Samuel had suffered an "apoplexy rupture of the cerebral blood vessel."[14]

As soon as Margaret and John, now the Reverend J. Agnew Crawford, D.D., were informed, they quickly made arrangements to be by his side.[15] They were joined in the evening by Reverend McConnell of St. Stephen's. Samuel W. Crawford passed away that Thursday evening near 8 o'clock. After a few hours in an unconscious state, he died from a stroke. A note was sent to "J. Clayton, undertaker," who, in turn, notified the superintendent of Laurel Hill Cemetery to prepare the gravesite. Interment would take place in the early afternoon of November 7.[16] The time for A.J. and Margaret was spent looking over the arrangements. Not surprisingly Samuel had prepared most of the details.

Ironically at the hour of his death, the citizens of Charleston were "reproducing the bombardment of Fort Sumter."[17] It had been 31 years since that fateful time when Assistant Surgeon Samuel W. Crawford stood by his honor, flag, and family.

John Agnew and Margaret most likely made arrangements to view the body privately as he lay in state in the vestry room before the viewing was opened to the public. The moments would be charged with emotion.

As they entered, they would have seen a cloth-covered casket with large silver handles. They then looked through the glass plate. His face displayed a calm peacefulness. What he meant to each of them was being mourned. They held hands as Margaret's tears dripped on the silver plate bearing his name. John probably tried to ease her pain, but he too would have been in anguish. He would have found solace in the fact that his brother was at peace, without pain, the pain that had afflicted him most of his adult life.[18]

The old soldier's coat lapels had the two insignias he had looked at the last evening of his life—The Military Order of the Loyal Legion of the United States along with his gold past commander's pin. Proudly resting against the lid of the coffin was a Maltese cross created from chrysanthemums. A handsomely draped national flag was placed carefully on the lid of the casket. Nearby was a magnificent floral arrangement from the Pennsylvania Reserves, dignified and appropriate.

As they departed, they were greeted by an overwhelming number of well-wishers, friends, and old war buddies, some dressed in their old uniforms.

The siblings went to St. Stephen's Episcopal Church where the service would be held at 10 a.m. on November 7. After speaking with the four ministers about the funeral plans and procedures, the conversation turned to the topic of their individual experiences with Samuel. Much was made of his Holy Land visits. John remembered that after his brother's visits to Asia Minor, his interest in the classics was revived and stirred. Samuel had been flabbergasted by the ruins and stones from thousands of years ago that made the biblical stories come alive. Reverend McCullough remembered Samuel's recounting of how he had to change his itinerary to escape the plague in Assyria.[19]

Another of the ministers undoubtedly recalled the great pride Samuel took in his geographical and historical honorary memberships in associations in the United States, Mexico and Great Britain, and of course, Pennsylvania—the first membership from Mexico, nearly 35 years ago and the last one only a few years ago.[20] Much of his life had been devoted to the human environment.

Alex arrived on the morning of the seventh and likely spent some quiet moments at the casket. The younger brother had practiced a stern demeanor, but his emotions were stronger; he could not choke back the tears. Their time together represented a bond that none of the other family members had known. Upon leaving he saluted and whispered, "No more bandages, General, and no more pain."[21]

The next day as the overcast skies broke; the old soldier's casket was borne by men Alex readily recognized. However, the thing that jumped out at Alex was the American flag—the flag that was paramount in his brother's life. He could still remember after the passage of all this time how Samuel once wrote in a letter to him that the Sumter troops might perish, but they would maintain the honor of their flag to the end. As they entered the church the "Dead Man's March" was played.[22] The tune had been very familiar. His pallbearers, Dr. Reed, Dr. Collins, Major George Myers, Major J. T. Coates, Major J. W. Scott, and Sergeant J. H. Ash of the 7th Pennsylvania Reserves, moved slowly with the casket draped with the American flag and a Maltese cross fashioned with white chrysanthemums, violets, and red roses. Mr. A. K. McClure was an honorary pallbearer and was easily recognized by the family.[23]

The casket was placed onto a catafalque and the scriptures based on a passage from Corinthians were read. It stressed the necessity of man's need to continue the search for the self. The conflict between finding a proper balance between his soul and his occupation followed him into the hereafter.[24]

After the rites came to a close, the 75 military men and a guard of Bucktails carrying draped flags led the way to Laurel Hill. Many of the over 200 prominent men of social, civil, and military circles followed the hearse led by the Secretary of Internal Affairs. "The soldier's funeral" included the audience singing his favorite hymn, "Lead Kindly Light."[25]

Samuel, along with his father and A.J., had selected the site for his mortal remains with care. Water was near, he faced the mountains, and now, Meade was his neighbor. The large spreading maples provided shade for the warriors, and Pa afforded Ma security. Years later when his headstone was finished, its simplicity would speak volumes—Fort Sumter on one side and Gettysburg on the other with the Maltese cross etched between them.

Since Alex was his brother's aide at the Battle of Cedar Mountain, he could have probably retold the story the soldiers had heard about General Stuart and the hat. With certainty he could never forget that miserably hot day in August 1862. General Stuart and his brother had been friends before the war and met again that day. As the truce ended, General Stuart said that the Northern press would call this a Northern victory. Samuel disagreed vehemently. Finally "Jeb challenged the wager of a new hat and Crawford took him up."[26] A short time after the wager, Alex brought Samuel a copy of the *New York Herald*, which did, indeed, give the victory to the Northern troops. Samuel sent his brother flying for a brown plumed hat, no expense spared. After he found one and brought it back, he placed the article in the hat and had him deliver it to Stuart. It took some time finding General Stuart as he was having dinner at Jackson's headquarters and the "said bet" was delivered up. Later it was heard that Stuart had lost the hat in an encounter with Union cavalry, jumping a fence on a "get away."[27]

As the ceremony ended and the family started for home, it did not escape any of them that their brother would have celebrated his 65th birthday tomorrow morning. It was now just after noon on Monday, November 7, 1892.

Two years later Major General Samuel Crawford, in spirit, would be in Gettysburg once more as the Reserves dedicated their encampment, Camp Samuel Crawford, with a "21 gun salute and a 99 percent attendance, many with empty sleeves and missing legs."[28] The Reserves bragged that never in the history had any other such numbers been attained.

In 1899 his devoted aide, Alex, was buried near him.

With all his meticulous attention to detail, with his knack for planning, and sense of family, who would have supposed that Samuel W. Crawford would have died intestate?[29] But his countrymen would remember him "for faithful and capable service."[30]

With this diagram, the Samuel Crawford story closes as he closed every letter:

This is the cut made by a *Franklin Repository* artist from a photo. It appeared in the paper upon the death of Crawford.

Franklin Repository. Courtesy of *Public Opinion*

Gettysburg Battlefield.

Author's photo

General Crawford's grave in Laurel Hill Cemetery. Notice the simplicity: the Maltese cross, Fort Sumter, and Gettysburg.

Author's photo

General George Gordon Meade's grave a short distance from Crawford's.

Author's photo

The Crawford Statue at Gettysburg. General Crawford faces Alandale and behind him is the rocky slope where the Reserves made their charge on the evening of July 2, 1863.

Photo by Karen Wagner

Appendix

"The bugle that calls the attack will echo along the slopes of the Alleghenies, amid the granite hills of the north, along the shores of the Great Lakes, and far away on the prairies of the west. The earth will shake with the tread of armed men."

—S. W. Crawford, February 3, 1861

"Go back with me for a moment and mingle in memory with scenes . . . that awoke this peaceful spot from years of quiet . . . to one of earth's fearful tragedies."

—S. W. Crawford (Antietam), May 30, 1874

PREFACE

A TRAGIC story is easily told. Battle pictures are not hard to paint with words or brush. It is more difficult to trace with accuracy the beginning of revolutionary movements, for these are from their very nature secret, and hidden from the common view, and often the more carefully concealed in proportion to their importance. It has been my pleasure and my purpose to seek into these hidden things. In these pages I have undertaken to touch the spring of a fresh impulse, and to unfold the story of those events which led to the great national stuggle between the North and the South in the war for the union of the States. I had a singular intoduction to the scenes which ushered in the mighty conflict...

S. W. CRAWFORD
Brevet Major-General, U. S. A.

UNIVERSITY OF PENNSYLVANIA,
PHILADELPHIA, April 12, 1887.

Inside Page of *Genesis of the Civil War.* Two things are evident in Crawford's preface page: The first is the desire to have history passed to subsequent generations; and secondly, his long association with the University of Pennsylvania.

ॐ Genealogy ॐ

Father

Reverend Samuel Wylie Crawford, Sr. Born January 7, 1793, Charleston, South Carolina. Died June 7, 1876, at Alandale. Interred in Laurel Hill Cemetery, Philadelphia, Pa., February 19, 1879.

Mother

Jane Agnew. Born 1797 New York City and died March 15, 1867. Interred Laurel Hill Cemetery, March 16, 1867.

They were married August 28, 1820, in New York City.

Seven children 1822–1833.

Children

John Agnew Crawford. Born Philadelphia June 24, 1822, and died in Chambersburg, Pa., September 19, 1907. Interred in Falling Spring Presbyterian Cemetery, Chambersburg, Pa.

Married

Susan Monroe Gilbert. Born 1830. Died February 4, 1908, in Chambersburg and is also interred in Falling Spring Presbyterian Cemetery in Chambersburg.

Issue: Jean, Susan, Hazlett, Ellen Anderson.

Margaret Wylie Crawford. Born Philadelphia November 28, 1823, and died December 13, 1912, in Alandale, Fayetteville, Pa.

Married

Edward Crawford Washington. Born January 26, 1820, and died May 16, 1863, Vicksburg, Miss.

Issue: Reade Macon, Samuel Crawford, Norris, Jane "Jennie."

Anne Stavely Crawford. Born November 4, 1825, in Alandale and died 1877, Orange County, N.Y.

Married

Andrew Wilson.

Issue: Andrew, Anne, Maggie.

Samuel Wylie Crawford, Jr. Born in Alandale, November 8, 1827, and died November 3, 1892, in Philadelphia. Buried in Laurel Hill Cemetery, Philadelphia, November 7, 1892.

No Issue

Alex McLeod Crawford. Born May 11, 1829. Died October 20, 1899, in Campbell, N.Y. Buried in Laurel Hill Cemetery, October 23, 1899.

No Issue

Cornelius Nathan Crawford. Born in Philadelphia 1831 and died 1840. Interred in Laurel Hill Cemetery.

Jane Elizabeth Crawford. Born and died in 1833. Interred in Laurel Hill Cemetery.

ᛊᐤ Major Events in Life of Samuel Wylie Crawford ᛋ

1827	November 8. Born at Alandale, Fayetteville, Pennsylvania.
1842–46	Bachelor of Arts Degree, University of Pennsylvania.
1845–46	Moderator of the Philomathean Society, University of Pennsylvania.
1846–48	Graduate Degree, M.A., Penn.
1850	Medical Degree, M.D., from the University of Pennsylvania.
1851–61	Assistant Surgeon in the United States Army, Captain 8th U.S. Infantry.
1856	Temporary Staff Member of the United States Embassy in Mexico; Extensive Collection of Natural History Treatise on Fauna and Flora published by U.S. Congress.
1857	Climbed two Mexican volcanoes and sent specimens to West Point.
1858	Elected as an Honorary Member to Mexico's Geographical Society.
1858–59	Assigned to accompany W. T. Sherman to Texas; Kansas
1860	September. Assigned to Fort Moultrie in Charleston Harbor, South Carolina.
1860	December 26. The 1st U.S. Artillery secretly moved to Fort Sumter.
1861	April 12–13. The bombardment of Sumter by Southern batteries.
1861	May 14. Promoted to Major, Regular Army, 13th U.S. Infantry.
1861	September. Appointed Inspector General on General William S. Rosecrans' Staff in western Virginia.

1862	Waiting for a Command, Crawford was a Reconnaissance Scout for General Nathaniel P. Banks.
1862	April 25. Promoted to Brigadier General of Volunteers.
1862	August. Commanded a Brigade in the Battle of Cedar Mountain.
1862	September. While leading a Division at Antietam he was wounded (XII Corps).
1863	Spring. Worked on a Court-Martial Court. Selected as a member of Academy of Science.
1863	June. Appointed to command a division of the Pennsylvania Reserves.
1863	July 2. Brevet Colonel in the Regular Army.
1863	July 2–3. Battle of Gettysburg.
1864	February 17. Lieutenant Colonel of 2nd Infantry.
1864	Summer. Commanded the Reserves/others in Overland Campaign (V Corps).
1864	June 16. Crossed the James River.
1864	December. Brevet Major General of Volunteers.
1865	October and January. Division and Briefly Corps Commander in Appomattox Campaign.
1865	January 13. Brevet Major General in Regular Army.
1865	Honorary Member of the Military Order of the Loyal Legion. Commanded the Pennsylvania group.
1866	Honorable discharge from the Volunteer Army.
1867	Honorary Law Degree, L.L.D., from the University of Pennsylvania.
1869	February 22. Colonel of the 16th U.S. Infantry (March 15 to 2nd Infantry).
1870	Vice President of the University of Pennsylvania Alumni Association.
1872	Purchased 50 acres of land in Gettysburg to honor the Reserves.
1873	February 19. Retired from the Regular Army as a Colonel of the 2nd Infantry.
1875	March 3. Promoted to Brigadier General on retirees list.

1875–87	World Traveler. For health and to the Holy Land.
1870s, 80s	Attended reunions of the Pennsylvania Reserves at Gettysburg.
1879	Honorary Member of the Royal Geographical Society of Great Britain.
1879–81	Pennsylvania Historical Society; New York Historical and Geographical Society.
1887	April 12. Finished the writing of his book *Genesis of the Civil War*.
1892	November 3. Died in Philadelphia.
1892	November 7. Interred in Laurel Hill Cemetery, Philadelphia.
1988	125th Anniversary of the Battle of Gettysburg. A statue to General Crawford was dedicated.

ℰ Abbreviations ℛ

ACHS	Adams County Historical Society, Gettysburg, Pa.
AL	Antietam National Battlefield Library
CFL	Coyle Free Library, Chambersburg, Pa.
CWTI	*Civil War Times Illustrated*
GNPA	Gettysburg National Military Park Archives
GNPL	Gettysburg National Military Park Library
HSC	Historical Society of Charleston
HSP	Historical Society of Pennsylvania, Philadelphia, Pa.
KHS	Kittochtinny Historical Society, Chambersburg, Pa.
LHA	Laurel Hill Cemetery Archives, Philadelphia, Pa.
LOC	Library of Congress, Washington, D.C.
MA	Moultrie Archives, Moultrieville, S.C.
NA	National Archives, Washington, D.C.
NCWM	National Civil War Museum, Harrisburg, Pa.
NYPL	New York Public Library
OR	*The War of the Rebellion: A Compilation of Official Records of the Union and Confederate Armies*
PSUL	Penn State University Library
SUL	Shippensburg University Library
UPA	University of Pennsylvania Archives, Philadelphia, Pa.
USAMHI	United States Army Military History Institute, Carlisle, Pa.
WCA	Wilson College Archives, Chambersburg, Pa.

ꙮ Notes ꙮ

CHAPTER ONE: A SUMMER'S RETREAT TO ALANDALE

1. Samuel Wylie Crawford to his family, or in his diary, January 24, 1861; February 2, 12, 24, 1861. The expressions varied but the basic idea was the same, and they were always associated with illness, "I need the mountains of Pennsylvania." "To get better I must have the fresh air of the Pennsylvania mountains." Crawford Papers, LOC, Washington, D.C.
2. Crawford Family Genealogy, KHS; Alfred Nevin, *Men of Mark of the Cumberland Valley 1776–1876* (Philadelphia: Fulton Publishing Co., 1876), 160–63, CFL; Genealogy, KHS; Article "Stranger in the Graveyard," Edward James (Author's possession). The couple retrieved the children in 1800 and adopted them.
3. Nevin, *Men of Mark*, 160. In two towns the services were held in schools and in the others in churches, CFL; Letter from Reverend Crawford to Philadelphia Presbytery Synod, April 1, 1831. CFL.
4. Genealogy file. John Agnew born in 1822 and Margaret November 1823, KHS.
5. Nevin, *Men of Mark*, 161, Crawford Genealogy, KHS.
6. Nevin, *Men of Mark*, 161; Reverend Crawford Letter to Philadelphia Presbytery Synod 1831, CFL. It contained over 300 acres of land; James Dickson, Kittochtinny Papers, vol. 19, 172.
7. Crawford file, CFL. According to the owner at the time of writing, Gerald Eberly, logs were carved with the date 1823 and Crawford did not move in until March or April 1824. Interview, December 2001 with Mr. and Mrs. Gerald Eberly; Reverend Crawford letter to synod, April 1, 1831.
8. Nevin, *Men of Mark*, 161.
9. James Dickson, "Major General Samuel Wylie Crawford," Kittochtinny Papers, vol. 19 (1989): 173–80. The name comes from an area in Scotland, Great Britain, near his ancestral home. It was spelled "Alandale." Sometimes newspapers had it "Allan dale" (two words) or "Allandale." Other times it was seen as "Allendale." I use "Alandale" because that is the way Reverend Crawford wrote it. Before the homestead was rebuilt it was called "Crawford-John."
10. Crawford Genealogy, KHS. Anne Stavely Crawford, November 4, 1825. Samuel Wylie, Jr., November 8, 1827, and Alex McLeod, May 11, 1829.
11. Letter to Philadelphia Presbytery Synod, April 1, 1831, on pending resignation from Rev. S. W. Crawford, April 1, 1831, CFL. He wrote that when he arrived home Sunday evenings, he then had to prepare for his academic duties.
12. Ibid.
13. Nevin, *Men of Mark*, 161; Dickson wrote that he was "eminently successful in managing the academy." KHS, vol. 19, 177.

289

14. Rev. Samuel Crawford sermon #33, HSP.
15. Presentation by Jane Washington Wiestling and Janet Wiestling Sharpe to KHS (copy date is November 7, 1938); *War of the Rebellion, A Compilation of the Official Records of the Union and Confederate Armies* (Washington, D.C.: Government Printing Office, 1891) vol. 46, series 2, 630. Hereinafter it will be written *OR*, vol./series, p. Meade to Grant, February 22, 1865.
16. Nevin, *Men of Mark*, 162.
17. Crawford Family Genealogy, Nathan Cornelius 1831–1840, Jane Elizabeth 1833. Indications are that one died of yellow fever and the other due to trauma of childbirth.
18. The children were re-interred when the sister of Samuel, Sr., died. She was buried 5'8" deep and they 12' deep. North Laurel Hill, Permit No. 830, LHA.
19. Crawford Genealogy, KHS, 1822 to 1833. Five lived: three boys and two girls. Two died: one boy and one girl.
20. Diary, Jennie Washington Wiestling, Samuel's niece, given to me by Mr. and Mrs. Eberly. She always wrote of transportation with the hired man. However it seems possible that John Clark, the tenant, could have done the honors. The Jane Wiestling and Janet Sharpe presentation, KHS. It is possible that they were referring to the same person.
21. Nevin, *Men of Mark*, "Major General S. W. Crawford," 436–40. No place was found that indicated his weight. He was referred to as thin.
22. Dickson, Kittochtinny Society Papers, vol. 19, October 1986, 177. 500 yards from Alandale; Gerald Eberly interview; Diary of Jennie Washington Wiestling, CFL.
23. Personal tour of the home provided by the Eberlys. The landscape was also included in the tour. Also some photos and drawings, KHS. A Pictorial History of Franklin County has a photo of Alandale in 1890, p. 75.
24. Many stories of the owls swooping down from the hill were told to me by locals, especially Geoff Crawford.
25. Personal visit; Footnote on Jane Wiestling and Janet Sharpe presentation, KHS.
26. Abstract of the regulations of the University Department of Arts, 1846. S. Wylie Crawford, Jr., graduates in the Arts. Senior essay, Ornithology, University of Pennsylvania Archives, UPA. Most University of Pennsylvania Post-Graduation and Medical School Records indicate Samuel Wylie Crawford, Jr., to differentiate between him and his father.
27. Tour provided by Mr. and Mrs. Gerald Eberly to Karen and Richard Wagner.
28. Personal tour. Such seems the case as the owner found bricks in the dirt and the ovens were mentioned in their letters; Diary of Jennie Washington Wiestling.
29. Jane Wiestling and Janet Sharpe presentation, KHS. The girls had to read the Bible and memorize verses.
30. Crawford's Letter to the Adjutant General, October 12, 1871, correcting birth date. He spelled his birthplace as "Allandale Farm"; a second letter was later found dated October 12, 1891.
31. Abstract of the Regulations of the University Collegiate Department, UPA. This lists all classes for all years. To be admitted into the Freshman Class, one must be qualified for examination in Latin, Greek, English, and math. At the time this research was done, the student records of those who graduated before 1850 were located in an upstairs room under the Franklin Field bleachers.
32. Department of Arts Regulations, University of Pennsylvania; Falling Spring Presbyterian History, 108. Both men taught Greek. Reverend Crawford in University of Pennsylvania, and John Crawford in Wilson College in later years. One letter indicated John had a special capacity in teaching Greek poetry. The reverend taught Latin, Greek, and Hebrew. The December 1897 *Pharetra* of Wilson College indicated he occupied a chair of philosophy. WCA.
33. Nevin, *Men of Mark*, 160, CFL. Samuel, Sr., had taught in this school in the years before he was sent to New York where he was ordained in 1823.
34. Papers of Samuel W. Crawford, LOC. Notes and letters throughout stress the importance of this family trait.

35. Abstract of the Regulations of the University, Department of Arts. The school year was divided into three terms.
36. Ibid., 6, 7. The duties of Rev. Samuel Crawford, D.D., are listed as teacher of classics, professor of Greek and Latin, and vice-provost. The subjects he would teach were Horace's Satires, Epistles to Hebrews, Herodotus, Roman and Grecian Antiquities.

CHAPTER TWO: THE MENTOR, THE PLAN, AND PHILO

1. The *Pharetra* (Wilson College Newsletter), vol. 21 (#1), (November 1907), 22, WCA; Falling Spring Presbyterian Church history, 1904. Rev. John Agnew Crawford, D.D., 1867–1882. This information in the Falling Spring Presbyterian church chapel with a portrait.
2. Crawford Family Genealogy, KHS.
3. Samuel W. Crawford to John Agnew Crawford, December 12, 1860, Samuel Crawford Papers, LOC.
4. Tombstone: Falling Spring Presbyterian Church, Chambersburg, Pa.; *The Pharetra*, vol. 21, 1907, 22, WCA. "I have fought a good fight, I have finished my course, I have kept the faith."
5. *The Pharetra*, vol. 11 (#2), (December 1897), 65, WCA.
6. Crawford Genealogy, KHS. In his letters Samuel calls her "Suzie."
7. Nevin, *Men of Mark*, 163. Father took definite stands on controversial issues.
8. John Agnew's belief as cited in S. W. Crawford's responses in letters.
9. Samuel W. Crawford to John Agnew Crawford, December 12, 1860, Samuel Crawford Papers, LOC. No human foresight can tell what the end of this issue will bring. February 24, 1861; Notes in Crawford Papers, LOC.
10. Abstract, Regulations of the University Collegiate Department (1845–1850). The courses ran the gamut from the study of classics in their native language, mathematics, literature, moral philosophy, sciences, rhetoric, history, and government. On Saturdays, the seniors delivered essays on current topics. UPA. There are no dates, but the archivist said they ran for periods of five years.
11. Ibid. Modern Languages will cost "a moderate additional expense."
12. Abstract, Department of the Arts: Graduates in the Arts, 1846. The states are listed individually. Students from outside the United States were listed as students from Canada, West Indies, and East Indies.
13. Crawford Letter to John Agnew, December 12, 1860. "I am sympathetic with the Southern states in that I do honestly believe all states should be treated with justice and equal rights." Later he would write that "the state did not want justice only revolution."
14. Philomathean Society folder. University of Pennsylvania Archives for those who graduated before 1850.
15. Abstract, Department of the Arts: Section Master of Arts: S. Wylie Crawford, July 1848, UPA. When a document dealt with a Penn matter, he signed "Samuel W. Crawford, Jr." to avoid conflict with his father's name.
16. Nevin, *Men of Mark*, 160. Father studied under Dr. Samuel Smith for a brief period and then entered the study of theology. At one point he wrote he could not get through Smith's course. CFL. Ironically Samuel's grandparents died of yellow fever in Charleston, S.C., where he would be stationed at the beginning of the Civil War, and even provided medical services in that city. KHS.
17. Honorary Degree Records, University of Pennsylvania, Samuel Wylie Crawford, Jr.; Crawford Papers, LOC.
18. Folder: Philomathean Society; Archivist UPA.
19. Crawford Papers, Historical Society of Pennsylvania, HSP.
20. Honorary Degree records list his admission into Philo and the fact he was selected moderator. UPA; Historical Society of Pennsylvania, Crawford Papers, HSP.
21. Philomathean Society notes. S. Wylie Crawford and others to Peter McCall, Esq., September 24, 1845, Crawford Papers, HSP.

22. Abstract Department of the Arts, List of Graduates, July 1846, S. Wylie Crawford, Ornithology, UPA.

CHAPTER THREE: BACK TO PHILADELPHIA AND PENN

1. Crawford File, Genealogy, KHS. Three children: two girls and a boy. In her diary Jennie mentions going to their place at different times during the war. The last time she visited, she said they sold photos of Lincoln after his assassination. Two of the children would represent Anne in the deed ceremony of the Gettysburg Crawford property in July 1894.
2. Crawford Papers, LOC. With the exception of a note here and there in letters it was difficult to find information about Alex. Most information comes from his service records, genealogy, and Samuel's letters. The letters contained words that indicated a close relationship.
3. Constance Wagner, *Ask My Brother* (New York: Harpers and Brothers Publisher, 1959). Throughout the book the author describes the geography and social climate of the times in Chambersburg.
4. Nevin, *Men of Mark*, 162. Later he held the job of professorship of divinity for two or three years.
5. Laurel Hill Cemetery brochure, LHA, Philadelphia, Pa. This was a Sunday occurrence according to the officials at Laurel Hill Cemetery.
6. Amey Hutchins, Public Service Archivist, University of Pennsylvania; Van Pelt Collection, a drawing, UPA.
7. Abstract, Regulations Medical Department, UPA; Medical Faculty, 1850, inside page, and report of the Medical Department, 1850. The readings and courses were to aid the applicant to get into medical school, UPA.
8. Laurel Hill's Cemetery's Sales Book #1, 201. The lot number, section number, May 2, 1847, $50.
9. Abstract; Regulations of the Medical Department of the University, session 1849–1850, UPA.
10. Ibid.; Honorary Degree Records, UPA. The A.M. was finished in 1849.

CHAPTER FOUR: MEDICAL SCHOOL UNIVERSITY OF PENNSYLVANIA

1. Medical Faculty, ed. *Report on the Medical Department, University of Pennsylvania* (Philadelphia: R. L. Bailey, 1850), UPA.
2. Ibid.
3. Amey Hutchins, Public Service Archivist, University of Pennsylvania Archivist.
4. Medical Faculty, ed., *Report on the Medical Department, University of Pennsylvania*. This may have been the Mr. H. Smith that communicated with Samuel in Fort Sumter. UPA.
5. Diseases that can be cured by use of drugs.
6. Abstract, Surgical and Medical Cases and Procedures, University of Pennsylvania, 1850, Philadelphia, Pa. UPA. Chloroform is listed with medicines at Fort Sumter. Crawford Papers, LOC.
7. Ibid.
8. Medical Department Report, 4; Medical Department Faculty, 8. Crawford's list of medicines at Sumter is listed in his papers. Among them lavender, cinnamon oil, peppermint, mustard seed, cayenne pepper, olive oil, and citric acid. Crawford Papers, LOC.
9. Crawford Papers, LOC.
10. Arthur Schlesinger, Jr., ed., *The Almanac of American History* (New York: Barnes and Noble, 1993), 254; David Potter, *The Impending Crisis* (New York: Harpers, 1976), 1–6.
11. Notes, Dr. Bernard Hogg, Shippensburg College, Personal; Dave Heidler and Jeanne Heidler, *Encyclopedia of the American Civil War* (New York: Norton, 2000), 2121.
12. Philip Klein, *President James Buchanan* (Newtown, Conn.: Political Biography Press, 1962), 290.
13. Merle Curti, et al. *A History of American Civilization* (New York: Harpers, 1953), 287. In Crawford's Papers were letters from James Buchanan, LOC; Crawford folder, HSP.

14. Abstract listing graduates, April 6, 1850, 24. Crawford, S. Wylie, Jr., Philadelphia. Hypertrophy and Atrophy. Samuel's preceptors were Horner and Smith; Atrophy: the muscles decrease in size because of disease or non-usage; and hypertrophy: abnormal enlargement of organs, elephantiasis, for example; according to Medical Regulations of the University, the thesis was presented to the preceptor, who, if in favor of the document, presented it to the committee.
15. Abstract listing graduates compared with those who had entered. UPA.
16. Medical School Graduate Bulletin, 1850; Honorary Degree Records. Ludlow was listed as provost. UPA.

CHAPTER FIVE: MILITARY, MEDICINE, AND ADVENTURE ON THE FRONTIER

1. James Dickson, vol. 19; Nevin, *Men of Mark*, 436, CFL. This was a grueling 2-day oral exam.
2. Throughout Samuel's life there was confusion in regard to his birth year, particularly in the Civil War years. Many listed his birth year as 1829, but it was finally correctly listed as 1827. In a letter to the Retirement Board (Adjutant General) October 12, 1871, he acknowledged being born November 8, 1827, at "Allandale farm," Franklin County, Pa. M1395, NA. His sevens and nines often looked similar; pay information from Scott Hartwig, Gettysburg National Park Historian. In a later search, another letter concerning his birth was dated October 12, 1891. NA; Adjutant General's Office, File ACP 1873, assistant surgeon; James Dickson, 173, KHS.
3. James Dickson, 173, vol. 19, KHS; Jeff Coy speech, Pa. House of Representatives, 9/08/1986.
4. Paul Boyer, ed., *Oxford Companion to American History* (New York: Oxford, 2001), 149, 150; Ken Davis; *Don't Know Much About Civil War* (New York: Bantam Doubleday Dell Audio, 1996); McPherson, James, *Battle Cry of Freedom* (New York: Oxford University Press, 1988), 82. The 1850 compromise provided concessions to both North and South, some based on the concept of popular sovereignty to decide the slavery issue in territories. These were mentioned in a number of Samuel's letters to John Agnew, and in his interviews with Judge J. S. Black, a member of Buchanan's second cabinet. Crawford Papers, LOC.
5. Holman Melcher, *With a Flash of His Sword* (Kearny, N.J.: Belle Grove Publishing, 1994), 219, 220; Burke Davis, *Jeb Stuart, The Last Cavalier* (New York: Wing Books, 2000), 157–60.
6. James Dickson, 173, KHS; speech to Pennsylvania House of Representatives, Jeff Coy, September 8, 1986.
7. Crawford Papers, LOC.
8. S. W. Crawford to A.J., March 15, 1861. This was in response to a drawing sent to Crawford by his brother. He added, "Our little band stands out in bold when one thinks of Twiggs and his treachery."
9. Ibid. In January of 1854 Samuel sent a drawing to John Crawford. Years later, he sent it back to Samuel. Prior to March 15, 1861; James Dickson, 173.
10. Nevin, *Men of Mark*, 436. Nevin gives the time 1853 to 1856. CFL; Coy speech, Sept. 8, 1986.
11. Nevin, *Men of Mark*, 436; Samuel Bates, Library, Sharpsburg, Md.
12. Bates, *Martial Deeds of Pennsylvania* (Philadelphia, Pa.: Davis Publishers, 1870), 810, AL; Nevin, *Men of Mark*, 436, CFL. Collections of natural history entitled "The Flora and Fauna." Some of this area was unexplored; Dickson, 173.
13. Nevin, *Men of Mark*, 436; James Dickson, KHS; Bates, *Martial Deeds*, 810; Crawford Papers, CFL, LOC. Language at Penn was a specialty and indications are that he learned to speak Spanish fluently while in Texas the prior years.
14. Nevin, *Men of Mark*, 436; Coy speech, Sept. 8, 1986.
15. Nevin, *Men of Mark*, 436; *Harper's Weekly* Journal (Bedford, Mass.: Applewood Books, 2001), disc one, March 23, 1861; Crawford Papers, LOC. The Prussians had published the results of

a scientist who provided the dimensions of the volcano to confirm the findings of Humbold. The Prussian government wanted to verify the dimensions.
16. Bates, *Martial Deeds*, 810, AL; Nevin, *Men of Mark*, 436, 437, CFL.
17. James Dickson, 173, KHS. Sent to West Point. The first person to carry a barometer to the summit of Popocatepeti, the grand volcano of Mexico. The second volcano he climbed was Iztuchihuat, which means the Sierra Nevada of Mexico; Nevin, *Men of Mark*, 437.
18. Nevin, *Men of Mark*, 437, CFL; Honorary Degree Records, UPA.
19. Bates, *Martial Deeds*, 810, AL; *Harper's Weekly*, March 23, 1861 (disk no. 1).
20. Exhibit, USAMHI, Carlisle, Pennsylvania.
21. Merle Curti, et al., *History of American Civilization* (New York: Harpers, 1953), 316–19; Jean Baker, *James Buchanan* (New York: Holt and Co., 2004), chapters 1, 2; lecture notes American History, Robert Bloom, Gettysburg College, personal; Klein, *James Buchanan*, 271–72.
22. Samuel Crawford to Dear Brother, February 3, 1861, Crawford Papers, LOC. In Charleston harbor the policy that developed until December 27, 1861, was to do nothing to make the state feel threatened. Through this non-aggression policy, they believed war would be averted. Secretary of War Floyd was one of this policy's fondest advocates.
23. Samuel W. Crawford to Alex (the introduction probably was meant for either A.J. or Mac), January 17, 1861, Crawford Papers, LOC. "I do not stand for republicanism, but do not mistake I do not go with the ultra south at all."
24. Stephen Oates, *To Purge This Land with Blood* (Amherst: University of Massachusetts, 1984), 132–37; James McPherson, *Battle Cry of Freedom* (New York: Oxford Press, 2002), 119.
25. S. W. Crawford to A.J. (John Agnew), March 15, 1861. Later Samuel would mention the treason and treachery of Twiggs and how it broke their hearts. Twiggs was one of his commanders for a brief time when Crawford was in the Southwest; Dickson, 174; Coy speech.
26. Samuel Crawford, *Genesis of the Civil War* (New York: Webster Co., 1887), preface, v. Fort Adams was his frequent transfer base.

CHAPTER SIX: THE CALL TO MOULTRIE

1. Jennie Washington Wiestling Diary, Crawford file, CFL. This is Margaret and Edward Crawford Washington's daughter, Samuel's niece. She married a Wiestling.
2. Woodstock Mill, Painting in Alandale. The gristmill was an integral part of the rural area economy.
3. Iron furnace of Caledonia file, KHS. Samuel and A.J. communicated later in letters about the furnace and the need to repair and maintain it. The first letter was March 7, 1861.
4. Iron Works folder, KHS. The shop near the furnace operation sold and took orders for this type of equipment. Brochure Caledonia Park and personal tours.
5. Samuel W. Crawford to Dear Brother, March 4, 1861, Crawford Papers, LOC. He writes of the Twigg treachery again.
6. Samuel Crawford to Dear Brother, March 4, 1861. He admits he is "sad for the condition of the country."
7. *Valley Spirit*, July 16, 1859, August 29, 1860. Chambersburg, Pa. The latter is the one of this incident.
8. Crawford, *Genesis of the Civil War* (New York: Webster, 1887), v.
9. Samuel wrote about this in his later letters to his brothers and family. When he received packages from home he expressed his gratefulness for "goodies from Ma," and the home-style food he missed that Margaret and Anne sent him.
10. Abner Doubleday, *Reminiscences of Forts Sumter and Moultrie in 1860–61* (Charleston, S.C.: Nautical and Aviation, 1998), 23. Captain Abner Doubleday would say of Crawford, "He was genial, studious, and full of varied information." His sense of history is evident in many of his writings. See address delivered at Antietam National Cemetery, Decoration Day, 1874.

11. *Valley Spirit*, August 24, 1859. The *Valley Spirit* was active in following the Brown story. KHS.
12. Stephen Oates, *To Purge this Land with Blood* (Amherst: University of Massachusetts, 1984), 297. Updated reports in modern newspapers indicate there is no doubt that Frederick Douglass conferred with Brown at a quarry in Chambersburg; *Valley Spirit*, October 26, 1859.
13. Oates, *To Purge This Land*, 307–11.
14. Crawford, *Genesis*, preface, v.
15. Ibid.
16. Crawford, *Genesis*, vi.
17. Crawford, *Genesis*, vi, vii; Doubleday, *Reminiscences*, 19.
18. Crawford, *Genesis*, vi.
19. Crawford, *Genesis*, vi.
20. Crawford, *Genesis*, vi.
21. Crawford, *Genesis*, 4–8.; *Fort Moultrie, Constant Defender*, National Park Handbook, 136 (Washington, D.C.: U.S. Department of Interior, 1985), 30, 31.
22. W. A. Swanberg, *First Blood* (New York: Scribner's Sons, 1957), 2, 102; *OR*, vol. 1/1, 75, Anderson's evaluation of the situation; Doubleday, *Reminiscences*, 14.
23. Crawford, *Genesis*, vii. Crawford wrote that the servant had attended an officer he thought had died with yellow fever.
24. Crawford, *Genesis*, vii.
25. Crawford Papers, LOC.
26. Richard Hatcher, Moultrie historian, provided lists of personnel. These were created by Rick Calhoun. One source indicated Crawford had other aides; if so, they must have been temporary appointments. MA.
27. Gordon Dammann, *Medical Instruments and Equipment*, vol. 2 (Missoula, Mont.: Pictorial Histories Publishing Co., 1988), 50.
28. Doubleday, *Reminiscences*, 24, 32, 97, 130; Swanberg, *First Blood*, 102; Maury Klein, *Days of Defiance* (New York: Alfred Knopf, 1997), 332.
29. Doubleday, *Reminiscences*, 23.
30. Doubleday, *Reminiscences*, 97, 130; Swanberg, *First Blood*, 10–11; Klein, *Defiance*, 332.
31. Nevin, *Men of Mark*, 160; Crawford, *Genesis*, 7; Crawford Genealogy, KHS.
32. John Waugh, *Class of 1846* (New York: Warner Books, 1994), 183. The drawings that appeared in *Harper's* are in the Crawford Papers in the LOC; Crawford, *Genesis*, 279, 291.
33. Crawford, *Genesis*, 56.
34. Crawford, *Genesis*, 56; Doubleday, *Reminiscences*, 18.
35. Crawford, *Genesis*, Porter Report, 60; *OR*, vol. 1/1, 70–72.
36. Crawford, *Genesis*, 7.
37. Doubleday, *Reminiscences*, 30; Crawford, *Genesis*, 37; *OR*, vol. 1/1, 69.
38. Crawford, *Genesis*, 57–59; *OR*, vol. 1/1, 68, 69; In *Annals of the War* Crawford wrote that a large number of the workers came from Charleston, 319; Doubleday, *Reminiscences*, 36.
39. Crawford, *Genesis*, 57–60; Doubleday, *Reminiscences*, 30, 31; Waugh, *Class of 1846*, 184, 185; *OR*, vol. 1/1, 69.
40. *OR*, vol. 1/1, 69–71; Klein, *Buchanan*, 354; Doubleday, *Reminiscences*, 30, 31.
41. Klein, *Buchanan*, 354–58, 377, 378; *OR*, vol. 1/1, 70, 72.
42. Doubleday, *Reminiscences*, 17, 18. The garrison was ecstatic when Floyd resigned on January 1. President Buchanan's cabinet later took on a different aura.
43. Crawford, *Genesis*, 12–14; Klein, *Buchanan*, 354; Doubleday, 45, believed these officials had made up their mind to secede and used the Lincoln election as an excuse.
44. Doubleday, *Reminiscences*, 25; Crawford, *Genesis*, 11.

Notes to Pages 57–64

45. *OR*, vol. 1/1, 73, Special Order 137; Doubleday, *Reminiscences*, 41, 42; Crawford, *Genesis*, 61; Ezra Warner, *Generals in Blue* (Baton Rouge, La.: Louisiana State University Press, 1964), 7, 8; Swanberg, *First Blood*, 34–37; Klein, *Defiance*, 106.
46. Waugh, *Class of 1846*, 189; Crawford, *Genesis*, 61; *OR*, vol. 1/1, 76.
47. *OR*, vol. 1/1, 76, dated November 24, 1860.; Crawford, *Genesis*, 2, fort description.
48. Crawford, *Genesis*, 2, 62; *OR*, vol. 1/1, 72, 74–75, 78.
49. Fort Sumter, *Anvil of War* (Washington, D.C., National Park Service, 1984), 7; Doubleday, *Reminiscences*, 34.
50. Doubleday, *Reminiscences*, 34, 35; Crawford, *Genesis*, 62.
51. *OR*, vol. 1/1, 74, 75, 93–95; Crawford, *Genesis*, 70. Robert Anderson to rector of a Trenton church, December 19, 1860. A story was told that a cow had once walked into the fort on a sand hill.
52. *OR*, vol. 1/1, 78–80. November 28 dispatch to Col. S. Cooper, Adjutant General.
53. Doubleday, *Reminiscences*, 58, 59; *OR*, vol. 1/1, 75; *Battles and Leaders*, 42, "burn the dwellings"; Doubleday, *Reminiscences*, 58.
54. *OR*, vol.1/1, 75.
55. Johnson and Buel, eds., *Battles and Leaders*, 41.
56. Crawford, *Genesis*, 71; *OR*, vol. 1/1, 87–89; Klein, *Buchanan*, 354, 355.
57. *OR*, vol. 1/1, 74, 93–95; Jeff Coy speech to the Pennsylvania House of Representatives, September 8, 1986. Crawford wrote to A.J. that they were trying to make the position as strong as possible with what they had to use; Crawford, *Genesis*, 70.
58. Crawford, *Genesis*, 73, memorandum; *OR*, vol. 1/1, 89, 90, 117; Klein, *Buchanan*, 376.
59. Crawford, *Genesis*, 74.
60. Telegram War Department to Anderson, December 23, 1861; Crawford, *Genesis*, 75; *OR*, vol. 1/1, 103.
61. Crawford, *Genesis*, 77; *OR*, vol. 1/1, 69, 96, 100, 101.
62. *OR*, vol. 1/1, 101, December 20, 1860; Pettigrew Letter in Crawford Papers; In Anderson's reply he said he had not responded until 1:30 a.m. on the 20th; *OR*, vol. 1/1, 67, 68, Haugh, *Class of 46*, 193; Crawford, *Genesis*, 69.
63. Crawford, *Genesis*, 81–84, 88, 89; Klein, *Buchanan*, 375.
64. Crawford Diary, December 2, 1860, Crawford Papers, LOC; *OR*, vol. 1/1, 81. One wonders if this could have been a friend of the Crawford family.
65. In numerous letters, Samuel defends limited States Rights but not these "ultra Carolinians"; Doubleday described Anderson as proslavery but opposed to secession. LOC; Doubleday, *Reminiscences*, 42. Anderson is opposed to secession and Southern extremists.
66. Samuel W. Crawford to Dear Brother, December 12, 1860. Crawford Papers, LOC. It can't be established when the tour was taken. The role of the power of the state was a continuing idea in Crawford's thinking as was the fear of the results of ending slavery.
67. Crawford, *Genesis*, viii, 48. This story is for the most part in Crawford's Diary also.
68. Crawford, *Genesis*, 50; Crawford Diary, December 19, 1860, LOC.
69. Crawford, *Genesis*, 45.
70. Crawford, *Genesis*, 51, 52, 53; Crawford Diary, December 19, 1860, LOC; McClure, ed., *Annals of the Civil War*, 320.
71. Crawford, *Genesis*, 45, 52; Crawford Diary, December 20, 1860, LOC.
72. Crawford, *Genesis*, 53, 54; Crawford, Diary, December 20, 1860, LOC.
73. Crawford, *Genesis*, 53, 54; *OR*, vol. 1/1, 99. Robert Anderson acknowledged the passing of the ordinance.
74. Crawford, *Genesis*, 55; Crawford Diary, December 20, 1860.
75. Crawford, *Genesis*, 55.
76. Doubleday, *Reminiscences*, 56.
77. Letter to Dear Brother, January 2/3, 1861.
78. W. A. Swanberg, *First Blood* (New York: Scribner's Sons, 1957), 95, 96; Crawford Diary, December 25, 1860.

CHAPTER SEVEN: THE CROSSING, DECEMBER 26, 1860

1. Crawford Diary, December 1, 1860; *OR*, vol. 1/1, 81, December 1, 1860.
2. S. W. Crawford Letter to Brother, December 12. Samuel had been called to Sumter by the engineers when two workers had been struck by cannon they were trying to mount. They had died before he was able to attend them. The militia was brash enough to say they were going to inspect Moultrie next. They were stopped at Moultrie. In a note dated December 21, 1860, Foster indicated Crawford was caring for his workers. *OR*, vol. 1/1, 104, 105; *OR*, vol. 1/1, 90; Crawford, *Genesis*, 68.
3. Crawford, *Genesis*, 74.
4. S. W. Crawford Letter to Brother, March 7, 1861. Anderson had predicted it much earlier; *OR*, vol. 1/1, 75; Crawford, *Genesis*, 110; *OR*, vol. 1/1, 3.
5. Letter, Crawford to Brother, December 12, 1860, LOC.
6. Crawford, *Genesis*, 103, footnote; Crawford Diary, December 26, 1860. A second letter written on January, 2/3, 1861, is in the MA. The one used will be denoted as MA or LOC. This one in MA.
7. Crawford, *Genesis*, 104; Diary, December 26, 1860, LOC. Anderson originally planned to move the 25th of December but weather prevented the move.
8. Crawford, *Genesis*, 104; Letter, January 2/3, 1861; December 30, 1860, Letter to Family.
9. Klein, *Defiance*, 254; Crawford, *Genesis*, 103. In his diaries, Samuel refers to these men as spies.
10. Crawford Diary, LOC; Crawford, *Genesis*, 103, 105; Crawford Letter, January 2/3, 1861, MA.
11. Doubleday, *Reminiscences*, 62; Crawford, *Genesis*, 104.
12. Doubleday, *Reminiscences*, 62, 63, 67.
13. Crawford, *Genesis*, 104.
14. Crawford, *Genesis*, 104; Crawford Diary, December 26, 1860, LOC; Doubleday, 63, LOC.
15. Swanberg, *First Blood*, 98. The storm flag cost $17 to replace. MA; Doubleday, *Reminiscences*, 64, 65. Since Chaplain Harris was a non-combatant, he was not notified.
16. Crawford Diary, December 26, 1860, LOC; Letters, January 2/3, 5, 1861, LOC; Crawford, *Genesis*, 106. The original source in Crawford's Papers was written by Doubleday.
17. Crawford, *Genesis*, 102–12; Johnson and Buel, eds. *Battles and Leaders of the Civil War*, vol. 1 (New York: Yoseloff, Inc., 1956), 51, 54; Doubleday, *Reminiscences*, 65.
18. Doubleday, *Reminiscences*, 66.
19. Johnson and Buel, eds., *Battles and Leaders*, 53.
20. Johnson and Buel, eds. *Battles and Leaders*, 53–54; Crawford, *Genesis*, 130–32, tells the placement of guns, etc.
21. Crawford Letter, January 2/3, 5, 1861. The entire move is in these letters.
22. Crawford, *Genesis*, 106; Samuel Crawford to Brother, January 5, 1861, LOC. This 12-page letter deals almost exclusively with the move. (As stated previously, this was probably added to the letter of January 2/3.)
23. Samuel Crawford to Brother, January 2/3, 1861, LOC. Samuel Crawford, Letter to Brother and Alex, January 17, 1861. "Today I had a cane made from the Moultrie flagstaff that I cut off after we leveled it." Crawford wrote that five guns were destroyed the next day.
24. Crawford, *Genesis*, 105. Crawford wrote the boat was *Emma*.
25. Crawford, *Genesis*, 132.
26. Crawford, *Genesis*, 106; *OR*, vol. 1/1, 2.
27. Crawford, *Genesis*, 107, 471; Anderson wrote in *OR*, vol. 1/1, 2, that Foster was sent to destroy all ammunition that could not be sent over.
28. Crawford Diary, January 2, 1861, Letter "amputating table" prepared January 2/3, 1861, MA. Samuel brought with him a medicine chest that stocked over 75 medicines and herbs. List in Crawford Papers, LOC.
29. Samuel Crawford Letter to the Family, through his brother, January 2/3, 1861; Letter to A.J., December 30, 1860, LOC.

30. Crawford Diary, December 28, 1860, LOC.
31. Diary and Letter, January 5, 1861, LOC. Many times the diary entry will follow in a letter a few days later. At times he sends a letter to A.J. and Mac on the same day. The basic concepts are the same, but at times stated differently.
32. Samuel Crawford to A.J., January 17, 1861.
33. Albert Castel, *Fort Sumter 1861* (Harrisburg, Pa.: Historic Times, 1976), 6–14; Fort Sumter-Anvil of War (U.S. Dept. of Interior, Washington, D.C., 1984), 8, 9, 11–13; Sumter Notes from MA.
34. Johnson and Buel, eds., *Battles and Leaders*, 54.
35. Crawford, *Genesis*, 131; Fort Sumter Handbook, Anvil of War.
36. Letter to Brothers, January 2, 3, 5, 1861; Mary Chesnut, *A Diary from Dixie* (Boston: Houghton Mifflin Company, 1949), 35.
37. *OR*, vol. 1/1, 185.
38. *OR*, vol. 1/1, 4; Crawford, *Genesis*, 109, 110–12
39. Crawford, *Genesis*, 109, 110, 112; *OR*, vol. 1/1, 3, 4; Samuel Crawford Letter, January 5, 1861, to Brother, LOC; Doubleday, *Reminiscences*, 79.
40. Crawford, *Genesis*, 110; Crawford notes in Crawford Papers. LOC.
41. Crawford, *Genesis*, 110.
42. Crawford, *Genesis*, 111; Crawford notes.
43. Crawford, *Genesis*, 111; Crawford notes.
44. Crawford, *Genesis*, 111.
45. Crawford, *Genesis*, 111; Crawford notes.
46. Crawford, *Genesis*, 111; Doubleday, *Reminiscences*, 81; *OR*, vol. 1/1, 3.
47. Samuel Crawford, Letter to his Brothers, January 2/3, 1861, LOC. While researching his book, Crawford wrote Ellison Capers for information pertaining to the agreement. The conclusion was inconclusive.
48. Crawford Letters, January 5, 17, 1861 (on the 17th, Samuel was officer of the day, which meant a long letter); Crawford, *Genesis*, 132.
49. Crawford Letter, January 17, 1861. This letter was to Alex.
50. Doubleday, *Reminiscences*, 71.
51. Klein, *Defiance*, 164, 165; *OR*, vol. 1/1, 3, 4; McClure, ed., *Annals*, 320–21.
52. *OR*, vol. 1/1, 112. December 28, 1860. This is reality, but it was still a war between brothers that was to be gentlemanly in the beginning; Crawford, *Genesis*, 126.
53. Crawford to his Brother Mac on January 2/3, 5, 1861, MA; Crawford, *Genesis*, 133.
54. Crawford to his Brothers on January 2/3, 5, 1861, MA.
55. Crawford to his Brothers on January 2/3, 1861.
56. Crawford, *Genesis*, 107. Letter said "case after case."
57. Johnson and Buel, eds., *Battles and Leaders*, 65; Doubleday, *Reminiscences*, 71, 72.
58. Crawford Diary, December 27, 1860, LOC; Letter, January 16, 1861, Crawford, *Genesis*, 130.
59. Johnson and Buel, eds., *Battles and Leaders*, Sergeant Chester, 52–55.
60. Letters to Family, December 31, 1860, and January 2/3, 1861, MA. Samuel asked his minister brother to write to Anderson during the commander's most difficult times. LOC.
61. Ibid.
62. Crawford Letter to Brother, January 2, 3, 1861; Crawford Diary December 31, 1860.

CHAPTER EIGHT: FORT SUMTER: SYMBOL AND PRISON

1. Crawford Diary, December 30, 1860; January 3, 1861, LOC. The five temporary buildings had been destroyed for fuel by March; the others had been used, and the apparatus from the blacksmith shop taken to a casemate for warmth; Crawford, *Genesis*, 295. Temporary structures were torn down and were used for firewood.

2. Crawford Letter, January 2/3, 1861, one to the family and one to Dear Brother.
3. Doubleday, *Reminiscences*, 89; Crawford Letter to Brother, January 2/3, 1861. Crawford in his diary wrote that they ordered the inspector of lighthouses out of the state [Captain Hunter] on December 31; Crawford Diary, December 31, 1861; On February 15, 1861, the Fresnel Lights were removed from the Morris Island Lighthouse. Crawford, *Genesis*, 210.
4. Crawford Diary, January 3, 1861. LOC.
5. Crawford Letter, January 17, 1861.
6. Crawford Diary, March 14, 1861; *OR*, vol. 1/1, 195, 232; Diary, January 4, 1861. Now dysentery was beginning to be a problem. On January 19, Crawford recorded that by regulation he was to issue meat 4 out of 10 days. LOC; Fatigue was mentioned. Diary, January 29, 1861.
7. Doubleday, *Reminiscences*, 114–15.
8. Samuel Crawford Letter to John Agnew, February 24, 1861. The diary entries and then letters encompassed: January 24, 1861, quite sore throat; January 30, throat sore for weeks; February 2/3, throat burns like coal; February 12, thin and need a change; February 24, need air of Pa. mountains. LOC.
9. Composite of January, and February letters, and diary entries; Crawford, *Genesis*, 295.
10. Crawford Letters to Brother and Mac, January 2, 3, 5, 1861.
11. Crawford Letter to Mac, January 2, 3, 1861.
12. Diary, March 9, 1861; January 24, Letter and Diary; January 20, Letter, soap candles gone; January 24, vinegar and salt; Diary, 19th.
13. Crawford, *Genesis*, 133. Mrs. Anderson was an invalid and the round trip took an extreme toll on her health. Diary, January 3, 1861.
14. Crawford Diary, January 5, 7, 1861. This sounded as though Crawford had taken part in the practice. In a letter he said, "we had great practice." LOC.
15. Diary, January 19; Crawford to Alex, January 24, 1861, LOC.
16. Crawford Diary, January 19, 1861. Talbot came back with the message from Washington; Crawford, *Genesis*, 204.
17. S. Crawford to Dear Brother, January 17, 1861, LOC.
18. Crawford, *Genesis*, 133, 175–86; Crawford Diary, January 8, 9; Klein, *Defiance*, 198. *OR*, vol. 1/1, 130. Act 9 hostility unparalleled in history of our country.
19. Crawford, Diary and *Genesis*, 185–86. Oakes is the gunner, the same soldier who is at the Hough gun in the explosion during the flag salute. The gun was an 8-inch howitzer. The entire story is in Crawford, *Genesis*, 175–86; Doubleday, *Reminiscences*, 103; Crawford Notes, *Star of the West*, LOC.
20. Crawford, *Genesis*, 187–88; Crawford Diary, January 9, 1861.
21. Crawford, *Genesis*, 187; Crawford Diary, January 9, 1861; Crawford Notes on the *Star of the West* incident.
22. Doubleday, *Reminiscences*, 89, 106.
23. Doubleday, *Reminiscences*, 106; Crawford, *Genesis*, 187.
24. Crawford Diary, January 9, 1861; Crawford, *Genesis*, 188; Crawford Notes, *Star of the West*.
25. Swanberg, *First Blood*, 150; Crawford, *Genesis*, 188.
26. *OR*, vol. 1/1, 134.
27. Crawford, *Genesis*, 189, 190; *OR*, vol. 1/1, 135, 136.
28. Letter, January 17, 1861, LOC. While Samuel supports the major, Doubleday questions the policies of the commander; Doubleday, *Reminiscences*, 104; Crawford Notes, *Star of the West*.
29. Crawford Diary, January 12; January 17, 1861, to Dear Brother.
30. Crawford, *Genesis*, 193. "Why not exhaust diplomacy?"
31. *OR*, vol. 1, 140, dated January 16. Holt became secretary of war when John Floyd resigned at the end of December 1860. With the additions of Judge Black and Holt, Buchanan was given different information.

Notes to Pages 81–84

32. Louis Wigfall notified the Carolina officials, "It means war. Cut off supplies to Anderson and take Sumter as soon as possible." *OR*, vol. 1/1, 252, Confederate correspondence.
33. *New York Tribune*, January 13, 1861, PSUL; Crawford Papers, *Star of the West* notes. LOC.
34. Crawford Diary, January 10, 11, 12, 1861, LOC; Crawford, *Genesis*, 194, 195.
35. Crawford, *Genesis*, 191, 192. Dispatch from the executive office of South Carolina, January 11, at noon and then a call for surrender of the fort. Pickens to Anderson.
36. Letter, January 24, 1861; espionage, Diary, January 16, 1861.
37. Crawford Letter, March 4, 1861.
38. Crawford, *Genesis*, 203. His first inspection was January, 15, 1861; Crawford Diary, January 17, 1861; *OR*, vol. 1/1, 154. Indications are that Crawford was meticulous and thorough. Anderson was surprised at the difference in provisions that were available compared to what he thought were available. The inventory itemized pork, flour, bread, beans, coffee, sugar, vinegar, candles, soap, and salt.
39. Letter to Brother, January 17, 1861, LOC.
40. Diary and Letter, January 24, 1861, LOC.
41. Crawford, Letter home, March 4, 1861, LOC.
42. Diary entries January 30, 1861, and in a letter to A.J. Samuel asks if he supports the Crittenden amendment (January 17). Crawford is concerned about Kentucky and the West. Samuel summarized the states that had left the Union in a January 6 entry. In a diary entry he used the phrase, "for the union all hope would be gone if Border States are lost." LOC.
43. Pension Service Records, NA. John Doran I U.S. Artillery, Battery H.
44. Crawford, *Genesis*, 203; Crawford Diary, January 20, 24, 1861.
45. Crawford Diary, January 28, 1861 (left the fort), February 9 (heard of safe arrival). A number of dates were negotiations with the steamboat company. Samuel maintained very detailed records as can be seen in his personal papers. LOC. Crawford letter to family to alert Anne, February 3, 1861.
46. *OR*, vol. 1/1, 144. Another time he called it a "fratricidal war"; *OR*, vol. 1/1, 191.
47. According to his diary the arrangements were confirmed January 28. On the first of February, Samuel listed 20 women, 17 children, 5 infants. In Crawford, *Genesis*, 206–7, he reports that the South Carolina officials were asked for permission as an act of humanity on January 19; Doubleday, *Reminiscences*, 100, when wives reported.
48. Diary and Letter to Brother, February 2–3, 1861. This was a response to a question by A.J. as to why the garrison had not been reinforced; Diary, January 17, 1861.
49. Crawford Diary, February 20, 1861, "they are humiliated by their men of war."
50. Tombstone, Ellen Anderson Crawford, Falling Spring Presbyterian Cemetery, Chambersburg, Pa.; Crawford Diary, February 12, 1861; letters to family February 2, 12, 1861.
51. Letters to Family, February 2, 12, 1861. Sometimes he asks A.J. not to share certain things with Ma as she would get upset. He said similar words on January 17; On February 24, 1861, Samuel thanks Jennie (Margaret's daughter) for all she is doing.
52. To Adjutant General Cooper from Major Anderson, February 24, 1861; *OR*, vol. 1/1, 185. Crawford was surgeon, quartermaster, commissary officer, as well as pulling officer-of-the-day duties. Lieutenant Snyder and Lieutenant Meade were also given kudos.
53. Letter to Dear Brother, March 14, 1861. (Officer of the Day) Around the beginning of the year he understands that Dr. Simmons is coming and Samuel would be the medical doctor for the workers. This did not transpire. In one letter he said he would exchange the knife for the musket; Diary, March 14, 1861.
54. Louis Duncan, *"General Crawford," Military Surgeon*, ed. John Hoff, vol. 34 (Washington, D.C., November 1916), 568, addenda.
55. Crawford Letter, March 14, 1861, to Dear Brother, LOC.
56. Diary, March 9, 1861. Crawford, Officer of the Day. Given the tensions of the time in that place, little incidences loomed colossal. This was the eighth time officer-of-the-day or guard duty was listed in his diary. LOC.

Notes to Pages 84–90

57. Crawford Diary, March 9, 1861, LOC.
58. Ibid.; Letter, March 14, 1861, LOC.
59. Crawford Letter, March 14, 1861. Attachment, "make sure Pa sees this."
60. Diary, February 3, 1861. Samuel suspected a spy was in the group that came to take the photo. Letter to Brother, March 14, 23, 1861. He probably felt so ill that he did not proofread as he wrote he could "harily" stand. Normally his letters had almost perfect spelling and grammar. LOC; Doubleday, *Reminiscences*, 123. They were amused by those who played their parts.
61. Crawford Diary, March 30, 1861.
62. Crawford, *Genesis*, 375–76; *OR*, vol. 1/1, 236–38. The ship was the *Rhoda B Shannon* of Boston.
63. Crawford, *Genesis*, 381; Anderson to the U.S. War Department April 6, 1861.
64. Crawford, *Genesis*, 468. Lincoln's speech to Congress.
65. Klein, *Defiance*, 396; *OR*, vol. 1/1, 251, 252, 291.
66. Klein, *Defiance*, 397; *OR*, vol. 1/1, 297; Castel, *Fort Sumter 1861*, 39, 40.
67. Crawford, *Genesis*, 399fn. Samuel said the artillery explosion was a part of a national salute on February 22. That is the only source that indicates this.
68. Roy Meredith, *Storm over Sumter* (New York: Simon & Schuster, 1957), 155; Wylie Crawford in McClure, ed., *Annals of War*, 325.
69. Crawford Letter, March 14, 1861; Castel, *Fort Sumter*, 40, 41.
70. Crawford, *Genesis*, 422, 423; *OR*, vol. 1/1 13, 300, 301.
71. Crawford Diary, April 11. The major then read from a December 21 confidential document that gave him power to capitulate when the occasion demanded; Klein, *Defiance*, 401.
72. Letter to Dear Brother, midnight, April 13, 1861.
73. Crawford, *Genesis*, 423; *OR*, vol. 1/1, 301. Beauregard notified Secretary of War Walker; Enclosure of Anderson's reply.
74. Crawford, *Genesis*, 423–25.
75. Crawford, *Genesis*, 425–26; *OR*, vol. 1/1, 18.
76. Johnson and Buel, eds., *Battles and Leaders*, 58, 59.
77. Fuel restricted, December 31, 1860, vegetables and fresh meat was sent back if not ordered, 20 January no soap candles, also vinegar and salt rationed, last of March planks burned; In his Official Report, Anderson said that on March 29 they issued their last barrel of pork.
78. Crawford Diary, April 12, 1861; Crawford, *Genesis*, 426.
79. Klein, *Defiance*, 402.
80. Crawford Diary, March 15, 1861; Letter to A.J. dated same day.
81. Johnson and Buel, eds., *Battles and Leaders*, 66; Crawford, *Genesis*, 427.
82. Crawford, *Genesis*, 427; Beauregard, *OR*, vol. 1/1, 305, 306; Foster, 18, 139; Doubleday, *Reminiscences*, 144.

CHAPTER NINE: "GOD BLESS THE POOR NOBLE FELLOWS"

1. Samuel Crawford to his Brother, April 13, 1861, and Diary entry.
2. Crawford Diary, April 11, 1861, LOC.
3. Crawford Letter, March 23, 1861, to brother A.J. In his letter of the 15th and 16th John tried to defend the Lincoln administration, LOC.
4. Each battery is given the leader's name. Doubleday, *Reminiscences*, 147, 148; Crawford, *Genesis*, 427–29; Klein, *Defiance*, 410; *OR*, vol. 1/1, 18. This did not count the 5 Columbiads on the parade ground; Swanberg, 305. Foster noted 43 workers and almost all volunteered to aid in some way.
5. Crawford Diary, April 12, 1861. First shot from Fort Johnson 2,250 yards. In Crawford, the time is 4:30 a.m.; in *Genesis*, 427. Some letters noted the time as 4:27 a.m.

6. Doubleday, *Reminiscences*, 145.
7. Letter to A.J., March 19, 1861; *New York Tribune*, April 13, 1861. Samuel expresses his belief that Greeley and his vile party want to blame Anderson for everything.
8. Crawford, *Genesis*, 429. "it was not until 7 that Sumter opened its fire." Charleston Press article. Handwritten copy located in the South Carolina Historical Society, Charleston. No other information could be interpreted.
9. Doubleday, *Reminiscences*, 145; Chester wrote 7:30 a.m. in *Battles and Leaders*, 67; Castel, *Sumter*, 45.
10. Louis Duncan, "General Crawford," *Military Surgeon* (vol. 39, 1916), 566–69; Chester's military service began on December 1, 1854, 1st U.S. Artillery description book, NA; Crawford, *Genesis*, 429; Doubleday, *Reminiscences*, 146.
11. Crawford, *Genesis*, 430; *Battles and Leaders*, 67; four hours later relieved by Lieutenant R. K. Meade; *OR*, vol. 1/1, 18, 19 (see for location and size of Sumter's guns).
12. Crawford, *Genesis*, 430, 431. Effect of the fire on the floating battery was slight. The battery was replaced by one commanded by Lt. R. K. Meade. Captain Seymour relieved Doubleday. Doubleday, *Reminiscences*, 147. The gunners aimed with handmade notched sticks that Doubleday devised.
13. Doubleday in *Battles and Leaders*, 48; Foster, *OR*, vol. 1/1, 19.
14. Doubleday, *Reminiscences*, 148. The English Whitworth also provided firepower but, according to Doubleday and Chester, ran low on ammunition; Swanberg, 287; Crawford, *Genesis*, 397; *OR*, vol. 1/1, 20, 21.
15. Crawford Diary, April 12; Doubleday, *Reminiscences*, 148; Samuel spells it "Kernan." Hatcher agrees with Doubleday. This Irishman began active duty January 26, 1856. On Richard Hatcher's list, John Schweirer, mason, MA. (Total list of wounded, killed, and mortally wounded is in Crawford, *Genesis*, 470.) Foster identifies the worker as Swearer from Baltimore, wounded by a shell that burst near the casemate.
16. Duncan, *Military Surgeon*, 567; *OR*, vol. 1/1, 21. Foster reported that coarse paper and extra hospital sheets were used to make cartridges.
17. Crawford, *Genesis*, 432, 433.
18. Medicinal potassium. He would discover later that his illness was more than a sore throat. Foster said since coming into the fort the weather had been bad. *OR*, vol. 1/1, 139.
19. Crawford, *Genesis*, 399. This same day a potato that Doubleday was saving was tramped.
20. *Battles and Leaders*, 56. According to Doubleday a tobacco shipment was made to the men, but the Southerners confiscated it for their own smoking pleasure. Doubleday also revealed the men missed tobacco very much. In one letter Crawford indicated that the Carolinians confiscated a tobacco shipment.
21. Milby Burton, *The Siege of Charleston 1861–1865* (Columbia: University of South Carolina, 1994), 49; *OR*, vol. 1/1, 21, 22.
22. Crawford, *Genesis*, 435; Doubleday, *Reminiscences*, 157; Swanberg, *First Blood*, 316; *OR*, vol. 1/1, 22.
23. Klein, *Defiance*, 415; Crawford, *Genesis*, 437; *OR*, vol. 1/1, 22, 23.
24. Alan Gaff, "Two dead at Sumter," *CWTI*, Harrisburg, Pa. (March 2001), 48; Crawford, *Genesis*, 437; *OR*, vol. 1/1, 22.
25. Crawford Diary and Letter, April 13, 1861; *OR*, vol. 1/1, 12, 22.
26. Crawford, *Genesis*, 439–41; *OR*, vol. 1/1, 57. The first of January, Wigfall was an ex-Texas senator.
27. Klein, *Defiance*, 169. Wigfall approached Secretary Floyd concerning a plot to kidnap Buchanan in the last week of December 1861; Klein, *Buchanan*, 378.
28. Chester in *Battles and Leaders*, 72, 73. A story about Crawford replacing the flag and receiving singed eyebrows was told to me at Kittochtinny, but I found no proof of such an event. General Beauregard had taken command of the Confederate batteries in the Charleston area in early March.

29. Klein, *Defiance*, 417; Crawford, *Genesis*, the entire story, 439–42.
30. Crawford, *Genesis*, 440; Foster in *OR*, vol. 1/1, 23.
31. Duncan, *Military Surgeon*, 567, 568.
32. The mines, demijohns filled with powder, had been removed but Samuel tried to place fear in the three commissioners. Crawford Diary, April 12, 1861. One source reported the commissioners were angry that they were not properly received. *OR*, vol. 1/1, 62.
33. Duncan, *Military Surgeon*, 567; Crawford, *Genesis*, 441; *OR*, vol. 1/ 1, 62.
34. Crawford, *Genesis*, 445; Doubleday, *Reminiscences*, 166; *OR*, vol. 1/1, 12.
35. Duncan, *Military Surgeon*, 567, 568. One source said Crawford provided the brandy when they awakened the next morning. Staying with procedures established the evening before seems more likely.
36. Crawford entry in his Diary, April 13, 1861 (almost like an attachment). Letter to his brother of same date, LOC; *OR*, vol. 1/1, 25.
37. Crawford Letter home, March 23, 1861, and reported March 30, 1861, in another letter. This was written at a time the garrison expected to be evacuated.
38. Doubleday, *Reminiscences*, 172–73.
39. Doubleday, *Reminiscences*, 172, 173. Corporal Bringhurst came back to inform Abner they were calling his name. He had previously received a letter from Charleston saying if he appeared they would tar and feather him. A regular soldier who switched to the Confederates told his men of Doubleday's abolitionist views and encouraged them to hang him.
40. Ibid. Known for his exaggerations, Abner stretched the enemy number and shrank the Union size slightly.
41. Crawford, *Genesis*, 446–47.
42. *Harper's Weekly*, April 27, 1861.
43. Crawford Diary, April 13, 1861, LOC.
44. Crawford Letters, March 23, 1861; March 30, 1861.
45. McClure, ed., *Annals of the War*, 329.
46. Crawford, *Genesis*, 369, 370.
47. Klein, *Defiance*, 378–84; Crawford, *Genesis*, 421. The story of the 632-mile mission to Fort Sumter is covered in Crawford's book, 402–20.
48. Burton, *Siege of Charleston*, 46–47. Those guns were placed off limits due to the danger. It was because of this that Crawford told his brother he doubted if a parallel case could be found of such heavy firing for so long with no one killed. John Carmody had been in the service since June of 1854; Chester, *Battles and Leaders*, 69; Doubleday, *Reminiscences*, 152.
49. David Detzer, *Allegiance* (New York: Harcourt, 2001), 35. As assistant surgeon, pay equals $2,046 a year.
50. Hatcher's list, MA; Burton, 60; Gaff, *CWTI*, 51; Daniel began active duty in November of 1854. He was a private in Company E, First U.S. Artillery. He listed home as Tipperary, Ireland. Hough's file, MA. Oakes was Francis Oakes, a corporal in Co. E, a Bostonian who had served in the U.S. service for three years. MA. At one point he served time in a mental institution in Washington, D.C.
51. Burton, *Siege of Charleston*, 60; Gaff, *CWTI*, 50–52; Crawford, *Genesis*, 470. Sgt. James Edward Galway: died the 15th under the care of Dr. Chisolm and was buried in St. Lawrence Cemetery. George Fielding: private from Waterford, Ireland. 5 years a United States artilleryman. John Irwin, Co. E., Irish, 6 years in the U.S. service. MA.
52. Crawford, *Genesis*, 442fn.; Brian Kelly, *Best Little Stories from the Civil War* (Nashville: Cumberland House, 1998), 39, 40.
53. Crawford Letter, April 13, 1861. The "shells received" is the same number as used in Doubleday, 166.
54. Crawford Letter, April 13, 1861. March 15, 1861, he wrote, "See you soon" because he felt the fort was going to be evacuated.

Notes to Pages 100–112

55. Reverend Crawford to Major Anderson, February 4, 1861, Anderson Papers, LOC. Father also was discouraged about the Buchanan policies as he referred to the president as "an imbecile"; Swanberg, *First Blood*, 208–9.
56. Swanberg, *First Blood*, 324.
57. Jacob Hoke, *Reminiscences* of the War (Chambersburg: Foltz, 1884), 8.

CHAPTER TEN: FROM ASSISTANT SURGEON TO MAJOR, U.S. INFANTRY

1. S. W. Crawford, Note to August Belmont, September 15, 1888. He is referring to April 1861. NYPL.
2. Ibid.
3. Johnson and Buel, eds., *Battles and Leaders*, 48, 49.
4. *New York Tribune*, April 19, 1861, front page, PSUL.
5. Meredith, *Storm over Sumter*, 190.
6. Personnel List, previously cited, MA. Foster wrote they initially arrived April 17; *OR*, vol. 1/1, 24.
7. *New York Times*, April 20, 1861. He had written home, "God be thanked. I've escaped injury." PSUL. The one flag was carried out on the broken staff. PSUL.
8. *New York Herald*, April 19, 1861, PSUL.
9. Doubleday, *Reminiscences*, 175; Swanberg, *First Blood*, 332.
10. Crawford note to August Belmont, September 15, 1888, NYPL.
11. Personnel List. MA. During my research I have found his name spelled different ways. I used Rick Calhoun's list from Fort Moultrie. Doubleday lists a musician James Galway; Others, Gallway, Galloway. Crawford confirms James E. Galway, MA; *OR*, vol. 1/1, 66.
12. Detzer, *Allegiance*, 312; Crawford, *Genesis*, 450; *OR*, vol. 1/1, 12.
13. Crawford, *Genesis*, 450. The telegram is misdated, 1801.
14. *OR*, vol. 1/1, 12, dated April 18, 1861. New York, April 19, 1861.
15. S. W. Crawford, Letter to Brother. January 2/3, 1861, LOC. The Christian-Warrior Model was the lesson he learned from Robert Anderson.
16. Lincoln's message to the 37th Congress. Crawford, *Genesis*, 468.
17. S. W. Crawford, Letter to Mac, January 2/3, 1861, LOC.
18. S. W. Crawford, Letter to Brother, March 9, 1861.
19. Franklin Repository, November 5, 1892; Service Records, Record Group 94, Adjutant General's Office; Crawford Papers, LOC. Assigned to 13th United States Infantry as major. May 14, 1861. Based on Winfield Scott recommendation, Dickson, KHS. Promotion, May 14, 1861, Adjutant General's Records, NA.
20. Crawford Letters; February 12, February 24, 1861, LOC.
21. Jennie Washington Diary, 13th Infantry, Company C, "John Agnew Union Chaplain from 1862–1864"; *The Pharetra*, vol. 11, 66, WCA; Nevin, *Men of Mark*, 163.
22. Information obtained from S. Crawford Letters; January 2, 3, 17; February (5), 20; March 4, 9, 1861.
23. Expressed in S. Crawford's Letter, January 2/3, 1861.
24. All information obtained about Jane Agnew Crawford was that she was a kind, gentle human. The simulation is thus constructed from Nevin.
25. Letter from S. Crawford, March 9, 14, 1861, LOC.
26. Heidler and Heidler, *Encyclopedia of Civil War*, 1677; *OR*, vol. 5/1, 252, 256, 258; Warner, *Generals in Blue*, 410, 411.
27. Richard Sommers Interview, USAMHI. The role of the inspector general.
28. *OR*, vol. 5/1, 75, 254, 275; From H.Q. Department Western Virginia.
29. *OR*, vol. 5/1, 275.
30. *OR*, vol. 5/1, 259, 275.

31. *OR*, vol. 5/1, 275.
32. *OR*, vol. 5/1, 254, 255, 275.
33. *OR*, vol. 5/1, 251, 258, 277. General Rosecrans had two plans in case the first did not work by November 12, 1862.
34. *OR*, vol. 5/1, 277.
35. *OR*, vol. 5/1, 277; *OR*, vol. 5/1, 251, 258, 259; Heidler and Heidler, *Encyclopedia of Civil War*, 1677.
36. *OR*, vol. 5/1, 259. Sergeant Haven was also given kudos.

CHAPTER ELEVEN: CEDAR MOUNTAIN OR SLAUGHTER MOUNTAIN

1. *OR*, vol. 5/1, 692. To Crawford and Captain Hartranft: "I am favorably impressed with these two as men with large views and worthy of consideration of the country."
2. Adjutant General's Office, Special Orders 102, May 8, 1862. The promotion was dated April 25, 1862; Crawford Papers, LOC.
3. *OR*, vol. 12/1, 552. Maj. Gen. Nathaniel P. Banks, commanding Shenandoah Dept., June 1862; Warner, *Generals in Blue*, 17–18; *OR*, vol. 15/1, 526.
4. Crawford Papers. Crawford called it the most beautiful animal he ever laid eyes on. It was a beautiful blood. It was reported that Rosecrans noticed Crawford's ability to handle mounts. LOC.
5. Quaife, ed., *Cannon's Mouth*, 99; *OR*, vol. 12/2, 145.
6. *OR*, vol. 12/2, 152, 153; Service Records, NA; *Franklin Repository*, November 22, 1864. His enlistment date was April 4, 1862, commissioned first lieutenant. Crawford Papers, LOC.
7. *OR*, vol. 12/3, 510, 511.
8. *OR*, vol. 12/2, 109, July 26, 1862. Enclosure (July 27) from captain of commanding scouts, John Kester.
9. *OR*, vol. 12/3, 510, 511. Appears he placed the times on the envelopes.
10. *OR*, vol. 12/3, 522.
11. Gould Papers, June 15, 1862; September 3, 1862, AL, Sharpsburg, Md.
12. Culpeper Chamber of Commerce Pamphlet, Battles in the Area.
13. *OR*, vol. 12/2, 149, 150; *OR*, vol. 12/3, 526.
14. *OR*, vol. 12/2, 149, 150; Quaife, ed., *Cannon's Mouth*, 100.
15. Quaife, ed., *Cannon's Mouth*, 100.
16. Gary Gallagher, ed., *The Second Day at Gettysburg* (Kent, Ohio: Kent State University Press, 1993). "No Troops on the Field Had Done Better." Scott Hartwig, 136–71. Scott analyzes the role of the brigade in combat; *OR*, vol. 12/2, 149, 150.
17. *OR*, vol. 12/2, 150, 161. Knap wrote that the artillery ended about 5:30 p.m.
18. *OR*, vol. 12/2, 150.
19. *OR*, vol. 12/2, 146; *OR*, vol. 12/2, 151.
20. Robert Krick, *Stonewall Jackson at Cedar Mountain* (Chapel Hill, N.C.: University of North Carolina, 1990), 143; *OR*, vol. 12/2, 151.
21. *OR*, vol. 12/2, 151.
22. *OR*, vol. 12/2, 151; Battlefield plaque.
23. *OR*, vol. 12/2, 151, 152; Krick, *Stonewall Jackson at Cedar Mountain*, 232.
24. *OR*, vol. 12/2, 152–53.
25. *OR*, vol. 12/2, 152, 153.
26. Krick, *Stonewall Jackson at Cedar Mountain*, 181.
27. Battlefield plaque; *OR*, vol. 12/2, 183; Krick, *Stonewall Jackson at Cedar Mountain*, 151, 238; *OR*, vol. 12/2, 153. The troops that were to be used for reserve appeared about 2 hours later.

28. Gould Papers, August 11, 1863, AL, Sharpsburg, Md.
29. Krick, *Stonewall Jackson*, 343. General Jackson originally agreed to 2 p.m. and then extended the deadline to 5 p.m., *OR*, vol. 12/2, 184, 185.
30. Davis, *Last Cavalier*, 158–60; W. W. Blackford, *War Years with Stuart*, 98.
31. Davis, *Last Cavalier*, 159.
32. Davis, *Last Cavalier*, 159.
33. *OR*, vol. 12/2, 148.
34. *OR*, vol. 12/2, 137–38, 147, 152. 88 officers and 1,679 men into battle and 56 officers and 811 men casualties.
35. *OR*, vol. 12/2, 147, 148.
36. *OR*, vol. 12/2, 151, 153.
37. *OR*, vol. 12/2, 147, 148. Williams called Crawford and Gordon "prompt, ready, zealous, and cooperative."
38. *OR*, vol. 12/2, 47, 134.
39. General Pope's report, *OR*, vol. 12/2, 134.
40. Crawford Papers, LOC.
41. Battlefield plaque.
42. General Pope. Army of Virginia, June 26, 1862, to September 12, 1862; Report, *OR*, vol. 12/2, 134.

CHAPTER TWELVE: ANTIETAM: FROM A WHEATFIELD TO A CORNFIELD

1. James McPherson, *Antietam Crossroads of Freedom* (New York: Oxford Press, 2002), 12; James McPherson, *Illustrated Battle Cry of Freedom* (New York: Oxford, 2003), 221, 222.
2. Robert Denney, *The Civil War Years* (New York: Sterling Publishing, 1994), 36.
3. Frances Kennedy, ed., *Civil War Battlefield Guide* (New York: Houghton Mifflin, 1998), 5, 44–45, 52.
4. Heidler and Heidler, *Encyclopedia of Civil War*, 692–95.
5. McPherson, *Illustrated Battle Cry*, 378.
6. Jim Miles, *Forged in Fire* (Nashville, Tenn.: Cumberland House, 2000), 235, 239, 241; James McPherson. *Antietam Crossroads of Freedom*, 42–44.
7. Frank Owsley, *King Cotton Diplomacy* (Chicago: University of Chicago, 1959), 142; James Murfin, *Gleam of Bayonets* (Baton Rouge: Louisiana State University Press, 1993), 64–70. Murfin analyzes the reasons for Lee's invasion in detail; McPherson, *Illustrated Battle Cry*, 320, 459.
8. Murfin, *Gleam of Bayonets*, 64–70; McPherson, *Illustrated Battle Cry*, 483–84 (results of the election).
9. James McPherson. *Crossroads of Freedom: Antietam* (New York: Oxford Press, 2002), 85, 86, 90, 91; Stephen Sears, *Landscape Turned Red* (New York: Ticknor and Fields, Houghton Mifflin Co., 1994), 64, 69.
10. Jim Miles, *Forged in Fire* (Nashville: Cumberland House, 2000), 356. Lee's proclamation is recorded in total.
11. *OR*, vol. 19/2, 223.
12. *OR*, vol. 19/2, 224.
13. *OR*, vol. 19/2, 224.
14. 46th Pennsylvania Volunteer Infantry regiment history, File AL.
15. *OR*, vol. 19/2, 224.
16. *OR*, vol. 19/1, 179. First Brigade: 5 Connecticut [not in Antietam], 10 Maine [Col. G. L. Beal], 28 New York [Capt. W. H. Mapes], 46 Pa. [Col. J. F. Knipe], 124 Pa. [Col. J. W. Hawley], 125 Pa. [Col. J. Higgins], 128 Pa. [Col. S Croasdale]; *OR*, vol. 19/1, 484.

17. John Priest, *Antietam: The Soldiers' Battle* (New York: Oxford University Press, 1993), 25, 26.
18. Stephen Sears, *Landscape Turned Red*, Antietam, 106–9.
19. John Priest, *Antietam: The Soldiers' Battle*, 4; *Richmond Enquirer*, 16, 18, September 1862.
20. *The Pharetra*, vol. 11 (#2), 1897, WCA; Nevin, *Men of Mark*, 163.
21. Sears, *Landscape*, 90–92, 112, 113; James McPherson, *Antietam*, 106–9.
22. Crawford speech at Antietam, May 30, 1874, NYPL; *OR*, vol. 19/2, 281.
23. Warner, *Generals in Blue*, 309, 310; Quaife, ed., *Cannon's Mouth*, 123; Heidler and Heidler, *Encyclopedia of Civil War*, 1248.
24. James McPherson, *Antietam*, 109, 115. This author believes McClellan missed two opportunities to deal Lee a severe setback.
25. Stephen Sears, *Landscape*, 125; *OR*, vol. 19/1, 951. 8 a.m. Two messages had been sent; one the possibility of surrender, and this one of the reality of the surrender, September 15, 1862. Lee received it slightly before noon.
26. Sears, *Landscape*, 175, 176; Murfin, *Gleam of Bayonets*, 208; McPherson, *Illustrated Battle Cry*, 463.
27. *OR*, vol. 19/1, 484; story by Eugene Boblitz in 125 Pennsylvania History by Milton Lytle, Carman Collection; Private Frederick Crouse, 128th Pennsylvania Volunteer Infantry, An Account of the Battle of Antietam, AL; Sears, *Landscape*, 177.
28. *OR*, vol. 19/1, 484.
29. Sears, *Landscape*, 177; *OR*, vol. 19/1, 494; Crouse, 128 Pa., AL.
30. Crawford, *Genesis*, 442; numerous letters from Captain Crawford to his brother John Agnew from Fort Sumter in 1861; Murfin, *Gleam of Bayonets*, 343–73.
31. Quaife, ed., *Cannon's Mouth*, 125; Murfin, *Gleam of Bayonets*, 209; Crouse, 128 Pa., AL.
32. Quaife, ed., *Cannon's Mouth*, 125.
33. *OR*, vol., 19/1, 494; Crouse, 128 Pa., AL.
34. Crawford speech, May 30, 1874, NYPL.
35. C. B. Gilliam, 28 New York. Carman Collection, AL.
36. Sears, *Landscape Turned Red*, 180, 181; Murfin, *Gleam of Bayonets*, 211, 212; Samuel Crawford speech, May 30, 1874, Antietam Cemetery, NYPL; *OR*, vol. 19/1, 244.
37. *OR*, vol., 19/1, 494; McPherson, *Illustrated Battle Cry*, 464; Luvass, Nelson, eds. *A Guide to the Battle of Antietam* (Lawrence: University of Kansas, 1987), 119. Many bemoaned the piecemeal attack. Some authors credited the fact that McClellan could not see this part of the battlefield clearly from his headquarters due to geography and smoke; James McPherson, *Antietam* (New York: Oxford Press, 2002), 116, 119.
38. New York soldier, C. B. Gilliam, Carman Collection, AL.
39. *OR*, vol., 19/1, 475, 484, 494; Crouse, 128 Pa., AL; Letter of a 28 New York soldier (name unrecognizable), date November 22, 1892, AL.
40. C. B. Gilliam, 28 New York, Carman Collection, AL; Crouse, 128 Pa., AL.
41. *OR*, vol., 19/1, 484; Crouse, 128 Pa., AL.
42. Quaife, ed., *Cannon's Mouth*, 125; *OR*, vol., 19/1, 484, almost every *OR* of the brigade reported the mass movement. Sometimes it was referred to as "enmass"; *OR*, vol. 19/1, 475; the times of deployment ranged from dawn to 6:30 a.m. o'clock; *OR*, vol. 19/1, 484, 489.
43. *OR*, vol. 19/1, 487.
44. *OR*, vol. 19/1, 485.
45. *OR*, vol. 19/1, 489. Report of the Tenth Maine was written by J. S. Fillebrown, the officer who was kicked by Beal's horse and had been twice wounded.

46. Battlefield plaque, Antietam, personal visit; Letter by H. T. Smith of the 10th Maine in Carman collection; H. K. Hentin, 128 Pa., May 5, 1894, Gould Papers, AL; *OR*, vol. 19/1, 491; Surgeon Flood of 107 N.Y., Letter to Mrs. Mansfield in Carman Papers, chapter 12, pp. 54, 55, 56, AL. Colonel Higgins, 125th Pa. in Carman Papers, AL.
47. Crouse, 128 Pa., AL; *OR*, vol., 19/1, 493; the report of the 128 Pa. was written by Maj. Joel Wanner; *OR*, vol., 19/1, 477; Warner, *Generals in Blue*, 309; Priest, *Antietam*, 83.
48. *OR*, vol., 19/1, 491.
49. Ibid., 492.
50. McPherson, *Antietam*, 119.
51. *OR*, vol. 19/1, 476, 485. Carman Papers, chapter 12, 53; 124th Pa. history, Gould Collection, AL.
52. *OR*, vol. 19/1, 484; *OR*, vol.19/1, 476, 477; McPherson, *Antietam*, 120, 122; Sears, *Antietam*, 222, 223, 227; Murfin, *Gleam of Bayonets*, 236; Crawford, Antietam Speech, May 30, 1874, NYPL.
53. Battlefield plaque; *OR*, vol. 19/1, 492.
54. *OR*, vol. 19/1, 485, 486; *OR*, vol. 19/1, 492; Sears, *Antietam*, 224; Murfin, *Gleam of Bayonets*, 238.
55. *OR*, vol. 19/1, 492; Crouse, 128 Pa., AL.
56. *OR*, vol. 19/1, 492; Carman Papers 125th Pa. history, AL.
57. *OR*, vol. 19/1, 485; Sears, *Landscape Turned Red*, 208. It appears that Crawford was trying to aid the 17th Indiana when he was shot. A number of wounded in that area had shotgun-type wounds. The 3rd North Carolina had a number of shotgun-type weapons but it did not report its movements at this time. General Williams reported he saw the hole and that it was not large, but he saw where it entered not where it exited.
58. *OR*, vol. 19/1, 485.
59. *OR*, vol. 19/1, 497.
60. John M Priest, Antietam: *The Soldiers' Battle*, 341, 342.
61. *OR*, vol. 19/1, 496; Sears, *Antietam*, 296. 12 hours and roughly 23,000 casualties; McPherson, *Antietam*, 177n. 56; *OR*, vol., 19/1, 497; Robert Denney, *The Civil War Years*, 213; *OR*, vol. 19/1, 486; Priest, *Antietam*, 341. As the 10th Maine marched back to the woods it occupied in the morning, their number was 70 less. The other two Slaughter Mountain veterans lost half that number. The 124th and 128th Pa. lost nearly 200 in casualties. The gallant 125th Pa. was hit hardest, losing 226.
62. Crouse, 128 Pa., AL.
63. *OR*, vol. 19/1, 497.
64. Miles, *Forged in Fire*, 406–8; McPherson, *Illustrated Battle Cry*, 480–81.
65. Ron White, *The Eloquent President* (New York: Random House, 2005), 171.
66. McPherson, *Antietam*, 137–55.
67. Sears, *Antietam*, 355; Denney, *Civil War Years*, 215.
68. John Schildt, *September Echoes* (Middletown, Md.: The Valley Register, 1960), 97.
69. Welsh, *Medical Histories of the Union Generals* (Kent, Ohio: Kent State Press, 1996), 80–81. What seemed like a slight wound was infected, and bone damage gave him problems for the rest of his life. The wound seeped debris for years after the incident.
70. *New York Times*, September 20, 1862, PSUL.
71. *Valley Spirit*, October 1, 1862, Dickson, KHS; Jennie Washington Wiestling Diary, CFL.
72. Hoke, *Reminiscences*, 24, 26. One newspaper report recorded Hoke going to see Crawford after South Mountain battle.
73. Hoke, *Reminiscences* of War, 24, 26.
74. Ibid.

75. Note in Crawford Papers. Rather difficult to read, which was unlike most of Crawford's documents, LOC; William Stewart, *A Pair of Blankets* (Wilmington, N.C.: Broadfoot Press, 1990), 94, 95. The author notes that Dr. Senseny is the doctor for all Union troops in the area. Indications are that a daughter visited Crawford in Gettysburg. Nevin, *Men of Mark*, writes that the wound "bids fair to cripple him for the rest of his life," 438.
76. Nancy Heefner, et al., eds. *The Tuscarora Reader* (Mercersburg Historical Society, 2002), "Jeb Stuart's Raid Into Pennsylvania," Thomas Steiger, Jr., 193, 194; *OR*, vol., 19/2, 52.
77. Heefner, et al., *The Tuscarora Reader*, 193, 194.
78. Hoke, *Reminiscences*, 29.
79. Ibid., 30, 31.
80. *Star and Sentinel*, August 28, 1907, ACHS.
81. John Thompson, *Horses, Hostages and Apple Cider* (Mercersburg, Pa.: Mercersburg Printing, 2002), 74; *Star and Sentinel*, August 28, 1907, ACHS.
82. *Star and Sentinel*, August 1907, ACHS.
83. Telegram from General S. W. Crawford, October 16, 1862, Crawford Papers, LOC.
84. *Star and Sentinel*, August 28, 1907, ACHS.
85. *Star and Sentinel*, August 28, 1907, ACHS.
86. *Star and Sentinel*, August 28, 1907, ACHS.
87. *Star and Sentinel*, August 28, 1907, ACHS.
88. *OR*, vol., 19/1, 486.
89. Hoke, *Reminiscences*, 29–32.

CHAPTER THIRTEEN: GETTYSBURG, ON A ROCKY RIDGE AND BEYOND

1. Donald Cartmell, *Civil War 101* (New York: Gramercy Books, 2001), 5, 17, 28 different names are listed.
2. Alice Fahs, *The Imagined Civil War* (Chapel Hill: University of North Carolina, 2001), 17. Walt Whitman's Poem.
3. James McPherson, *Antietam*, 155.
4. Bruce Catton, *America Goes to War* (Middletown, Conn.: Wesleyan University Press, 1958), 28–47.
5. Ibid.
6. Robert Denney, *The Civil War Years* (New York: Sterling Publishing, 1994), 263.
7. Ibid., 261, 264.
8. Ezra Warner, *Generals in Blue*, 57–58, 233–34, 290–91, 315–17.
9. Allan Nevins, ed., *Diary of a Battle*; Journals of Charles Wainwright (Gettysburg: Stan Clark Military Books), 182.
10. Randall Bedwell, *Brink of Destruction* (New York: Random House, 1999), 125. Charles Wainwright in his Personal Journal quotes Hooker, "He was sure to whip him [Lee] badly,"182.
11. Edwin Coddington, *The Gettysburg Campaign* (New York: Charles Scribner's Sons, 1984), 6–24.
12. William Davis, *Look Away* (New York: Free Press, 2002), 333.
13. Edwin Coddington, *The Gettysburg Campaign*, 8–10; Joseph Stevens, *1863, Rebirth of a Nation* (New York: Bantam, 1999), 216–17; Walter Taylor, *General Lee 1861–1865* (Dayton, Ohio: Morningside Press, 1975), 180.
14. A number of Franklin Repositories carried articles concerning recruiting. Jacob Hoke in *Reminiscences* called it "usual recruiting." The change in community response to the recruits differed greatly from the beginning of the war until 1864 (pp. 7–9).
15. The 120-foot flagpole was placed in the Chambersburg square in 1861. It would later be cut down before Lee's army arrived. Hoke, *Reminiscences*, 8.

16. Samuel Crawford Letter to August Belmont in 1888. He reflects the feelings of the early war period. NYPL.
17. Wiestling Diary. Anne urged the girls to sell photos of Lincoln for five cents and send the money to a local Union hospital. Crawford Papers, LOC.
18. Telegram to the United States War Department, December 17, 1863, Service records, NA. Interview, Dr. Paul Orange. Ecchmotic: inflammation of the blood cells can develop tissue death, and Erythematous: skin lesions with large blisters that often break and ooze and form scar tissue.
19. Crawford service records, NA. On May 19, 1863, General Crawford relieved from the court-martial board and assigned to serve under General Heintzelman in the defense of Washington, D.C.; *OR*, vol. 25/2, 587.
20. *OR*, vol. 25/2, 507, Special Order 224; *OR*, vol. 51/1, 1043, Special Order 99; Nicholson, ed., *Pennsylvania at Gettysburg*, September 2, 1890, Reserve Day vol., 85; A. K. McClure wrote that he had talked to the governor concerning Crawford's appointment. *The Annals of War* (Philadelphia Times, 1879).
21. Evan M. Woodward, *Our Campaigns: The Second Regiment of the Pennsylvania Reserve Volunteers* (Shippensburg, Pa.: Burd Street Press, 1995), 14; Josiah Sypher, *A History of the Pennsylvania Reserves* (Lancaster, Pa.: Elias Barr, 1865), 93; Fox Regimental Losses, chapter 9, 114. The Reserves had fought in Mechanicsville, Gaines Mill, 2nd Manassas, South Mountain, Antietam, and Fredericksburg.
22. Little Round Top Seminar by Gettysburg Battlefield Guides, booklet and notes, 1995, personal.
23. Evan Woodward, *Our Campaigns* (Shippensburg, Pa.: Burd Street Press, 1995), 204, 205; Nicholson, ed., *Pennsylvania at Gettysburg*, Reserve Day vol., 226.
24. Crawford Papers, LOC; *OR*, vol. 27/1, 57. Letter to Major General Hooker from H. W. Halleck, June 25, 1863. The Second Brigade will not be a part of the Crawford command.
25. Henry Minnigh, *History of Company K* (Gettysburg: Thomas Publications, 1998), 48 (lower page number and 22 upper page number from now on it will be indicated 48/22).
26. Itinerary in Crawford Papers. LOC; Woodward, 206–8.
27. Franklin Repository, July 8, 1863; Hoke, *Reminiscences*, 41. This count was based on Ewell's and Hill's corps, not Longstreet's.
28. Jennie Washington Wiestling Diary.
29. Jennie Washington Wiestling Diary.
30. Jennie Washington Wiestling Diary.
31. Jennie Washington Wiestling Diary.
32. Caledonia files, KHS. When Sweeney told Early that the Iron Works were losing money, he replied, "Yankees don't do business that way." He then ordered the torch. Sears, *Gettysburg*, 112.
33. Evan Woodward, *Our Campaigns*, 205, 229, 230; Meade, *Life and Letters*, vol. 2, 12.
34. Harry Pfanz, *Gettysburg: The First Day* (Chapel Hill: University of North Carolina, 2001), 43–49.
35. Warner, *Generals in Blue*, 492–93; Crawford Papers, LOC. His memos in my possession are short and curt.
36. James P. Smith, *With Stonewall Jackson* (Gaithersburg, Md.: Zullo and Van Sickle, 1982), 56; Charles Marshall, *Lee's Aide-De-Camp*, 217–19.
37. Joseph Stevens, *1863: The Rebirth of a Nation* (New York: Bantam Books, 1999), 222–24.
38. Michael and John Peterson, *The Devil's To Pay: General John Buford* (Gettysburg: Farnsworth Military Impressions, 1995), 26, 30–33; Glenn Tucker, *High Tide at Gettysburg* (Dayton, Ohio: Morningside Press, 1983), 80–82.
39. Joseph Stevens, *1863: The Rebirth of a Nation* (New York: Bantam Books, 1999), 222–24; Charles Marshall, *Lee's Aide-De-Camp* (Lincoln, Neb.: University of Nebraska Press, 2000),

217–19; Glenn Tucker, *High Tide at Gettysburg* (Dayton, Ohio: Morningside Press, 1983), 80–82.

40. Hoke, *Reminiscences*, 67–69; James Longstreet, *From Manassas to Appomattox* (New York: De Capo Press, 1992), 346, 347; Marshall, *Lee's Aide*, 218–20.
41. Moxley Sorrel, *Recollections of a Confederate Staff Officer* (Wilmington, N.C.: Broadfoot Publishing Co., 1995), 152, 155–56.
42. Harry Pfanz, *Gettysburg: The First Day*, 21, 22.
43. Marshall, *Lee's Aide*, 218.
44. Adams County Census 1860, ACHS; Harry Pfanz, *Gettysburg: The Second Day* (Chapel Hill, N.C.: University of North Carolina Press, 1987), 13; Glenn Tucker, *High Tide at Gettysburg*, 100, 101; Clyde Wilson, *Carolina Cavaliers* (Athens, Ga.: University of Georgia, 1990), 191.
45. Clyde Wilson, *Carolina Cavaliers* (Athens, Ga.: University of Georgia, 1990), 191, 192. General Hill said he was just from General Lee and it was not believed the Federal army was in the area. *OR*, vol. 27/1, 923, 924; Bradley Gottfried, *Brigades at Gettysburg* (Cambridge, Mass.: De Capo Press, 2002), 604, 605.
46. Phipps and Peterson, *Devil's to Pay*, 24; *OR*, vol. 27/1, 922, 924. Included in Buford's intelligence was a pass signed by General Lee in Chambersburg on June 28, 1863. He informed General Pleasonton of the units in his front. *OR*, vol. 27/1, 924, 925.
47. Mike Riley, *For God's Sake Forward* (Gettysburg, Pa.: Farnsworth Impressions, 1995), 17–20, 42; Harry Pfanz, *Gettysburg: The First Day* (Chapel Hill, N.C.: University of North Carolina, 2001), 42.
48. Day one seminar, Gettysburg, Pa. Personal notes.
49. Pfanz, *The First Day*, 42; Eric Campbell and Scott Hartwig. Separate Day One walks and First Day Seminar.
50. Harry Pfanz, *Gettysburg, The First Day* (Chapel Hill, N.C.: University of North Carolina, 2001), 77, 78; Edwin Coddington, *The Gettysburg Campaign* (New York: Touchstone by Simon & Schuster, 1997), 269, 270.
51. Edwin Coddington, *The Gettysburg Campaign*, 270–76; Nicholson, ed., *Pennsylvania at Gettysburg*, Reserve Day vol., September 2, 1890, 249.
52. *Mr. Lincoln's Army*, Programs at the Sixth Annual Gettysburg Seminar, GNMP, 1997, 108; Coddington, 323. The result of the first two days provided the Union with a configuration in the "fish hook" that provided its leaders with the inside track, making it easier to move troops more quickly and communicate more effectively. Some historians believe the in depth concept was not planned but events transpired in such a way as to make it seem planned.
53. Bradley Gottfried, *Brigades of Gettysburg*, 272, 275.
54. Nicholson, ed., *Pennsylvania at Gettysburg*, Reserve Day vol., September 2, 1890, 249.
55. Joseph Gibbs, *Three Years in the Bloody Eleventh* (University Park, Pa.: Penn State University Press, 2002), 217.
56. Nicholson, ed., *Pennsylvania at Gettysburg*, Reserve Day vol., September 2, 1890, 249.
57. Woodward, *Our Campaigns*, 208; *Franklin Repository*, July 29, 1863; Nicholson, ed., *Pennsylvania at Gettysburg*, Reserve Day vol., 227.
58. John Nicholson, ed., *Pennsylvania at Gettysburg*, Reserve Day vol. (Harrisburg, Pa.: Stanley Ray Printer, 1889), 227; Woodward, *Our Campaigns*, 208; Gottfried, *Brigades at Gettysburg*, 270; Samuel Bates, *History of Pennsylvania Reserve Volunteers* (Harrisburg, Pa.: Singerly, 1869), 552, 553.
59. Nicholson, ed., *Pennsylvania at Gettysburg*, Reserve Day vol., 227, 281; *OR*, vol., 27/1, 592; Gottfried, 270, 271; Some of the soldiers of the Pa. Reserves were upset by the comment that they could not keep up. They pointed out that they could not leave early because of long wagon trains and then those trains slowed them; Coddington, 334. Crawford did his best to catch up.
60. Nicholson, ed., *Pennsylvania at Gettysburg*, Reserve Day vol., 279. The sword was presented to General Reynolds' sister by Sergeant Hayes Grier.
61. Minnigh, *History of Company K*, 48.

62. Nicholson, ed., *Pennsylvania at Gettysburg*, Reserve Day vol., 228, 259; Minnigh, *History of Company K*, 49. Arrival times differed: Minnigh said it was morning, Crawford about noon, and one 83 Pa. soldier gave the time as about 1 p.m.
63. McCandless, *OR*, vol. 27/1, 657; Nicholson, ed., *Pennsylvania at Gettysburg*, Reserve Day vol., 259. In 28 hours with only 3 hours of rest the regiment had marched 42 miles.
64. Coddington, *The Gettysburg Campaign*, drawing, 332. While this drawing has another purpose, it shows the battle configuration often referred to as a fishhook.
65. *OR*, vol. 27/1, 653; Nicholson, ed., *Pennsylvania at Gettysburg*, Reserve Day vol., 297; *OR*, vol. 27/1, 553; Pfanz, *Day Two*, 392; Gibbs, *Three Years*, 220.
66. *OR*, vol. 27/1, 653, 657.
67. Nicholson, ed., *Pennsylvania at Gettysburg*, Reserve Day vol., 260, 280.
68. *OR*, vol. 27/1, 653; Nesbitt, *35 Years*, 153. Horner was a member of the 12th Reserves.
69. *OR*, vol. 27/1, 653, 657; Nicholson, ed., *Pennsylvania at Gettysburg*, Reserve Day vol., 297, 280; Woodward, *Our Campaigns*, 272; Pfanz, *Gettysburg: The Second Day*, 391.
70. Nicholson, ed., *Pennsylvania at Gettysburg*, Reserve Day vol., 260.
71. Crawford Letter to Professor Jacobs, Dec. 1863. Crawford Papers, LOC; Crawford sent Louis Livingston of his staff to ask Sykes for orders. Crawford Papers, LOC; *OR*, vol. 27/1, 653; Pfanz, *Day Two*, 398; Nicholson, ed., *Pennsylvania at Gettysburg*, Reserve Day vol., 280, 281; *OR*, vol. 27/1, 653. Enemy skirmishers reached foot of rocky ridge. General Sykes in his Official Report said that he ordered the charge.
72. Gibbs, *Three Years*, 222; *OR*, vol. 27/1, 654, 657; Pfanz, *Second Day*, 398. In a letter to Professor Jacobs, Crawford used the term "fearful struggle."
73. *OR*, vol. 27/1, 662; Minnigh, Company K, 52/26; *OR*, vol. 27/1, 399–400; Nicholson, ed., *Pennsylvania at Gettysburg*, Reserve Day vol., 114; Gibbs, *Three Years*, 222; Gottfried, *Brigades at Gettysburg*, 273.
74. *OR*, vol. 27/1, 662; Gibbs, *Three Years*, 222. Called the shot buck and ball; Glenn LaFantasie, *Twilight at Little Round Top* (Hoboken, N.J.,: John Wiley, 2005), 197.
75. Letter to Rothermel, March 8, 1871, Blair and Pencak, eds. *Making and Remaking Pennsylvania's Civil War* (University Park: Pennsylvania University Press 2001), 240; Crawford Papers, LOC; Samuel Bates, *The Battle of Gettysburg* (Philadelphia: Davis Publishers, 1875), 133; Woodward, *Our Campaigns*, 213; Nicholson, ed., *Pennsylvania at Gettysburg*, Reserve Day vol., loud hurrahs; *OR*, vol. 27/1, 657; Coddington, *Gettysburg Campaign*, 409.
76. *Harper's Weekly*, August 8, 1863; Woodward, *Our Campaigns*, 213; Gibbs, *Three Years*, 224; Pfanz, *Second Day*, 398. The first painting was done by Rothermel and the latest by Dale Gallon, entitled "Encounter at Plum Run." Many details concerning the incident are different. Some say the original bearer was wounded and the flag was turned over to Swope; another says the flag was stuck and Crawford originally went to give aid to the bearer. General Crawford wrote that the bearer did not recognize him, having been commander only a few weeks.
77. Stephen Sears, *Gettysburg* (New York: Houghton Mifflin Co., 2003), 321.This was in a letter from one of Crawford's staff members, Capt. Richard Auchmuty; letter to Rothermel, March 8, 1870, Crawford Papers, LOC; Pfanz, *Second Day*, 398.
78. *OR*, vol. 27/1, 654, 657; Pfanz, *Second Day*, 398. In a letter to Professor Jacobs, Crawford used the term "fearful struggle"; Minnigh, Company K, 51/25; *OR*, vol. 27/1, 654, 657.
79. Nicholson, ed., *Pennsylvania at Gettysburg*, Reserve Day vol., 113, 304; *OR*, vol. 27/1, 655.
80. Nicholson, ed., *Pennsylvania at Gettysburg*, Reserve Day vol., 281. Jackson said Crawford complimented his regiment in most exaggerated terms. This story appears long after the battle.
81. Pfanz, *Second Day*, 402; *OR*, vol. 27/1, 618, 654, 658. This was after other regiments had a toehold on the big round top. Both Crawford and Fisher came under attack for not being more aggressive and claiming they had achieved more than they had. This will be more closely observed later.
82. Nesbitt, *35 Days to Gettysburg* (Mechanicsburg, Pa.: Stackpole Books, 1992), 162; Nicholson, ed., *Pennsylvania at Gettysburg*, Reserve Day vol., 259, 298, 299; Crawford to Colonel Fisher,

Notes to Pages 166–173

December 22, 1863. In this letter and to Colonel Rice, Crawford tried to show that two different charges took place; *OR*, vol. 27/1, 625, 632, 654, 658; Pfanz, *Second Day*, 401, 403. Lack of a unifying commander, darkness, and rough terrain prevented the plan from working according to Colonel M. Hardin and Colonel J. Chamberlain.

83. Letter to Samuel W. Crawford from Evan Woodward. Crawford Papers, LOC; Gettysburg Historical Articles of Lasting Interest, "The Terrible Impetuosity," Jeff Sherry, vol. 16, 75. Sometimes the surgeon's name was spelled Reed.
84. Nicholson, ed., *Pennsylvania at Gettysburg*, Reserve Day vol., 116.
85. A good third day source on Pickett and the charge that bestows his name by Cathy George Harrison, *Nothing But Glory*; Norman Hall fought with the II Corps, Second Division, Third Brigade commander; *OR*, vol. 27/2, 222, 223, 416, 417; *OR*, vol. 27/1, 457, 654; Coddington, *Gettysburg Campaign*, 477, 478.
86. *OR*, vol. 27/2, 416, 417, 422, 423; *OR*, vol. 27/1, 654.
87. Woodward, *Our Campaigns*, 215, 216; *OR*, 27/1, 654–57.
88. *OR*, vol. 27/1, 657; Nicholson, ed., *Pennsylvania at Gettysburg*, Reserve Day vol., 118; Woodward, *Our Campaigns*, 216; *OR*, vol. 27/1, 658.
89. *OR*, vol. 27/1, 657; Woodward, 216;
90. *OR*, vol. 27/2, 417, 423.
91. Gibbs, *Three Years*, 226; *OR*, vol. 27/1, 657–58. Crawford originally listed the count at 7,000 but in the breakdown listed 3,672 and one 12-pound Napoleon and 3 caissons. 139th Pennsylvania claimed the recapture of a brass Napoleon and 3 caissons. Also listed as James of the First Rifles; Nicholson, ed., *Pennsylvania at Gettysburg*, Reserve Day vol., 117–19; *OR*, vol. 27/1, 655–57; Gibbs, *Three Years*, 226; Woodward, *Our Campaigns*, 215–17; Colonel DuBose does not mention the lost flag.
92. *OR*, vol. 27/2, 422–24; *OR*, vol. 27/2, 423, 424; *Mr. Lincoln's Army*, Sixth Gettysburg Seminar, 193.
93. Jennie Washington Wiestling Diary and note. The date had to be the same time period, for it became public knowledge at the end of July in the Franklin Repository. She believed the body would be transferred to Cincinnati. Margaret's youngest son would die within nine months on Christmas Day. Crawford Papers, LOC; Adjutant General's records, July 2, 1863, February 17, 1864, NA.
94. *OR, vol.* 27/3, 563.Story found in the *Franklin Repository*, July 29, 1863, KHS. I chose parts of the story as it covers almost 7 columns.
95. General Orders General G. G. Meade, Letters of Meade, vol. 2, 122, 123; Nicholson, ed., *Pennsylvania at Gettysburg*, Reserve Day vol., 225.
96. *Philadelphia Inquirer*, July 7, 1863, PSUL.
97. Woodward, *Our Campaigns*, 222, 223; Gibbs, *Three Years*, 230.
98. Clyde Wilson, *Carolina Cavalier* (Athens, Ga.: University of Georgia Press, 1990), 198–200. Pettigrew was shot July 14 and died July 17, 1863. Crawford Papers, LOC.
99. Samuel Crawford, *Genesis of the Civil War*, 113–16.
100. Ibid.
101. Crawford, *Genesis*, 113–16.
102. Woodward, *Our Campaigns*, 226; Nicholson, ed., *Pennsylvania at Gettysburg*, Reserve Day vol., 233.
103. Woodward, *Our Campaigns*, 229.
104. Woodward, *Our Campaigns*, 229. Crawford was a believer in strict discipline but at times he was accused of accentuating trivials, *CWTI*, June 2002. Article by William Marvel, 46f.
105. Woodward, *Our Campaigns*, 230. Most of the story is in the Woodward book; Wainwright, *Our Campaigns*, 277.
106. Woodward, *Our Campaigns*, 229–31; Crawford Papers, LOC.
107. Crawford Papers, LOC.

108. Capt. G. G. Meade, ed., *The Life and Letters of General George Gordon Meade*, 2 vols. (New York: Scribner's Sons, 1913), vol. 2, 313, entire speech; Freeman Cleaves, *Meade of Gettysburg* (Norman: University of Oklahoma Press, 1991), 192..
109. Woodward, *Our Campaigns*, 230–33; Meade speech, 230; Nevins, ed., *Diary of a Battle*, 277. Wainwright felt Curtin's speech was one for reelection.
110. Nevins, ed., *Diary of a Battle*, 277. Wainwright was not pleased with the conduct of many officers and Governor Curtin's staff.
111. Woodward, *Our Campaigns*, 233, 234; Crawford Itinerary with notes. Crawford Papers, LOC; Theodore Gerrish, *Army Life* (Baltimore, Md.: Butternut and Blue, 1995), 123, 124.
112. Robert Alotta, *Civil War Justice* (Shippensburg, Pa.: White Mane Publishing Co., Inc., 1989), 77.
113. William Powell, *Fifth Army Corps* (Dayton, Ohio: Morningside, 1984), 572, 573.
114. Ted Gerrish quoted in Alotta, *Civil War Justice*, 79.
115. *Composite of Gerrish*, 125–28; Alotta, *Justice*, 77–80; Woodward, *Our Campaigns*, 233, 234.
116. Quaife, ed., *Cannon's Mouth*, 255, 295.
117. Quaife, ed., *Cannon's Mouth*, 255; Marvel article, *CWTI*, June 2002. Griffin, a West Pointer, was not fond of Crawford, who had not been trained at West Point.
118. Medical Records, NA; Surgeon Reed suggested a treatment, Crawford Papers, LOC.
119. Heidler and Heidler, *Encyclopedia of Civil War*, 285–86; William Hassler, *Lee's Forgotten General* (Chapel Hill: University of North Carolina, 1962), 180.
120. Welsh, *Medical Histories*, 81; Army Medical Records, NA; Crawford Papers, LOC; *Franklin Repository*, October 28, 1863.
121. Jennie Washington Wiestling Diary.
122. Jennie Washington Wiestling Diary
123. Jennie Washington Wiestling Diary
124. Hoke, *Reminiscences*, 90–92, 100–102.
125. Jennie Washington Wiestling Diary.
126. *Franklin Repository*, November 11, 1863, KHS; Letter to Sanitary Commission from General Crawford, November 16, 1863. The commission provided tobacco for the troops.
127. Captain Alex Crawford service records, NA.
128. Hoke, *Reminiscences*, 174–76.
129. Hoke, *Reminiscences*, 174–76.
130. Woodward, *Our Campaigns*, 238–40; Gibbs, *Three Years*, 241.
131. Woodward, *Our Campaigns*, 240; Gibbs, *Three Years*, 243–44.
132. Note in Crawford Papers, LOC; *OR*, vol. 29/1, 978. December 13, 1863, Warrenton Junction.
133. Letter to Professor Jacobs from General S. W. Crawford, December 1863. Crawford tried to explain the differences in the two charges; The letters to Brig. Gen. James Rice were written on December 11 and 23, 1863. At Gettysburg Rice was a colonel; Undated Letter to Professor Jacobs. Crawford Papers, LOC.
134. Letter to Professor Jacobs, December (?), 1863.
135. Letter to Professor Jacobs. Crawford Papers, LOC. The accusation continued to bother the Reserves, and in 1886 a resolution was adopted to confirm their role in the Little Round Top charge.
136. Woodward, *Our Campaigns*, 205.
137. Nicholson, ed., *Pennsylvania at Gettysburg*, Reserve Day vol., 226; *Franklin Repository*, July 29, 1863, KHS; Crawford Papers, LOC.
138. Pfanz, *The Second Day*, 393; *OR*, vol. 27/1, 653–57.
139. Minnigh, Company K, 50/24; Nicholson, ed., *Pennsylvania at Gettysburg*, Reserve Day vol., 303; Richard Auchmuty Letter in the Crawford Papers, LOC.

140. *OR*, vol. 27/1, 653, 657, 662; Nicholson, ed., *Pennsylvania at Gettysburg*, Reserve Day vol., 281.
141. Crawford Letter to Jacobs, December 1863; Crawford Letter to Stover, May 14, 1867. Crawford Papers, LOC.
142. Coddington, *Gettysburg Campaign*, 409, 410; Nicholson, ed., *Pennsylvania at Gettysburg*, Reserve Day vol., 281, 282; *OR*, vol. 27/1, 685.
143. *OR*, vol. 27/1, 592; Bill Hyde, ed., *The Union Generals Speak* (Baton Rouge: Louisiana State University Press, 2003), 346, 347.

CHAPTER FOURTEEN: SPRING IN THE WILDERNESS AND SPOTSYLVANIA

1. William McFeely, *Grant* (New York: W. W. Norton, 1982), 152; Letter from Edwin Stanton to Oliver W. Holmes; McPherson, *Illustrated Battle Cry*, 625.
2. McPherson, *Illustrated Battle Cry*, 625, 626. The age was now 17 to 50. Conscription Act of February 17, 1863; Robert Denney, *The Civil War Years* (New York: Sterling Publishing, 1994), 261.
3. Tracy Power, *Lee's Miserables* (Chapel Hill: University of North Carolina, 1998), 8–9, 260, 261; McPherson, *Illustrated Battle Cry*, 625.
4. Power, *Lee's Miserables*, 10. The reported number of officers lost varied greatly, but most indicate significant problems in that area.
5. McPherson, *Illustrated Battle Cry*, 627–28; McFeely, *Grant*, 157.
6. Military records, NA; Warner, *Generals in Blue*, 99, 100, 541, 542; David Jordon, *Happiness Is Not My Companion* (Bloomington, Ind.: University of Indiana, 2001), 97, 120; Crawford tombstone.
7. Michael Kelly, *I Will Have Justice Done* (Gettysburg: Farnsworth Impressions, 1997), 37; David Jordon, *Happiness Is Not My Companion*, 99. Does not totally agree with this assessment.
8. *Franklin Repository*, March 12, 1863, KHS; Gibbs. *Three Years*, 255; Crawford Papers, LOC.
9. Crawford, Medical Records, NA. Alex McLeod Crawford would serve until he was discharged as disabled, 11/21/64, and then came back to the Veterans Reserve Corps, 2/21/65 until 1/3/67. Military Records, NA; Crawford Papers, LOC.
10. *OR*, vol. 33/1, 738; Samuel was reassigned Third Division commander in V Corps on March 25, 1864. General Order; *OR*, vol. 36/2, 360, signed by Robert McCoy.
11. *OR*, vol. 36/2, 355; Nevins, ed., *Diary of a Battle*, 347.
12. Theodore Gerrish, *Army Life* (Baltimore: Butternut and Blue, 1995), 156; *OR*, vol. 36/2, 370, May 4, 1864.
13. *OR*, vol. 36/1, 1070.
14. *OR*, vol. 36/2, 360. Crawford's division was made up of two brigades of Pennsylvania Reserves under Colonels McCandless and Fisher and a brigade of artillery under Capt. Augustus Martin. Ten regiments of infantry made up the Reserves. The number was 3,460 in officers and men; Woodward, *Our Campaigns*, 243–45; Howard Thomson and William Rauch, *History of the Bucktails* (Philadelphia: n.p., 1906), 291; *OR*, vol. 36/2, 359. Locke Assistant Adjutant General.
15. Humphreys, *Virginia Campaign*, 9–12. He lists the Union army at 99,438 and the Army of Northern Virginia at just under 62,000; *OR*, vol. 36/1, 189, General Meade; McFeely, *Grant*, 165. The campaign was hideous in every way but it worked; Grant's letter to Halleck, chief of staff, expressed doubt as to what Lee's intentions were. *OR*, vol. 36/2, 370.
16. Lyman, *Grant and Meade*, 85, 87, 89, 180; Woodward, *Our Campaigns*, 243–45; Thomson, *Bucktails*, 291.
17. Woodward, *Our Campaigns*, 243–45; McFeely, *Grant*, 165; John Vautier Diary, 88th Pennsylvania Infantry. May 4 and May 9, 1864, USAMHI; Gerrish, *Army Life*, 156, 157.

18. Gerrish, *Army Life*, 156, 157; Vautier USAMHI; Private John Haley, 17th Maine, *The Rebel Yell and The Yankee Hurrah* (Camden, Me.: Down East Books 1985), 142.
19. Gordon Rhea, *The Battle of the Wilderness* (Baton Rouge: Louisiana State University Press, 1994), 74; *OR*, vol. 36/2, 378. William Ray Diary, May 4, 1864. He was a member of the 7th Wisconsin in the Fourth Division of the V Corps. USAMHI.
20. *OR*, vol., 36/2, 378, 379; *OR*, vol. 36/1, 283; Maj. Ben Fisher, Chief Signal Officer.
21. Nevins, ed., *Diary of a Battle*, 349; Crawford Papers, LOC.
22. Gibbs, *Three Years*, 256; Nevins, ed., *Diary of a Battle*, 348. The cavalry was the Third Division of J. H. Wilson; *OR*, vol. 36/2,377; Noah Trudeau, *Bloody Roads South* (Baton Rouge: Louisiana State University, 2000), 46–47.
23. *OR*, vol. 36/2, 417. The Reserves had been to Parker's Store the year before.
24. Rhea, *Wilderness*, 117; Noah Trudeau, *Bloody Roads South*, 46; Josiah Sypher, *History of the Pennsylvania Reserve Corps* (Lancaster, Pa., 1865), 510.
25. *OR*, vol. 36/2, 418. One mile of Parkers, brisk skirmishing, halted in good position. This was received by Humphreys and sent to Meade as Warren was aiding Griffin on the turnpike. About an hour was lost in the transfer.
26. Rhea, *Wilderness*, 104.
27. *OR*, vol. 36/2, 418.
28. *OR*, vol. 36/2, 418, 419; Warren's Journal #98, Washington Roebling in Warren collection, as cited in Rhea, *Wilderness*, 116.
29. *OR*, vol. 36/2, 420. The time was 12 noon; Gibbs, *Three Years*, 257.
30. Woodward. *Our Campaigns*, 246; Gibbs, *Three Years*, 258, 259; *OR*, vol. 36/1, 539, 540.
31. Woodward, *Our Campaigns*, 247. One source indicated Crawford was informed by a signal corps messenger of his peril.
32. Rhea, *Wilderness*, 223; Josiah Sypher, *History of the Pennsylvania Reserve Corps* (Lancaster, Pa.: n.p., 1865), 522; Woodward, *Our Campaigns*, 246, 247.
33. *OR*, vol. 36/1, 539–40. #98 Warren's Journal.
34. *OR*, vol. 36/2, 457.
35. Minnigh, Company K, 58/32. [I will refer to the bottom page number]
36. Theodore Lyman, *With Grant and Meade* (Lincoln: University of Nebraska, 1994), 89.
37. Vautier, May 13, 1864, USAMHI; John Cannan, *The Spotsylvania Campaign* (Conshohocken, Pa.: Combined Books, 1997). A quote from Horace Porter, 15, 16.
38. Bruce Catton, *Grant Takes Command*, 189; Haley, *Rebel Yell*, 144; John Vautier, May 5, 1864.
39. McPherson, *Illustrated Battle Cry*, 631; Edward Steere, *The Wilderness Campaign* (Mechanicsburg, Pa.: Stackpole Books, 1960), 297–300; Rhea, *Wilderness*, 268.
40. *OR*, vol. 36/2, 457; Rhea, *Wilderness*, 322; *OR*, vol., 36/1, 540.
41. Rhea, *Wilderness*, 329.
42. Woodward, *Our Campaigns*, 247.
43. Jeffry D. Wert, *General James Longstreet* (New York: Simon & Schuster, 1993), 387; James Longstreet, *From Manassas to Appomattox* (New York: Da Capo Press, 1992), 563, 564; Rhea, *Wilderness*, 370; Moxley Sorrel, *Recollections of A Confederate Staff Officer* (Wilmington, N.C.: Broadfoot Publishing, 1995), 233, 234.
44. *OR*, vol. 36/1, 540; Lyman, *Grant and Meade*, 98. Lyman said the Pennsylvania Reserves were sent to the rescue; Woodward, *Our Campaigns*, 247.
45. Gibbs, *Three Years*, 261; Nevins, ed., *Diary of a Battle*, 354.
46. Cannan, *Spotsylvania Campaign*, 16 (more of the Porter quote); Horace Porter, *Campaigning With Grant* (New York: Konecky and Konecky, 1992), 65; Rhea, *Wilderness*, 436.
47. *OR*, vol. 36/1, 190, 191; Dr. James Frick, Gettysburg, Battlefield Guide.
48. McPherson, *Illustrated Battle Cry*, 633; Grant's Memoirs, 534; Letter to H. W. Halleck, Chief of Staff, May 7, 1864.

Notes to Pages 197–203

49. Nevins, ed., *Diary of a Battle*, 354; *OR*, vol. 36/2, 481; Catton, *Grant Takes Command*, 202, 203.
50. Thomson and Rauch, *Bucktails*, 297; *OR*, vol. 36/2, 504, 505; *OR, vol. 36/2*, 481. Prepare for night march.
51. William Ray Diary, May 7. Ray was in the Iron Brigade in the V Corps. A couple of months later, the Iron Brigade would become a part of Crawford's division. USAMHI; Sypher, *Pennsylvania Reserves*, 520; Catton, *Grant Takes Command*, 208. Crawford listed the time leaving at 10 p.m.; Gerrish, *Army Life*, 170, 171.
52. John Vautier and Avery Harris. Both expressed the conditions similarly. Letters, Pennsylvania regiments, USAMHI; Nevins, ed., *Diary of a Battle*, 355; Rhea, *Spotsylvania*, 38.
53. *OR*, vol. 36/1, 540. Lyman (Grant and Meade) tells how Sheridan and Warren had words over the delays. Sheridan said nothing was in the way and infantry behavior was disgraceful. Lyman adds maybe this was the beginning of the dislike for Warren and ill feelings against Meade (pp. 105–6).
54. Thomson and Rauch, *Bucktails*, 299; John Vautier Diary, USAMHI.
55. Rhea, *Spotsylvania*, 43, 44.
56. Gerrish, *Army Life*, 174.
57. Gibbs, *Three Years*, 264; Rhea, *Spotsylvania*, 62, 63; Sypher, *Pennsylvania Reserves*, 522.
58. Rhea, *Spotsylvania*, 152 drawing.
59. *OR*, vol. 36/1, 541; Gibbs, *Three Years*, 255.
60. Rhea, *Spotsylvania*, 64, 65; *OR*, vol. 36/2, 539, 540, 541, 542; Matrau, Letters Home, 78.
61. Rhea, *Spotsylvania*, 65.
62. Gibbs, *Three Years*, 264, 265; *OR*, vol. 36/2, 540, 541, 542, 543. The report of deaths of fellow officers was noted in his report before his statements of dejection.
63. Woodward, *Our Campaigns*, 248, 249.
64. Catton, *Grant Takes Command*, 189; Lyman, *Grant and Meade*, 91; *OR*, vol. 36/2-#10, Washington, May 9, 1864.
65. Welsh, *Medical Histories*, 81; medical records S.W. Crawford, NA; Crawford Papers, LOC.
66. Jeff Sharpe, *Last Full Measure*, (N.p.: 1998, Audio Cassette, unabridged).
67. Rhea, *Wilderness*, 118; Woodward, *Our Campaigns*, 252; *OR*, vol. 36/2, 819. Seth Williams, May 16, 1864. The confusion resulted in the consideration of two muster dates. The Reserves mustered in just after Fort Sumter in 1861, but the Union did not give them enlistment credit until they joined the Federal army.
68. Nevins, ed., *Diary of a Battle*, 353; *OR*, vol. 36/2, 459.
69. Rhea, *Spotsylvania*, 94, 95; Lyman, *Grant and Meade*, 107–8; Humphreys, *Virginia Campaign*, 71; James Thomas 107 Pa., USAMHI.
70. Sypher, *Pennsylvania Reserves*, 524–26; *OR*, vol. 36/1, 541; Gibbs, *Three Years*, 265.
71. Rhea, *Spotsylvania*, 127–29, 161. Rhea suggests the aggressive manner was to make up for the piecemeal performance on May 8 at Laurel Hill; John Cannan, *The Spotsylvania Campaign*, 87; Nevins, ed., *Diary of a Battle*, 362.
72. Nevins, ed., *Diary of a Battle*, 362; John Vautier Diary, USAMHI; Gibbs, *Three Years*, 266.
73. *OR*, vol. 36/2, 606, 607; Rhea, *Spotsylvania*, 127, 129, 130.
74. *OR*, vol. 36/2, 607; Rhea, *Spotsylvania*, 130.
75. Minnigh, *Company K*, 61.
76. Gibbs, *Three Years*, 266; *OR*, vol. 36/1, 541.
77. Gibbs, *Three Years*, 266, 267; Catton, *Grant Takes Command*, 220, 221.
78. John Gibbon, *Personal Recollections of the Civil War* (Dayton, Ohio: Morningside Press, 1988), 218; Rhea, *Spotsylvania*, 147; Cannan, *Spotsylvania*, 87; David Jordon, *Happiness Is Not My Companion*, 148.
79. Gibbs, *Three Years*, 267; Sypher, *Pennsylvania Reserves*, 524, 525; Rhea, *Spotsylvania*, 147.

80. Rhea, *Spotsylvania*, 146; Cannan, *Spotsylvania Campaign*, 89; Gibbon, Personal Recollections, 218.
81. Rhea, *Spotsylvania*, 177.
82. *OR*, vol. 36/1, 541; Cannan, *Spotsylvania Campaign*, 89, 91. D. Bloodgood of 141 Pa. quote.
83. Woodward, *Our Campaigns*, 249; Nevins, ed., *Diary of a Battle*, 364; Grant, *Memoirs and Letters*, 549; *OR*, vol. 36/1, 541.
84. Denney, *Civil War Years*, 406; Rhea, *Spotsylvania*, 211; Cannan, *Spotsylvania Campaign*, 118, 119.
85. Cannan, *Spotsylvania Campaign*, 121; Rhea, *Spotsylvania*, 232; *OR*, vol. 36/1, 192. Warren: "at daylight Hancock surprised Johnson in his lines and captured nearly all of it, with 18 pieces of artillery."
86. Cannan quote by W. G. Tyler, 164; Rufus Dawes, *A Full Blown Yankee* (Lincoln: University of Nebraska), 254–56, 266.
87. *OR*, vol. 36/2, 669, 670, 671; Rhea, *Spotsylvania*, 189, 289, 290.
88. John Vaultier Diary, USAMHI
89. Grant, *Memoirs and Letters*, 550.
90. Gibbon, *Personal Recollections of the Civil War*, 221.
91. *OR*, vol. 36/1, 197.
92. *OR*, vol. 36/1, 197.

CHAPTER FIFTEEN: THE SUMMER OF 1864

1. Nevins, ed., *Diary of Battle*, 372.
2. *OR*, vol. 36/2, 716. May 12 had been spent trying to determine the enemy position and strength. Enough firing had been done for Warren to report to Humphreys that Crawford's .52-caliber ammo was exhausted.
3. *OR*, vol. 36/1, 541, 542; Gerrish, *Army Life*, 184; Nevins, ed., *Diary of a Battle*, 372. Warren spells the river "Ny." Roebling wrote they were in the midst of an Egyptian darkness; *OR*, vol. 36/2, 721, 722.
4. Rhea, *North Anna*, 81.
5. Rhea, *Spotsylvania*, 319. From May 5–12 and including Burnside the 33,000 casualties translated into 28% of the force. The V Corps losses were 21,578 from 5 to 22 May; *OR*, vol 36/3, 146; William Ray Diary, May 14, 1864, USAMHI; Tracy Power, *Lee's Miserables* (Chapel Hill: University of North Carolina, 1998), 28. William McFeely, *Grant*, 169; *OR*, vol. 36/2, 812. The Union medical director counted 6,000 wounded in Fredericksburg.
6. *OR*, vol. 36/2, 819. The soldiers did not leave until the 17th. It was at this time the other Pennsylvania Reserves date was calculated for discharge; Tracy Power, *Lee's Miserables*, 36; *OR*, vol. 36/2, 818, 819.
7. Vautier Diary, May 17, 1864, USAMHI; *OR*, vol. 36/2, 850; Rhea, *North Anna*, 155.
8. *OR*, vol. 36/2, 873; Dawes, *Full Blown Yankee*, 257; Rhea, *North Anna*, 159; Thomson and Rauch, *Bucktails*, 307–9; Rhea, *North Anna*, 159; Woodward, *Our Campaigns*, 251.
9. Rhea, *North Anna*, 185; Trudeau, *Bloody Roads*, 208; Grant, *Memoirs and Letters*, 559; *OR*, vol. 36/2, 922; Woodward, *Our Campaigns*, 251; Sypher, *Pennsylvania Reserves*, 536; Grant, *Memoirs*, 559.
10. Gibbs, *Three Years*, 271; Catton, *Grant Takes Command*, 242; McPherson, *Illustrated Battle Cry*, 641; Rhea, *North Anna*, 191, 192; Trudeau, *Bloody Roads South*, 210; Gibbs, *Three Years*, 271.
11. Rhea, *North Anna*, 228; Nevins, ed., *Diary of a Battle*, 380, 381.
12. *OR*, vol. 36/1, 542. Warren reported he was up all night because of the many changes in orders. Ewell had reached the Telegraph Road which was the V Corps original route. Times ranged from 3 p.m. to 5 p.m.

13. Thomson and Rauch, *Bucktails*, 312; Gibbs, *Three Years*, 271; Woodward, *Our Campaigns*, 251.
14. Sypher, *Pennsylvania Reserves*, 538–39; *OR*, vol. 36/1, 542; Vautier Diary, USAMHI; *OR*, vol. 36/3, 90, 91.
15. Nevins, ed., *Diary of a Battle*, 383; Lyman, *Grant and Meade*, 118.
16. Locke, *Story of Regiment*, 340–43; David Jordon, *Happiness Is Not My Companion* (Bloomington: University of Indiana, 2001), 155; *OR*, vol. 36/1, 543; *OR*, vol. 36/3, 126.
17. Locke, *Story of Regiment*, 340–43; Nevins, ed., *Diary of a Battle*, 383; Woodward, *Our Campaigns*, 252; *OR*, vol.36/3, 129, 130.
18. Sypher, *Pennsylvania Reserves*, 540–44; Nevins, ed., *Diary of a Battle*, 101; *OR*, vol. 36/3, 132; Vautier Diary, USAMHI. One soldier in the 46th Pennsylvania, at Antietam, suggested Crawford was probably hiding behind a tree.
19. Locke, *Story of Regiment*, 343; Nevins, ed., *Diary of a Battle*, 387; Trudeau, *Bloody Roads*, 238; Jordon, *Happiness is Not My Companion*, 156; *OR*, vol. 36/3, 128, 159.
20. Trudeau, *Bloody Roads South*, 223, 239.
21. Gerrish, *Army Life*, 192.
22. Woodward, *Our Campaigns*, 252; Trudeau, *Bloody Roads South*, 242.
23. John Vautier Diary, USAMHI.
24. Thomson and Rauch, *Bucktails*, 319.
25. Humphreys, *Virginia Campaign*, 168; Gibbs, *Three Years*, 276–77; Thomson and Rauch, *Bucktails*, 319, 320.
26. Thomson and Rauch, *Bucktails*, 319–20; Gibbs, *Three Years*, 276–77; Minnigh, *Company K*, 64; Woodward, *Our Campaigns*, 253; Trudeau, *Bloody Roads South*, 257; Orndorff, 52nd Va. Woodward wrote that the general was Ransom from North Carolina. I could not identify him.
27. Vautier Diary, USAMHI.
28. Woodward, *Our Campaigns*, 254; *Philadelphia Inquirer*, June 6, 1864.
29. Woodward, *Our Campaigns*, 254.
30. Woodward, *Our Campaigns*, 254–55; *Pennsylvania at Gettysburg*, vol. 1, 85; Dickson, KHS; McClure, *Lincoln and Men of War*, 453, 454.
31. Woodward, *Our Campaigns*, 256.
32. Woodward, *Our Campaigns*, 260.
33. Woodward, *Our Campaigns*, 259.
34. Dawes, *Full Blown Yankee*, 282.
35. Nevins, ed., *Diary of a Battle*, 396. Later Wainwright experiences Warren's explosion again. The colonel indicated that the V Corps was operating in fear (p. 405); Rhea, *Cold Harbor*, 260. Special Order, 131, June 2, 1864; *OR*, vol. 36/3, 494, 495.
36. Rhea, *Cold Harbor*, 260–61.
37. *OR*, vol. 36/2, 714–15. Warren gave credit to a number of his division commanders, who were Ayres, Cutler, and Crawford. *OR*, vol. 40/3, 319.
38. *OR*, vol. 36/3, 614. Hardin, Lyles, and Bates would command Crawford's brigade.
39. James Thomas, June 6, USAMHI. Civil War Letters, First Brigade.
40. Horace Porter, *Campaigning with Grant* (New York: Konecky, et al., 1992), 195–97.
41. Trudeau, *Last Citadel*, 17, 18.
42. Gerrish, *Army Life*, 197; Humphreys, *Virginia Campaign*, 203; Lyman, *Grant and Meade*, 159; Nevins, ed., *Diary of a Battle*, 417; William Swinton, *The Army of the Potomac* (Secaucus, N.J.: Blue and Grey, 1988), 500.
43. *OR*, vol. 40/1, 188. No entry for the 15th, which is the day they were likely in this place; John Vautier Diary, June 14, USAMHI.
44. McPherson, *Illustrated Battle Cry*, 649; Heidler and Heidler, *Encyclopedia of Civil War*, 1496, 1497.

45. John Vautier, USAMHI. Good description of army life during the early phase of Operation Overland.
46. Nevins, ed., *Diary of a Battle*, 431.
47. James Robertson, *Soldiers Blue and Grey* (Columbia: University of South Carolina Press, 1988), 143; Theodore Lyman, *With Grant and Meade* (Lincoln: University of Nebraska, 1994), 181, 182.
48. *OR*, vol. 40/3, 393, 394.
49. *Southern Revenge* (Chambersburg, Pa.: Chamber of Commerce, and Shippensburg, Pa.: White Mane Publishing Co., Inc., 1989), 101. Jubal Early ordered the burning of the town to counter the destructive policies of Union General David Hunter in the Shenandoah Valley. The story of the burning is taken from chapter six of this source.
50. Heidler and Heidler, *Encyclopedia of Civil War*, 1272; James Thomas, August 2, 1864; Hoke, *Reminiscences*, 115, 116.
51. *Franklin Repository*, July 27, 1864.
52. Jacob Hoke, *The Great Invasion* (Gettysburg: Stan Clark Military Books, 1992), 582–84; *Southern Revenge*, chap. 6; Ted Alexander, *The Burning of Chambersburg and McCausland's Raid* (Columbus, Ohio: Blue and Gray Magazine, 2004), 20, 29; Hoke, *Reminiscences*, 104–20.
53. Hoke, *Great Invasion*, 582–84; *Southern Revenge*, 104.
54. Jennie Washington Wiestling's Diary. Averil [sic] for Averell.
55. Hoke, *Invasion*, 582. *Southern Revenge*, map directory and legend of burning, 130, 131; Alexander, *Burning of Chambersburg*, 44, 60.
56. Hoke, *Reminiscences*, 105; *Southern Revenge*, 132.
57. Avery Harris Letter, USAMHI; Crawford Papers, LOC.
58. *Franklin Repository*, August 24, 1864; *Southern Revenge*, 132; Crawford Papers, LOC.
59. Hoke, *Reminiscences*, 137–40.
60. John Vautier Diary, USAMHI.
61. *OR*, vol. 42/1, 491. The report was written on September 25 but included activities for August 18, 19, and 21; *OR*, vol. 42/2, 278; Henry Matrau, *Letters Home*, 95.
62. *OR*, vol. 42/1, 492, 494. General Hartranft's troops captured a Rebel flag belonging to a North Carolina regiment in this charge; Al Gambone, *Major-General John Frederick Hartranft* (Baltimore, Md.: Butternut and Blue, 1995), 113.
63. U.S. Medical Records, NA; Jack Welsh, *Medical Histories of the Union Generals* (Kent, Ohio: Kent State Press, 1996), 81; Crawford Papers, LOC.
64. *OR*, vol. 42/1, 506, 518, 519, 522, 523, report that George Reed captured the 24th North Carolina flag; Major Sheaffer names the 18th North Carolina; Mary Thomas, ed., *The Civil War Letters of First Lieutenant James B. Thomas* (Baltimore, Md.: Butternut and Blue, 1995), 234–45. McCoy's report mentioned Hottenstein.
65. *OR*, vol. 42/2, 433.
66. William Ray Diary, USAMHI; Special Orders 207. *OR*, vol. 42/2, 453. The orders were cut on the 24th, but William Ray cites the 25th in his diary.
67. *OR*, vol. 42/1, 494; *Franklin Repository*, November 22, 1864. Alex was brevetted Major in March of 1865. Retired January 3, 1867.
68. Crawford Papers, LOC. The expression for the need of discipline is evident in a note to another officer toward the end of his military career in 1873; William Ray Diary mentions the different inspections and drills in different months in the winter of '64. USAMHI.
69. James Thomas letters, October 21, 1864, and November 10, 1864. USAMHI. I found these before I had access to the book. See #64.
70. Lyman, *Grant and Meade*, 242. Lyman said it did not go down well with Griffin and Ayres as they were old school and Crawford got his star because of Sumter.
71. *OR*, vol. 42/3, 106; *OR*, vol. 42/1, 450.

72. Richard Sommers, "The Battle No One Wanted," *Civil War Illustrated Times* 14 (August 1975), 11–18; *OR*, vol. 42/1, 450; *OR*, vol. 42/3, 127.
73. Sommers, *CWTI* (August 1975), 11–18.
74. Sommers, *CWTI* (August 1975), 11–18; *OR*, vol. 42/1, 450; *OR*, vol. 42/3, 127.
75. Sommers, *CWTI* (August 1975), 11–18.
76. *OR*, vol. 42/1, 450; *OR*, vol. 42/3, 127; Warner, *Blue*, 359; Sommers, *CWTI* (August 1975), 11–18. Parke had attended the academy Samuel's father taught and went to Penn, graduating the year before Samuel, and then went to West Point, ranking second in his class.
77. Sommers, *CWTI* (August 1975), 12–18; *OR*, vol. 42/1, 450.
78. Lyman, *Grant and Meade*, 251; *OR*, vol. 42/1, 495, 496. In the November 2 report the dates were October 27 and 28.
79. *OR*, vol. 42/1, 495, 496, 497; Heidler and Heidler, *Encyclopedia of Civil War*, 945; William Ray Diary, October 27, 1864; USAMHI; Lyman, *Grant and Meade*, 250, 251.
80. *OR*, vol. 42/3, 402, 403.
81. Private Haley, February 7, 1865, 241; Henry Matrau, *Letters Home*, 105.
82. Heidler and Heidler, *Encyclopedia of Civil War*, 333. The original idea was created by the late Phil Kearny; James Robertson, *Soldiers Blue and Grey* (Columbia, S.C.: University of South Carolina, 1988), 24. Colors: 1st division red, 2nd blue, and 3rd white; *OR*, vol. 42/3, 503. Crawford inadvertently dated the memo November 3, 1861; Warren responded on November 4, 1864.
83. Heidler and Heidler, *Encyclopedia of Civil War*, 546; *OR*, vol. 36/1, 96, 97; Matrau, *Letters Home*, 108, 105; Haley, *Rebel Yell*, 241.
84. William Ray Diary, USAMHI. December 16, 1864; January 14, 1865; January 27, 1865.
85. William Ray Diary, January 1, 1865.
86. *OR*, vol. 42/3, 207. In four or five different reports Crawford sends information to his commander received from Confederate soldiers that turned themselves in.
87. William Ray Diary, December 16 and 21; Lyman, *Grant and Meade*, 299, December 13, 1864; Matrau, *Letters Home*, 110.
88. *OR*, vol. 42/3, 1095, Special Order 473, December 29, 1864. The list had been submitted.

CHAPTER SIXTEEN: AN END AND A BEGINNING

1. Ulysses Grant, *Memoirs and Letters*, 651; Robert Denney, *The Civil War Years*, 551; Tracy Power, *Lee's Miserables*, 216, 218.
2. Robert Denney, *The Civil War Years*, 484, 507. The Electoral College vote was 212 to 21 for McClellan; Grant, *Memoirs*, 651.
3. Crawford Service Records, NA, August 1864; January 1865. Medical Records, NA. In a letter supporting Crawford's retirement, a doctor in Huntsville indicated mental confusion that stemmed, he believed, from the wound and the malaria.
4. Haley, *Rebel Yell*, 144, 145. Many stories of wounded soldiers asking their fellow soldiers to shoot them appear in many battles.
5. *OR*, vol. 46/2, 94, 162.
6. Letter from Jack A. to a P. Daul in 107th Pa. Folder, USAMHI. Both had been in the 107 Pa. This was a letter from Jack telling Daul he was glad he was not in the outfit since his buddy would tell of his stunts he had pulled. The reason for this leave was stated to get married, which he never intended.
7. Abner Small, 16th Maine, USAMHI. William Ray, March 3, 1865; Private John Haley, 17th Maine, February 27, 1865.
8. Sam Cauller Letter, USAMHI.
9. Matrau, *Letters Home*, 102; Lyman, *Grant and Meade*, 303.
10. Lyman, *Grant and Meade*, 313.

11. *OR*, vol. 46/1, 798; Haley, *Rebel Yell*, 254; *OR*, vol. 46/3, 225, 226. The troops carried eight days' supply of coffee, sugar, salt. The division had three days' supply of beef on the hoof and forage for the animals for eight days; Chris Calkins and Ed Bearss, *The Battle of Five Forks* (Lynchburg, Va.: Howard, 1985), 25.
12. *OR*, vol. 46/1, 884–85, 893; Calkins and Bearss, *Battle of Five Forks*, 14, 25, 26. This was also called the Battle of Lewis Farms.
13. *OR*, vol. 46/1, 602.
14. Calkins and Bearss, *Battle of Five Forks*, 29, 59–62; *OR*, vol. 46/1, 602; *OR*, vol. 46/2, 485.
15. Melcher, *Flash of His Sword*, 210; *OR*, vol. 46/3, 370; *OR*, vol. 46/1, 602.
16. Sylvanus Cadwallader, *Three Years with Grant* (Lincoln: University of Nebraska, 1996), 299; *OR*, vol. 46/3, 301. Opinions differ as to the reasons Crawford was silent. See William Marvel's article in *CWTI*, June 2002, 60; Jordon, *Happiness Is Not My Companion*, 217; Wainwright Diary, 508, 509.
17. Calkins and Bearss, *Battle of Five Forks*, 69, 70; Jordon, *Happiness Not Companion*, 229.
18. Calkins and Bearss, *Battle of Five Forks*, 75, 87. Crawford, Griffin and Warren worked to get the troops into a battle line.
19. Chris Calkins, *The Appomattox Campaign* (Conshohocken, Pa.: Combined Books, 1997), 30, 89; *OR*, vol. 46/1, 797.
20. Calkins, *Appomattox Campaign*, 30–32; *OR*, vol. 46/1, 880, 881; Grant *Memoirs and Letters*, 701.
21. Sheridan Report. Samuel also received commendations for Wilderness, Spotsylvania, Jericho Mills, and Bethesda Church. Adjutant General Records, NA; *OR*, vol. 46/1, 1106; Nevins, ed., *Diary of a Battle*, 518.
22. Matrau, 114; *Philadelphia Inquirer*, April 4, 1865, PSUL; Nevin, eds., 518.
23. Melcher, *Flash of His Sword*, 217.
24. Secretary of War Stanton Invitation, Crawford Papers, LOC.
25. Matrau, *Letters Home*, 259; Cauller Letter, USAMHI.
26. Haley, *Rebel Yell*, 262; Gerrish, *Army Life*, 253.
27. Gerrish, *Army Life*, 259.
28. Haley, *Rebel Yell*, 265; Melcher, *Flash of His Sword*, 217; Matrau, Letters, 114.
29. Frank Cauble, *Biography of Wilmer McLean* (Lynchburg, Va.: H. E. Howard, Inc., 1987), Introduction.
30. *New York Herald*, April 17, 1865, PSUL.
31. Robert Anderson, Fort Sumter, April 14, 1865; *The Trip of the Steamer Oceanus* (Brooklyn, N.Y.: Union Steam Printing House, 1865), Introduction.
32. Crawford Papers from a Mr. White who had learned of his presence at Sumter in 1865, LOC. This was the last order dated until late in the month; *OR*, vol. 46/3, 706.
33. Crawford, *Genesis*, 112; Swanberg, *First Blood*, 106; *Oceanus*, 47.
34. Crawford Papers, LOC. He wrote he had twice gone back to Moultrie and Sumter in *Genesis*, 463; later in the 1880s to give aid to earthquake victims. Southern Historical Society Papers, vol. 14, 220–21.
35. *Oceanus*, 34–39; Charleston carriage tour. The tour was designed to show the results of the Civil War on the city. Personal.
36. Crawford, *Genesis*, 55.
37. *Oceanus*, 45; Crawford, *Genesis*, 114.
38. Crawford, *Genesis*, 430.
39. *Oceanus*, 50–52.
40. *Oceanus*, 6–8, 23–33; Reverend Beecher's Penn State Library Program of Events, April 14, 1865; Story in *Oceanus*, 40.

41. Crawford, 449; *OR*, vol. 1/1, 12; *Oceanus*, 50–51.
42. *Oceanus*, 50–52, PSUL.
43. *Oceanus*, 51.
44. *Oceanus*, 52.
45. *Oceanus*, 63.
46. Klein, *Defiance*, 419.
47. Gaft, 49–51; Richard Wheeler, *A Rising Thunder* (New York: HarperCollins, 1994), 102–3; *OR*, vol. 1/1, 66.
48. Crawford Papers, LOC.
49. Quote from Morris Schaff, author of *The Sunset of the Confederacy*, in *Military Surgeon*; Duncan, *Medical Department*, 568.
50. George Sheets, *The Grand Review* (York, Pa.: Bold Print, 2000), 43; Nevins, ed., *Diary of a Battle*, 524–30. Colonel Wainwright has an excellent description of the events from May 20 until the end of the second day of reviews.
51. Sheets, *Grand Review*, 42.
52. Part of Farmers and Merchants Bank display by Mrs. Janet Wiestling Sharpe who owned the sword at the time. It was later reported in the possession of a Maryland doctor.
53. Joshua Chamberlain, *The Passing of the Armies* (Dayton, Ohio: Morningside, 1992), 122, 347; Artillery commander Charles Wainwright also wrote that Crawford was "quite a politician."
54. Sheets, *Grand Review*, 43; Tour: John Wilkes Booth's Escape Route. Personal.

CHAPTER SEVENTEEN: THE YEARS OF PASSING
FLAGS, FRIENDS, AND CAREER

1. Crawford to Reserves, June 1, 1864.
2. William Talley to Crawford, June 28, 1865, HSP.
3. *New York Herald*, April 17, 1865; Melcher, *Flash of His Sword*, 219.
4. July 4, 1866: Richard Sauers "Advance the Colors," 27–31 (*Philadelphia Inquirer*, July 5, 1866.
5. Nicholson, ed., *Pennsylvania at Gettysburg*, Reserve Day vol., 238.
6. Woodward, *Our Campaigns*, 255; *OR*, vol. 33/1, 636.
7. Sauers, "Advance the Colors," 27–31.
8. Sauers, "Advance the Colors," 27–31.
9. Sauers, "Advance the Colors," 27–31.
10. Program of the entire ceremony, PSUL.
11. The 16th and 2nd U.S. Infantry were consolidated as the wartime army was reduced. February 22, 1869, Samuel was a colonel in the 16th Infantry and transferred March 15, 1869, to the combined 2nd Infantry as colonel. NA.
12. Crawford's Retirement Records and Medical Records, NA.
13. The obituary was in a U.S. Army Paper Deputy of Quartermaster, Crawford Papers, HSP.
14. Crawford, *Genesis*, 103–5.
15. Medical Records, NA.
16. Dr. Ned Taylor's final letter and report to Adjutant General, NA.
17. Meade, *Life and Letters*, vol. 2, 303–6.
18. Meade, *Life and Letters*, vol. 2, 305.
19. Meade, *Life and Letters*, vol. 2, 304.
20. Woodward, *Our Campaigns*, 232; Meade, *Life and Letters*, vol. 2, 313.
21. Woodward, *Our Campaigns*, 232.

Notes to Pages 251–261

22. Meade, *Life and Letters*, vol. 2, 313–15.
23. Meade, *Life and Letters*, vol. 2, 313–15.
24. Service Records, Dr. Ned Taylor Letter to Adjutant General, NA.
25. Service Records, Dr. Ned Taylor Letter to Adjutant General, NA.
26. Dr. Ned Taylor Letter to Adjutant General, NA.
27. Dr. Ned Taylor Letter to Adjutant General, NA.
28. March 3, 1875. He had been honorably discharged from the Volunteer Army, January 16, 1866. Adjutant's records. The first correspondence with the retirement board concerning retirement upgrade was January 20, 1874, to Charles Albright, Service Records, NA.

CHAPTER EIGHTEEN: THE WORLD TRAVELER

1. Crawford Papers, HSP.
2. 3:30 p.m. Laurel Hill Cemetery certificate. Laurel Hill Certificate 8749, 70 years, no days or months. This was only one day after her death.
3. Nevin, *Men of Mark*, 162. Words for Jane Crawford in article about her husband, Reverend S. W. Crawford.
4. Honorary Degree Record, UPA. Crawford had also served as vice president of the Alumni Association for a number of years.
5. C. Kelton, acting adjutant general, October 15, 1888. Introduction to Foreign State Departments, NA; Crawford Papers, LOC.
6. Europe, Asia Minor, Bermuda, 1876, 1884, 1885, 1888, KHS. Many of the applications were requested for the benefit of his health. Adjutant General Files, NA.
7. Honorary degree information on Samuel Wylie Crawford, Jr., UPA.
8. Dickson, KHS.
9. A series of articles written for the newspaper. Most of the papers have been destroyed by fire. *Franklin Repository*. The remaining are difficult to read and without dates. KHS.
10. A. K. McClure, *Annals of the War* (Philadelphia Times Publ. Co., 1892), CFL.
11. Crawford Papers, KHS, June 9/10, 1876, *Franklin Repository*.
12. Genealogy and note by Margaret, KHS; Nevin, *Men of Mark*, 163, wrote he suffered from "the infirmities of four score years."
13. Permit for interment, North Laurel Hill, February 19, 1879 (13016) 11 a.m.
14. Crawford Papers, HSP.
15. Laurel Hill burial, permits for mother, 1867, and father, 1876. Graves, south 2 and 3. Genealogy, married 1820, KHS.
16. Laurel Hill Cemetery Permit for Reinterment, 1853. Their aunt was buried at 12 feet deep and the children were buried at a depth of 6 feet in same grave.
17. June 22, 1876, land and homestead executed to Margaret, KHS.
18. Presentation of Jane Wiestling and Janet Sharpe, 1938, KHS.
19. Born 1825 and died 1877, Genealogy, KHS.
20. Nevin, *Men of Mark*, 163. Father was an abolitionist, mostly refused pay for ministerial duties, provided ministry at prisons and penitentiaries.
21. S. W. Crawford, Jr., Letter to Father. It was dated November 20, 1871, and signed Wylie. CFL.
22. Crawford Papers, CFL, letter in hands of the author. It was written November 20, 1871. Huntsville, Ala.
23. Cadwallader, *Three Years*, 299–301. Some believe that Cadwallader let his dislike for Warren exaggerate the conversation.
24. Cadwallader, *Three Years*, 299–301.
25. Kelly, *Justice Done*, 56; Wainwright Diary, 508, 509.
26. Cadwallader, *Three Years*, 299–301.

27. Marvel, *CWTI* (June 2002), 60.
28. Samuel Crawford to Warren, Crawford Papers, July 2, 1872, LOC.
29. Jordon, *Happiness Not Companion*, 268.
30. Warren Court of Inquiry. Transcript in the *New York Times* and *Herald*, PSUL. June 1880. Crawford took great pains to explain he understood the spirit of his orders; Crawford Papers, LOC, "Later Warren would testify that he had confidence in Crawford and Griffin."
31. Samuel attended the funeral of Warren. *New York Times*, August 13, 1882, PSUL.
32. Address given by S. W. Crawford at Antietam, May 30 [Decoration Day], 1874. Printers M'gill and Witherow. Washington 1874, NYPL.

CHAPTER NINETEEN: A LIFE'S COMMITMENT

1. S. Crawford Letter to Professor Stover, May 14, 1867, LOC.
2. William Frassanito, Plate #48 in Early Photography of Gettysburg, 135, 137.
3. Crawford Letter to Professor Stover, May 14, 1867, LOC.
4. Letter to A. K. McClure, June 27, 1886, HSP. McClure attended a lecture by Sickles on the Pennsylvania Reserves while Samuel went to Gettysburg to attend a Pennsylvania Reserve encampment. LOC.
5. Story in Crawford Papers and Nicholson, ed., *Pennsylvania at Gettysburg*, Reserve Day vol., September 2, 1890. Report of the Committee, 107. McLaws' claim is also in the report, 100–108.
6. Letter to Locke, April 10, 1863, LOC. *OR*, vol. 27/1, 655. 7,000 small arms, 1 Napoleon gun, and 3 caissons. [In his report Crawford listed the small arms captured at 3,672.] The ammunition was used or destroyed.
7. Record Books of Property Purchased 1893–1912, GNPA. Samuel wanted a museum built in honor of the Reserves.
8. Kathy Georg drawing and Gettysburg Battlefield Commission, 45 acres, 152 perches (after land given to electric RR).
9. Deed, ACHS.
10. The record book of property purchased 1893–1912, GNPA.
11. John Agnew's Project began in 1877. Falling Spring Presbyterian Church History. Sam corresponded with the state and the Adjutant General in 1891. He offered the site for any monument to the Reserves, and in April of 1892 he received word that the subject was before Congress.
12. June 25, 1988.
13. John Earnest, Superintendent, Gettysburg National Park dedication ceremony.
14. Crawford files, KHS, CFL.
15. July 10, 1913, Lutheran Copy, ACHS.
16. S. Crawford Letter to Professor Stover in May of 1867.
17. March, May, September 1892, Crawford Papers, LOC.
18. 1894: Information from the deed and the proceedings. The deed was recorded July 21, 1894. John and Alex later recorded the deed in Franklin County and Campbell, N.Y. GNPA.

CHAPTER TWENTY: THE END IS NEAR

1. Samuel to A.J. about writing a book in relation to his experiences at Sumter. Letter to Brother, March 4, 1861.
2. Webster Publishing Company History, 1.
3. Crawford, *Genesis*, preface.
4. Medallion given, April 19, 1861. *New York Times and Herald*, April 20, 23, 1861.
5. Crawford, *Genesis*, preface.

6. Note dated September 15, 1888. Belmont collection, NYPL.
7. Duncan, *Military Surgeon*, 568.
8. May 23, 1992, note from Army Navy Club in Washington "disabled and go about little." Crawford Papers, LOC.
9. Letters from R. N. Haights, and a number concerning the Gettysburg land; Jesse Burx. The drug appeared to be spelled "lamzesic." Crawford Papers, LOC, HSP.
10. Haights, March 1, 1892, and a number from veterans.
11. Dr. William Pepper, *Franklin Repository*, November 4, 1892.
12. *Franklin Repository*, November 5, 1892, "General Crawford's Funeral."
13. Crawford was inducted in the prestigious society before his Honorary Degree was given because it is listed in his awards by Penn. He requested the award be pinned on his lapel when he was buried. The award first appeared on his uniform in a photo from 1865.
14. Death Certificate, Dr. Pepper, Apoplexy ruptured blood vessels. Form of stroke. Dr. Pepper listed time of death as 7 p.m. Ecchymotic (inflamed blood cells that are purple) and erythematous (skin lesions with blisters); *Franklin Repository*, November 5, 1892.
15. Philadelphia Ledger, November 8, 1892, 6. One paper said his niece accompanied John. Most notes of the funeral come from this eulogy.
16. Laurel Hill Cemetery Burial Certificate, LHA. Quartermaster General publishes about the death of Crawford on November 9, 1892, NA. J. Clayton undertaker.
17. *Franklin Repository* from Philadelphia Paper, November 5, 1892.
18. *Philadelphia Ledger*, November 8, 1892, p. 6.
19. *Valley Spirit*, June 7, 1876, CFL, KHS.
20. Recorder's Office, Honorary Degree Department, UPA. Geographical in New York, Britain, Mexico, and Historical in New York, Pennsylvania.
21. Note in Crawford Family Papers, HSP. Ledger listed him in attendance.
22. *Philadelphia Ledger*, November 8, 1892, HSP.
23. *Philadelphia Ledger*, November 8, 1892, HSP.
24. Ibid.
25. *Philadelphia Ledger*, November 8, 1892, HSP.
26. Davis, *Jeb Stuart*, 159–60.
27. Davis, *Jeb Stuart*, 162.
28. *Franklin Repository*, August 11 and 14, 1894, KHS.
29. The land deed was presented to the family, February 5, 1894, GNPA. Dickson writes this was recorded in Philadelphia county deed, February 1894, KHS.
30. Dedication ceremony booklet, June 23, 1988. "Franklin County's Forgotten Hero." CFL.

⁂ Bibliography ⁂

Archival Sources

Adams County Historical Society. Gettysburg, Pa.

Star and Sentinel. Gettysburg, Pa., August 28, 1907.

S. W. Crawford. Sale of almost two acres of Crawford Park to Gettysburg Railroad, 1891, for $1.

Antietam National Battlefield Library. Sharpsburg, Md.

Interviews with Antietam Battlefield Historian Ted Alexander.

The Antietam Experiences of Frederick Crouse, 128 Pa. Infantry file.

Ezra Carman Papers.

John Gould Papers.

Childhood Home of Samuel Crawford. Alandale.

Interview and tour, Mr. and Mrs. Gerald Eberly, 2001.

Interview with new owner Chris Shorb, 2006.

Coyle Free Library. Chambersburg, Pa.

Crawford Family File.

Crawford, Reverend Samuel. Letter to Presbyterian Synod, April 1, 1831.

Crawford, Samuel Wylie. Letter to Reverend Crawford, November 20, 1871. Huntsville, Ala.

Interview with archivist Ruth Gembe.

Nevin, Alfred. *Men of Mark of the Cumberland Valley: General Samuel Crawford and Samuel Wylie Crawford, D.D. 1776–1876.* Philadelphia: Fulton Publishing Co., 1876.

Wiestling, Washington, Jennie. Diary. 1862–1865. Written in longhand. Chambersburg, Pa.: Crawford File. Also author's personal copy.

Falling Spring Presbyterian Church. Chambersburg, Pa.

Portrait of John Agnew Crawford hanging in the chapel.

Falling Spring Presbyterian Church History, ed., n.d.

Fort Moultrie National Military Park Library. Sullivan's Island, S.C.

Crawford, Captain Samuel. Letter to Dear Brother, January 5, 1861.

Interviews and e-mails with Richard Hatcher, National Military Park historian, 1990–1999.

Smith, Horace, of Philadelphia. Letter to Captain S. W. Crawford. 1861.

Valley Spirit. Chambersburg, Pa., July 16, 1859; August 24, 1859; October 26, 1859; November 2, 1859; November 9, 1859; December 7, 1859; August 29, 1860; October 1, 1862; June 7, 1876.

Gettysburg National Military Park Archives

Interviews with archivist Gregory Goodell.

Land purchased by Crawford from John Houck and John Timbers, 1872. Book of Records.

Record book of property purchased by Gettysburg National Park Association. 1893–1912.

S. W. Crawford. Land, 46.9 acres, to National Military Park, Gettysburg, Pa., February 5, 1894, by family members.

S. W. Crawford. Letter to Adjutant General, April 4, 1892, concerning land purchased from John Houck and John Timbers.

Gettysburg National Military Park Library

Interviews with military Historian Scott Hartwig.

Interview with Librarian John Heiser.

Historical Society of Pennsylvania. Philadelphia, Pa.

Professor Beaux. Letter to Samuel Crawford, 1892. Crawford Papers.

Crawford, Reverend Samuel, Sermon #3, 33. Crawford Papers.

Crawford, W. Samuel, Jr., moderator. Letter to Peter McCall from Philomathean Society, 1845. Crawford Papers.

Heights, R. N. Letter to Samuel Wylie Crawford, 1892. Crawford Papers.

Philadelphia Inquirer. July 7, 1863; June 6, 1864; April 4, 1865.

Philadelphia Ledger. November 5, 1892; November 8, 1892.

Talley, William. Letter to General Samuel W. Crawford. June 28, 1865. Crawford Papers.

Kittochtinny Historical Society. Chambersburg, Pa.

Coy, Jeff. "Dr. General Samuel Wylie Crawford U.S.A, AM, M.D., L.L.D." Pennsylvania State Legislature, September 8, 1986.

Dickson, Dr. James. "Major General Samuel W. Crawford." Vol. 19. Kittochtinny Society Papers. Talk was presented October 1986; published in 1989.

Franklin County's Forgotten Hero. Franklin County Foundation, 1988. Crawford File.

Franklin Repository. Chambersburg, Pa., March 12, 1863; July 8, 1863; July 29, 1863; Oct. 28, 1863; Nov. 6, 1863; Nov. 11, 1863; July 27, 1864; Aug. 24, 1864; Nov. 9, 1864; Nov. 22, 1864; June 9, 10, 1867; Nov. 4, 1892; Aug. 18, 1894.

Interviews with "Bud" Barkdoll, Larry Calimer, Lillian Colletta between 1990–1997.

Wiestling, Washington Jane, and daughter Janet Wiestling Sharpe. The paper was presented to Kittochtinny Historical Society, 1938.

Laurel Hill Cemetery Archives. Philadelphia, Pa.

Laurel Hill Cemetery Company Sales Book Number 1.

Laurel Hill Cemetery; the People and the Places.

Library of Congress. Washington, D.C.

Samuel Wylie Crawford Papers. 1860–1870.

Crawford, General S. W. Letter to Lieutenant Colonel Woodward, 1863.

Crawford, General S. W. Letter to Col. F. T. Locke, July 10, 1863.

Crawford, General S. W. Letter to Sanitary Commission, November 16, 1863.

Crawford, General S. W. Letter to Professor Jacobs. Gettysburg University, December 1863.

Crawford, General S. W. Letter to Colonel Fisher, December 22, 1863.

Crawford, General S. W. Letter to Brigadier General J. Rice, December 23, 1863.

Crawford, General S. W. Letter to Professor M. L. Stover. Gettysburg University, May 14, 1867.

Crawford, Samuel. Letter to John Agnew, January 30, 1861.

Crawford, Samuel W. Letter to A.J., December 12, 1860.

Crawford, Samuel W. Letter to Dear Brother, December 12, 1860.

Crawford, Samuel W. Letter to A.J. and family, December 30, 1860.

Crawford, Samuel W. Letter to Dear Brother, Mac, and family, January 2–3, 1861.

Crawford, Samuel W. Letter to John Agnew (A.J.), January 12, 1861.

Crawford, Samuel W. Letter to Alex and Dear Brother, January 17, 1861.

Crawford, Samuel W. Letter to Dear Brother, Alex, January 24, 1861.

Crawford, Samuel W. Letter to Dear Brother, February 2/3, 1861.

Crawford, Samuel W. Letter to Dear Brother, February 2/3, 1861.

Crawford, Samuel W. Letter to Dear Brother, February 10, 1861.

Crawford, Samuel W. Letter to John Agnew, February 24, 1861.

Crawford, Samuel W. Letter to Dear Brother, March 4, 1861.

Crawford, Samuel W. Letter to Dear Brother, March 7, 1861.

Crawford, Samuel W. Letter to Mac and Dear Brother, March 14, 1861.

Crawford. Samuel W. Letter to A.J., March 15, 1861.

Crawford, Samuel W. Letter to A.J., March 19, 1861.

Crawford, Samuel W. Letter to Brother (Alex and A.J.), March 23, 1861.

Crawford, Samuel W. Letter to Dear Brother, March 30, 1861.

Crawford, Samuel W. Letter to Dear Brother, April 11, 1861.

Crawford, Samuel W. Letter to Dear Brother and A.J., April 13, 1861.

Portrait of Reverend Samuel Crawford.

Samuel Wylie Crawford Diary.

National Archives. Washington, D.C.

Adjutant General's Office. Letters 74 ACP, 1873.

Commission Branch Files.

Crawford, Samuel W. to Adjutant General, October 12, 1871. Military Records M 1395.

Interview with archivist David Wallace, 1999.

Medical Officers File.

Record Group 94 [74 ACP 1873]. Adjutant General's Records [AGO].

Taylor, Dr. Ned. Letters to U.S. War Department on behalf of Crawford's disability, 1872–73.

National Civil War Museum. Harrisburg, Pa.

Exhibits of Civil War Uniforms from 1860–1865.

Interview with archivist Elayne Goyette, 2002.

The New York Public Library. New York City, N.Y.

August Belmont. Belmont Papers.

Crawford, Samuel. Letter to August Belmont. September 15, 1888. Belmont Papers.

Crawford, Samuel W. Address, Antietam National Cemetery. May 30, 1874. Washington Printers M'gill and Witherow, 1874.

Penn State University Library. University Park, State College, Pa.

Documents of the journey of *Oceanus*.

New York Herald. April 19, 1861; April 21, 1861; April 17, 1865.

New York Times. April 20, 1861; April 23, 1861; Sept. 20, 1862; June 1–16, 1880; August 13, 1882.

New York Tribune. April 11, 1861; April 13, 1861; April 19, 1861.

Pennsylvania State Archives. Harrisburg, Pa.

Crawford, Samuel. Letter to Peter Rothermel. March 8, 1871.

Portrait of Reverend Samuel W Crawford. Also in the Crawford Papers in the Library of Congress.

Shippensburg University Ezra Lehman Library. Shippensburg, Pa.

Interview with Judith Culbertson, collection management and acquisition librarian.

Local History File.

South Carolina Historical Society. Charleston, S.C.

Folder on the burial of Daniel Hough.

Folder on incidents at Fort Sumter following the surrender of the fort in 1861.

Papers on Ed Ruffin.

Papers on Gordin Young.

United States Army Military History Institute. Carlisle, Pa.

Abner Small, 16 Me. Regimental Papers.

Avery Harris, 143 Pa. Volunteers, Pennsylvania Regimental Papers.

Crawford, Samuel. Letter to Gouverneur Warren, July 2, 1872.

Crawford Photos: Mollus, Nelsson Collection, Barrett Collection.

Interview with Richard Sommers, chief of patron services.

William McCandless Papers and Photos.

Medical Civil War Uniform of 1850s Exhibit.

John Vautier. 88th Pennsylvania Volunteers Pennsylvania regiments. Also manuscript form.

University of Pennsylvania Archives, Graduates. Philadelphia, Pa.

Abstract of Surgical and Medical Cases. University of Pennsylvania Press.

Department of the Arts. List of Graduates, July 1846.

Graduate List. Medical Department, April 6, 1850. Class Member Names with Preceptors.

Honorary Degree Records. S. Wylie Crawford.

Interview with Amey Hutchison, public service historian.

Medical Department. List of Matriculants, July 1849.

Regulations of the Medical Department. University of Pennsylvania, 1849–50.

Regulations of Pennsylvania University. Department of Arts.

Regulations of the University. Collegiate Department, 1845–50.

Regulations of the University. Department of Arts, July 1848.

Report on the Medical Department by the Medical Faculty. University of Pennsylvania, Philadelphia, Pa. Published by Bailey, 1850.

Wilson College Archives. Chambersburg, Pa.

Interviews with archivist Wanda Finney.

The Pharetra. Wilson College Newsletter. Vol. 11 (#2) 1897.

The Pharetra. Wilson College Newsletter. Vol. 21 (#1) 1907.

Printed Material

Books

Adams, George. *Doctors in Blue*. Dayton, Ohio: Morningside Press, 1985.

Bibliography

Alexander, Ted. *The Burning of Chambersburg and McCausland's Raid.* Columbus, Ohio: Blue and Gray Enterprises, 2004.

Alotta, Robert. *Civil War Justice.* Shippensburg, Pa.: White Mane Publishing Co., Inc., 1989.

Bachelder, John. *John Bachelder's History of the Battle of Gettysburg.* Edited by David and Audrey Ladd. Dayton, Ohio: Morningside Press, Inc., 1997.

Baker, Jean. *James Buchanan.* New York: Henry Holt and Company, 2004.

Bates, Samuel. *The Battle of Gettysburg.* Philadelphia, Pa.: Davis Publishers, 1875.

———. *History of Pennsylvania Volunteers, 1861–1865.* Harrisburg, Pa.: Singerly, 1869.

———. *Martial Deeds of Pennsylvania.* Philadelphia, Pa.: Davis Publishers, 1876.

Bedwell, Randall. *Brink of Destruction.* New York: Random House, 1999.

Blackford, Susan. *Letters from Lee's Army.* New York: A. S. Barnes, 1962.

Blackford, W. W. *War Years with Jeb Stuart.* New York: Charles Scribner's Sons, 1945.

Blair, William, and William Pencak, eds. *Making and Remaking Pennsylvania's Civil War.* University Park, Pa.: Pennsylvania University Press, 2001.

Boatner, Mark. *Civil War Dictionary.* New York: McKay Co., 1959.

Boyer, Paul, ed. *Oxford Companion of American History.* New York: Oxford, 2001.

Brennan, Patrick. *To Die Game.* Gettysburg, Pa.: Farnsworth House Military Impressions, 1998.

Burton, Milby. *The Siege of Charleston, 1861–1865.* Columbia: University of South Carolina Press, 1994.

Cadwallader, Sylvanus. *Three Years with Grant.* Edited by Benjamin Thomas. Lincoln: University of Nebraska Press, 1996.

Calkins, Chris. *The Appomattox Campaign.* Conshohocken, Pa.: Combined Books, 1997.

———. *Lee's Retreat.* Richmond Va.: History Publications, 2000.

Calkins, Chris, and Edwin Bearss. *The Battle of Five Forks.* Lynchburg, Va.: Howard, 1985.

Cannan, John. *The Spotsylvania Campaign*. Conshohocken, Pa.: Combined Books, 1997.

Cartmell, Donald. *Civil War 101*. New York: Gramercy Books, 2001.

Castel, Albert. *Fort Sumter 1861*. Harrisburg, Pa.: Historic Times, 1976.

Catton, Bruce. *America Goes to War*. Middletown, Conn.: Wesleyan University Press, 1958.

———. *Grant Takes Command*. New York: Little Brown and Company, Inc., for Book of the Month Club, 1994.

Cauble, Frank. *Biography of Wilmer McLean*. Lynchburg, Va.: H. E. Howard, Inc., 1987.

Chamberlain, Joshua. *The Passing of the Armies*. Dayton, Ohio: Morningside, 1992.

Chesnut, Mary. *A Diary from Dixie*. Edited by Ben Ames Williams. Boston: Houghton Mifflin Co., 1949.

———. *Mary Chesnut's Civil War*. New Haven, N.J.: Yale Press, 1981.

Cheyney, Edward. *History of the University of Pennsylvania*. New York: Arno Press, 1977.

Cleaves, Freeman. *Meade of Gettysburg*. Norman: University of Oklahoma Press, 1991.

Coddington, Edwin. *The Gettysburg Campaign*. New York: Charles Scribner's Sons, 1984.

Commanger, Henry. *The Blue and the Grey*. Indianapolis, Ind.: Merrill, 1950.

Corner, George. *Two Centuries of Medicine*. Philadelphia, Pa.: Lippincott, 1965.

Crawford, Samuel. *Genesis of the Civil War*. New York: Webster Co., 1887.

Curti, Merle, et al. *A History of American Civilization*. New York: Harpers, 1953.

Dammann, Gordon. *Medical Instruments and Equipment*. Missoula, Mont.: Pictorial Histories Publishing Co., 1988.

Davis, Burke. *Jeb Stuart, the Last Cavalier*. New York: Wings Books, 2000.

Davis, Ken. *Don't Know Much About History*. New York: Avon Press, 1990.

Davis, William. *Jefferson Davis: The Man and His Hour*. New York: HarperCollins, 1991.

———. *Look Away*. New York: Free Press, 2002.

Bibliography

Dawes, Rufus. *A Full Blown Yankee*. Lincoln: University of Nebraska Press, 1999.

Denney, Robert. *The Civil War Years*. New York: Sterling Publishing, 1994.

Desjardin, Thomas. *Stand Firm Ye Boys from Maine*. Gettysburg, Pa.: Thomas, 1995.

Detzer, David. *Allegiance*. New York: Harcourt, 2001.

Donaldson, Francis. *Inside the Army of the Potomac*. Mechanicsburg, Pa.: Stackpole, 1998.

Doubleday, Abner. *Reminiscences of Forts Sumter and Moultrie in 1860–61*. Charleston, S.C.: Nautical and Aviation, 1998.

Douglas, Henry. *I Rode with Stonewall*. Chapel Hill: University of North Carolina Press, 1987.

Dowdy, Clifford, ed. *The Wartime Papers of Robert E. Lee*. New York: Bramhall House, 1961.

Duncan, Louis. *Medical Department of the United States Army in the Civil War*. Gaithersburg, Md.: Butternut Press, Inc., 1985.

Eicher, David. *The Longest Night*. New York: Simon & Schuster, 2001.

Engle, William. *Andrew Gregg Curtin*. Philadelphia: Avil Printing, 1895.

Fahs, Alice. *The Imagined Civil War*. Chapel Hill: University of North Carolina Press, 2001.

Foote, Shelby. *The Civil War, A Narrative*. New York: Random House, 1958.

Fort Sumter: Anvil of War. Washington, D.C.: National Park Service, Handbook No. 127. 1984.

Frassanito, William. *Antietam*. Gettysburg, Pa.: Thomas Publications, 1978.

———. *Early Photography of Gettysburg*. Gettysburg, Pa.: Thomas Publications, 1998.

Freeman, Douglas. *Lee's Lieutenants*. New York: Scribner, Simon & Schuster, 1998.

Gallagher, Gary, ed. *Antietam: Essays on 1862 Maryland Campaign*. Kent, Ohio: Kent State, University Press, 1989.

———. *The Second Day at Gettysburg*. Kent, Ohio: Kent State University Press, 1993.

Gallagher, Gary. *The Wilderness Campaign*. Chapel Hill: University of North Carolina Press, 1997.

Gallman, M., ed. *The Civil War Chronicle*. New York: Crown Publisher, 2000.

Gambone, Al M. *Major-General John Frederick Hartranft*. Baltimore: Butternut and Blue, 1995.

Gardner, Alexander. *Photographic Sketch Book*. New York: Dover Publications, 1959.

Gerrish, Theodore. *Army Life*. Baltimore: Butternut and Blue, 1995.

Gibbon, John. *Personal Recollections of the Civil War*. Dayton, Ohio: Morningside Press, 1988.

Gibbs, Joseph. *Three Years in the Bloody Eleventh*. University Park, Pa.: Pennsylvania State University Press, 2002.

Gottfried, Bradley. *Brigades at Gettysburg*. Cambridge, Mass.: Da Capo Press, 2002.

Grant, Ulysses S. *Memoirs and Selected Letters*. New York: Library Classics, 1990.

Green, R., ed. *History of the 124th Pa. Volunteers*. Philadelphia, 1907.

Haley, John. *The Rebel Yell and the Yankee Hurrah*. Edited by Ruth Silliker. Camden, Me.: Down East Books, 1985.

Harrison, Kathy, and John Busey. *Nothing but Glory*. Baltimore, Md.: Longstreet House by Gateway Press Inc., 1993.

Hassler, William. *Lee's Forgotten General*. Chapel Hill: University of North Carolina Press, 1962.

Heefner, Nancy, et al., eds. *The Tuscarora Reader*. Mercersburg, Pa.: Historical Society, 2002.

Heidler, Dave, and Jeanne Heidler. *Encyclopedia of the American Civil War*. New York: Norton, 2000.

Herdegen, Lance, and Sherry Murphy, eds. *William Ray, Four Years with the Iron Brigade*. Cambridge, Mass.: Da Capo Press, 2002.

Hoke, Jacob. *The Great Invasion of 1863*. Gettysburg, Pa.: Stan Clark Military Books, 1992.

———. *Reminiscences of the War*. Chambersburg, Pa.: Foltz Printer, 1884.

Humphreys, Andrew. *The Virginia Campaign of 1864–65*. New York: Da Capo Press, 1995.

Hyde, Bill, ed. *The Union Generals Speak*. Baton Rouge: Louisiana State University Press, 2003.

Johnson, Paul. *A History of the American People*. New York: HarperCollins Publishers, 1999.

Johnson, Robert, and Clarence Buel, eds., *Battles and Leaders of the Civil War*. Vol.1. New York: Thomas Yoseloff, Inc., 1956.

Jordon, David. *Happiness Is Not My Companion*. Bloomington: University of Indiana Press, 2001.

Kautz, August. *A Handbook of Duties for Officers of the Army*. Mechanicsburg, Pa.: Stackpole Books, 2002.

Kelly, Brian. *Best Little Stories from the Civil War*. Nashville, Tenn.: Cumberland House, 1998.

Kelly, Michael. *I Will Have Justice Done*. Gettysburg: Farnsworth Impressions, 1997.

Kennedy, Frances H., ed. *The Civil War Battlefield Guide*. New York: Houghton Mifflin, 1998.

Kirk, Robert. *Lee's Colonels*. Dayton, Ohio: Morningside, 1991.

Klein, Maury. *Days of Defiance*. New York: Alfred Knopf, 1997.

Klein, Philip. *President James Buchanan*. Newtown, Conn.: Political Biography Press, 1962.

Krick, Robert. *Stonewall Jackson at Cedar Mountain*. Chapel Hill: University of North Carolina Press, 1990.

LaFantasie, Glenn. *Twilight at Little Round Top*. Hoboken, N.J.: John Wiley and Son, 2003.

The Life and Letters of General George Gordon Meade. Captain George Gordon Meade. Edited by General George Gordon Meade. 2 vols. New York: Charles Scribner's Sons, 1913. Reprint, Butternut and Blue, Baltimore, 1994.

Locke, William. *The Story of the Regiment*. Philadelphia: J. B. Lippincott and Co., 1868.

Long, E., and Barbara Long. *The Civil War Day by Day*. New York: Da Capo Press, 1971.

Longstreet, James. *From Manassas to Appomattox*. New York: Da Capo Press, 1992.

Luvass, Jay, and Harold Nelson, eds. *A Guide to the Battle of Antietam*. Lawrence, Kansas: University Press of Kansas, 1987.

Lyman, Ted. *With Grant and Meade*. Edited by George Agassiz. Lincoln: University of Nebraska Press, 1994.

Marshall, Charles. *Lee's Aide-De-Camp*. Edited by Frederick Maurice. Lincoln: University of Nebraska Press, Bison Book Edition, 2000.

Matrau, Henry. *Letters Home, Henry Matrau of the Iron Brigade.* Edited by Marcia Green. Lincoln: University of Nebraska Press, 1993.

McClure, A. K. *Abraham Lincoln and Men of War.* Philadelphia: Philadelphia Times Publishing Co., 1892.

McClure, Alexander. *The Annals of the War.* Reprinted *The Annals of the Civil War.* New York: Da Capo Press, 1994.

McFeely, William. *Grant.* New York: W. W. Norton, 1982.

McPherson, James. *Battle Cry of Freedom.* New York: Oxford University Press, 1988.

———. *Crossroads of Freedom: Antietam.* New York: Oxford Press, 2002.

———. *Drawn by a Sword.* New York: Free Press, 2002.

———. *The Illustrated Battle Cry of Freedom.* New York: Oxford Press, 2003.

Melcher, Holman. *With a Flash of His Sword.* Edited by E. William Styple. Kearny, New Jersey: Belle Grove Publishing, 1994.

Meredith, Roy. *Storm over Sumter.* New York: Simon & Schuster, 1957.

Miles, Jim. *Forged in Fire.* Nashville: Cumberland House, 2000.

———. *Piercing the Heartland.* Nashville: Rutledge Hill Press, 1991.

Minnigh, Henry. *History of Company K.* Gettysburg, Pa.: Thomas Publications, 1998.

Morris, Roy. *Sheridan.* New York: Crown Books, 1992.

Murfin, James. *Gleam of Bayonets.* Baton Rouge: Louisiana State University Press, 1993.

Nesbitt, Mark. *35 Days to Gettysburg.* Harrisburg, Pa.: Stackpole Books, 1992.

Nevin, Alfred. *Men of Mark of the Cumberland Valley 1776–1876.* Philadelphia: Fulton Publishing Co., 1876.

Nevins, Allan, ed. *Diary of a Battle; Journals of Charles Wainwright.* Gettysburg: Stan Clark Books, 1962.

Nichols, Edward. *Toward Gettysburg, Reynolds.* State College, Pa.: Penn State, 1958.

Nicholson, John, ed. *Pennsylvania at Gettysburg.* Reserve Day volume. Harrisburg, Pa.: Stanley Ray Printer, 1889.

Nicolay, John. *The Outbreak of the War.* Wilmington, N.C.: Broadfoot, 1989.

Norton, Oliver. *Attack on Little Round Top*. Dayton, Ohio: Morningside, 1983.

Nye, Wilbur. *Here Come the Rebels!* Dayton, Ohio: Morningside Press, 1988.

Oates, Stephen. *To Purge This Land with Blood*. Amherst: University of Massachusetts Press, 1984.

Owsley, Frank. *King Cotton Diplomacy*. Chicago: University of Chicago Press, 1959.

Pennsylvania at Gettysburg. Vol. 1. Harrisburg, Pa.: General Assembly Pennsylvania, 1889.

Pfanz, Harry. *Gettysburg: The First Day*. Chapel Hill: University of North Carolina Press, 2001.

———. *Gettysburg: The Second Day*. Chapel Hill: University of North Carolina Press, 1987.

Phipps, Michael, and John Peterson. *The Devil's to Pay: General John Buford*. Gettysburg: Farnsworth Military Impressions, 1995.

Pierce, Tillie Alleman. *What a Girl Saw and Heard of the Battle*. Baltimore: Butternut and Blue, 1987.

Pinker, Steven. *The Blank Slate*. New York: Viking, 2002.

Piston, William. *Lee's Tarnished Lieutenant*. Athens: University of Georgia Press, 1987.

Porter, Horace. *Campaigning with Grant*. New York: Konecky and Konecky, 1992.

Potter, David. *The Impending Crisis*. Edited by Henry Commager and Richard Morris. New York: Harpers, 1976.

Powell, William. *The Fifth Army Corps*. Dayton, Ohio: Morningside House, 1984.

Power, Tracy. *Lee's Miserables*. Chapel Hill: University of North Carolina Press, 1998.

Priest, John. *Antietam: The Soldiers' Battle*. New York: Oxford University Press, 1993.

Quaife, Milo M., ed. *From the Cannon's Mouth, Civil War Letters of Alpheus Williams*. Lincoln: University of Nebraska Press, 1995.

Rhea, Gordon. *The Battles for Spotsylvania Court House and the Road to Yellow Tavern*. Baton Rouge: Louisiana State University Press, 1997.

———. *The Battle of the Wilderness*. Baton Rouge: Louisiana State University Press, 1994.

———. *Cold Harbor*. Baton Rouge: Louisiana State University Press, 2002.

———. *To the North Anna River*. Baton Rouge: Louisiana State University Press, 2000.

Riley, Mike. *For God's Sake Forward*. Gettysburg, Pa.: Farnsworth House Military Impressions, 1995.

Robertson, James. *Soldiers Blue and Gray*. Columbia: University of South Carolina Press, 1988.

———. *Stonewall Jackson*, New York: Simon & Schuster, 1997.

Roy, Andrew. *Fallen Soldier*. Edited by William Miller. Montgomery, Ala.: Elliott and Clark, 1996.

Sauers, Richard. *Advance the Colors*. Harrisburg, Pa.: Capital Restoration Committee, 1987.

Schildt, John. *September Echoes*. Middletown, Md.: Valley Register, 1960.

Schlesinger, Arthur, Jr., ed. *The Almanac of American History*. New York: Barnes and Noble, 1993.

Sears, Stephen. *Landscape Turned Red, Antietam*. New Haven, Conn.: Ticknor and Fields, Houghton Mifflin Co., 1983.

———. *Gettysburg*. New York: Houghton Mifflin Co., 2003.

Sheets, Georg. *The Grand Review*. York, Pa.: Bold Print, 2000.

Smith, Henry. *A System of Operative Surgery*. Philadelphia, Pa.: Lippincott, 1856.

Smith, James Powers. *With Stonewall Jackson*. Gaithersburg, Md.: Zullo and Van Sickle, 1982.

Sorrel, Moxley. *Recollections of a Confederate Staff Officer*. Wilmington, N.C.: Broadfoot Publishing, 1995.

Southern Revenge. Greater Chambersburg Chamber of Commerce. Shippensburg, Pa.: White Mane Publishing Co., Inc., 1989.

Stackpole, Edward. *From Cedar Mountain to Antietam*. Harrisburg, Pa.: Stackpole Books, 1993.

Steere, Edward. *The Wilderness Campaign*. Mechanicsburg, Pa.: Stackpole Books, 1960.

Stevens, Joseph E. *1863: The Rebirth of a Nation*. New York: Bantam Books, 1999.

Stewart, William. *A Pair of Blankets*. Edited by Benjamin Trask. Wilmington, N.C.: Broadfoot Publishing Co., 1990.

Strong, George. *The Diary of George T. Strong*. Edited by Allan Nevins. New York: Macmillan Publishing Co., 1962.

Swanberg, W. A. *First Blood*. New York: Charles Scribner's Sons, 1957.

Swinton, William. *The Campaigns of the Army of the Potomac*. New York: Charles Richardson, 1866.

Sypher, Josiah. *A History of the Pennsylvania Reserves*. Lancaster, Pa.: Elias Barr, 1865.

Taylor, Frank. *Philadelphia in the Civil War*. Glenside, Pa.: J. M. Santarelli, 1991.

Taylor, Walter. *General Lee 1861–1865*. Dayton, Ohio: Morningside Press, 1975.

Thomas, Mary, ed. *The Civil War Letters of First Lieutenant James B. Thomas 107 Pa*. Baltimore, Md.: Butternut and Blue, 1995.

Thompson, John IV. *Horses, Hostages, and Apple Cider*. Mercersburg, Pa.: Mercersburg Printing, 2002.

Thomson, Howard, and William Rauch. *History of the Bucktails*. Philadelphia: n.p., 1906.

Thrush, Ambrose. *Medical Men of Franklin County*. Franklin County: Medical Society, 1928.

The Trip of the Steamer Oceanus. Edited by Passenger Committee. Brooklyn, N.Y.: Union Steam Printing House, 1865.

Trudeau, Noah. *Bloody Roads South*. Baton Rouge: Louisiana State University Press, 2000.

———. *The Last Citadel*. Baton Rouge: Louisiana State University Press, 1991.

Tucker, Glenn. *High Tide at Gettysburg*. Dayton, Ohio: Morningside Press, 1983.

Wagner, Constance. *Ask My Brother*. New York: Harpers and Brothers Publisher, 1959.

War of the Rebellion: A Compilation of the Official Records of the Union and Confederate Armies. 128 vols. Washington, D.C.: Government Printing Office, 1880–1901.

Warner, Ezra. *Generals in Blue*. Baton Rouge: Louisiana State University Press, 1964.

———. *Generals in Grey*. Baton Rouge: Louisiana State University Press, 1959.

Warner. *History of Franklin County*. Chicago: Beers and Co., 1887.

Waugh, John. *The Class of 1846*. New York: Warner Books, 1994.

Welsh, Jack. *Medical Histories of Union Generals*. Kent, Ohio: Kent State Press, 1996.

Wert, Jeffry. *General James Longstreet*. New York: Simon & Schuster, 1993.

Wheeler, Richard. *A Rising Thunder*. New York: HarperCollins, 1994.

———. *Witness to Gettysburg*. New York: Harper Row, 1987.

White, Ronald. *The Eloquent President*. New York: Random House, 2005.

Wilson, Clyde. *Carolina Cavalier*. Athens: University of Georgia Press, 1990.

Woodward, Evan M. *Our Campaigns; The Second Regiment of the Pennsylvania Reserve Volunteers*. Edited by Stanley Zamonski. Shippensburg, Pa.: Burd Street Press, 1995.

Periodicals and Pamphlets

Periodicals

Civil War Times Illustrated

Gaff, Alan. "Two Dead at Sumter." Harrisburg, Pa., March 2001.

Marvel, Williams. "Thorn in the Flesh." Vol. 61. Harrisburg, Pa., June 2002.

Sommers, Richard. "The Battle No One Wanted." Vol. 14. Harrisburg, Pa., August 1975.

The Gettysburg Magazine

Sherry, Jeffrey. "The Terrible Impetuosity": The Pennsylvania Reserves at Gettysburg. Vol. 16. Historical Articles of Lasting Interest.

Stahl, Joe. Private David D. Alexander Co. G, 11th Pa Reserve Infantry, #30, January 2004.

Other Magazines

Duncan, Louis. "General Crawford," *Military Surgeon*. Edited by John Hoff. Vol. 34. Washington, D.C., November 1916.

Grant, Ulysses, 3rd "The Civil War," *National Geographic*. Washington, D.C., April 1961.

Harper's Weekly. February 9, March 23, 1861.

Hartwig, Scott. "We must fight them more vindictively." The Civil War in 1863. Gettysburg National Military Park, 2001.

Rhea, Gordon. "Butchery at Bethesda Church." America's Civil War. January 2002.

Pamphlets

Battle for Sumter. Charleston, S.C.: Charleston Press, Evans and Cogswell, 1861.

Civil War Battles Fought in Culpeper. Edited by Chamber of Commerce, 2000.

Crossroads of Destiny. Edited by Chambersburg Chamber of Commerce, 1964.

Falling Spring Presbyterian Church History. Falling Spring Church, Chambersburg, Pa., 1904.

Fort Sumter, 1861. Harrisburg, Pa.: Historical Times, 1981.

The Great Decision. The Centennial of Chambersburg. Chambersburg, Pa.: Chamber of Commerce, 1963.

Medical Alumni in the Civil War. University of Pennsylvania, 1961.

The Stuart Raid. Edited by Chamber of Commerce, Chambersburg, Pa., 1962.

Wilcox, Arthur, and Warren Ripley. *The Civil War at Charleston.* Post Courier booklet, 1991.

National Park Handbooks

Fort Moultrie, Constant Defender. National Park Handbook, 136. U.S. Department of Interior, Washington, D.C., 1985.

Fort Sumter, Anvil of War. National Park Handbook. Washington, D.C.: U.S. Department of Interior, 1984.

Tilberg, Frederick. *Antietam.* U.S. Department of Interior, Washington, D.C., 1960.

CD and CD-ROMs

Ayres, Edward, and Anne Rubin. *Valley of the Shadow.* Norton, 2000.

Confederate Military History. Guild Press of Indiana, 1997.

Harper's Weekly Journal. 3 vols. Bedford, Mass.: Applewood Books, 2001.

Mudd, Roger. *Great Minds in History.* New York: Simon & Schuster, 1999.

Shaara, Jeff. *Last Full Measure*. New York: Random House Audio Books, 1998.

Southern Historical Society Papers. Guild Press of Indiana, 1998.

The War of the Rebellion: A Compilation of Official Records. Guild Press of Indiana, 1996.

Miscellaneous

College Notes

Gettysburg College. 1957. American History. Dr. Robert Bloom.

Shippensburg College (now Shippensburg University), 1962. Pennsylvania History Seminar. Dr. Bernard Hogg.

Shippensburg College (now Shippensburg University), 1961. American Constitutional Law, Dr. Benjamin Nispel.

Gettysburg Battlefield Tours

Day One, Eric Campbell.

Day One, Scott Hartwig.

Day Two, The Wheatfield, Eric Campbell.

1 July 1863, Wayne Moats.

Little Round Top Seminar.

Index

Photos are listed in **bold** type.

A

Alandale, ix, 7, 15, 16, **22**, **24**, 38, 42, 48
  Alex, servant at, 155, 177
  first named Crawford-John, 4
  Hill, A. P., staff near, 154
Alexander, Ted, xi, xvi
Anderson, Robert, 56, 57, 78, 82, **101**, 109, **252**
  and Pierre G. T. Beauregard, 87, 88, 94, 95
  brevetted officers, 100
  and Don Carlos Buell, 59–60, 65
  clarifies President Buchanan's policies, 81
  S. W. Crawford, Jr., encourages brother to write Major Anderson, 75
  defense of Fort Moultrie, S.C., 58–59
  desires to avoid war, 80, 83, 87, 106
  dies in France, 248
  and John Floyd, 58, 59, 60
  at Fort Sumter, S.C., 1865, 238, 239, 240, 241; ceremony, 74–75; defense of, 92, 93, 94, 98; demand to surrender, 80, 87, 96; letter from Reverend Crawford, 100; official report, 107; personal memo before leaving, 108; surrender of, 96; transferring to, 65–66, 67, 69, 70
  and President Lincoln, 84, 85, 86, 109
  meeting with his officers, 71, 79, 87, 88
  in New York City, 105, 106, 107, 271
  and Johnston Pettigrew, 71–73
  quotes of, 59, 60, 65, 70, 73, 81, 83, 85, 87, 103
  receives telegram from Simon Cameron, 107
  relations with S. W. Crawford, Jr., 57, 61, 63–64, 66, 70, 74, 80, 81, 83, 84, 87, 90, 97
  and *Star of the West*, 78–80, 81
  tour of Charleston, South Carolina, forts, 57–58
  visit by wife and Peter Hart, 78
  and Louis Wigfall, 95
Antietam, 14, 53, 133
  28th New York, 138
  46th Pennsylvania, 138
  124th Pennsylvania, 134, 137, 138
  125th Pennsylvania, 138, 139, 140
  128th Pennsylvania, 140
  S. W. Crawford, Jr., at, 115, 133, 152; Crawford's First Brigade at, 133, 134, 137; 1874 speech Antietam National Cemetery, 151; moves troops, 140; Official Report, 147; wounded, 140–41, 149; wound controversy, 175; wound treatment, 143
  human results, 143
  landscape after the battle, 141
  Lee at, 133, 136, 150
  Lee moves north, 128, 129
  "lost order," 132
  old friends and old enemies, 134
  President Lincoln, Emancipation Proclamation, 142
  See also Crawford, Samuel Wylie, Jr.; Doubleday, Abner; McClellan, George
Ayres, Romeyn, 225, 234
  at Dabney's Mill, 226
  dislikes S. W. Crawford, Jr., 223
  at Five Forks, 234, 235
  at Gettysburg, 162, 163, 164
  "kudos" for, 227
  at Second Battle of Squirrel Level Road, 224
  Warren evaluation, 214

B

Baltic, U.S. steamer, 97, 105, 106, 241

345

Index

Bayard, George, 120, 121, 123
Beauregard, Pierre G. T., 87, 88, 94, 95, 99, 107, 216, 241
Beecher, Henry Ward, 240
Brown, John
  in Chambersburg, 49
  at Harpers Ferry, 50
  in Kansas, 43
Buchanan, James, 33, 41, 42, 56, 60, 94
  "don't initiate policy," 42, 43
  and Abner Doubleday, 57
  and Fort Moultrie, 56
  policies of, 81, 83
  policies of South Carolina strengthen, 73
  and "Wheatland," 42, 78
Buell, Don Carlos, 59–60, 65

C

Cedar Mountain, battle of, 120
  also called Slaughter Mountain, 120
  truce for burials, 123
  See also Crawford, Samuel Wylie, Jr.
Chambersburg, Pa., 151, 177, 256
  burning of, 218–19
  county seat, 4
  Crawford family at, 4, 5, 25–26
  Crawford, S. W., Jr., at, 47, 49, 100, 220, 227, 268
  invasions of, 145, 147, 154, 176
  Messersmith's Woods near, 156, 157, 158
  Southern retreat and wounded, 177
  telegraph office, 100, 145
Chester, James, 74, 78, 82, 91
  at bombardment of Fort Sumter, 88–89, 92, 94
  at ceremony, 75
  death and wounding of cohorts, 98–99, 107
  lands at Fort Sumter, 68, 69
Crawford, Alex McLeod, ix, **22**, 25, 38
  at Alandale, 15
  birth, 5
  genealogy, 282
  military life, 12th Pa. Cavalry, 119
  possible wounding, 222
  relations with brother Samuel, 6, 8, 9, 47, 69, 75, 83, 85, 143
  as Samuel's aide, 119, 122, 147, 178, 188, 191, 217
  sibling position, 6, 15
  and "Jeb" Stuart, 123
Crawford, Anne Stravely, ix, 8, 152
  at Alandale, 25
  birth, 5
  children, Gettysburg property, 267
  death, 258

  genealogy, 282
  married Andrew Wilson, 6
  mother of, 10, 143
  in Orange County, New York, 10
  reminder of Alandale, 25
  Samuel's bossy sister, 5, 83, 146, 147
Crawford, Jane Agnew (Ma), ix, 3, 4, 5, 15, 31, 83
  coming of the rebels, 143, 146
  death and burial, 255
  genealogy, 281
  homemaker, 8–10
  at Laurel Hill Cemetery, 27
  marriage to Reverend, 4
  move to Franklin County, 4
  personal characteristics, 6
Crawford, John Agnew (A. J.), ix, 14, 19, **21**
  at Alandale, 14
  discussions at Alandale, 38
  and Falling Spring Presbyterian Church, 267
  first born, 4
  genealogy, 281
  letters to and from A. J., 74, 77, 81, 83, 94, 109, 270
  married Susan Monroe Gilbert, 16
  pastor, ideas on race, 16
  relations with Samuel: nickname "A. J.," 12; mentor, 13; brother Samuel's death and funeral, 273, 274
  signs deed, Gettysburg land, 269
  as Union chaplain, 131
Crawford, Margaret (also Maggie), ix, 4, 5, 83, 267
  at Alandale, 5, 14
  and brother Samuel, 47, 168, 176; Samuel's death and funeral, 273; son, namesake, 255
  brothers and sisters of, ix
  at Crawford–John, 14
  daughter's photo, 22
  death, ix
  father of, 258
  genealogy, 281
  and A. P. Hill's staff, 154
  husband, Edward Crawford Washington, 5; with 13th U.S. Infantry, 110; death, 168, 176
  marriage, 47
  mother of, 10
  remembers Cornelius and Jane Elizabeth, 6
  sons of, 143, 176
Crawford, Reverend Samuel W., Sr. (Pa), 4, 12, **21**, 27
  abolitionist, 16
  buying burial plot, 27

Index

at Chambersburg Academy of Learning, 4
churches served in Franklin County, 4
death, 256, 257
at Fairmont Presbyterian Church, 5
family serving Union cause, 131
orphaned in South Carolina, 4
and Thaddeus Stevens Ironworks, 48
at University of Pennsylvania, 5
Crawford, Samuel Wylie, Jr., ix, x, 2, 10, 11, 12, 13, **22**, **44**, **101**, **116**, **228**, **230**, **276**, **278**

Military career of
8th U.S. Infantry, 38, 39
13th U.S. Infantry: acting inspector general, 111–13; and Nathaniel Banks, 118; brigade command, 118, 119; passed over for V Corps command, 236
American Embassy, Mexico City, Mexico, 40
in Antietam Campaign: to Alandale to heal, 143, 147; and Sallie Horner, 144–47; first brigade evening of September 16, 1862, 133, 134, 135; replaces losses, 129, 130, 131; wounded, 140, 141
assistant surgeon, 37
at Battle of Cedar Mountain, 116, 120–23; hat bet with Jeb Stuart, 123–24; results of Crawford's Brigade, 124–25
at Battle of Gettysburg: 139th Pennsylvania Infantry, 167; charge on the evening of the 2nd of July, 163–64; charge of McCandless, July 3, 167, 168; Fisher's Brigade, 165, 166; Meade Order 68, 170; role of, 165; and Bertless Slott, 165
commands Pennsylvania Reserves, 153
commissary and quartermaster duties, 82
court-martial board duty, 153
at Fort Moultrie, S.C., 50, 51; evaluation of movement, 71; problems with arsenal and Carolinians, 55, 56; relations with Robert Anderson, 56, 57, 84; relations with Doubleday and Seymour, 53, 54; relations with South Carolinians, 55; role in, 69, 70; treated dengue or bone fever, 52
at Fort Sumter, S.C., 63–69; Crawford and aide last to leave, 97; Crawford's battery, 91, 92; "long and weary vigil about to close …", 87; for letters to and from A. J. see Crawford, John Agnew; medical duties, 92; meets with Johnston Pettigrew and Ellison Capers, 72–73; miseries at, 76, 77, 78; refuses demand to surrender, 87
in Gettysburg Campaign: First and Third Pa. Reserves to Gettysburg, 160, 162;

Pennsylvania state line, S. W. Crawford, Jr., speech, 160–61
at Kansas, 43
Meade offers command of cavalry, 5
in Overland Campaign: at Bethesda Church, 211, 212; crosses the James River, 215; at North Anna, 208–10; says farewell to the Reserves, 212, 213; sculpture of, 233; second battle of Squirrel Level Road, 223, 224; at Spotsylvania, 198–204, 205; tongue lashing by Warren, 235; visits Robert E. Lee and James Longstreet at Appomattox Court House, 237, 238; Gouverneur Warren describes behavior, 214; at Weldon Railroad, 220; at Wilderness, 188–98

personal life of
birth, 11, 283
at burial of George Meade, 249–51
climbs volcanoes, 40, 41
death and funeral, 272–75
father: death and burial, 256–58; reaction to fighting, 101
favorite mount disappears, 248
genealogy, 282
goes back and purchases land at Gettysburg, 266–69
illness of, 93, 94
mountains of Pennsylvania, 3
observes secessionist session, 61, 62, 63
Genesis of the Civil War, 86, 270–71
Gettysburg statue of, 258, 278
Grand Review, 242–44
Harrisburg, July 4, 1866, 245–48
illness and wounds, 85, 88, 175–76, 177, 188, 198, 221
at Penn: admitted, 13; continuing relationship, 20; graduated June 1846, 20; Medical school graduation 1850, 34; national issues while at Penn, 32, 33, 38, 41; Philomathean Society, 19; physical appearance, 7; preparing for admission, 12; study of medicine, 29–32, 33, 34
Post-Gettysburg: death of Margaret's husband, 176; evaluates role of Pa. Reserves at Gettysburg, 180–82; harassment by guerillas, 180; presents sword to Meade, 172, 173
quotes of, v, 35, 45, 103, 115, 229, 253, 263, 279
searches for his father's genealogy, 258–60
sends research to Smithsonian, 40
speaks on behalf of G. Warren, 261, 262
reception in New York City, 106, 107
retirement of, 251

returns to Alandale, 47, 49, 143, 147, 245
trip to New York City, New York: Carmody incident, 98; Hough incident, 98, 99
world traveler, 255–56
Crouse, Frederick
  128th Pa infantry, 133, 138, 140
  at Antietam, 134, 135, 138, 141
  and S. W. Crawford, Jr., 136

D

Dabney's Mill, 226
Davis, Confederate President Jefferson, 129, 150
  and Robert E. Lee, 86, 128, 186
  opening of Civil War, 86
Doubleday, Abner, 53, 54, **101**
  and Robert Anderson, 67
  at Antietam and Gettysburg, 53, 159, 160
  and Mrs. Doubleday, 53, 67
  first shot from Sumter and after, 91, 92, 94
  at Fort Moultrie, S.C., 54, 58, 68
  at Fort Sumter, S.C., 56, 57, 58, 73, 77, 83, 88, 240
  leaving Sumter and after, 96, 105, 108
  relations with Carolinians, 53, 66, 72
  relations with S. W. Crawford, Jr., 53, 74, 78, 79, 99, 134, 271
  and *Star of the West*, 79
  thinking back, 242

E

Emancipation Proclamation, 142
executions, military, 132, 173–75

F

Fayetteville, Pa., xiii, 4, 15, 268
  compared with Philadelphia, 25
  S. W. Crawford, Jr., and Sally Horner, 145–46
  Reverend Crawford buys land, 4
Fisher, Joseph, 153
  departing of the Reserves, 213, 214
  at Gettysburg, 165, 166
  Third Brigade of Pennsylvania Reserves, 160, 162, 163, 194, 198, 254
Five Forks Battle, xiv, 233, 234, 235, 260–61
Floyd, John, 55–56, 58, 59, 111
  and Buchanan instructions, 60
  and Don Carlos Buell, 59–60
  as Confederate officer, 111, 113
  about Doubleday, 56
  replaced by Holt as secretary of war, 81
  and Wigfall's proposal to kidnap President Buchanan, 94
Fort Moultrie, Charleston, S.C., xiii, 60, 63, 73, 74, 76
  Anderson at, 58, 59, 67, 72, 74
  Chaplain Harris at, 51
  S. W. Crawford, Jr., at, 50, 51, 52, 54, 61, 65, 66, 69, 75
  Doubleday at, 53, 57–58
  during bombardment, 92
  John Gardner at, 52, 54, 56
Fort Sumter, Charleston, S.C., **36**, 65, 70, 71, 73, 97, 100, **101**
  Anderson report of, 107
  bombardment of, 88–90, 93, 94, 96
  build-up against, 86
  circle of fire, 91
  children and women leave, 83
  condition of, 93
  December 27, 1860, 74
  demands for surrender, 87, 88
  drawings and letter, 102, 114
  false beginning of war, 84
  first mortar, 89
  Fort Sumter 1865, 236, 238, 240, 241
  inspection by Anderson 58, 59
  landing December 26, 1860, 68
  Lincoln plan of relief, 85–86
  Roger Pryor incident, 95, 99
  shortage of cartridges, 92
  starvation at, 84, 87
  surrender proposal, 95
  talk of mining, 86
  See also Anderson, Robert; Doubleday, Abner; Crawford, Samuel Wylie, Jr.
Foster, John, 55, 57–58, 60, 64, 68, 85
Fox, Gustavus, 97, 107, 241
Franklin Repository, 187, 218, 256
  announced S. W. Crawford, Jr.'s promotion to brevetted Major General U.S. Volunteers, 227
  articles from the Holy Land, 256
  Battle of Gettysburg, 169
  drawing of S. W. Crawford, Jr., **276**
  personal servant shot in breast, 222

G

Galway, James, 99, 107, 242
Gardner, John
  descriptions by Doubleday and S. W. Crawford, Jr., 54
  relieved of duty from Fort Moultrie, 56
  request to arsenal storekeeper, 55, 56
  "Secession propensities," 56
  sick servant for S. W. Crawford, Jr., to treat, 52
Genesis of the Civil War, 46, 86, 104, 270–71, 280, 285
Gettysburg Battle of, 149
  big round top, 166

Index

charge across Plum Run, xiv, 165
S. W. Crawford, Jr., as battlefield preservationist, 260, 267, 269
little round top, 162–63, 164
overview day one, 158–60
role of Bucktails and Company K, 165
role of the Pennsylvania Reserves, 152, 153, 154, 156
See also Crawford, Samuel Wylie, Jr.; Doubleday, Abner; Meade, George
Gerish, Ted, 190, 197, 198, 206, 210, 237
Germanna Ford, 189
Plank Road, 190
Gordon, George
at Antietam, 135, 141, 142
General Williams gives credit to, 125
Grant, Ulysses, 150, 194, 203, 205, 206, 208, 270
appointed supreme commander of Union forces, 186, 187
at Appomattox, 237
and S. W. Crawford, Jr., 225, 236, 265
crosses James River, 215
at Grand Review, 243
and Lee, 192, 207, 211, 215, 233, 237
and Meade, 191, 194, 199, 200, 217, 223–24, 249
at North Anna, 209
quote of, 183
strategy of 1864, 187, 189, 231, 234, 260; May 6–7, 194, 195, 196, 197–98
and Warren, 235, 261
Greencastle, Pa., 4, 15
Griffin, Charles, 191, 192, 198, 203, 227
under S. W. Crawford, Jr.'s command, 224
dislike of Crawford's advance without West Point training, 223
at Five Forks, 261
has words with Meade, 200
honored with V Corps command, 236
marching conditions, 206
at Quaker Road, 233
Warren's evaluation, 214
at White Oak Road, 235

H

Hall, Norman, 55, 242
at Antietam and Gettysburg, 134, 167
S. W. Crawford, Jr., takes over duties for, 81
the crossing, 66, 69
to Governor Pickens, 80
and spies, 67
Star of the West incident, 79
Sumter flagstaff, 94
to Washington, 81

Hancock, Winfield, 194
and S. W. Crawford, Jr., and retirement board, 249
July 4, 1866, 246, 247
in Overland Campaign, 194, 195, 197, 203, 204, 208, 210, 223
at Petersburg, 225
Hardin, Martin
12th Reserves, 163
First Brigade commander, 208
at Gettysburg, 163
wounded, 180
Hart, Peter, 78, 92, 94
in New York, 106
at Sumter 1865, 240, 241
See also Anderson, Robert
Heintzelman, Samuel, 152
Higgins, Jacob
125th Pa. Infantry, 139, 141
brother Joseph, 140
color sergeant of 125th Pa. Infantry, 140
his men aid Mansfield, 138
Hoke, Jacob
at burning of Chambersburg, 219
and Lee's invasion 1863, 154
at Lincoln's Gettysburg Address, 178–79
results of battle of South Mountain, 143–44
store of, 26, 144–45
witnesses Jeb Stuart Cavalry invasion, 145, 146
Horner, Franklin, 12th Pa. Reserves, 163, 166
Horner, Sallie, 145, 146
Hough, Daniel, 96, 99
hypertrophy and atrophy, 33, 34

I

Isabelle, 96, 97

J

Jackson, Samuel
11th Pa. Reserves, Gettysburg, 163, 164
S. W. Crawford, Jr., to Jackson, 161, 166
Jackson, Thomas "Stonewall," 117–18, 124, 126, 128, 190
and S. W. Crawford, Jr., xiv, 119, 120–22, 123, 125, 134, 139
at Harpers Ferry, 133
wounded, 150
Jacobs, Michael, 180, 268

K

Knipe, Joseph, 123
at Antietam, 137; Pa. Infantry, 138–46
dislikes S. W. Crawford, Jr., 175
wounded at Cedar Mountain, 130

Index

L

Laurel Hill, Spotsylvania, Va., 198, 201
  S. W. Crawford, Jr., at, 202, 261
  Warren at, 199, 204, 205
Laurel Hill Cemetery, Philadelphia, Pa., 26, 27, **277**
  S. W. Crawford, Jr., buried at, 14
  Crawford family burials at, 6, 257, 275
  Meade burial at, 250
Lee, Robert E., xiii, 113, 117, 118
  in Antietam Campaign, 129, 132–33, 136, 141, 142
  toward Appomattox, 236, 237
  and Cedar Mountain, 120, 123
  at Chancellorsville, 150, 151
  in Gettysburg Campaign, 153, 154, 156–58, 167
  and Harpers Ferry, 50
  versus Meade and Grant, 179, 186, 189, 190, 191, 192, 196, 202, 204, 207
  in Peninsula Campaign, 128
  at Petersburg, 231, 232, 233
Light, John, 48–49
Lincoln, President Abraham
  and Anderson letter, 84, 86, 109
  S. W. Crawford, Jr., view of, 48, 256
  Doubleday view of, 53
  and Grant, 186, 187
  loss to Union, 242, 244
  Northern view of, 117, 149
  plan to liberate Sumter, 86, 97
  response to Sumter bombardment, 97
  Southern sentiments about, 56, 61, 90
  views about move to Sumter, 85
  war response, 126, 127, 128, 129, 200, 231
Locke, Frederick, 191, 199
Longstreet, James, 186
  at Antietam, 133, 134
  at Chambersburg, Pa., 156–57
  and S. W. Crawford, Jr., 38, 238, 266–67
  at Gettysburg, 182
  at Wilderness, 193–94,
  wounded, 195

M

Manifest Destiny, 33
Mansfield, Joseph, 132, 254
  at Antietam, 133, 135–36, 137, 139
  wounding and death, 137–38
Matrau, Henry, 227
  at Dabney's Mill, 226
  death of Lincoln, 243
  needed a furlough, 232–33
  toward the end of the war, 236, 237
  at Weldon Railroad, 220

McCandless, William, First Brigade Commander, 153, **184**, 254
  and S. W. Crawford, Jr., 163, 164,
  at Gettysburg, 162, 166, 167–68
  leaves the Army of the Potomac, 214
  at the Wilderness, 193, 194, 197
  wounded, 198
McClellan, George, 124, 149, 254
  at Antietam, 131, 136, 139
  and S. W. Crawford, Jr., 129
  "lost order," 132–33
  in Peninsula Campaign, 117, 128
McClure, Alexander, 219
  and S. W. Crawford, Jr., 143, 256, 263, 265, 274
McLaws, Lafayette, 167, 267
Meade, George, 174, 179, 209, 233, 247–48, **252**, 254
  command of Army of the Potomac, 156–57, 158
  and S. W. Crawford, Jr., 5, 171–72, 221, 222, 224, 227, 243, 246, 258, 275
  at Dabney's Mill, 225–26
  death and burial of, 249, 250
  at Gettysburg, 159, 160, 169–70
  and Grant, 200, 217, 223, 232, 235
  grave of, **277**
  and Pa. Reserves, 149, 152, 156, 172–75, 211, 251
  at Philadelphia, 250
  at Spotsylvania, 197, 199, 204, 205
  at the Wilderness, 188, 191, 192–93, 196
Meade, Richard, 68, 80, **101**, 171
Mercersburg, Pa. 144, 145
Minnigh, Henry
  with Company K, 153
  at Gettysburg, 162, 165
  in Overland Campaign, 194, 202
Moore, Alexander, 163

N

national issues
  Kansas, 43
  Manifest Destiny, 33
  Northwest Ordinance, 33
  popular sovereignty, 18, 33
  slavery moral and property issue, 33
  states rights and slavery, 62
  Wilmot proviso, 33
New York Times, 143, 180

O

Oceanus, liner, 240
Ordinance of Secession, 62, 63
  and S. W. Crawford, Jr., 46, 61, 62

P

Pennsylvania Reserves, xiv, 156, 222
  190th Pa. Reserves, 224
  at Bethesda Church, 211, 212, 247
  and burning of Chambersburg, 219
  and S. W. Crawford, Jr., 152, 160–61, 165, 210, 213, 229, 245, 246, 265–69
  at Gettysburg, 162–63, 164–65, 166–67
  history of, 152–53
  July 4, 1866, 247, 250, 251
  and Meade, 156, 173, 179
  in Overland Campaign, 195, 200, 201–3, 206, 207
  Philadelphia Inquirer evaluates, 170
  Post–Gettysburg, 172, 180
  role at Gettysburg, 180–82
  saying goodbye, 212, 214
Pepper, William, 272
Pettigrew, Johnston, 69, 73
  at Castle Pinckney, 170
  death, 170
  at Gettysburg, 158, 167
Philadelphia, 4, 5, 11, 20, 26, 97, 172, 188, 245–46
Pickens, Francis, 80, 86, 100, 170
  and Anderson's appeal, 81
  confiscates federal property, 73
  letter to President Buchanan, 60
  and Lincoln, 85
  orders gunboats to patrol Moultrie Sumter area, 60
Pope, John, 117, 120, 126, 128
  and S. W. Crawford, Jr., 119, 125, 129
Potts, Sam, 124th Pa Infantry, 131
Pryor, Roger, 95, 99, 134

R

Ray, William, 190, 222, 225, 232
  and Iron brigade, 207, 227
Reynolds, John, 156
  characteristics of, 159
  at Gettysburg, 159, 162
  and Pa. Reserves, 152, 162, 172, 250
Roebling, Washington, 192, 193, 194, 195, 232
Rosecrans, William, 111
  and S. W. Crawford, Jr., 111–12, 113, 118

S

Sedgwick, John
  at Antietam, 134, 139–40
  in Overland Campaign, 194, 195, 201
Seymour, Truman, 64, **101**, 271
  to arsenal in Charleston, S.C., 55
  and S. W. Crawford, Jr., 53, 54, 64, 134

  at Fort Sumter, 55–56, 68, 70, 78, 88, 94
Sheridan, Philip, 203, 234, 236
  and Grant, 235
  verbal exchange with Meade, 200
  and Warren, 214, 236, 260, 261
slavery, 33, 42, 148, 242
  and Crawford family, 16, 61, 155, 177, 218
  and integrity of the Union, 231
  as moral and property issue, 33
  possible compromise, 38
Spotsylvania, Battle of, 196, 198
  S. W. Crawford, Jr., at, 220
  Meade's statement, 205
  and Wainwright, 208
  and Warren, 199
  See also Meade, George
Star of the West, ship, 79–80
  cannonading of, a national disgrace, 81
  follows surrender demand, 80
States rights, 33
  and S. W. Crawford, Jr., 110
Stevens, Thaddeus, 48, 155
Stuart, "Jeb," 50, 128, 203
  at Antietam, 133
  and S. W. Crawford, Jr., 38, 123–24, 134, 145–46, 204, 275
  and Lee, 157–58
  raid into Pennsylvania, 144–45, 154
Sykes, George, 156, 161, 166, 182, 254
  and S. W. Crawford, Jr., 162–64, 167

T

Talley, William, 198, 199, 245–46
Taylor, Charles, 165
Taylor, Ned, surgeon, 251

U

United States Army Medical Board exam, 37
University of Pennsylvania, xiii, xv
  and Crawford family, 4, 5, 14
  and S. W. Crawford, Jr., 13, 18, 19
  medical school, 29–34

V

Valley Spirit, 218
Vautier, John, 88 Pa. Infantry, 190, 198, 205, 209, 210, 211–12, 214, 220

W

Wainwright, Charles, 172–73, 190, 191, 197, 200, 206, 209, 243, 254
  and S. W. Crawford, Jr., 203, 210, 216, 236
  and Hooker, 150
  at opening of Overland Campaign, 188
  and Warren, 196, 214, 236

Warren, Gouverneur, 187, 212, 234, 236, 247, 254
 and S. W. Crawford, Jr., 190, 192, 195, 196, 197, 201, 202–3, 204, 207, 209, 217, 220, 223, 226, 232–33, 234
 and Grant, 194
 and Meade, 187, 197, 202, 209, 216–17
 in Overland Campaign, 191, 193–94, 195, 196, 198, 199, 205
 and Sheridan, 200, 236
 and Wainwright, 214, 236
Waynesboro, Pa., 4, 15, 48
Williams, Alpheus, 119, 147, 254
 at Antietam, 134, 135, 137, 138, 139
 at Cedar Mountain, 120
 and S. W. Crawford, Jr., 125
 as a Crawford detractor, 175
 and Mansfield, 132, 136–37
Wilderness, Battle of
 S. W. Crawford, Jr., at, 210, 213
 and Grant: comment on, 185; objective of, 189; description of, 190
 Longstreet wounded at, 266
 Lyman's observations, 194
 May 5, 1864, 191, 193
 May 6, 1864, 194–95
 May 7, 1864, 196–98
 price in men, 196
 See also Meade, George

— OF RELATED INTEREST —

CONFEDERATE RETALIATION
McCausland's 1864 Raid
Fritz Haselberger

The Confederate army's destruction of Chambersburg, Pennsylvania, marked a watershed in the mounting violence of both sides against civilian populations. A new in-depth study that shows the burning in the context of the battles that led up to and followed that event. Combining military & social history, a comprehensive account of this psychological turning point in the war is provided.

ISBN 978-1-57249-113-7 • Hardcover $34.95

ECHOES OF THE FALLING SPRING
Dody Myers
Historical Novel Set in Chambersburg, Pa.

During the Civil War the Confederate army invaded the North, passing through Chambersburg three times. The invasions resulted in the Battles of Antietam and Gettysburg as well as the destruction of the town itself in 1864. Set in Pennsylvania, this novel follows two love stories that are constantly tested by the conflict of the Civil War—brought together by a war but bound to a culture that is no longer possible.

ISBN 978-1-57249-231-8 • Hardcover $24.95

CIVIL WAR CITY
Harrisburg, Pennsylvania, 1861–1865
William J. Miller

Centrally located & only a few hours from the front lines, Harrrisburg, Pennsylvania, became a very important crossroads for the Union war effort. During the invasion of 1862 and 1863, Harrisburg's Camp Curtin was critical in organizing the militia to stop the invaders.

ISBN 978-1-57249-237-0 • Softcover $19.95

— COVER ILLUSTRATION —
"ENCOUNTER AT PLUM RUN"
Image courtesy of Gallon Historical Art,
Gettysburg, PA, www.gallon.com

WHITE MANE PUBLISHING CO., INC.

To Request a Catalog Please Write to:
WHITE MANE PUBLISHING COMPANY, INC.
P.O. Box 708 • Shippensburg, PA 17257
e-mail: marketing@whitemane.com

Printed in the United States
200301BV00005B/82-261/A